D1199098

CHILDHOOD, YOUTH, AND SOCIAL WORK IN TRANSFORMATION

Childhood, Youth, and Social Work in Transformation

Implications for Policy and Practice

**Lynn M. Nybell,
Jeffrey J. Shook,
and Janet L. Finn, Editors**

COLUMBIA UNIVERSITY PRESS New York

Columbia University Press
Publishers Since 1893
New York   Chichester, West Sussex

Library of Congress Cataloging-in-Publication Data
Childhood, youth, and social work in transformation : implications for policy and practice /
edited by Lynn M. Nybell, Jeffrey J. Shook, and Janet L. Finn.
p. cm.
Includes bibliographical references and index.
ISBN 978-0-231-14140-6 (cloth : alk. paper) — ISBN 978-0-231-51852-9 (ebook)
1. Social work with children — United States.   2. Social work with teenagers—United
States.   3. Child welfare—Government policy—United States.   I. Nybell, Lynn M.
II. Shook, Jeffrey J. III. Finn, Janet L., 1956–
HV741. C5359 2009
362.7—dc22
2008029831

⊗

Columbia University Press books are printed on permanent and durable acid-free paper.
This book is printed on paper with recycled content.
Printed in the United States of America

c 10 9 8 7 6 5

To the children who have touched our lives.

You taught us so much once we found the humility to learn.

Contents

Foreword

Rosemary Sarri

Children and youth in the United States today, as well as in many other countries, are increasingly marginalized without having their physical and social needs met or their human rights honored. The social, political, economic, and cultural changes of the past quarter century have resulted in a substantial decline in the well-being of millions of children. Equally important, few policy decision-makers see meeting the needs of these children as a priority. As a result, the politics of childhood has shifted in the United States to emphasize responsibility for well-being far more heavily on the parental family than on the community or society. At the same time, institutions of social control in local communities have been granted great discretion in the ways they address children's behavior in schools and neighborhoods.

This book by a respected group of social workers and social scientists raises provocative questions regarding our perspectives about children and youth in postindustrial U.S. society. There is at present considerable ambiguity in our views about dependence and independence, about caring and being cared for, about risk taking and responsibility for one's actions, and about societal responsibility for the well-being of children and youth. Considering that most Western countries, including the United States, have rapidly growing, aging populations that will depend heavily on the support of young people, one would think that greater care would be shown about the conditions of so many children and youth.

Written for students and practitioners of social work, this edited volume provides knowledge about the many dimensions of childhood and the institutions devised to provide for the development, care, and control of children. It helps social workers understand what it is like to be a child in the United States today, how others view childhood, and how social policies and institutions influence the well-being of children. The book examines many of the important social services sectors affecting our understanding of childhood today, including adoption, foster care, juvenile justice, teen parenting, human and legal rights, school exclusion policy and preschool programming, health care, and youth participation in developing and operating programs. It also suggests some alternative ways for addressing the challenges that we face.

First, some context: there are 73 million children below the age of 18 in the United States today, including 20 million below the age of 5.[1] The proportion of children of color approaches 40%, and 20% have at least one foreign-born parent. These populations are distributed unevenly across the country, as are the 17% of children living below the poverty level. Problems are concentrated in urban centers, depressed rural areas, and a few states. The conception of childhood as a negative period is not limited to the poor or to children of color because some children grow up in great affluence but still experience profound problems, while other children are growing up homeless and in abject poverty.

Although predictions are always problematic, it is safe to estimate that before these 73 million children reach adulthood, about 5 million will have experienced out-of-home placement, another 3–4 million will have a parent or sibling who is or has been incarcerated, 25% may not have completed high school, about 51 per 100,000 will have died an accidental death as an adolescent, and nearly 100,000 will have been sentenced to placement in an adult jail or prison. Some 12% will have experienced maltreatment in the form of abuse or neglect, 21% will have a physical or mental health disability, and millions will have been victimized with no report filed of their victimization; although they suffer in silence, the impact is no less serious.

On the other side of the equation, assuming that we are entering a period when more federal policy will be directed to children and youth, we would expect that most young adults will have grown up with at least a national health care program for children. There will be millions of first- and second-generation immigrant children who are prepared for successful adult roles, and, when compared with children who matured in the 1990s and the early twenty-first century, many more will have benefited from quality child care. These children will also have benefited from entering adulthood at a time when racial and ethnic diversity is far more extensive in our society. Similarly, educational policy will have changed such that children and youth will be better prepared to participate effectively in a postindustrial society.

Last, and perhaps most difficult to estimate, is the type of physical and social environment these children will experience. It will probably have a more negative effect on children of color, poor children, and children with disabilities. The impact of the physical environment on childhood and youth is one of the elements that social workers seldom think about when considering social services for children and youth in the United States, but one needs only to point to the dramatic increase in childhood asthma to acknowledge the impact of environmental change on children, as many public health researchers have noted. On average, both children and youth are much more sensitive to the physical environment of their country and community than are adults, and it can be expected that they will demand that far more be done in the future than is being done now. Very young children are now keenly aware of environmental policies and encourage adult compliance, but they require the active involvement of adults in environmental protection for the decades ahead, as we struggle to develop a future world in which all can live. As a number of contributors to this volume show, young people are critically observing and assessing their worlds, and they are important contributors to changes in programs, communities, and public policies.

A growing and deeply troubling problem today is the trafficking and sexual exploitation of children and youth in the United States and many other countries. These boys and girls are so badly damaged that childhood has almost no meaning for them. Even in the United States there are cases of parents trafficking their own children; when the situation is identified, the child or youth is taken by the court and institutionalized for neglect, while, too often, the parent escapes legal consequences.

When the juvenile court was established in Chicago in 1900, society stated that children were immature and need to have the opportunity to develop in a nurturing environment if they were to become productive adults. In the latter half of the twentieth century we have moved away from that view and no longer acknowledge the differences between children and adults in critical areas that can have lifelong effects on youth. The risk of a child or youth being inappropriately treated as an adult challenges social workers and policy makers in the United States to give special attention to childhood and youth as a continuum with different tasks to be solved at each step in the maturation process. Some of these tasks reflect developmental requirements while others are a consequence of the social and cultural politics regarding childhood and youth in society. Several of the authors in this volume discuss the impact of globalization on childhood. Despite vast differences in children's life chances in "the developed" and "the developing" worlds, contributors point to the ways that children's everyday experiences around the globe are increasingly politically, socially, and spatially intertwined. The world population in 2006 included 2.1 billion children, most of whom reside in developing countries with few resources, limited opportunities for elementary education, and health care so problematic that life expectancies are in the forties, not the high seventies as in developed countries. The heralded "advances" of the developed world are too often built upon conditions of political and structural violence that affect poor children from Detroit to Darfur. For example, the developed countries have established economic and political barriers that limit interaction and exchange. What does childhood mean where children are often expected to support the family at age 8 or younger? It is perhaps difficult to understand fully that in most African countries today the median age of the population is 17, and at that age many must be prepared to accept substantial responsibility in their societies.

Children and youth in the developing world are active agents in the construction of social structures and processes, but their options are sharply constrained, as anyone who has observed a child street beggar selling small objects on a busy street knows. The story of Ishmael Beah, a child soldier in Sierra Leone, as he tells it in his autobiography, is a powerful and gripping story of what happened to a young boy when his family was killed and he was recruited by the guerillas.[2] It is also a story of his rehabilitation with the help of staff from UNICEF as he learned to forgive himself and to regain his humanity. He now resides in the United States, where his story profoundly influences our conception of childhood in warring countries.

Many children in Africa and South Asia are "double orphans" because of the death of both parents due to HIV/AIDS. At very young ages they become heads of households responsible for the rearing of their younger siblings. Some of these children are in immigrant families who have come to the United States legally or illegally, but they influence our political and cultural conceptions of childhood and youth. They also influence their communities and our entire society. Certainly their conception of childhood and youth is socially and culturally constructed from the many experiences they have had in a variety of communities. One wonders if some of the children who are required to assume adult responsibilities at very early ages are not entitled to be dependent for a few years—if not on family, then on society.

A careful study and review of the social work authors in this volume can provide the reader with new conceptions about childhood and youth that will benefit their practice and direct them to participate in the development of more effective and meaningful social policies for the challenges that we face today and will face tomorrow.

NOTES

1. The statistics cited in the foreword are taken from three sources: Federal Interagency Forum on Child and Family Statistics, *America's children: Key indicators of well-being 2007* (Washington, D.C.: Federal Interagency Forum on Child and Family Statistics, 2007); UNICEF, *State of the world's children, 2007* (New York: UNICEF, 2007); and U.S. Bureau of the Census, *Current population survey* (Washington, D.C.: U.S. Department of Commerce, 2007).

2. Ishmael Beah, *A long way gone: Memoirs of a boy soldier* (New York: Farrar, Straus and Giroux, 2007).

Acknowledgments

This project took root over the last decade as the editors, several of the contributors, and other colleagues engaged in practice with and research on children and youth. Some of us were struggling with the everyday dilemmas and contradictions in our practice and finding that the theoretical frames and intervention strategies we had in hand were insufficient for the challenges we faced. Others were exploring novel terrain of theory and practice and posing different questions. The pioneering work of Sharon Stephens (1952–1998) on the anthropology of childhood was a profound influence in our developing thought and practice, and we honor her memory here. Sharon Stephens inspired many of us with her teaching and generous personal encouragement, as well as her groundbreaking scholarly work. Her edited volume *Children and the Politics of Culture* (1995a) is a standard collection in this area, and her provocative introduction to the book (1995b) opens up the line of questioning pursued by many contributors to this volume. Her articles on children, risk, and the environment (1994, 1995c, 1996), children at risk (in Finn and Nybell 2001), and children and nationalism (1997a, 1997b) raise profound and still generative questions for social workers and researchers. Over the years we have kept the dialogue going, engaged a diverse group of scholars and practitioners, and learned about the creative and critical work of others who were also grappling with these questions, several of whom agreed to contribute to this volume.

The editors are indebted to the many mentors, both children and adults, who have shaped our thinking over the years. We pay homage to Rosemary Sarri, whose indefatigable force and dedication to the well-being of children around the world continues both inspire and challenge us. Ongoing debates with Rosemary have made us better thinkers, practitioners, and advocates. Janet Finn thanks Connie Waterman, Miriam Morgan, Vince Matule, and Dick Rosenleaf, remarkable social workers who have dedicated themselves to healing, empowerment, and advocacy for children and families of Montana, and she pays special tribute to Margaret Stuart (1926–2005) whose legacy as a social work educator and child welfare practitioner lives on through two generations of Montana social workers.

Lynn Nybell gratefully acknowledges her debts to the many talented and dedicated child and youth advocates in Michigan who so generously shared their concerns, critiques, and visions, including Ashley Gray, Michelle Williamson, Derrick Jackson, Greg Pratt, and Lori Fryzel. She recognizes her colleague Sylvia Sims Gray, whose vision and wisdom have enriched so many efforts, including this one. Lynn's work on this project was supported in part by a Sabbatical Leave Award from Eastern Michigan University, and she thanks the university for this opportunity.

Jeff Shook thanks his parents Carole and Jim and his sister Lori, whose tireless work on behalf of children and youth have helped shape not only his career but his commitment, and his nephews Devan and Eric, whose development has helped ground his thinking and motivation. He offers a special thank you to his wife Sara and their two children, Maya and Zack, whose support has provided tremendous inspiration throughout this project. Jeff would also like to extend additional appreciation to Rosemary Sarri, not only for the example she has set, but for the time and attention that she has dedicated to his training and career.

The editors also thank Lauren Dockett, Christine Mortlock, and Roy Thomas at Columbia University Press, and our copyeditor Anita O'Brien, for their professional, responsive support and guidance as this book came to fruition.

CHILDHOOD, YOUTH, AND SOCIAL
WORK IN TRANSFORMATION

Introduction and Conceptual Framework

Lynn M. Nybell, Jeffrey J. Shook, and Janet L. Finn

Mike, an artistic, somewhat withdrawn African American
ninth-grader, was having academic difficulties. His mother
and I were permitted to watch from a one-way observation
studio while Mike was evaluated by a school psychologist.
During the reporting session, the psychologist indicated that
Mike was quite limited and very concrete in his thinking.
Yet, in response to the question, "How are a poem and a
statue alike?" Mike replied, "They both make you wonder."
When I said I thought his answer was not only abstract but
also very moving, the psychologist thumbed through the
protocol before saying, "That answer isn't scorable."

—Ruth Zweifler, student advocate

We, the editors of this volume, have been wondering for some time about questions of childhood and the nature of social work. With the colleague who told us Mike's story, we are eager to restore a place for "wondering" in the process of social work education. Like Mike, we hope to identify profound connections between apparently disparate things. In particular, in this text we hope to spur social workers to wonder about their work with children and youth and to connect this work with larger patterns of global transformation. We want to invoke wonder in both of its meanings: first, in its sense of experiencing amazed admiration and awe; and second, in its sense of speculating and being curious to know about something. We hope that the contributions to this edited volume reawaken a sense of admiration and awe for the present-day insights as well as the future possibilities of young people whom we meet as we practice social work. We wish to make the gifts of people like Mike more available, challenging the processes that so often make the talents and skills of such young people invisible to so many. We also intend to stimulate curiosity about how social policy and practice with American young people has come to be as it is, in this particular historical moment of global transformation. We particularly want to provoke critical questions about trends in contemporary social policy and practice that exclude, stigmatize, and leave behind large segments of the nation's youth. Finally, we wish to inspire speculation about how things might be otherwise.

Childhood, Youth, and Social Work in Transformation is the product of the conversations and concerns of social workers, anthropologists, lawyers, and youth workers who have wondered about the transformation of childhood, youth, and social work over the last decade. Each contributor explores a particular aspect of contemporary policy or practice. Each spent months or even years in a specific local context or studying a specific aspect of social policy with the aim of getting some purchase on larger questions of how childhood, youth, and social work are being transformed. Contributors seek to understand young people's experiences in school classrooms, detention centers, Head Start preschools, "teen mom" groups, youth centers, and community meetings. Some authors carefully document changing legal standards toward children in particular arenas of law; others follow and analyze specific media stories focused on youth. One author learns to play hockey in a mental health program for youth; another serves as "an ethnographic babysitter" to an upper-middle-class family; yet others devise programs in which young people resolve community conflicts, deliver "guerilla poetry," study their legal rights, or instruct their social workers. Few of the profound lessons that our authors have gained from these experiences are "scorable." But they all make you wonder.

One of the themes that unite these diverse contributions is the premise that in the context of a transforming global order, there is a profound shift under way in our assumptions about children and youth—about who they are, what they need, and how they can be helped. The authors are attempting to evoke our intense curiosity and speculation about the nature of this shift. Many of the contributors were prompted to undertake their studies or experiment with new practices because of a realization that we were witnessing the abandonment of a powerful set of modern ideas about the nature of childhood and youth and the possible emergence of something new (Fass 2007; Ruddick 2006; Scheper-Hughes and Sargent 1998; Stephens 1995). We believe that recent trends in social welfare policymaking demonstrate that our nation is in retreat from public commitments to protecting, educating, sheltering, and nurturing its young people. As many historians of social welfare have shown, the public institutions that the nation created to carry out these functions have often failed, as the intention to care for and uplift was transformed into an impulse to condemn or control (Abramovitz 1996; Finn, this volume; Lindsey 2004; Specht and Courtney 1994). Still, in contemporary times, a shared commitment to the ideal of a protected, nurtured childhood has been an important starting place, a moral ground from which to advocate for young people and their families.

Erosion of a commitment to these ideals regarding childhood and youth has particular significance for the social work profession and for each of us as social workers. Unlike scholars of childhood, who mostly observe such transformations, we, as social workers, take active part in them—dismantling, carrying forth, and reinventing policies, programs, and practices that affect the daily lives of young people. We are deeply implicated in the ongoing process of constructing and reconstructing childhood and youth for young people. At the same time, we are uniquely positioned both to witness the efforts that young people make to shape their own lives and to advocate on their behalf. The contributors explore ways in which social workers are both implicated in the construction of childhood and engaged with young people. They question the certainties that inform policies and practices, and they offer alternative possibilities for imagining and engaging with children and youth.

The central aims of this text are to help social workers to connect their understandings of childhood and youth to changing political and economic conditions; to critically examine the dynamic interplay among policies, institutions, and practices addressing the care and control of children and youth; and to imagine new possibilities for social work practice. The contributors provide conceptual tools, practical examples, and provocative stories that prompt readers to reexamine their own assumptions about and contributions to the institutions, policies, and practices that shape the experience of childhood and youth for young people.

In their writings, contributors draw on new paradigms of child research that are investigating the "cultural politics of childhood" (for example, Corsaro 1997; Hutchison and Charlesworth 2000; James and James 2004; James, Jenks, and Prout 1998; Jenks 1996; Qvortrup 2005; Qvortrup et al. 1994; Scheper-Hughes and Sargent 1998; Stephens 1995b). It is to the elements of this paradigm of "the cultural politics" of childhood and youth that we first turn. After introducing this paradigm, we take up our argument that specific modern Western ideas about childhood that have been taken as natural and universal understandings are eroding in the context of a globalizing world. Finally, we introduce the contributions to this text and preview the questions that they raise and the conceptual tools and strategies that they offer us as we seek to study the transformation of childhood, youth, and social work.

THE "CULTURAL POLITICS" OF CHILDHOOD AND YOUTH

A fundamental premise of this text is that notions of "childhood" and "youth" are socially and culturally constructed. Within social work, this is an unsettling proposition, as our profession's understandings of childhood have been drawn primarily from developmental psychology. Traditionally, developmental psychological approaches have represented child development as a natural, largely biological process that unfolds in chronological and linear stages (Burman 1994; Kessen 1990; Morss 1996; Walkerdine 1984). This approach roots the answer to questions such as "what is a child?" in biology, rather than in the social and cultural reality of a specific historical moment.

In contrast, this text is located in a burgeoning new scholarship of childhood in anthropology, sociology, history, and legal studies. The social historian Phillipe Ariès is credited with launching this new vein of scholarship of childhood with the publication of his striking assertion that in medieval society in western Europe, "men . . . did not dwell on the image of childhood, and that that image had neither interest nor even reality for them" (Ariès 1962:34). Ariès used depictions of children and data on children's clothing and games to argue that, prior to the fifteenth century, children were portrayed, dressed, entertained, and, in fact, conceptualized as "miniature adults."

Though Ariès's provocative thesis has been sharply debated, the body of scholarship it generated underscores the point that childhood has varied across both cultures and decades. Ariès's work provided a platform for rethinking the idea of childhood as "a particular cultural phrasing of the early part of the life course, historically contingent and subject to change" (James and James 2004). It provided impetus to explore the diversity that exists among children and their childhoods at any single historical moment. And it required acknowledgment of the ways that the ideas we hold about childhood shape how we behave toward young people and structure children's daily experiences.

Building on Ariès's insight, a new paradigm of child research took root in the late 1970s, pitched against the assumptions about children and childhood so firmly embedded in developmental psychology and uncritically embraced within social work and many other disciplines. Scholars studying the social and cultural construction of childhood rejected the degree of emphasis on children's biological makeup and the lack of attention to children's engagement with their social and cultural worlds (for a review of this work, see Boocock and Scott 2005). An important five-year project, *Childhood as a Social Phenomenon*, began in 1987 under the auspices of the European Centre for Social Welfare Policy and Research, organizing meetings of international scholars and publishing landmark reports and books (Qvortrup et al. 1994). Another landmark occurred in 1990, when Alan Prout and Allison James published a collection of studies on *Constructing and Reconstructing Childhood*. In the introduction to this volume, James and Prout defined the parameters of the new paradigm for child research, and by so doing shaped a great deal of subsequent research and theoretical debate. Here we summarize three key premises of a paradigm of research on the "cultural politics of childhood": that childhood is socially and culturally constructed; that children are and must be seen as active agents in the construction of their own lives; and that particular notions of "childhood" and "youth" must be understood in the specific political and economic contexts in which they emerge.

Childhood as Socially and Culturally Constructed

The first premise is that childhood, "as distinct from biological immaturity, is neither a natural nor universal feature of a human group" but a specific social and cultural institution instead (Prout and James 1990:9). Scholars working within this paradigm pay critical attention to "*discourses*" of childhood and youth, by which we mean the structures of knowledge and systematic ways of carving up reality that provide parameters for what can be said, thought, and known about young people (Chambon, Irving, and Epstein 1999; James and James 2004). Scholars researching the "cultural politics of childhood" also demonstrate that the study of childhood cannot be divorced from other social variables, such as class, gender, and race, stressing that research reveals a variety of childhoods rather than a single, universal one.

In part, social work's lack of engagement with this new paradigm of child research may reflect the degree to which these studies disturb ideas and assumptions that are deeply embedded within our profession. In particular, understanding childhood as socially and culturally constructed represents a challenge to powerful ideas imported into social work from developmental psychology. Assumptions rooted in developmental psychology underlie many social work interventions. For example, researchers within the new paradigm of child research have challenged John Bowlby's highly influential theories of the impact of maternal separation and attachment on children's needs, questioning to what extent the needs he postulates are universal and innate (James and James 2004; Woodhead 1990).

Within social work, a developmental psychological perspective on child development has competed with and been combined with "family" and "ecological" perspectives. These more sociological theories emphasize the ways that individuals and their environments exist in reciprocal relationships, each changing over time and mutually adapting to each other (Bronfenbrenner 1979; Garbarino 1992; Hartman 1979). Such approaches place much stronger emphasis on the family, community, and social context in which the child develops. However, these approaches have also been challenged by the new generation of child researchers. For example, child researchers such as Qvortrup have argued that these models frequently submerge the specific needs and interests of children with those of the family. As Qvortrup contends:

> All too often—in both research and policy—it is taken for granted that children and child families are more or less the same unit. . . . This problem arises not because of ill will, but is rather a problem of the sociology of knowledge in the sense that adults are often intoxicated with the view of children as dependents and themselves as fair representatives of children. Adults simply "forget" to raise other perspectives. It is more or less taken for granted that "what is good for the family is good for the child." (1990:87)

Challenging our theoretical perspectives means asking hard questions, reawakening us to wonder about what we have forgotten, what we have taken for granted, and what views might have "intoxicated" us and blurred our vision of children's needs and perspectives.

Children as Agents in Their Own Lives

Secondly, and very significantly, scholars examining the "cultural politics of childhood" have emphasized that children are and must be seen as active in the construction of their own social lives, the lives of those around them, and the societies in which they live. If childhood is not a strictly biological phenomenon but a largely social one, they argue, then the part that young people play in shaping their own and others' social worlds must be taken into account (James 2004). Prout and James urge researchers to understand children as active agents and not just passive subjects in the construction and reconstruction of social structures and processes (1990:8). Unified by a view of children as active and constructive members of society and childhood as an integral part of the social fabric, scholars stimulated by this new paradigm focused on the empirical circumstance of children's real, everyday lives and invited children themselves to explain how they are experiencing their lives (Boocock and Scott 2005).

Scholars working in this vein argue that their work will be as important to twenty-first-century scholarship as women's and racial and ethnic studies were to twentieth-century scholarship. One of the potentially most transformative characteristics of this scholarship is its attention to children's *voice* and *agency* (Boocock and Scott 2005, Prout and James 1990; Pufall and Unsworth 2004; Qvortrup 2005). By voice, scholars refer to "the cluster of intentions, hopes, grievances and expectations that children guard as their own" (Pufall and Unsworth 2004). By agency, they reference the fact that children are more self-determining than we have generally acknowledged. Children act as agents in their own lives, though they often act from positions of limited power. Nevertheless, children's actions affect their worlds, and they voice their views in efforts to affect or persuade others (Pufall and Unsworth 2004).

Thus, in addition to running against the grain of traditional theoretical ideas and assumptions, this emerging paradigm of child study challenges the way that the profession has engaged with young people. Recognizing that children and youth are fully human beings (rather than simply immature adults, or human *becomings*) alters the parameters of practice. For example, granting children voice and agency raises new questions about how they are (or are not) involved in choices that affect their lives—such as decisions about out-of-home placement, consent to medical treatment, meaningful participation in school governance, or voice in the management of programs designed to enhance their welfare. The paradigm also raises questions about how to undertake research efforts that recognize young people's experiences and take their perspectives into account.

Social workers in many other countries have been grappling with these concerns, propelled at least in part by their engagement with the United Nations Convention on the Rights of the Child (CRC). The CRC articulates an international response to questions about what a child is and what she needs. The convention describes rights that children have for special protection, but it also specifies children's rights to identity, to form and express views, to association, and to privacy. In the United States, one of the two countries that has not ratified the CRC, there has been a remarkable absence of debate or discussion about the convention. In our experience, most social workers in the United States have never heard of the CRC, a shocking situation in light of its influence abroad. Despite this lack of engagement with the CRC, some U.S. scholars and practitioners are beginning to raise important questions regarding children's voice and agency as citizens (see, for example, Checkoway and Guttierez 2006). Still, questions regarding children's voice and agency remain largely unexamined despite profound implications for social work practice with young people in the United States.

Childhood, Youth, and Politics

Finally, the third premise of this paradigm entails the notion that concepts of childhood and youth—like all other social and cultural ideas—emerge in the context of relations of political and economic power (Katz 2004; Qvortrup 2005; Scheper-Hughes and Sargent 1998; Stephens 1995). The discourses and practices of childhood and youth that shape our thinking and behavior toward them are inseparable from these political and economic relationships. When we say that childhood and youth are political and economic ideas, we reference the ways that governments, political parties, national and international organizations, media outlets, and marketers make use of notions of childhood and youth. In addition to being social and cultural institutions that structure the lives of young people, notions of childhood and adolescence have been invested with enormous symbolic power. To give just one example, several scholars have noted waves of popular hysteria over child abduction seemingly out of proportion to the rarity of these tragic instances (Fass 2007; Ivey 1995; Mintz 2004). These scholars argue that panics about missing children express a much more general sense of vulnerability and loss of innocence, functioning as powerful ways to express a less clearly focused sense of grievance and anxiety about other shifts in the economy, changes in the family, new sexual practices, and changing gender roles (Comaroff 1997; Fass 2007; Katz 2005). Yet, as adults respond to these panics by restricting children's freedoms and increasing surveillance of their activities, the symbolic uses of childhood by adults generate material effects on the minds and bodies of young people (Cross 2004).

When we say that childhood and youth are political and economic ideas, we also draw attention to the ways in which political and economic change affects the lived experiences of young people. Robert Coles, in his groundbreaking book *The Political Life of Children* (1986), argued vigorously that though children do not vote or hold office, they are not secluded or shielded from the effects of political and economic processes. Indeed, political processes produce changes in welfare laws, health provision, lunch programs, recreational centers, school outcomes measures, juvenile justice statutes, and public housing—all of which have direct and immediate effects on the everyday lives of young people. In fact, as Coles notes, it is possible to understand the ways that the nation's politics make up the individual child's psychology. Katz illustrates this point when she describes the ways that poor and working-class children in New York City in the 1990s "could see their declining 'values' in the dilapidated conditions of the city's public schools, in the city's litter, which was strewn in poorly maintained neighborhood parks and playgrounds, and in the unsafe and decaying public spaces of the residential city" (2004:160).

As social workers, we have opportunities to witness the ways in which laws, social policies, and social work practices are based on particular conceptions of who children are, what rights they do or do not have, and what they need. Within the profession, specific notions of childhood and youth are embedded in the ways that young people are talked about, the network of practices in which they are immersed everyday, and the laws and policies that frame these practices. While we may prefer to think of our work as rooted only in the objective basis of empirical evidence, this paradigm suggests that social workers are embroiled in the messier, value-based struggle over the meaning of childhood instead. We must make diligent efforts to expand our knowledge of children and youth and to assess the effectiveness of children's programs through means that are rigorous, ethical, and methodologically sound. However, acknowledging the cultural politics of childhood challenges us to recognize that beneath technical and methodological concerns lay important political and moral questions about the place of children in the broader society, the nature of their troubles, and our responsibilities in these matters.

This means that our daily practice as social workers is bound up with the cultural politics of childhood. It also means that the social work agencies, schools, community groups, and policymaking bodies that employ social workers can be understood as sites of struggle over understandings and practices of childhood and youth. These struggles have profound consequences for children, youth, and society. Acknowledging the existence of childhood as a cultural category, we argue, will aid social workers in these struggles by providing the tools to contest prevailing assumptions regarding the nature and needs of young people, and to develop new strategies of thought and action.

In summary then, we acknowledge that there is nothing new about studying children—the profession of social work has always rested on an abundance of research on young people. However, thinking through the "cultural politics of childhood" shifts the way that scholars engage with children and opens up new terrain for further research. It requires that we critically examine the discourses that structure our understandings of children and youth. It proposes that we consider young people as agents in their own lives and as participants in constructing our shared social worlds. Research in this paradigm also takes a new perspective on social work and social policy. It demands that we understand social policy and social work practice not as simple responses to the self-evident and natural needs of young people. Instead, the policies and practices of social work are considered as means by which childhood and youth are constructed for young people (James and James 2004). Finally, this paradigm prompts us to ask whether the specific, modern, Western notions about childhood so central to the emergence of U.S. social work in the twentieth century are "at risk" in the context of a globalizing world (Fass 2007; Katz 2004; Ruddick 2006; Schepher-Hughes and Sargent 1998; Stephens 1995).

THE RISE OF MODERN CHILDHOOD, YOUTH, AND SOCIAL WORK

Working within a paradigm of the "cultural politics of childhood" reorients social work's search for foundational knowledge toward questions of history, culture, and power. It challenges us to explore the relationship between a transforming global order and the evolving expectations and understandings of young people. Engagement with this literature offers us ways to understand how deeply the history of the profession of social work is entwined with the emergence of particular modern Western ideas about childhood and youth—a relationship that has been both taken for granted and left largely unexamined.

In concise and insightful recent essays on childhood in America, Paula Fass draws attention to three issues that have redefined the experience of childhood and youth for young people: the issues of children's work, the role of play in child development, and the problems of sexuality (2007:204). Beginning in the late nineteenth century, and gaining momentum in the twentieth century, the "century of the child," Americans defined a "proper childhood" to be one that was free of labor; devoted in substantial measure to education, play, and recreation; and free of abuse and exploitation. These protections of childhood originated as middle-class conceptions that were gradually extended to all, and sometimes imposed on families who had differing expectations of and relationships with their children.

The effort to extend this ideal of childhood and its protections to all young people was at the center of much of the social work profession's earliest campaigns. Fass enumerates a long list of the institutions and practices that "spilled out" from this vision of childhood, including Children's Aid Societies, a host of Societies for the Prevention of Cruelty to Children, orphanages, adoption and foster care, juvenile courts and detention centers, sports clubs and playgrounds, settlements and social centers, and the Children's Bureau (207). As Fass notes, while in Germany and Britain it was the needs of the worker that served as the foundation of the welfare state, in the United States it was the figure of the mother and the child that prompted the development of Mother's Pensions and served as the entering wedge in the development of welfare provision (249; see also Gordon 1994; Skocpol 1992). In addition, it was the idea of the child and the extension of childhood to adolescents that necessitated the creation of universal public schools as symbols of democracy and community pride and important sites for the extension of social work to young people (Fass 2007; Tyack 2003).

As Viviana Zelizer (1985) has pointed out, at the core of this proliferating set of policies, practices, and programs was a cultural shift from the economic to the emotional valuing of children. American young people, valued in the seventeenth and eighteenth centuries for their economic contributions, were transformed into "priceless" children, beings whose worth could not be evaluated in monetary terms. Children's value was understood in sentimental terms that then obligated their parents, communities, and society to a commitment to protect their well-being. As Fass summarizes, "In shifting the child from a ledger where he or she could participate in economic calculations and to which even his or her small contribution had weight, to a ledger in which the only legitimate calculation was how well he could be sheltered and provided for, the society experienced a paradigm shift" ((2007:206). Social work was intimately involved in bringing about this paradigm shift and in elaborating institutions and practices that sheltered, provided for, controlled, and contained young people outside of the marketplace. As we enter the twenty-first century, we seem to be experiencing another paradigm shift in conceptions of and directions for childhood, youth, and social work as a powerful new logic of the market penetrates all aspects of social life.

NEOLIBERAL GLOBALIZATION

In this section we explore the concept of globalization and the relationship to the logic and practices of neoliberalism, which we contend are key to understanding not only the contemporary context of practice with children and youth but also the very ways in which childhood and youth are being constructed. Globalization—new arrangements and alignments of nations and regions, enabling new flows and conjunctures of people, ideas, culture, and politics—has impacted children beyond making McDonald's hamburgers, Levis, and rap music internationally available, though those are not insignificant developments. Globalization has entailed the international circulation of images of children's plights and the development of global networks of concern for children's welfare that produced the United Nations Convention on the Rights of the Child (Fass 2007). Even more profoundly, however, in the context of a globalizing world, we believe that modern ideas about who children are and what they need are being displaced. We follow Stephens in proposing that "we should take very seriously the possibility that we are now witnessing a profound restructuring of the child within the context of a movement from state to global capitalism, modernity to postmodernity" (1995:19).

Critical theorists of late-twentieth-century global capitalism have drawn attention to globalization as both an *ideology*, or set of beliefs, regarding the "inevitability" of the new world order and a *political strategy*, a systematic effort to consolidate power, create "flexible" workers, and open borders to the movement of corporate interests (Korten 2001; Piven and Cloward 1997). They recognize the transnational penetration of "neoliberal" economic politics and practices as a driving force in the production of new forms of social exclusion and political conflict (Alvarez, Dagnino, and Escobar 1998; Lowe and Lloyd 1997). We see evidence of this profound restructuring in our observations of the policy revolution that has reshaped young people's access to food, shelter, health care, education, and social services over the last decade (Giroux 2003; Grossberg 2001; Ruddick 2006). Critical understanding of and attention to these broader political and economic processes are essential to contemporary social work with children and youth, even in its most "local" and "personal" forms. (For further discussion, see Clarke [2003], Finn and Jacobson [2008], and Ferguson, Lavalette, and Whitmore [2005].)

The discussion of globalization cannot be divorced from that of neoliberalism. The central, powerful neoliberal idea is that human well-being is best advanced when individuals are free to apply their entrepreneurial skills and freedoms in a market economy. This philosophy holds that the social good will be maximized by maximizing the reach and frequency of market transactions and so seeks to extend the market into all arenas of social life (Harvey 2005). Neoliberal political and economic ideas are premised on the belief that private enterprise and individual initiative are the keys to the creation of wealth, the elimination of poverty, and the improvement in human welfare. Competition—among individuals, businesses, cities, or nations—is held to be a primary virtue. According to neoliberal theory, freedom of individuals, businesses, and corporations to act in unrestricted ways within the market will deliver a higher living standard to everyone, as the "rising tide" of productivity will "lift all boats."

From a neoliberal perspective, many of the social institutions that have been central to our profession—social insurance, welfare benefits, and social services—have become positioned as economically and socially costly obstacles to maximizing economic performance and productivity (Burchell 1996). Individual success in this context is held to be a product of each person's enterprise and ability to "entrepreneur" for himself or herself within the free market. Conversely, lack of success is attributed to individual failings and deficiencies, not to the effects of broader structural inequalities. Thus, from a perspective that celebrates engagement with the market, welfare provision is conceived as a barrier to initiative, trapping recipients in patterns of dependency and need.

Neoliberal ideas became widely accepted as "common sense" at the end of the millennium. Under the influence of neoliberal ideas, nearly all governments, either voluntarily or under coercive pressure, embraced aspects of neoliberalism and changed policies to roll back taxes, reduce welfare spending, and deregulate labor markets (Harvey 2005). Of course, the variation and unevenness among governments is substantial, and no state or government clung to neoliberal theory all the time (Clarke 2003). Nevertheless, it is possible to trace an emphatic global turn in political and economic practices and thinking that resulted in the withdrawal from many areas of social welfare, and the deregulation and privatization of other arenas.

Neoliberal strategies of government have a profound impact on contemporary social work. Fisher and Karger argue in their text *Social Work and Community in a Private World* (1997) that the neoliberal approach is to transfer government roles to business and to reorient social, cultural, and political institutions to corporate values. To that end, numerous public social welfare agencies (as well as prisons, schools, universities, and other social institutions) have been replaced by private profit-making businesses or at least placed under increasing pressure to view their efforts in "quasi-business terms," considering their efforts to provide care for the nation's neediest and most vulnerable members in terms of markets, margins, competitors, and bottom lines (Burchell 1996; Harvey 2005; Rose 1996). Sometimes moves to transfer public responsibilities and resources to the private sector were direct and obvious, as in the privatization of school districts, welfare programs, or prisons; other times, perhaps less so. For example, Karger draws attention to the dramatic recent expansion of the "fringe economy" in the context of a diminishing welfare state:

> While TANF work requirements force former recipients into low-wage work, they also allow fringe economy businesses to assume some welfare-state functions, such as providing emergency cash assistance through payday loans, pawns, and other short-term credit. Hence, the fringe economy has taken on the functions of a privatized—and expensive—welfare state by offering former recipients emergency financial services no longer provided by government. It's also one of the only economic sectors that primarily serve the poor. (2005:24)

Neoliberal approaches to government have transformed the structure of social welfare institutions, encouraged the expansion of privatized alternatives, and raised new and challenging questions for social work practice. For example, Fisher and Karger question how we will practice *social* work in a world that is increasingly antagonistic to the social sphere. They ask, "how do we create empowered citizens in a context that values independent and self sufficient family members, workers, and consumers?" (1997:4). Epstein argues that in this context, social work has broadly and much too uncritically disseminated the idea of individual initiative and personal autonomy as the solutions to problems of living in ways that make these strategies appear "believable." She notes, "The view holds that *you can do it, you can have it, it is up to you to pull yourself together to get the skills to learn the stuff, get on with your life, do it*" (1999:10).

In the context of a neoliberal ethic that celebrates self-sufficiency, pathologizes dependency, and advocates market solutions to personal and social problems, how do we think about young people? The modern notions of "the child" that were built into twentieth-century welfare programs assumed that children's dependency made it incumbent upon adults to make arrangements for their protection, education, guidance, and nurture. Meanwhile, children were extracted from the streets, the labor market, and other locations where they might be "self sufficient." Do we expect children and youth to "pull themselves together" and "get on with their lives"? Dependent by social, cultural, and legal definition, where do children and youth fit in contemporary social, cultural, and political worlds? What are the effects of reform on the life experiences of diverse young people across the nation? So far, scholars who have productively explored the implications of neoliberal globalization for the profession have paid surprisingly scant attention to shifts and changes in social work's relationship to children and youth. These transformations are central concerns for the authors who contribute to this book.

CHILDHOOD AND YOUTH IN NEOLIBERAL GLOBALIZATION

The complicated constellation of neoliberal reforms affects children in local settings in complex ways. The contributors to this volume are involved in the process of tracing the impacts of these reforms on discourses of childhood and on practice with children in particular contexts. However, as an introduction to these very specific explorations, we want to highlight some general trends here. We draw attention in particular to a growing indifference to the material plight of segments of the nation's youthful population; an increasing reliance on strategies of exclusion, punishment, and stigma; and an escalating sense of panic and anxiety over "children at risk" who are also understood to be "risky children" (Stephens 1995).

Children, Youth, and Intensifying Inequality

First, implementation of neoliberal political and economic theory has had material impact on children's lives. Neoliberal interventions have not delivered on promises to "lift all boats" or to generate productivity that would "trickle down" and eliminate poverty. In fact, a neoliberal reform has produced intensifying levels of inequality, particularly for young people. Analysts offer a variety of ways to illustrate these patterns of inequality. For example, by 2004 the richest 5% of all U.S. households received more than 20% of total income. What is more, the average after tax income of the richest 1% of households was 50 times that of the bottom 20% of households. Neoliberal policies resulted in the redistribution of wealth upward: these wealthy households saw their after-tax income increase by 140% since 1979—65 times more than the gains seen by the typical household and 370 times the average income gain for the 22.2 million American households with the lowest incomes (Children's Defense Fund 2005:4).

The effects of this intensifying inequality have been particularly harsh on children. Despite the heralded "success" of welfare reforms, for example, in 2005, the U.S. Census Bureau reported that 13.3 % of all persons lived in poverty, which was pegged at an income level of $15,577 for a family of three persons. Rates of child poverty were substantially higher than the average for all persons: 18.5 % of all those under 18 were poor. Conditions were worse for the youngest children: more than a fifth (21.3%) of all of the nation's children under 5 years of age were poor (Child Welfare League of America 2007). The number of children in extreme poverty—defined as living at less than half of the poverty level, with an annual income below $7,610 for a family of three—increased to its highest level in more than 30 years, affecting almost 5.6 million children (Darling-Hammond 2007; Children's Defense Fund 2005). Though children's poverty is often attributed to lack of parental enterprise and work effort, more than 7 out 10 poor children lived with at least one employed relative (Children's Defense Fund 2005).

The impact of deep inequalities on poor children was made harsher by increasing barriers to quality education, decent housing, and adequate health care for many of the nation's young people. Under the dramatically altered welfare rules, only one-quarter of poor children receive benefits under the provisions of Temporary Assistance for Needy Children (TANF), though the number of children living in poverty has increased nearly 13% since 2000 (Children's Defense Fund 2005; National Center for Children in Poverty 2006). As public budgets tightened, states aggressively retrenched public health care to poor families and children. As states reduced Medicaid rolls and tightened benefits, infant mortality, a key index of child health, which had declined for four decades, showed significant and sometimes dramatic increases in 2005 in regions with poor populations and particularly minority populations (Eckholm 2007). Patterns of public disinvestment in children's welfare in poor and working-class neighborhoods produced deteriorating public schools, playgrounds, recreation centers, and public spaces (Katz 2005; Kozol 2005; McLaren and Farahmandpur 2006). Amid a crisis in affordable housing, 40% of homeless persons were members of families with children. Another 5% of the homeless population were unaccompanied youth, age 18 or younger. Higher education became significantly less accessible to working- and middle-class families, and young people who succeeded in higher education emerged with escalating levels of personal debt (Toppo 2005). Because of this debt load, many young people are increasingly reliant on their family members into their mid-to-late twenties or early thirties as they work at low-paying, entry-level jobs or assume unpaid internships (Jennings 2007). Young people without this family support struggle to find a foothold in society.

One central and profoundly troubling effect of neoliberal policy, then, is a deepening inequality in the material circumstances of the nation's young people. This dismal result has occurred in the world's richest nation, during a period that has been heralded for its prosperity. What is very striking is not only that this injustice has occurred, but that it has produced so little comment. As Grossberg notes, "this intolerable situation is tolerated, not only by politicians but also by the general population" (2001:113). He suggests that this indifference to the plight of young people indexes a shift in our conception of children, and an abandonment of our belief in and commitment to our collective future. He proposes that throughout most of the twentieth century, our faith in our collective future was embodied in children and youth. Our national investment in their welfare was a sign of hope for that future. In the contemporary context of neoliberal globalization, the attack on programs for youth is also an assault against our commitment to that collective modern social vision (135).

We agree with Grossberg that public indifference to the material plight of so many of the nation's young people indexes a profound change in our shared notions of childhood and youth. Shared commitments to the well-being of all the nation's children have eroded in the context of neoliberalism, altering our view of who children are, and what we owe them. Evidence of this displacement of concern for the welfare of "the child" is evident in the tendency to "change the subject" of policy once aimed at children. As "Aid to Dependent Children" is replaced by the "Personal Responsibility and Work Opportunity Reconciliation Act" (PRWORA), for example, children and youth are displaced as the explicit subjects of reform discourse as the spotlight focuses on the "work effort" of their parents. In contemporary welfare provision, benefits to children are conditioned on the willingness and ability of their parents to become "self-sufficient" by complying with stringent demands for "work effort" and other punitive requirements. Members of families whose adult members cannot or do not comply with these demands and requirements are "sanctioned" as benefits are reduced or terminated.

In addition, PRWORA targeted benefits to full citizens, restricting benefits to legal and undocumented immigrants. As of 2001, many (about 15%) of the nation's children are native citizens with immigrant parents; another 4% are foreign-born children with at least one immigrant parent (Leiter, McDonald, and Jacobson 2006). New immigrant children are excluded from benefits. Native-born children of immigrant parents are eligible; however, scholars have documented an erosion of access to benefits by second-generation children, following their parents' loss of benefits. In other words, children of immigrants, who are among the most likely young people to need a safety net because their parents are poor and uninsured, are now less likely to access it (Leiter, McDonald, and Jacobson 2006).

In summary, children's status as children no longer protects them from the withdrawal of even minimal levels of public support. Instead, proponents of welfare reform such as William Bennett degraded the provision of aid to poor children as a product of "the nanny state," an arrangement that "has eroded self-reliance and encouraged dependency, crowding out the character-forming institutions and enfeebling us as citizens" (Bennett 1998). The disappearance of concern for the material well-being of children from such debate about welfare reform bears heavily on the minds and bodies of young people, even as the evidence of these impacts escapes the frame of reference of policy debate.

Children, Youth, and Exclusion

As the infrastructure of support for many of the nation's young people eroded in recent years, punitive responses to the problems of children and youth gained momentum, revealing erosion of protectionist ideas about shielding young people from the full, adult consequences of their actions. Juvenile justice reforms "got tough" on young people, making it easier to try children as adults and stiffening their sentences (Sealander 2003; Shook 2005). School districts across the country enacted school discipline policies that enforced "zero tolerance" in schools. Mandatory expulsion laws, enacted to remove dangerous young people from schools, seemed to take on lives of their own. However, as these policies were implemented, evidence arrived of more and more districts removing children from school under the law on the basis of vague offenses with vague criteria for reentry, a practice that undermined the vision of universal education (Zweifler and DeBeers 2002). Practices of monitoring and surveillance of youth intensified. For example, in 1995, the U.S. Supreme Court upheld the right of schools to test all members of sports teams for drug use, even when individuals were not suspected of using drugs; in 2002, the Court upheld random drug testing for all students involved in extracurricular activities (Mintz 2004).

When investment in social welfare was withdrawn, prison populations soared as states invested in building new prisons and expanding their criminal and juvenile justice systems. In 2006, approximately 7 million Americans were in prison or jail, on probation, or on parole (Sarri and Shook 2006). As a result of the expansion of the justice system, increasing numbers of young people, particularly poor youth and youth of color, spend considerable portions of their adolescence and early adulthood in the juvenile and criminal justice systems. The erosion of a range of public social welfare institutions and organizations focused on youth development has been accompanied by an expanding criminal justice system, so that the justice systems are becoming a primary public site for youth development for a large population of young people. These youth are often those whose families did not have the resources to access or purchase the programs and services provided in the private sector.

In these policy moves, children and youth are subject to a range of strategies that evict young people from the conceptual categories of childhood. Young people who are judged to have made "bad choices" are no longer subject to the protections we once sought to guarantee to children. Children who are disciplined under zero-tolerance policies are denied the access to the education once guaranteed to the young (Zweifler, this volume); juvenile detainees are held responsible as adults without ever having experienced the rights of adulthood (Shook, this volume). The direction of much of this reform supports the claims of some researchers that notions about the innocence and vulnerability of children are being replaced with policies that are hostile to children, and that powerful interests are "at war" with the nation's youth (Giroux 2003; Grossberg 2001; Scheper-Hughes and Sargent 1998) or at least with "some people's children" (Hutchison and Charlesworth 2000).

Childhood, Youth, and Panic

The tone of all policy reform is not "child hostile." For example, in the face of this harshening of children's policy in the 1990s, calls for integrating children's services at the level of "the community" soared. Advocates from across a broad political spectrum converged upon a vision of reform in which local people would provide comprehensive, collaborative, community-based care that could respond flexibly to family needs (for example, Clinton 1996; McKnight 1995; Schorr 1997). Yet, these harmonious visions of children and youth ensconced in communities are starkly at odds with the broader trends in social policy reform that leave parents in poor and working-class communities overworked and overwhelmed, as demands of the workplace increase and the public infrastructures of schools and neighborhoods deteriorate. In addition, idyllic visions of community-based commitment to the needs of individual troubled local children are regularly disturbed by panics about the welfare of young people in these settings. Alarm about teenage pregnancy, juvenile crime, and child abduction powerfully impacted local communities in spite of the declining rates of teenage pregnancy (Mintz 2004) and juvenile crime (Snyder 2006), and the relative rarity with which children are kidnapped by strangers (Sedlak et al. 2002).

Parents and children had other worries, too, as an increasing portion of the youthful population was perceived to be suffering from emotional disturbance. In an era when support for welfare provision, schools, and social services for children dwindled, alarm over the status of children's mental health flourished. In 2000, the surgeon general of the United States, David Satcher, developed a national "action agenda" to respond to "public crisis in mental health for infants, children, and adolescents" that was conveyed as afflicting all children across lines of class, race, and culture. Experts at the conference quoted studies reporting that about one of every five young people suffered with diagnosable mental disorders (Kelleher 2000; Offord 2000). Evidence of parental concern for children's mental health problems was in evidence as an increasing proportion of the youthful population was diagnosed and treated pharmacologically. In 1996, for example, it was estimated that 1.5 million of the 38 million schoolchildren (or 3–5%) took Ritalin to treat attention deficit and hyperactivity disorder (ADHD) (Kolata 1996). By 2003, the Center for Disease Control estimated that approximately 4.4 million children (or close 8% of all children in the United States) were reported to have a history of ADHD diagnosis, with 2.5 million of them taking medication for the disorder (CDC, 2005). In addition to surging increases in prescriptions for Ritalin, an increasing number of children were diagnosed and treated for what have traditionally been considered adult disorders, particularly bipolar disorder, during this same period. Researchers reported in 2006 that a fivefold increase in the use of potent antipsychotic drugs to treat children for problems such as aggression and mood swings occurred between 1993 and 2002 (Carey 2006).

Nor was concern for young people limited to children with diagnosed disorders. Changing conditions of childhood affected the materially privileged as well as disadvantaged young people in other ways, too, as adult insecurity and fearfulness generated what observers dubbed "domestic fortressing," "household hypervigilance" (Katz 2005), or "paranoid parenting" (Lavalette 2005:154). Parents were drawn to strategies and devices that they hoped would protect their children from threat—private play corrals, highly structured and supervised activities, and home surveillance cameras (Katz 2005). Motivated by fear, parents restricted children's activities, limited their ability to play independently, and conveyed them to and from school and recreational activities (Lavalette 2005).

THE CHAPTERS IN THIS BOOK

We argue that this proliferation of policy reform, punitiveness, and panic indexes a transformation in notions of childhood and youth that has had profound, if largely unexamined, impacts on the daily practice of social workers. Reconstructions of childhood and youth also reconstruct the roles of those who care for young people—parents, teachers, social workers. In particular, we propose that the instability of these ideas presents new problems for the social work profession. Though social work practice with young people has historically been embedded with contradiction, in the transforming global order of the twenty-first century, social workers are encountering a particularly demanding set of competing claims about the needs and rights of children and youth. Workers are facing unprecedented and often excruciating dilemmas in policy and practice with young people. For example, child welfare workers are urged to serve children's best interests in the face of the realities of welfare systems that are overburdened, and economic, health care, and education systems that grow more precarious and privatized. School social workers are incited to "leave no child behind" even as they are asked to implement "zero-tolerance" policies that exclude young people from educational settings. Youth workers are asked to prevent the development of delinquency among "children at risk" while they are charged with holding juveniles accountable for their behavior and protecting communities from "risky children." In special education, social workers mobilize support for the inclusion of children with diverse needs in schools and communities, while school systems face increasing pressures to exclude children who will jeopardize average test scores and achievement records. In local communities, practitioners struggle to make innovative community-based programs work as the income, employment, and housing infrastructure grows more precarious.

Contributors to this text explore specific ways in which our perceptions of and discourses about children and youth have shifted and changed over time, particularly in the context of neoliberal policy, and they illustrate the implications of these shifts for work in specific local contexts. In addition, they highlight a few of the many possibilities for reinventing social work with young people. Here we elaborate, in turn, the three central themes around which the book is structured: the changing discourses of childhood and youth, the various contexts and settings in which notions of childhood and youth are contested, and the prospects for reinventing social work with young people.

Exploring Changing Discourses of Childhood and Youth

Contributors to part 1 of this volume inspire us to think critically about the contemporary "common sense" of childhood and youth. They illustrate a variety of strategies for making the familiar unfamiliar and making visible what we take for granted (Chambon 1999). Their work suggests that preparation in strategies for "interrupting this message" in order to think reflectively should be part of the education of all social workers. They illustrate and analyze particular discourses of childhood and youth, examining ways of carving up reality that structure what can be said, thought, and known about young people.

One means of calling into question what we take for granted at present is the study of the "history of the present." In part 1, Janet Finn follows the philosopher Michel Foucault's observation that "recourse to history is meaningful to the extent that history serves to show how that-which-is has not always been: that the things that seem most evident to us are always formed in the confluence of encounters and chances, during the course of a precarious and fragile history" (1983:206). Finn offers a historical perspective on the social construction of childhood in relation to notions of trouble. She examines the interplay among shifting representations of children and youth, beliefs about problems and pathology, and technologies of social work intervention. In particular, she speaks to the role of social work in both the consumption and production of images of trouble.

Several contributions to part 1 critically examine particular discourses that structure social work policy and practice with young people, illustrating how these ways of thinking and talking about young people are both shaped and constrained by social structures. These chapters examine how particular stories that we tell about young people shape the social work practices and social policies and institutions that we create to care for or control them. For example, Lynn Nybell critically examines representations of "missing children," exploring the circulation of these images and the ways in which they map onto a host of adult anxieties. Nybell raises important questions regarding the race- and gender-based nature of these images.

Linwood Cousins takes readers inside a predominantly African American public high school and critically examines the disconnect between the discourse of "moral entrepreneurs" and the complex realities of everyday life for many young people of color in the United States. His analysis speaks to the hypocrisy of public policy and policymakers who fail to acknowledge these complexities. To illustrate ways in which young people are actively challenging and changing the discourses of childhood, youth, and trouble, Jennifer Tilton focuses on the collective action of young people to stop the building of a "super jail" for California youth. Tilton's case study offers provocative insights into emerging youth voices, organizing strategies, and forms of power. Deborah Lustig presents an ethnographic perspective on young mothers, showing how parenting teens give meaning to their experience; claim rights, responsibility, and agency; and talk back to a dominant discourse that both pathologizes and silences them. Finally, Kerrie Ghenie and Charlie Wellenstein's contribution concludes part 1 as they probe shifting discourses and practices of attachment in relationship to the welfare of children. Their historical overview sets the stage for their critical reading of contemporary child welfare policy and the contradictory messages regarding attachment therein.

Contexts and Settings

Contributors to part 2 focus on a critical examination of specific policies and practices in particular locations and settings. A primary goal of these contributors is to examine the connection between macro and micro processes, in order to show how broader economic, political, and cultural transformations have influenced policy and practice toward children and youth. At the same time, each contributor attends to the importance of geography. In doing so, they collectively demonstrate that contestations and negotiations over the cultural parameters of childhood are ongoing across multiple sites and locations, involving actors representing a diverse array of interests, values, and resources. As each piece demonstrates, these contests and negotiations are not merely symbolic but have substantial consequences for children and youth.

Policy is often defined as a course of action directed toward a problem, issue, or group of people. However, contributors to part 2 demonstrate that policy itself often constitutes a particular problem, issue, or group. For example, policy can serve to establish who or what is considered to be a child, define the problems facing those who fall into this category, specify the rules for addressing these problems, and allocate resources to carry out these rules. Embedded within these categories, definitions, rules, and allocations are meanings regarding the nature and needs of children and youth. These meanings serve not only to shape understandings of the nature and needs of children and youth, but also to guide how social workers and other professionals practice and engage with children and youth.

In addition to acknowledging the role that policy plays in shaping understandings of the nature and needs of children and youth, contributions to part 2 explore how practitioners accept, modify, or resist these understandings. Attention to the meanings that practitioners construct and employ, as well as the organizing fields of knowledge they draw from in constructing and employing these meanings, reveals the tremendous fluidity of the cultural category of childhood and shows how its meanings vary across and within different contexts and settings.

Thus, these contributors make obvious the role of place in helping to produce meanings regarding the nature and needs of childhood and demonstrate how these meanings vary across or within different institutional settings and local contexts. Further, they demonstrate the constitutive role of practice, thereby revealing the power that social workers and other professionals hold in the production of the cultural category of childhood. Even more importantly, however, they reveal the power of social work and other professionals in reifying or altering social and structural inequalities, thereby offering the potential for a new course of action.

To begin Part 2, Jeffrey Shook explores the notion of "childhood by geography" through critical inquiry into variability within and across states regarding the decisions to treat juvenile offenders as adults. He builds from this critique to offer readers a framework for a more just and equitable balancing of the rights and responsibilities of young people. Luke Bergman continues the exploration of juvenile justice, taking readers to Detroit and into the political history of a new juvenile detention facility. Bergman demonstrates how the brick-and-mortar construction of the detention facility represents the physical embodiment of a political shift in attitudes toward and treatment of young offenders. Ruth Zweifler shows the ways in which punitive disciplinary policies are impacting the lives and educational futures of children in public school. Drawing from her work as a student advocate in Michigan, Zweifler also shows how young people are talking back, asserting their agency, and contesting the punitive policies and practices that shape and constrain them.

Part 2 continues with explorations of practice with children in a variety of specific settings. Patricia Jessup offers readers an ethnographic journey into a rural Head Start program and the ways in which teachers, administrators, children, and parents construct and negotiate meanings of childhood and disability. Jessup illuminates not only the social construction of childhood, but also the social construction of disability and the profound consequences of practices of labeling. Ben Stride-Darnley takes readers inside two mental health programs for children and youth, offering a nuanced picture of the ways in which young people give meaning to experiences in mental health systems, engage with professional helpers, negotiate the boundaries between institutional and noninstitutional spaces, and exercise agency within the confines of these spaces. Lynn Nybell draws on her ethnographic study of community-based intervention with "at-risk" children to raise questions about the ways in which notions of risk and concomitant practices of intervention are constructed. She questions narrow conceptualizations of risk in terms of children's behaviors and attitudes and asks readers to examine critically the implications of such reductionist concepts in light of larger shifts toward devolution and dismantling of social welfare systems.

Finally, Rachel Heiman shifts our attention away from social work's more traditional sites of engagement by turning her gaze to middle-class family life, problematizing how children learn the habits, tastes, and styles of their class positioning in ways that go without saying. In so doing, she helps us to think more critically about the making of childhood and about the concept of risk therein. Heiman demonstrates ways in which children are learning to be particular *kinds* of consumers, students, workers, and social subjects.

Reinventing Social Work with Children and Youth

Contributors to part 3 go beyond critique to open and explore possibilities for critical and creative social work practice with children and youth. They recognize the ways in which young people assert their agency, even in the most constrained circumstances, and they point to the power of intergenerational relationships where adults engage with young people as allies, advocates, and, most importantly, colearners.

In exploring creative directions for practice with children and youth, the contributors do not offer naïve or simplistic interpretations of the problems at hand. Contributors not only resist the pressure toward context stripping, they actively probe the very specific historical, cultural, social, geographical, and political spaces of young people's experiences. Their inquiries provide readers with intimate encounters with children and youth at home and in schools, treatment centers, court rooms, and correctional facilities. They take us to public sites of youth action, resistance, and performance and to private moments of reflection and dialogue that offer a more nuanced understanding of the tensions, fears, and hopes that shape young people's lives.

Janet Finn's contribution to part 3 offers a framework for social justice–oriented social work, grounded in the key themes of meaning, context, power, history, and possibility, to illustrate the challenges and possibilities for social work practice that honors the voices, views, and rights of children. This framework provides a structure through which to view more specific examples of creative work with young people. Derrick Jackson follows by describing his own journey into social justice–oriented social work with young people, as he joined youth in Ypsilanti, Michigan, to build Project SpeakOUT. Jackson's account of the evolution of Project SpeakOUT demonstrates the unexpected and dynamic ways that youth-led initiatives can transform communities, institutions, social workers, and the young participants themselves.

In the chapters that follow, contributors describe their own ventures in pioneering new forms of collaboration with children and youth. Maryam Ahranjani outlines the development of a project that seeks to inspire young people to care about the Constitution by showing them how if affects them in schools. Ahranjani's work also demonstrates how joining the energies of young law students and youth in the nation's low-income public schools and detention centers transforms all participants. Sara Goodkind draws from her ethnographic work on "gender-specific" programs in juvenile justice settings for young women. She challenges her readers to think critically about social work practices that center on concerns for young women's "self-esteem" or "independence" while failing to challenge the structural inequities that impinge on their lives. Goodkind concludes by offering guidelines for interventions that reconnect the "personal" with the "political" in residential programs for adolescent girls. In her description of the Youth Uprising Center in Oakland, Jennifer Tilton brings the program's philosophy of "gritty youth leadership development" to life as she describes how young people led both the initial campaign and the planning process for a center that uses youth music, language, and culture—often framed as the sources of neighborhood problems—as the tools for personal and community transformation. Charles Garvin draws from a long-term participatory research project with youth to demonstrate young people's capacities for leadership and conflict resolution. Finally, Lori Fryzel and Jamie Lee Evans describe their work in California's Y.O.U.T.H. Training Project, which brings together the grassroots efforts of current and former foster youth with a successful formal social work training institution. Fryzel and Evans demonstrate ways in which a youth-led social work training movement can challenge and change child welfare practice, and they offer a powerful set of guiding principles for this work.

Questions for Discussion

Through careful attention to the social, historical, cultural, and political contexts of young people's lives and the possibilities of human agency therein, these contributors challenge the *inevitability* of contemporary policies, programs, and practices. Social work practice guided by marketization, managerialism, and the medicalization of trouble is a relatively recent phenomenon (Ferguson, Lavalette, and Whitmore 2005), and one that is open to resistance and challenge by critical practitioners and by young people themselves. Contributors challenge us to be critical consumers of policies and practices, to question received wisdom, and to probe the ways in which our "common sense" about the concerns and capacities of young people is constructed. They provide poignant illustrations of the capacities of young people as both makers of meaning and bearers of rights. They recognize children and youth as critical actors, able to reflect on their experiences, resist interventions that claim to be "in their best interests" yet deny them their voice, and respond individually and collectively in making rights claims.

As the contributors carefully examine aspects and examples of contemporary social work practice and policy with children and youth, each intends to inspire critical reflection and action. In support of that intent, we introduce discussion questions at the end of each chapter, based on a framework for critical reflection. This framework asks, first, that you consider connections between the very particular, situated accounts of work with children and youth included in this book and your own experiences. It challenges you to explore the implications of each chapter for your own social work practice. It prompts you to raise questions about what you have taken for granted in contemporary social work with young people. For example, questions push you to reconsider what you are most certain about, historicize your "here-and-nows," deconstruct your dichotomies, or "complexify" your simple answers. Furthermore, a framework for critical reflection asks you to reconsider our practice from the perspective of children and youth themselves, whose insights often challenge our perceptions and aims. Finally, this framework invites you to consider the lessons, visions, or aspirations for the future that are inspired by each account.

We are eager to broaden the conversation about the transformation of childhood, youth, and social work currently under way and to collectively imagine new possibilities for action. We believe that the work of the contributors to this volume can inspire a dialogue that makes a difference. We invite you to wonder with us.

REFERENCES

Abramovitz, M. (1996). *Regulating the lives of women: Social welfare policy from colonial times to the present.* Boston: South End Press.

Alvarez, S., E. Dagnino, and A. Escobar. (Eds.) (1998). *Cultures of politics and politics of culture: Revisioning Latin American social movements.* Boulder: Westview Press.

Ariès, P. (1962). *Centuries of childhood.* Trans. R. Baldick. London: Jonathan Cape.

Bennett, W. J. (1998). Welfare reform will benefit children. In C. Wekesser, ed., *Child welfare: Opposing viewpoints,* 45–59. San Diego: Greenhaven.

Best, J. (1990). *Threatened children: Rhetoric and concern about child-victims.* Chicago: University of Chicago Press.

Boocock, S. S., and K. A. Scott. (2005). *Kids in context: The sociological study of children and childhoods.* Lanham, Md.: Rowman and Littlefield.

Bronfenbrenner, U. (1979). *The ecology of human development: Experiments by nature and design.* Cambridge: Harvard University Press.

Burchell, G. (1996). Liberal government and techniques of the self. In A. Barry, T. Osborne, and N. Rose, eds., *Foucault and political reason: Liberalism, neo-liberalism and rationalities of government.* Chicago: University of Chicago Press.

Burman, E. (1994). *Deconstructing developmental psychology.* London: Routledge.

Carey, B. (2006). Use of antipsychotic drugs by the young rose fivefold. *New York Times,* June 6.

Center for Disease Control (2005). *Morbidity and mortality weekly report* 54: 842–47. Washington, D.C.: U.S. Government Printing Office (September 2).

Chambon, A. (1999), Foucault's approach: Making the familiar visible. In A. Chambon, A. Irving, and L. Epstein, eds., *Reading Foucault for social work.* New York: Columbia University Press.

Chambon, A., A. Irving, and L. Epstein. (1999). *Reading Foucault for social work.* New York: Columbia University Press.

Checkoway, B. N., and L. M. Gutierrez. (2006). Youth participation and community change: An introduction. *Journal of Community Practice* 14: 1–9.

Child Welfare League of America. (2007). National fact sheet 2007 (America's children: a snapshot). Accessed June 1, 2007, at http://www.cwla.org/advocacy/national factsheet07.htm.

Children's Defense Fund. (2005). The state of America's children. Accessed June 1, 2007, at http://www.childrensdefensefund.org//site/DocServer/Greenbook_2005 .pdf?docID = 1741.

Chin, E. (2003). Children out of bounds in globalising times. *Postcolonial Studies 6:* 309–17.

Christenson, P., and A. James. (2000). *Research with children.* London: Falmer Press.

Clarke, J. (2003). Turning inside out? Globalization, neoliberalism and welfare states. *Anthropologica 45:* 201–14.

Clinton, H. R. (1996). *It takes a village and other lessons children teach us.* New York: Simon and Schuster.

Coles, R. (1986). *The political life of children.* Boston: Atlantic Monthly Press.

Comaroff, J. (1997). Consuming passions: Nightmares of the global village. In E. Badone, ed., Body and self in a post-colonial world [special issue]. *Culture 17* (1–2): 7–19.

Corsaro, W. (1997). *The sociology of childhood.* Thousand Oaks, Calif.: Pine Forge Press.

Cousins, L. (1999). "Playing between classes": America's troubles with class, race and gender in a black high school and community. *Anthropology and Educational Quarterly 30:* 294–316.

Cross, G. (2004). *The cute and the cool.* Oxford: Oxford University Press.

Darling-Hammond, L. (2007). Evaluating "No Child Left Behind." *Nation 284* (20): 11–20.

Eckholm, E. (2007). In turnabout, infant deaths climb in South. *New York Times,* April 22.

Epstein, L. (1999). The culture of social work. In A. S. Chambon, A. Irving, and L Epstein, eds., *Reading Foucault for social work.* New York: Columbia University Press.

Fass, P. (2003). Children and globalization. *Journal of Social History 26:* 963–77.

———. (2007). *Children of a new world: Society, culture and globalization.* New York: New York University Press.

Ferguson, I., M. Lavalette, and E. Whitmore. (2005). *Globalisation, global justice, and social work.* New York: Routledge.

Finn, J.L., and M. Jacobson, M. (2008). *Just practice: Social justice approach to social work.* 2nd ed. Peosta, Ia: Eddie Bowers.

Finn, J. L., and L. Nybell. (Eds.) (2001). Capitalizing on concern: The making of troubled children and troubling youth in late capitalism (special issue). *Childhood: A Global Journal of Child Research 8* (2).

Fisher, R., and H. J. Karger. (1997). *Social work and community in a private world: Getting out in public.* White Plains, N.Y.: Longman.

Foucault, M. (1983). Structuralism and poststructuralism: An interview with Gérard Raulet. *Telos: A Quarterly Journal of Critical Thought 55:* 195–211.

Garbarino, J. (1992). *Children and families in the social environment.* 2nd ed. New York: Aldine de Gruyter.

Giroux, H. (2003). The abandoned generation: Democracy beyond the culture of fear. New York: Palgrave Macmillan.

Goodkind, S. (2005). Gender-specific services in the juvenile justice system: A critical examination. *Affilia* 20: 52–70.

———. (forthcoming). "You can be anything you want, but you have to believe it": Commercialized feminism in gender-specific programs for girls. *Signs.*

Gordon, L. (1994). Pitied but not entitled: Single mothers and the history of welfare. New York: Free Press.

Griffin, C. (2001). Imagining new narratives of youth. *Childhood 8:* 147–66.

Grossberg, L. (2001). Why do neoliberals hate kids? The war on youth and the culture of politics. *Education/Pedagogy/Cultural Studies 23:* 111–36.

Halfon, N. (2000). *Preschool and identification of mental health needs. Report of the Surgeon General's conference on children's mental health: A national action agenda.* Washington, D.C.: U.S. Department of Health and Human Services.

Hartman, A. (1979). *Finding families: An ecological approach to family assessment.* Beverly Hills, Calif.: Sage.

Harvey, D. (2005). *A brief history of neoliberalism.* Oxford: Oxford University Press.

Hutchison, E. D., and L. W. Charlesworth. (2000). Securing the welfare of children: Policies past, present and future. *Families in Society: The Journal of Contemporary Human Services 8:* 576–85.

Hyman, S. E. (1997). Director of the National Institute of Mental Health. *Statement before the House Subcommittee on Labor-DHHS, Education and Related Agencies Committee on Appropriation, 195th Congress.* October 29.

Ivey, M. (1995). Have you seen me? Recovering the inner child in late twentieth-century America. In S. Stephens, ed., *Children and the politics of culture.* Princeton: Princeton University Press.

James, A. (2004).Understanding childhood from an interdisciplinary perspective: Problems and potentials. In P. B. Pufall and R. P. Unsworth, eds., *Rethinking childhood,* 25–37. New Brunswick, N.J.: Rutgers University Press.

James, A., and A. L. James. (2004). *Constructing childhood: Theory, policy and social practice.* New York: Palgrave Macmillan.

James, A., and A. Prout. (Eds.) (1990). *Constructing and reconstructing childhood: Contemporary issues in the sociological study of childhood.* London: Falmer Press.

James, A., C. Jenks, and A. Prout. (1998). *Theorizing childhood.* Cambridge: Polity Press.

Jenks, C. (1996).*Childhood.* London: Routledge.

——. (2005). *Childhood: Critical concepts in sociology.* New York: Routledge.

Jennings, A. (2007). Emptying nest eggs, not the nests. *New York Times,* July 14.

Jones, G. (2005).Children and development: Rights, globalization, and poverty. *Progress in Development Studies 5:* 336–42.

Karger, H. (2005). Shortchanged: Life and debt in the fringe economy. San Francisco: Berrett-Koehler.

Katz, C. (2004). *Growing up global: Economic restructuring and children's everyday lives.* Minneapolis: University of Minnesota Press.

——. (2005). The terror of hypervigilance: Security and the compromised spaces of contemporary childhood. In J. Qvortrup, ed., *Studies in modern childhood: Society, agency, culture,* 99–114. New York: Palgrave Macmillan.

Kelleher, K. (2000). *Primary care and identification of mental health needs. Report of the Surgeon General's conference on children's mental health: A national action agenda.* Washington, D.C.: U.S. Department of Health and Human Services.

Kessen, W. (1990). *The rise and fall of development.* 1986 Heinz Werner Lecture Series. Worcester, Mass.: Clark University Press.

Kolata, G. (1996). Ritalin use is lower than thought. *New York Times,* December 17.

Korten, D. C. (2001). *When corporations rule the world.* 2nd ed. San Francisco: Berrett-Koehler.

Kozol, J. (2005). *Shame of the nation: The restoration of apartheid schooling in America.* New York: Three Rivers Press.

Lansdown, G. (2000). *Promoting children's participation in democratic decision-making.* Florence, Italy: United Nations Children's Fund.

Lavalette, M. (2005). "In defense of childhood": Against the neo-liberal assault on social life. In J. Qvortrup, ed., *Studies in modern childhood: society, agency, culture,* 147–66. New York: Palgrave Macmillan.

Leiter, V., J. L. McDonald, and H. T. Jacobson. (2006). Challenges to children's independent citizenship: Immigration, family and the state. *Childhood: A global journal of child research 13:* 11–27.

Lindsey, D. (2004). *The welfare of children.* New York: Oxford University Press.

Link, R. (1999). Infusing global perspectives into social work values and ethics. In C. Ramanathan and R. Link, eds., *All our futures: Social work practice in a global era,* 69–93. Belmont, Calif.: Wadsworth.

Lowe, L., and D. Lloyd. (1997). *The politics of culture in the shadow of capital.* Durham: Duke University Press.

McKnight, J. (1995). *The careless society: Community and its counterfeits.* New York: Basic Books.

McLaren, P., and R. Farahmandpur. (2006). The pedagogy of oppression: A brief look at "No Child Left Behind." *Monthly Review 58* (3): 94–99.

Mintz, S. (2004). *A history of American childhood.* Cambridge: Belknap Press of Harvard University Press.

Morss, J. (1996). Growing critical: Alternatives to developmental psychology. London: Routledge.

———. (2003). The several constructions of James, Jenks and Prout. *International Journal of Children's Rights, 10:* 39–54.

National Center for Children in Poverty. (2006). Basic facts about low income children birth to 18. (September). Accessed June 1, 2007 at http://www.nccp.org/publications/pub_678.html

Nunn, K. B. (2002). The child as other: Race and differential treatment in the juvenile justice system. *DePaul Law Review, 51:* 679–714.

Offord, D. (2000). Identification of mental health needs. In *Report of the Surgeon General's conference on children's mental health: A national action agenda.* Washington, D.C.: U.S. Department of Health and Human Services.

Parton, N. (1999). Reconfiguring child welfare practices: Risk, advanced liberalism and the government of freedom. In A. Chambon, A. Irving, and L. Epstein, eds., *Reading Foucault for social work,* 101–30. New York: Columbia University Press.

Piven, F. F., and R. Cloward. (1997). *The breaking of the American social compact.* New York: New Press.

Prout, A., and A. James. (1990). A new paradigm for the sociology of childhood? Provenance, promise and problems. In A. James and A. Prout, eds., *Constructing and reconstructing childhood: Contemporary issues in the sociological study of childhood,* 216–37. London: Falmer Press.

Pufall, P. B., and R. P. Unsworth. (2004). Introduction: The imperative and the process for rethinking childhood. In P. B. Pufall and R. P. Unsworth, eds., *Rethinking childhood,* 1–24. New Brunswick, N.J.: Rutgers University Press.

Rose, N. (1996). Governing "advanced" liberal democracies. In A. Barry, T. Osbourne, and N. Rose, eds., *Foucault and political reason: Liberalism, neo-liberalism and rationalities of government.* Chicago: University of Chicago Press.

Qvortrup, J. (1990). A voice for children in statistical and social accounting? A plea for children's rights to be heard. In A. James and A. Prout, eds., *Constructing and reconstructing childhood: Contemporary issues in the sociological study of childhood.* London: Falmer Press.

———. (2005). *Studies in modern childhood: Society, agency, culture.* New York: Palgrave Macmillan.

Qvortrup, J., M. Bardy, G. Sgritta, and H. Wintersberger. (1994). *Childhood matters: Social theory, practice and politics.* Aldershot: Avebury.

Rains, P., L. Davies, and M. McKinnon. (2004). Social services construct the teen mother. *Families in Society 85:* 17–27.

Reynolds, P., O. Nieuwenhuys, and O. Hanson. (2006). Refractions of children's rights in development practice: A view from anthropology. *Childhood: A global journal of child research, 13:* 291–302.

Ruddick, S. (2006). Abnormal, the "new normal," and the destabilizing discourses of rights. *Public Culture 18* (1): 53–77.

Sarri, R. C., and J. J. Shook. (2006). The future of social work in juvenile and criminal justice. *Advances in Social Work 6:* 210–20.

Scheper-Hughes, N., and C. Sargent. (Eds.) (1998). *Small wars: The cultural politics of childhood.* Berkeley: University of California Press.

Schorr, L. B. (1997). *Common purpose: Strengthening families and neighborhoods to re-build America.* New York: Doubleday.

Sedlak, A. J., D. Finkelhor, H. Hammer, and D. J. Schultz. (2002). *National estimates of missing children: An overview.* Washington, D.C.: U.S. Department of Justice, Office of Juvenile Justice and Delinquency Prevention.

Sealander, J. (2003). *The failed century of the child: Governing America's young in the twentieth century.* New York: Cambridge University Press.

———. (2004). The history of childhood policy. *Journal of Policy History 16:* 176–87.

Shook, J. J. (2005). Contesting childhood in the U.S. justice system: The transfer of juveniles to adult criminal court. *Childhood: A global journal of child research 12:* 461–78.

Skocpol, T. (1992). *Protecting soldiers and mothers: The political origins of social policy in the United States.* Cambridge: Belknap Press of Harvard University Press.

Snyder, H. N. (2006). *Juvenile arrests 2004.* Washington, D.C.: U.S. Department of Justice, Office of Juvenile Justice and Delinquency Prevention.

Specht, H., and M. Courtney. (1994). *Unfaithful angels: How social work has abandoned its mission.* New York: Free Press.

Stephens, S. (1994). Children and the environment: Local worlds and global connections. *Childhood 2:* 1–21.

———. (Ed.) (1995a). *Children and the politics of culture.* Princeton: Princeton University Press.

———. (1995b). Introduction: Children and the politics of culture in "late capitalism." In S. Stephens, ed., *Children and the politics of culture,* 3–48. Princeton: Princeton University Press.

———. (1995c). The cultural fallout of Chernobyl radiation in Norwegian Sami regions: Implications for children. In S. Stephens, ed., *Children and the politics of culture,* 292–318. Princeton: Princeton University Press.

———. (1996). Reflections on environmental justice: Children as victims and actors. *Social Justice* (special issue: *Environmental Victims*) 23 (4): 62–86.

———. (1997a). Editorial introduction: Children and nationalism. *Childhood 4:* 5–17.

————. (1997b). Nationalism, nuclear policy and children in Cold War America. *Childhood 4:* 103–23.

Taylor, S., M. J. Austin, and E. A. Mulroy. (2004). Evaluating the social environment component of social work courses on human behavior and the social environment. *Journal of Human Behavior in the Social Environment,* 10 (3): 61–84.

Thomas, N. (2000). *Children, family and the state: Decision-making and child participation.* New York: St. Martin's Press.

Toppo, G. (2005). College graduates see their debt burden increase. *USA Today.*

Townsend, J., E. Zapata, J. Powlands, P. Alberti, and M. Mercado. (1999). *Women and power: Fighting patriarchies and poverty.* London: Zed Books.

Tyack, G. (2003). *Seeking common ground: Public schools in a diverse society.* Cambridge: Harvard University Press.

Walkerdine, V. (1984). Developmental psychology and the child-centred pedagogy. In J. Henriques, W. Hollway, C. Urwin, C. Venn, and V. Walkerdine, eds., *Changing the subject: Psychology, social regulation and subjectivity.* London: Methuen.

Weinberg, M. (2006). Pregnant with possibility: Paradoxes of "help" as anti-oppression and discipline with a young single mother. *Families in Society 87:* 161–70.

Woodhead, M. (1990). Psychology and the cultural construction of children's needs. In A. James and A. Prout, eds., *Constructing and reconstructing childhood: Contemporary issues in the sociological study of childhood.* London: Falmer Press.

Zelizer, V. (1985). *Pricing the priceless child.* New York: Basic Books.

Zweifler, R., and J. DeBeers. (2002). The children left behind: How zero tolerance impacts our most vulnerable youth. *Michigan Journal of Race and Law 8:* 191–220.

Exploring Changing Discourses of
Childhood and Youth

PART I

Making Trouble | ONE

Representations of Social Work,
Youth, and Pathology

Janet L. Finn

As social workers we often spend our days engaged in the hard work of investigation, advocacy, and intervention with children and families. The urgent demands of the work rarely allow for the luxury of stepping back and reflecting on practice and the contradictions we face everyday. But it is important to pause and ask: What are we doing in the name of intervention with kids and families? What do we believe about the sources of their troubles and why? Are interventions done in the "best interests" of other people's children ones that we would support for our own children? In this chapter I invite you to step back in time and take a look at how we think about children, youth, and "trouble." How have we tried to make sense of "trouble," define problems, and develop interventions? How have we come to hold certain beliefs regarding what is "right" and "true" about kids and trouble? How have our beliefs changed over time, and how have they remained the same? How has the profession of social work been implicated in both the production and consumption of particular notions of trouble at particular times? How might a historical perspective provide food for thought regarding the challenges and opportunities we face today? In this chapter I highlight some moments in the history of the care and control of children and youth. My goal is to provoke our thinking and practice so that we can become more critical consumers in the marketplace of images regarding children and youth. In addition I challenge us to be mindful of the ethical and political consequences of our roles as social workers in the *production* of images of children, youth, and trouble. I conclude with critical reflection on twenty-first-century practice regarding children, youth, and trouble.

Why history? Critical reflection on the past can provide important food for thought regarding our practices in the present. A historical perspective can help us see common themes and patterns that play out over time. History can help us understand the workings of power and inequality. It can serve as a warning device, as we are able to see with 20/20 hindsight the consequences of previous policies and practices purportedly implemented to serve the "best interests" of children and youth (Finn and Jacobson 2008: 63–64; Reisch 1988; Zinn 1970). The past can be illuminating in helping us see what truths we held dear and what "certainties" informed and constrained our practice (Sarri and Finn, 1992). After taking a step back in time, I ask you to imagine yourselves in the year 2058, presenting a talk on intervention with children and youth. What would you be saying about the ideas we held about children, youth, and trouble in 2008? What will practitioners of the future say about the practices we embrace today?

THE MAKING OF CHILDHOOD AND TROUBLE IN THE MID-NINETEENTH CENTURY

As discussed in the introduction to this volume, the concept of childhood is socially and historically constructed, with differing meanings and values in differing times and places. I begin this story of the making of childhood and trouble in the mid-nineteenth-century United States, when so-called modern notions of childhood were emerging.[1] In the mid-1800s views about children, youth, and trouble were being shaped in the context of a rapidly changing world. Immigration, urbanization, and the rise of industrial capitalism created convulsive changes in the nation's urban centers. Millions of foreign workers and their families were immigrating to the United States. Differences of nationality, ethnicity, and religion intersected with class- and gender-based differences, and children as well as adults were marked by those differences. Children of the immigrant poor and working classes were especially vulnerable, given their crowded and unsafe living conditions and lack of supervision as parents worked long hours. From the mid-1800s we see a growing public concern for unsupervised children and youth and the need to contain and control them. Concerned reformers deemed young children, often referred to as street waifs and little wanderers, to be at risk of falling into a life of deviance and crime (see Brace 1872; Holloran 1989). Older youth were labeled "dangerous," poised to prey on "innocent" young people migrating to the city from the countryside.

As Kett (1977) and Griffin (1993, 2001) have argued, lower-class children and youth, in contrast to the offspring of the middle and upper classes, were represented as inherently dangerous, corruptible, and potentially corrupting. They were viewed as an affront to images of childhood innocence and a potential threat to that innocence (Griffin 1993:101). Given their presumably limited capacity for self-discipline, they were seen to be in need of social control. Moreover, these emerging ideologies of children and youth incorporated racialized notions of Euro-white superiority that equated whiteness with normalcy (Griffin 1993:14). Lower-class children and youth were, by definition, a source of potential trouble and thus in need of disciplinary intervention. By midcentury, a cadre of reformers was poised to respond to that need.

At the same time, the emerging middle class was reconfiguring meanings of childhood and practices of parenting with the advice of parenting manuals and child-rearing guides that were becoming all the rage. Peter Holloran (1989:31) writes, "As Victorian America discovered the importance of careful child-rearing, the deviant child—whether delinquent or merely homeless—received greater attention from the anxious elite." Child-rearing "experts" conveyed a sense of urgency to middle-class parents regarding the importance of proper discipline and the dangers awaiting their young should they fall in with the "wrong class." Youth counselors wrote advice books targeting an audience of young men of the emerging middle class, warning them of the dangers of city life and their risk for seduction into a world of vice and temptation at the hands of lower-class youth.[2] Thus the making of middle-class childhood was in relationship and response to anxieties about "other" people's children. I pay particular attention to this historic period, given its instructive value for present-day challenges.

By the 1830s, early child-savers had begun their work in earnest, first taking up the cause of child placement. Reformers challenged the practice of confining poor children and adults together in almshouses. They first sought to separate children from the contaminating influence of adults and to develop institutions that focused on the care, discipline, and reform of children of the poor. A proliferation of children's asylums, orphanages, and reform schools followed. Reformers advocated for containment in special institutions where young people would be separated from "noxious moral influences," and where their character could be re-formed through rigid daily routines, hard work, and surveillance. Early youth institutions utilized uniforms, strict schedules, fixed programs of activities, and heavy-handed moral instruction as the preferred modes of inter-vention (Boyer 1978; Katz 1986). The prevailing philosophy of the early child-savers was that firm discipline and moral guidance could cure the ills of a faulty family and social environment (Holloran 1989).

Immigration pressures accelerated in the 1840s, as thousands fled desperate poverty in Ireland and other politically and economically oppressed countries. Fueled by a sense of Christian mission, the child-savers redoubled their efforts, seeking out the children of the new urban poor before they fell prey to the evils of the street. For the children of Irish Catholic immigrants, their salvation was spiritual as well as material, with conversion to Protestantism part of the bar-gain. Supported by religious groups and the new world of private philanthropy, child-savers took to the streets of New York and Boston in the search of little wanderers in need of rescue. As they faced a seeming endless supply of children, reformers began to debate the most efficient and effective way to intervene. Some argued for the value of the asylum where a rigid discipline and moral code could be paired with industrial training. Others began to raise questions about the "contagion effect" in the containment of troubled children as well as the costs of building and maintaining institutions for their care (Herman 2005; Lindsey 2004).

Charles Loring Brace, a preeminent reformer and founder of the Children's Aid Society of New York, wrote persuasively about the "dangerous classes" of children and youth in New York and their threat to "innocents" (Brace 1859). Brace used images of contamination and contagion to evoke the threat posed by these youngsters. Brace's treatises on youth and danger reflect a mix of pity for and condemnation of the children of poor immigrant families and the fear of the potential social and political force of this group as it comes of age. He graphically illustrated the inevitable downward trajectory from street waif to street gang, dereliction, and prison, if children were left to their own devices, and he argued persuasively against the institutionalization of these children (Brace 1872). In the New York Children's Aid Society's first circular, Brace writes:

> As Christian men, we cannot look upon this great multitude of unhappy, de-serted, and degraded boys and girls without feeling our responsibility to God for them. We remember that they have the same capacities, the same need of kind and good influences, and the same Immortality as the little ones in our own homes. We bear in mind that One died for them, even as for the children of the rich and happy. Thus far, alms-houses and prisons have done little to affect evil. But a small part our vagrant population can be shut up in our asylums, and judges and magis-

trates are reluctant to convict children so young and ignorant that they hardly seem able to distinguish good and evil. The class increases. Immigration is pouring in its multitude of foreigners, who leave these young outcasts everywhere abandoned in our midst. . .

These boys and girls, it should be remembered, will soon form the great lower class of our city. They will influence elections; they may shape the policy of the city; they will, assuredly, if unreclaimed, poison society all around them. They will help to form the great multitude of robbers, thieves, vagrants, and prostitutes who are now such a burden upon the law respecting community. (1872:91–92)

Following the lead of the Children's Mission of Boston, Brace argued against institutionalization as the response to the troubling problem of "homeless" children, advocating instead for the "placing out" of children with rural farm families in need of help with home and field labor. In 1850 the Children's Mission of Boston had hit upon the idea of shipping "rescued" children of the urban immigrant poor by train to destinations in rural New Hampshire (Holloran 1989: 44). Brace borrowed this idea and launched the "orphan train" system, in effect the nation's first foster care program, whereby children were sent en masse to western rural communities. Brace and his fellow reformers convinced the charitable organizations and their benefactors supporting the effort that the practice was a modern, efficient, and economical solution to the problem of troubled children and troubling youth on the streets of New York, Boston, and other urban industrial centers (Brace 1872; Holloran 1989). Between 1850 and 1929, nearly 200,000 children were shipped by train to fill the growing labor force needs of westward expansion (Nebraska State Historical Society). Brace states:

The founders of the Children's Aid Society early saw that the best of all Asylums for the outcast child, is the *farmer's home.* The United States have the enormous advantage over all other countries, in the treatment of difficult questions of pauperism and reform, that they possess a practically unlimited area of arable land. The demand for labor on this land is beyond any present supply. Moreover, the cultivators of the soil are in America our most solid and intelligent class. From the nature of their circumstances, their laborers, or "help" must be members of their families, and share in their social tone. It is, accordingly, of the utmost importance to them to train up children who shall aid in their work, and be associates of their own children. . . .With their overflowing supply of food also, each new mouth in the household brings no drain on their means. Children are a blessing, and the mere feeding of a young boy or girl is not considered at all. (225)

Brace and his fellow reformers also realized the need to create a demand for this supply of children, and thus they engaged in marketing campaigns to promote placing out. As Brace describes:

> To awaken the demand for these children, circulars were sent out through the city weeklies and the rural papers to the country districts. Hundreds of applications poured in at once from the farmers and mechanics all through the Union. At first, we made the effort to meet individual applications by sending just the kind of child wanted; but this soon became impracticable. . . .
>
> [Instead] we formed little companies of emigrants, and, after thoroughly cleaning and clothing them, put them under a competent agent, and, first selecting a village where there was a call or opening for such a party, we dispatched them to the place. (231–32)

Reverend S. S. Cummings of the New England Home for Little Wanderers shared Brace's zeal for the orphan trains as a modern, efficient, cost-effective solution to the problem of troubled children and troubling youth. As Cummings describes:

> There is system and order about it as there should be about every good work. These homes are not engaged beforehand as some have supposed. It is surprising to some that we will start off with a company of thirty or forty children, not knowing where we shall find a home for them. The process is simple. We look over the map of the country, and line of railroads, and decide on some town, make our first point, and then write to the pastors of the churches that we will be there at a given time, generally arriving on Saturday, and ask them to make arrangements for our holding services in their churches on the Sabbath. . . .
>
> The children at the church in the presence of the people and an appropriate talk of our duty to provide for, and take care of, orphan children, brings our work and the object of our visit before the public prepatory for the work of adoption on Monday. We invite the people to meet us on Monday and see the children and make a selection if desirable. (Baylor and Monachesi 1939:524)

Advertisements for child placement, such as one printed in the *Tecumseh Chieftain* in 1893, appeared in newspapers throughout the Midwest (Nebraska State Historical Society). Popular magazines, such as *Harper's News Monthly,* promoted and praised this "ingenious" plan for dealing with destitute children.[3] The orphan trains were hailed as a win-win solution to the problematic proliferation of children among the urban poor and the need for farm labor. In

Homeless .. .. Children.

THE CHILDRENS' HOME SOCIETY

HAS PROVIDED

2990 Children With Homes, in Families.

All children received under the care of this Association are of **SPECIAL PROMISE** in intelligence and health, and are in age from one month to twelve years, and are sent **FREE** to those receiving them, on ninety days trial, **UNLESS** a special contract is otherwise made.

Homes are wanted for the following children:

8 BOYS Ages, 10, 6 and 4. Brothers, all fine, healthy, good looks. Of good parentage. Brothers 6 and 4 years; English parents. blondes. Very promising, 2 years old, blonde, fine looking, healthy, American; has had his foot straightened. Walks now O. K. Six years old, dark hair and eyes, good looking and intelligent, American.

10 BABES Boys and girls from one month to three months. One boy baby, has fine head and face, black eyes and hair, fat and pretty; three months old. Send two stamps.

REV. M. B. V. VAN ARSDALE,
General Superintendent.

Room 48, 280 La Salle Street, CHICAGO.

reality, few of these children were orphans; rather, they were the offspring of the immigrant poor, and their parents were deemed unfit to raise them, by reason of poverty and "difference."

The child-saving campaigns were informed by very particular constructions of childhood, trouble, and difference, and they bore the marks of the reformers' privileged race and class positioning. For example, despite his pleas for the plight of poor children, Charles Loring Brace made judgments informed by class, ethnic, and religious prejudices. In his view, the most "dangerous" children were those of Irish and German immigrants (Brace 1872:27). He was especially critical of Catholicism, viewing Catholic parents as virtually unfit by definition. In Brace's discourse and that of his contemporaries, we see a blending of a preoccupation with environmental causality of children's troubles with belief in the inheritability of trouble. They argued that inherited traits and tendencies were powerful sources of deviance, a view that was to become ever more powerful in the ensuing years as emerging knowledge of genetics began to influence the social as well as biological sciences.

These early white reformers focused their attention on saving white children while by and large ignoring the plight of young people of color. In the post–Civil War era, child rescue efforts for children of color generally took the form of separate and unequal institutions. In contrast to the systematic neglect of African American children by the state and charitable reformers, the late 1800s saw the development of a partnership of church and state in a "civilizing mission" targeting American Indian children. From the 1870s well into the mid-1900s, church- and government-run boarding schools played a powerful role in the "education" of American Indian children in the United States. In the mid-1800s, many American Indian groups were forcibly relocated to reservations to make way for economic development of the western United States. Not long afterward, developers saw that reservation lands themselves had value for logging, mining, and cattle interests, and tribal organization was an impediment to that development. A new thrust in federal Indian policy (through the General Allotment Act) emerged, calling for the "assimilation" of American Indians through "reduction to citizenship," establishment of individual property rights, and education into mainstream white culture (Smith 1985; Takaki 1979, 1993). Boarding schools played a key role in this effort. By 1890 there were 140 federal boarding schools with an enrollment of nearly 10,000 students (Morgan 1890, as cited in Washburn 1973:44). Children were removed from families and tribal communities, often by force, and placed in boarding schools where they were to be systematically stripped of language and cultural ties and then filled like empty vessels with white middle-class values and patriotic fervor. The following quotes from commissioners of Indian affairs regarding American Indians reveal dominant white assumptions about the "Indian Problem" and the solution of child removal and indoctrination. In 1888 Commissioner John H. Oberly declared:

> He (the Indian) should be educated to labor. He does not need the learning of William and Mary, but he does need the virtue of industry and the ability of the skillful hand. . . . And the Indian should not only be taught how to work, but also that it is his duty to work; for the degrading communism of the tribal reservation system gives to the individual no incentive to labor, but puts a premium on idleness and makes it fashionable. Under this system, the laziest man owns as much as the most industrious man, and neither can say of all the acres occupied by the tribe, "This is mine." The Indian must, therefore, be taught how to labor; and, that labor may be made necessary to his well being, he must be taken out of the reservation through the door of the General Allotment Act. And he must be imbued with the exalting egotism of American civilization, so that he will say "I" instead of "We," and "this is mine" instead of "This is ours." (Oberly 1888, as cited in Washburn 1973:422)

His sentiments were shared by his successor, T. J. Morgan, who in 1889 proclaimed:

> It is of prime importance that a fervent patriotism should be awakened in their minds. The stars and stripes should be a familiar object in every Indian school, national hymns should be sung, and patriotic selections be read and recited. They should be taught to look upon America as their home and upon the United States Government as their friend and benefactor. They should be made familiar with the lives of great and good men and women in American history, and be taught to feel a pride in all their great achievements. They should hear little or nothing of the 'wrongs of the Indians' and the injustice of the white race. If their unhappy history is alluded to it should be to contrast it with the better future that is within their grasp. The new era has come to the red men through the munificent scheme of education, devised for and offered to them, should be the means of awakening loyalty to the Government, gratitude to the nation, and hopefulness for themselves. (Morgan 1889, as cited in Washburn 1973:434)

Similar to the orphan trains, the practice of removal of Indian children to boarding schools remained popular through the 1920s (Adams 1988; Ellis 1987; Szasz 1974).[4] However, criticism of both practices was growing more widespread as concerns were voiced about the conditions of care and the well-being of children; as new understandings of childhood, trouble, and intervention emerged; and as hard economic times shifted public attention away from the particular needs of children to the widespread problem of poverty wrought by the Great Depression.

THE MAKING OF TROUBLE AND MODERN CHILDHOOD AT THE TURN OF THE TWENTIETH CENTURY

The start of the twentieth century marked a profound moment in the making of children, youth, trouble, and intervention. On the one hand, this was a time of growing concern about the environment and its impact on children and youth and their families and communities. New understandings of health and disease informed emerging public health campaigns, with maternal and child health central concerns (Bremner 1970). The early work of the child-savers was subsumed under a broader banner of public concern regarding the welfare of children. The early twentieth century saw the development of a range of protective policies and practices regarding children and youth, including child-welfare and juvenile-justice systems (Kett 1977; Platt 1969; Sutton 1988). In addition, child labor laws and compulsory public education were reconfiguring the time, space, and special status of childhood and youth. Advocates for these efforts were looking to improve the context of everyday life for children and families, to address the vulnerabilities exacerbated by poverty and economic inequality, and to respond proactively to the needs of children and youth. For example, the first Juvenile Court, established in Cook County, Illinois in 1899, sought to intervene as a concerned parent, looking at environmental factors, rehabilitation, and the best interests of young offenders. Once again, however, the attention of mainstream child advocates focused on the plight of white children, largely ignoring the broader context of racism that intersected with classism in shaping the life chances of children and youth.

A definitive moment in the Progressive Era came in 1909 with the assembly of the first White House Conference on Children. The twentieth century was declared the "Century of the Child," and advocates decried the removal of children from their families and communities "for reasons of poverty" (Lindsey 2004). They called instead for economic and social supports that would enable families to stay together. The conference served as the impetus for the establishment of the U.S. Children's Bureau, a federal agency concerned with research and advocacy for the well-being of children (Holloran 1989, Lindsey 2004). Supporters of these efforts recognized the impact of larger social, political, and economic conditions in the lives of children. They looked beyond popular notions of personal deficits and congenital deviance to the troubling structural arrangements that produced and maintained inequality.

During this era we also see ideas regarding children and youth developing hand in hand with specialization in the social sciences, emerging ideologies of efficiency and scientific management, and practices of diagnosis, testing, and measurement. Studies of psychopathology, personality development, and individual differences were capturing the imagination of the emerging helping professions in the early 1900s (Day 2006; Gould 1981; Reisch and Wenocur 1986). A range of helping professions (including social work, child guidance, mental hygiene, and education), embracing a "scientific" approach to diagnosis and treatment, began to concern themselves with the welfare of "at-risk" children and the discipline of risky youth. At the same time, there was growing preoccupation with "normal" childhood and the need for professional guidance in child rearing. The child guidance movement, emerging in this era, served to further the problematizing of childhood and professionalizing of child rearing, thus fueling a sense of urgency and anxiety among the middle class regarding proper parenting. Professionals responded with the expansion of training programs to produce practitioners skilled in identifying trouble and in charge of developing disciplinary technologies of care and control.

Many practitioners turned their attention to youth and the shaping of young people's proper trajectories to adulthood and place in the social and economic order. Some appropriated knowledge from the biological sciences and applied it in the social realm, often in problematic ways, as exemplified by Social Darwinism, the eugenics movement, and an infatuation with tests and measurements that served to justify and reinforce racist, classist, and gendered assumptions about difference (Gould 1981). Through the influence of these professionals, an environmental perspective on the troubles of children and youth was eclipsed by belief in the power of heredity. It is on this stage that specific theories of both adolescence and deviance were articulated and disciplinary practices were elaborated and justified.

Psychologist G. Stanley Hall (1904) is widely credited with the "invention" of adolescence at the turn of the twentieth century. In his two-volume treatise entitled *Adolescence, Its Psychology, and Its Relations to Physiology, Anthropology, Sociology, Sex, Crime, Religion, and Education,* Hall put forth his view of adolescence as a biologically driven time of stress and storm—a period of inevitable psychological and social turmoil. Further, Hall offered a "recapitulation" theory of adolescence wherein he argued that adolescence was a "second birth" and a critical measure of human progress. Hall held that the development of the individual paralleled the development of the race, and that adolescence was thus key to racial and cultural betterment (Adams 1997). His notions served both to justify and to promote racialized notions of biological determinism regarding youth and deviance. Hall gave form and content to adolescence as a dynamic and salient social category to be variably developed, diagnosed, and disciplined by the nascent social sciences and helping professions. The very concept of adolescence was charged from the start with the portent of pathology and shaped by assumptions of hereditary destiny. From Hall's perspective, it seems that all adolescents are vulnerable to corruption and in need of guidance as they negotiate the turbulent transition to adulthood. However, poor and working-class youth are at risk by virtue of their heredity while middle-class, "white" youth are vulnerable to the corrupting potential of the world around them. Hall had wide-ranging influence in the emerging fields of child guidance and juvenile reform, and he was very influential in the eugenics movement. His work inspired troubling new directions in professional discourse and practice regarding the containment and control of "deviant" youth—generally those marked by differences of race and class.

Places of youth confinement became sites of surveillance where professional interventionists brought moral judgment and "scientific" observation to bear on the scrutiny of young "deviants." For example, psychologist Arthur MacDonald, a protégé of Hall's, proposed a study of the physical and mental characteristics of delinquents to the U.S. Senate in 1908 (MacDonald 1908, as cited in Bremner 1970). MacDonald appealed to Congress for funds to establish a laboratory for conducting anthropometrical measurements of juvenile delinquents. His request was denied, but his discourse offers a glimpse into the thinking influencing public policy regarding youth and trouble in the early 1900s. MacDonald writes:

> In the study of man the individuals themselves must be investigated. As the seeds of evil are usually sown in childhood and youth, it is here that all inquiry should commence, for there is little hope of making the world better if we do not seek the causes of social evils at their beginning. . . . The time has come when it is important to study a child with as much exactness as we investigate the chemical elements of a stone or measure the mountains on the moon. . . . As an illustration of such investigation I give the following plan: To study 1,000 boys in industrial schools, ages from 6 to 15; 1,000 boys in reformatories, ages 15 to 30; this investigation to consist in a physical, mental, moral, anthropological, social, and medico-social study of each boy, including such data as . . . Age, date of birth, height, weight, sitting height, color of hair, eyes, skin; first born, second born, or later born; strength of hand

grasp, left handed; length, width and circumference of head; distance between zygomatic arches, corners of eyes; length and width of ears, hands and mouth; thickness of lips, measurements of sensibility to heat and pain; examination of lungs, eyes, pulse and respiration; nationality, occupation, education, and social condition of parents; whether one or both parents are dead or drunkards; stepchildren or not, hereditary taint, stigmata of degeneration. All data gathered by the institutions as history and conduct of inmates might be utilized. (as cited in Bremner 1970:562)[5]

MacDonald's proposed project encapsulated both the anxieties around troubled youth and the fixations with bodily form and "defective ancestry" that informed much of the professional discourse and intervention of the times. His language exemplifies the seductive power in the melding of containment and surveillance with the authority of science and the moral and political imperative of corrective intervention. Through detailed measurement and classification, judgments about the deviance and justifications about the containment of particular groups of youth could be made.

Some professional reformers took a more optimistic, growth-oriented perspective on troubled youth. For example, William Healy, a pioneer in the investigation of juvenile delinquency, the formation of the youth court system, and the child guidance movement, advocated for an individualized, case-study approach to the diagnosis of troubled and troubling youth. Healy, a neurologist, was the first director of the Juvenile Psychiatric Institute of Chicago, where he engaged in clinical work with juvenile offenders. He argued for the need to consider the various influences—social, psychological, hereditary—that shape the delinquent. Healy (1915) contended that troubled youth were also malleable and thus salvageable. He called for preventive efforts to guide children away from the potential dangers of delinquency.[6] Healy's work was influential in promoting the rehabilitative perspective on discipline in the emergent juvenile justice system.[7] While Healy helped refocus on social and environmental factors that contributed to adolescent "trouble," he also incorporated powerful views about adolescence, gender, and deviance that remain with us today. Healy described delinquency and deviance in boys in terms of their petty crime, while he saw girls' delinquency or deviance in terms of their sexuality. For example, in describing a young girl referred to him, Healy writes that Maria X (age 12 1/2) had a pleasant face, good features, beautiful skin, and the broad hips and prominent bust of a developed young woman, but she was found to be "dull by reason of excessive sex practices" (1915:190–91). It is a message that has not changed much in 100 years or more; girls continue to be defined as deviant by reason of their sexuality and "sexual promiscuity."

Young children did not escape the gaze of eugenicists. Eugenics, or the "science of race improvement," emerged in the late nineteenth century and gained popularity in the early twentieth century. Advocates of eugenics called for the "scientific regulation of human breeding" as a means of preventing individuals and groups judged to be "unfit" from reproducing. Throughout the country, states passed sterilization laws to "relieve towns of their poor, their disabled, and their orphaned, neglected, or indigent children" (Gallagher 2001).[8] Those labeled "unfit" and targeted for reproductive regulation included the poor, people of color, immigrants, and people with disabilities. Thus the shadow side of "progressive" calls for family preservation was the regulation of which families were worthy of preservation. For example, Henry H. Goddard, director of the Training School for Feeble-Minded Girls and Boys in Vineland, New Jersey, argued that child adoption was fraught with eugenic danger. According to Goddard (1911), a child of unknown and suspect pedigree could be taken in by a well-meaning and respectable family only to carry the hidden taint of feeble-minded parentage within. Goddard plays out the scenario of an adopted girl who appeared so "normal" that "not even the experts can discover anything wrong with her":

> She grows up as one of the family, except that all know that she is not their own child. She comes to young womanhood, the son of the family falls in love with her, and there being no visible objections to a union, they are married. In due course of time a child is born and then another and another. As the years go by these children grow up and to the horror of all interested it is discovered that one or possibly two, even three of them, are feeble-minded. (1003–6)

Thus, contends Goddard, foster care and adoption of children of unfit or unknown "pedigree" should be only a last resort as these children and the offspring they may conceive are "dangerous from a hereditary standpoint." Goddard advocates providing for such children in "colonies" to avoid the risk of "contaminating the race by the perpetuation of mental and moral deficiency.... It is neither right nor wise for us to let our humanity, our pity, and sympathy for the poor, homeless, and neglected child, drive us to do injustice and commit a crime against those yet unborn" (1006).

In sum, early twentieth-century images of children, youth, and trouble were laden with tensions and contradictions that mapped nineteenth-century anxieties onto twentieth-century science. On the one hand, evocative references to "seeds of evil" and "stigmata of degeneration" played with fears regarding particular classes of young people and utilized technologies of knowledge and modes of intervention to classify and contain them. On the other hand, an optimistic, if somewhat anxious, view of all young people as malleable and therefore both vulnerable to corrupting influences in their environment and salvageable with proper guidance and discipline was being advocated. Both views promoted the cause of modern, scientific intervention and the expansion of the helping professions' involvement with all children and youth. And both were informed by class, race, and gender biases in the determination of troubled children and troubling youth.

CHILDREN, YOUTH, AND TROUBLE AT MID-TWENTIETH CENTURY

Let us fast forward now to the post–World War II era, a time of optimism on the home front and expansion of U.S. economic and political influence on a global scale. The postwar years saw a new configuration of capitalism, supported by state intervention, a long postwar economic boom, and a privileged workforce, reach maturity. However, the surface promises of progress thinly masked the underlying fissures in U.S. society and the growing discontent among groups who had been excluded from the American dream. Adams (1997) argues that youth came to symbolize what was both good and bad about the postwar years. On the one hand, youth were emblematic of postwar progress; on the other, discourse of the "youth problem" revealed white, middle- and upper-class anxieties about growing social unrest and the potential volatility stemming from social and economic inequality.

New psychosocial theories of child and adolescent development were emerging in the postwar years. Erik Erikson's (1959, 1968) classic theory of psychosocial development conceptualized childhood as a time of developing trust, industry, and initiative, and adolescence as a period of identity formation, wherein young people "tried on" on future adult roles. Those who failed to properly negotiate these "crises" would likely experience distrust, a sense of inferiority, and a crisis of identity, troubling precursors to deviance and delinquency. Erikson's model located child and adolescent development soundly in the dominant postwar middle-class script of upward mobility achieved through successful, sequential negotiation of the challenges posed at each life stage. Erikson reinforced beliefs in a proper trajectory for development, explaining failure in terms of individual deficits or circumstances rather than in structural inequalities (Erikson 1968; Griffin 1993). In contrast, African American psychologists Kenneth and Mamie Clark were challenging the class and race boundaries of Erikson's theory and redefining the sense of "inferiority" experienced by poor children and children of minority groups in terms of structural inequalities and exclusions rather than personal deficits (Markowitz and Rosner 1996; Nybell 2002). Despite these significant challenges, the dominant professional discourse on children, youth, and trouble continued to focus on individual rather than structural causes of trouble and directions for intervention.

The postwar years also saw growing attention to theories of family (Hartman and Laird, 1983). Theories of childhood bonding and attachment offered a renewed focus on the mother-child relationship (Ainsworth 1967; Bowlby 1951, 1968; Ghenie and Wellenstein, this volume). This work provided the theoretical frame for speculation regarding the linkages between maternal deprivation and juvenile crime. Researchers became preoccupied with questions of "attachment." Griffin (1993) notes that John Bowlby's speculations on connections between maternal deprivation and juvenile crime (1968) generated a boom in studies on working-class family life, which implicated working mothers in the development of delinquency and deprivation, incorporating psychological, social, and cultural (but not structural) themes into the increasingly popular "broken home" thesis (1993).

The 1950s also saw the emergence of the modern child welfare system and the professionalizing of the staff of public child welfare services (Lindsey 2004). Economic hardship remained the primary reason for the out-of-home placement of children, and yet the problem was more likely to be named in psychosocial terms of parental neglect than in economic terms (Ferguson 1961, cited in Lindsey 2004:33). The problem of child neglect was addressed with a combination of foster care for children and casework services for parents to "improve their situations." However, without attention to the structural barriers that kept poor parents living in poor housing with little income, inadequate health care, and few opportunities, "improvement" was an elusive goal. As Lindsey notes, "Thus, the children lingered in 'temporary' foster care for long periods of time, often extending over many years. Joseph Reid [then director of the Child Welfare League of America] termed such children languishing in foster care *orphans of the living*" (33).

Once again, larger structural questions were ignored, and views of white, middle-class ideal types informed inquiry and obscured the ways in which these constructions of childhood, youth, and pathology were shaped along lines of race, class, and gender difference. "Troubled" children and youth in need of containment and control continued to be largely "other" people's young. For example, let's consider the ways in which these midcentury notions of trouble and intervention were shaping policies and practice regarding Native American children. In the 1950s we see the institutionalization within child welfare system of the removal of Indian children from their families and tribal communities through adoption. In 1958 the Bureau of Indian Affairs and Child Welfare League of America entered into a contractual agreement for the adoptive placement of Indian children—90% of whom were placed with non-Indian families. The adoption of Indian children became a booming enterprise. A *Good Housekeeping* article written in 1966 captures the spirit of popular images of Native American children and their perceived troubles:

> Neither is there any balance scale that can weigh the difference between the life these children would have experienced had they been left to grow up, without parents, on an Indian reservation and the life they will now know as adopted sons and daughters. But this much is certain: the bare earth will never be the floor of their house—unless they go camping for a lark. They will never live huddled in tiny cabins with neither water nor heating. They will have more than eight years of schooling and their dropout rate will be 50 times less. They will not be ravaged by disease, and they can expect to live well beyond the 43 years that would be their life expectancy on the Indian reservation. All the intangibles that are part of parental love and care will also be theirs. (cited in Walker 1980:197)

This depiction renders Native American mothers, fathers, and kinship networks invisible. It is devoid of the history of exploitation of Native American peoples and the century-long practices of systematic removal of Indian children. Moreover, it makes no reference to 1950s' federal government policies of termination of reservation land rights and urban displacement that exacerbated poverty conditions on reservations and further disrupted Indian families. The racism behind public policies remained invisible to white child welfare advocates and the general public at the same time as its consequences were deeply felt by Native American children, families, and communities.

By the 1960s, the professional discourse of transmitted degeneracy, so popular at the turn of the century, had been supplanted by a kinder, gentler view of the process as one of transmitted deprivation via the "broken home" and the concomitant pathology of the poor single mother (Abramovitz 1996; Griffin 1993; Hays 2003). Growing preoccupation in the 1960s regarding the "culture of poverty" and the "pathology" of the black, female-headed family served to further racialize constructions of at-risk children and risky youth. These hostile representations were challenged by the political mobilizations of the civil rights movement and the War on Poverty. Some professionals and youth advocates were articulating the connections among poverty, racism, and the physical and mental well-being of children and youth and calling for radical new directions in the practice of intervention that championed community action and structural transformation (Cloward and Ohlin 1960; Kepel 1995; Nybell 2002). Aid to Families with Dependent Children, food stamps, and Medicaid programs saw increased use as more women claimed their rights to public assistance for themselves and their children (Abramovitz 1996; Hays 2003). Families disenfranchised by racism and poverty were staking claims to political and economic as well as civil rights. Young people were asserting themselves as political actors, taking a collective stand in opposition to the Vietnam War. Despite these efforts to locate discourses of youth and trouble in a larger social, political, and historical context, the efforts of helping professionals remained largely focused on psychologized models and the concomitant practices of individual care, containment, and control.[9]

Perhaps one of the most powerful examples of what Dennis Saleebey (2006) refers to as "context stripping" and the individualizing of pathology occurred in the wake of the "discovery" of child abuse. Just as child welfare professionals were being challenged to recognize the economic underpinnings of their work, public attention was drawn dramatically to the discovery of the "battered child syndrome," so named by C. Henry Kempe, a physician who recognized a long-overlooked pattern of physical abuse of children by a parent or caregiver. Kempe's recognition of the problem of battered children was important in awakening professional and public concern for the well-being of children. It had the effect, however, of drawing attention away from the structural arrangements that left many children "at risk," focusing public attention instead on the problem of individual adults who harm their children. As Lindsey (2004:122–23) notes, the "discovery" ignited a broad-based national effort to protect children. Within four years every state had adopted child-abuse legislation and mandatory reporting laws. In a short time the nation's child welfare system was transformed into a child protective service system with the bulk of professional time and resources dedicated to the investigation of reports of child abuse (Lindsey 2004).

The 1960s also saw a growing concern for the mental health of young people and the link to delinquency. The neglect of children's mental health was coming to be viewed as a harbinger of future problems, when that troubled child grew into a troubling teen. There were very few psychiatric hospital beds set aside for children through 1950s. But that changed in the 1960s. The assassination of President Kennedy served as a motive force for action when the Warren Commission reported that Lee Harvey Oswald had been a troubled child and did not receive mental health services. Senator Abraham Ribicoff, who held a deep commitment to addressing issues of poverty, mental health, and child welfare, proposed new legislation to establish a commission on children's mental health, which was passed in 1965. Initially, the commission took a strong environmental focus addressing issues of poverty, hunger, poor health care, poor education, and racism. A number of mental health experts had articulately argued the link between childhood poverty and emotional and behavioral problems of young people. However, questions of political economy were eventually bracketed out of the discussion, and it was a more individualized, depoliticized, and medicalized view that came to define a national "crisis in children's mental health" by 1966. Professional concern focused broadly on children "at risk" and the need for detection, diagnosis, and intervention. For example, in 1969 the Joint Commission on Mental Health reported that "using the most conservative estimates, the National Institute of Mental Health estimates that 1,400,000 children under 18 needed psychiatric care" (Joint Commission 1970). In sum, the 1960s was a decade marked by political activism, and the voices and actions of young people were central to struggles on multiple fronts. In spite and because of these struggles, anxieties about troubled children and youth and discourses of individual pathology continued to capture the imagination of professional helpers. While new alarms had sounded regarding the physical safety and mental health of all young people, old practices of care, containment, and control continued to differentiate troubled and troubling children and youth along axes of race, class, and gender. At the same time, the new alarms resurrected old fears that all young people are potentially "at risk," harboring as-yet-undetected seeds of pathology.

CLOSING A CENTURY OF TROUBLE

In the last quarter of the twentieth century we witnessed another shift in the logic and workings of capitalism, this time to a global system characterized by industrial decline, growth of a service economy, the shrinking role of the state, privatization of state-based services, growing economic inequality, and a significant loss of ground for the middle classes (Ehrenreich 1989; Ferguson, Lavalette, and Whitmore 2005; Harvey 1989, 2005; Korten 2001). As debt loads increase and job futures look uncertain, more people are concerned not with getting ahead but with getting by. Along with these economic shifts we have also witnessed a heightened preoccupation with troubled and troubling children and youth, and the proliferation of new forms of pathology, diagnostic categories, and intervention strategies by which to classify, contain, and cure them (Finn and Nybell 2001; Males 1996; Stephens 1995). Since the late 1970s, child and adolescent pathology has become a major growth industry in an expanding service economy, as ever increasing proportions of young people are being deemed in need of care and control (Lerman 1990; Males 1996; Weithorn 1988). As I have argued elsewhere, we are experiencing a medicalization of youthful difference, defiance, and distress such that adolescence itself has become equated with pathology (Finn 2001). I now contend that both childhood and adolescence are becoming equated with pathology. However, the forms of intervention continue to play out differently along class and color lines through separate and unequal systems of intervention.

Let us consider the expanding arenas of child and adolescent mental health. In 1982 it was being reported that at "least ten million children are in need of mental health services, and many more have yet to be identified" (Knitzer 1982). By 1986 there were more than 150,000 young people age 10–17 in inpatient psychiatric care for mental disorders. And between 1987 and 1996 the rate of psychotropic drug use in the treatment of child and adolescent disorders had tripled. Thus in 20 years' time, childhood itself had been identified as the fertile breeding ground of adolescent pathology. For example, in 1995 the Carnegie Council on Adolescent Development declared that half of America's 10–14-year-olds are "at risk" due to their problem behaviors (Males 1996).

These expanding indicators of youthful pathology coincided with a proliferation of new psychiatric diagnostic categories by which to label their troubles in terms of disease. Along with this move came a shift in hospital regulatory practices resulting in greater scrutiny of medical services. Child and adolescent psychiatric treatment remained a relatively unregulated arena, and hospital management specialists encouraged strategic moves into this relatively undeveloped treatment niche. A proliferation of diagnostic labels accompanied a rapid expansion of adolescent psychiatric bed space in the 1980s (Dalton and Forman 1987; Eisenberg 1984; Gaylon 1985; Philips and Jemerin 1988). The clientele competing for these spaces were largely white, middle- and upper-class children and youth whose parents' health insurance covered the bulk of the costs (Males 1996).

Aggressive marketing campaigns promoted the need for adolescent residential treatment to parents and professionals, feeding their fears (see Finn 2001). As a child welfare worker in the 1980s, I found myself as a member of the target audience for these campaigns. I was bombarded with glossy brochures claiming both the benefits of the latest residential treatment facility and the folly in failing to provide such treatment. I later engaged in a critical reading of selected advertisements for adolescent treatment programs printed in the journal *Social Work* during the late 1980s and early 1990s, when placement rates were soaring. The ads provided graphic illustrations of the ways in which pathologies of adolescence were marketed. Some ads played to race- and class-based fears of young people falling in with the "wrong crowd." Some ads encoded gendered assumptions regarding youth and trouble, voicing fears over young women's potential for "promiscuity." Others put forth alarming predictions regarding the consequences of failing to "treat" "chronically difficult" teens, as the text from one ad illustrates: "There are some teens who just can't seem to get out of the way of trouble. The law, drugs, school, even their families are always crossing them. Depression, disruptiveness, even violence are always the result" (cited in Finn 2001:183). In sum, marketing strategies of private residential treatment centers played on deeply felt anxieties of middle-class parents and professionals. Meanwhile, poor youth and youth of color continued to be disproportionately represented in state-based juvenile correctional facilities. As Mike Males writes:

> (K)id-fixing services erupted to meet the market. They were of two kinds. Prison gates opened wide in the 1980s to receive tens of thousands more poorer teens, three-fourth of them non-white. . . . At the same time, mental health and other treatment centers raked in huge profits therapizing hundreds of thousands of health-insured children of the affluent, nearly all white. ((1999:12)

By the mid-1980s, placements of white youth in juvenile detention facilities had significantly declined while their placement rates in psychiatric facilities and private residential treatment programs soared. The 1990s also saw a shift toward more punitive, get-tough policies in juvenile justice, with young people of color bearing the brunt of the punishment. Meanwhile, for-profit youth care was on its way to becoming a 25 billion dollar a year industry by the end of the twentieth century (Kearns 1998:4).

The 1990s' bull market in treatment for troubled teens was fed and sustained by the fevered pitch of popular media and professional discourse of youthful menace. Near hysteria surrounded the various depictions of youth as violent thugs, druggies, superpredators, and suicide risks, who are constructed as basically to blame for a "national moral melt down" (Males 1999; Zimring 1998). Articles in magazines such as *Atlantic Monthly* voiced fear and loathing over the coming of the "Adolescent Apocalypse" (Powers 2002). While racialized and class-based images of dangerous youth remained prevalent, fears were also growing regarding the violence within those young people previously presumed to be "innocent"—middle- and upper-middle-class white youth from suburbia and Middle America "on the right track" to adulthood (Finn 2001, 2004). While placement rates in treatment and disciplinary facilities have soared, communities have increasingly become sites of youth discipline through the surveillance and restriction of young people in privatized spaces such as shopping malls, enforcement of strict curfews, and zero-tolerance policies in schools.

TWENTY-FIRST-CENTURY TROUBLES

I would like to report that the dawn of the new century ushered in a new era regarding children, youth, and trouble. Thus far, however, that does not appear to be the case. The twenty-first century is shaping up to be a curious and troubling sequel to the "Century of the Child" that could perhaps be characterized as the "Century of the Troubled Child." It seems that the "little wanderers" of the 1800s have been replaced by the little worriers of today. What we have witnessed thus far is a trend toward earlier and earlier diagnosis of child psychopathology. According to Johnson (2003), approximately 26% of preschoolers meet at least one diagnostic category as described in the *Diagnostic and Statistical Manual of Mental Disorders (DSM-IV)*. In addition, Johnson reports an increased prevalence of the diagnosis of bipolar disorder in young children, with claims of onset of manic symptoms at age 5 or younger. Johnson does not raise questions about these claims but calls instead for increased public awareness and early intervention. James et al. (2006) report that 300,000 children now enter foster care each year, with more children going to short-term residential treatment as a result of managed-care policies. Overall, we seem to be experiencing a medicalization of everyday life in general and of childhood in particular, with sickness and pharmaceutical intervention being sold to parents, professionals, and children themselves at every turn.

Consider, for example, the explosive increase in the attention deficit and hyperactivity disorder (ADHD) diagnosis and the use of Ritalin over the past 20 years. ADHD diagnosis in the United States has grown from 500,000 in 1985, to 900,000 in 1990, to 5–7 million in 2004. The production of Ritalin increased 450% in the 1990s, and the United States consumes 90% of the world Ritalin supply (Carle 2000; Transit, 2004). According to Eben Carle (2000:17), particularly high levels of Ritalin use have been reported among children in affluent communities. For example, Carle cites a recent report showing that nearly 20% of children in Virginia Beach are on Ritalin for ADHD, a rate nearly six times higher than the national average, yet typical for many wealthier U.S. communities. Supposedly, parents turn to Ritalin to force their children to "pay attention" and sustain their focus, a key to future success. It appears that parents are fighting for the label, as having an "average" child is simply unacceptable. Critics decry the practice as forced, chemically induced "concentration" (Carle 2000).

Rachel Ragg (2006) offers a scathing critique of the medicalization of childhood and the absolute neglect of attention to the toxic environments in which far too many children live. Ragg cites a *Journal of the American Medical Association* study from 2000 reporting a 200–300% increase in the prescription of antidepressants and stimulants to children under age 3, including some as young as 15 months. According to U.S. psychologist and attorney Bob Jacobs, a critic of the Ritalin rage, "Drugs ensure the conformism that Western society demands. . . . Public consciousness is offended by seeing a child in physical restraints, but because chemical restraints are internal they are a much less 'sexy' issue, even though they are arguably more destructive" (cited in Ragg 2006:42). Jacobs notes that it is not so much our children's behavior that has changed but the way in which it is viewed in capitalist society. As Ragg aptly puts it, the exuberance of childhood is now frowned upon as inappropriate behavior. She contends that children are being pathologized and medicated for a broad and ever-changing range of behaviors deemed inappropriate. Ragg describes "inappropriate" as "one of the most weasel words of the 21st century, almost always meaning 'when it doesn't fit the prevailing agenda'" (42). Even more troubling, Ragg argues, is the complete lack of attention to the toxic environments in which children live, play, eat, and study. Ragg saves her strongest criticism for drug companies, which, she contends, are the "ones who market the disorders in the first place before providing the 'miracle cure'" (46).

As we complete the first decade of the twenty-first century, we find that for-profit treatment of children and youth continues to be big business, whether the profits go to residential-care enterprises, private boarding schools, or drug companies. We have witnessed both a widening of the scope of pathologies of everyday life and increasingly finer distinctions of difference and deviance calling for intervention. "Other" people's children still face more punitive and blaming interventions, but the net has been cast broadly, with virtually all children deemed "at risk" of some manifestation of trouble requiring professional intervention. It seems that children and youth have been reduced to commodities in an ever-expanding marketplace of care, containment, and control. It is imperative that we confront the fact that the production, marketing, and treatment of the troubles of children and youth are intimately connected to the logic and consequences of the prevailing political economic order of things. We can no longer afford "context stripping" approaches to understanding and action (Saleebey 2006:6). Further, in the post 9/11 era, we must critically examine the production of fear as a way of life and the implications for children and youth. If our professional practices serve to reduce more and more children to "bundles of pathology," what is at stake in terms of the rights and capacities of children and youth as social actors? How might we muster the political will and moral courage to challenge the dominant professional and popular discourse and take a long, hard look at the deeply entrenched structures of poverty, inequality, and difference that shape and constrain the lives of so many young people? How might we resist context-stripping assessment of trouble and treatment and dedicate ourselves instead to challenging and changing the toxic environments in which young people live? If we were to hold a conference in 2009 and declare the twenty-first century the new "Century of the Child," what would our vision be?

QUESTIONS FOR DISCUSSION

1. What are some further examples of practices in the history of intervention with children and youth that have fallen out of favor over time? How do those shifts in practices relate to shifts in the values and assumptions of professionals?

2. Are there aspects of your own practice with children and youth that raise ethical questions for you? How do you respond to those questions? What course of action might you take? How might a historical perspective inform your thinking and actions?

3. What other examples can you think of that illustrate ways in which social workers and other human-service professionals are implicated in the production of images regarding young people and "trouble?" What are the implications for practice with children and youth?

4. Where do you see examples of "context stripping" in interventions with children and youth? Where do you see examples of contextually grounded practice? What are the differences?

5. What is your vision of the "Century of the Child" for the twenty-first century? What policy and practice directions would you advocate in translating that vision into reality? Where might you anticipate meeting resistance? Where might you find allies?

NOTES

1. This discussion of history incorporates excerpts from a chapter previously published book chapter: J. Finn (2004), Troubled in paradise: A critical reflection on youth, trouble, and intervention. In R. Transit, ed., *Disciplining the child via the discourse of the*

professions, 90–129 (Springfield, Ill.: Charles C. Thomas). The excerpts are used here with permission of the publisher.

2. The concept of youth has historically been a strongly gendered concept associated with masculinity and male experience. A number of scholars have critically addressed the gendering of youth. See, for example, Griffin (1993; 1997) and Adams (1997).

3. "Homeless Children" image used here with permission of the Nebraska State Historical Society Archives.

4. Federal boarding schools lasted well beyond the 1920s. However, the 1928 Merriam Report, documenting the poor conditions of many schools and the systematic neglect of children in residence, diminished the popularity of boarding schools as the primary solution for the "problem" of Native American assimilation. The ensuing years would see a shift to more "efficient" policies—the sterilization of Native American women and the adoption of Indian children into non-Indian homes.

5. It is interesting to note the flexibility of the category of youth here in terms of age span. The fuzzy boundaries of chronological age and the concept of youth have added to the concept's ambiguous power.

6. Healy's work also reveals ways in which representations of adolescent trouble are marked by gender. While delinquent boys were discussed in terms of stubbornness, disorderly conduct, and, at times, mental slowness, the most troubling aspect of female "deviance" was their sexuality.

7. The institutionalized practices of the juvenile justice system, which expanded rapidly in the early twentieth century, helped to establish adolescence as a new social category and legitimize the role of the state and intervention professionals in their care and control (Shook 2005).

8. See Gallagher, Vermont eugenics: A documentary history (2001), for an excellent archival resource on the eugenics movement and legislation of the early twentieth century. The Vermont story is typical of legislation that was passed throughout the United States at the time. Of particular note here is the pamphlet entitled "Proposal for improving social legislation," published by the Vermont Conference on Social Work, Committee on Legislation, January 1, 1927.

9. See Nybell (2002) for an insightful summary of this period and a detailed examination of the depoliticization of the problem of children's mental health.

REFERENCES

Abramovitz, M. (1996). *Regulating the lives of women: Social welfare policy from colonial times to the present.* Rev. ed. Boston: South end Press.

Adams, D. (1988). Fundamental considerations: The deep meaning of Native American schooling, 1880–1900. *Harvard Educational Review 58* (1): 1–28.

Adams, M. (1997). *The trouble with normal: Postwar youth and the making of heterosexuality.* Toronto: University of Toronto Press.

Ainsworth, M. (1967). *Infancy in Uganda: Infant care and the growth of love.* Baltimore: Johns Hopkins University.

Baylor, E., and E. Monachesi. (1939). *The rehabilitation of children: The theory and practice of child placement.* New York: Harper.

Bowlby, J. (1951). *Maternal care and mental health.* World Health Organization Monograph Series No. 2. Geneva: World Health Organization.

———. (1968). *Attachment.* London: Pelican.

Boyer, P. (1978). *Urban masses and moral order in America, 1820–1920.* Cambridge: Harvard University Press.

Brace, C. L. (1859). *The best method of disposing of pauper and vagrant children.* New York: Wynkoop and Hollenbeck.

———. (1872). *The dangerous classes of New York and my twenty years' work among them.* New York: Wynkoop and Hollenbeck.

Bremner, R. (Ed.). (1970). *Children and youth in America: A documentary history.* Vols. 1–3. Cambridge: Harvard University Press.

Carle, E. (2000). ADHD for sale. *Psychology Today 33* (3): 17.

Cloward, R., and L. Ohlin. (1960). *Delinquency and opportunity.* Glencoe, Ill: Free Press.

Dalton, R., and M. Forman. (1987). Conflict of interest associated with psychiatric hospitalization of children. *American Journal of Orthopsychiatry,* 57: 12–14.

Day, P. (2006). *A new history of social welfare.* 5th ed. Boston: Allyn and Bacon.

Ehrenreich, B. (1989). Fear of falling: The inner life of the middle class. New York: Pantheon.

Eisenberg, B. (1984). The case against for-profit hospitals. *Hospital and Community Psychiatry 35:* 1009–13.

Ellis, H. (1987). From the battle in the classroom to the battle for the classroom. *American Indian Quarterly* (Summer): 255–64.

Erikson, E. (1959). *Identity and the life cycle: Selected papers.* New York: International Press.

Erikson, E. (1968). *Identity, youth, and crisis.* New York: Norton.

Ferguson, D. (1961). Children in need of parents: Implications of the Child Welfare League study. *Child Welfare 40:* 1–6.

Ferguson, I., M. Lavalette, and E. Whitmore. (2005). *Globalisation, global justice, and social work.* New York: Routledge.

Finn, J. (2001). Text and turbulence: Representing adolescence as pathology in the human services. *Childhood 8* (2): 167–92.

———. (2004). Troubled in paradise: A critical reflection on youth, trouble, and intervention. In R. Transit, ed., *Disciplining the child via the discourse of the professions,* 90–129. Springfield, Ill.: Charles C. Thomas.

Finn, J., and M. Jacobson. (2008, 2d ed.). *Just practice: A social justice approach to social work.* Peosta, Iowa: Eddie Bowers Publishing.

Finn, J., and L. Nybell. (2001). Introduction: Capitalizing on concern: The making of troubled children and troubling youth in late capitalism. *Childhood* 8 (2): 139–48.

Gallagher, N. (2001). Vermont eugenics: A documentary history. Accessed January 12, 2007, at www.uvm.edu/~eugenics.

Gaylon, S. (1985). The coming of the corporation and the marketing of psychiatry. *Journal of the American Academy of Child and Adolescent Psychiatry 36:* 154-59.

Ghenie, K., and C. Wellenstein. (2008). *The well being of children and the question of attachment.* In L. Nybell, J. Shook, and J. Finn, eds., *Childhood, youth, and social work in transformation.* New York: Columbia University Press.

Goddard, H. (1911). Wanted: A child to adopt. *Survey 27* (October 14): 1003–6.

Gould, S. J. (1981). *The mismeasure of man.* New York: W. W. Norton.

Griffin, C. (1993). *The study of youth and adolescence in Britain and America.* Cambridge: Polity Press.

———. (1997). Troubled teens: Managing disorders of transition and consumption. *Feminist Review 55* (1): 4–21.

———. (2001). Imagining new narrative of youth: Youth research, the "new Europe," and global youth culture. *Childhood 8* (2): 147–66.

Hall, G. S. (1904). Adolescence, its psychology and its relations to physiology, anthropology, sociology, sex, crime, religion, and education. Vol. 1. New York: Appleton.

Hartman, A., and J. Laird. (1983). *Family-centered social work practice.* New York: Free Press.

Harvey, D. (1989). *The condition of postmodernity.* Oxford: Basil Blackwell.

———. (2005). *A brief history of neoliberalism.* Oxford: Oxford University Press.

Hays, S. (2003). Flat broke with children: Women in the age of welfare reform. New York: Oxford University Press.

Healy, W. (1915). *The individual delinquent: A text-book of diagnosis and prognosis for all concerned in understanding offenders.* Boston: Little, Brown.

Herman, E. (2005). The adoption history project, Department of History, University of Oregon, Eugene, OR. Accessed January 13, 2007, at http://www.uoregon.edu/~adoption/timeline.html.

Holloran, P. (1989). *Boston's wayward children: Social services for homeless children, 1830–1930.* Boston: Northeastern University Press.

James, S., L. Leslie, M. Hurlburt, D. Slymen, J. Landsverk, I. Davis, S. Mathiesen, and J. Zhang. (2006). Children in out-of-home care: Entry into intensive or restrictive mental health and residential placements. *Journal of Emotional and Behavioral Disorders* 14 (4): 196–208.

Johnson, M. (2003). Prevalence of psychopathology in preschool-age children. *Journal of Child and Adolescent Psychiatric Nursing* 16 (4): 147–52.

Joint Commission on Mental Health of Children. (1970). *Crisis in child mental health: Challenges for the 1970s.* New York; Harper and Row.

Katz, M. (1986). *In the shadow of the poorhouse.* New York: Basic Books.

Kearns, R. (1998). Finding profits in at-risk kids, *Children's Voice* (Fall): 4–5, 14–16.

Kepel, B. (1995). *The work of democracy: Ralph Bunche, Kenneth B. Clark, Lorraine Hansberry, and the cultural politics of race.* Cambridge: Harvard University Press.

Kett, J. (1977). *Rites of passage: Adolescence in America, 1790–1970.* New York: Basic Books.

Knitzer, J. (1982). *Unclaimed children: The failure of public responsibility to children and adolescents in need of mental health services.* Washington, D.C.: Children's Defense Fund.

Korten, D. (2001). *When corporations rule the world.* 2nd ed. Bloomfield, Conn.: Kumarian Press.

Lerman. P. (1990). *Counting youth in trouble living away from home: Recent trends and counting problems.* New Brunswick, N.J.: Rutgers University School of Social Work.

Lindsey, D. (2004). *The welfare of children.* 2nd ed. New York: Oxford University Press.

MacDonald, A. (1908). Juvenile crime and reformation, including stigmata of degeneration, 60 Cong., 1 Sess (1908). Senate Doc. 532, 16–17. Washington, D.C. In R. Bremner, ed., *Children and youth in America: A documentary history.* Cambridge: Harvard University Press: 1970.

Males, M. (1996). *The scapegoat generation.* Monroe, Me.: Common Courage Press.

———. (1999). *Framing youth: Ten myths about the next generation.* Monroe, Me: Common Courage Press.

Markowitz, G, and D. Rosner. (1996). *Children, race, and power: Kenneth and Mamie Clark's Northside Center.* Charlottesville: University of Virginia Press.

Morgan, J. T. (1889). Annual report of the Commissioner of Indian Affairs. In W. Washburn, ed., *The American Indian and the United States: A documentary history.* Vol. 1. New York: Random House.

Nebraska State Historical Society Web Site (n.d.). Orphans trains. Accessed January 13, 2007, at http://www.nebraskahistory.org/sites/mnh/orphans/.

Nybell, L. (2002). Remaking children's mental health: On children, community, and care in reform. Ph.D. dissertation, University of Michigan.

Oberly, J. (1888). Annual report of the Commissioner of Indian Affairs. In W. Washburn, ed., *The American Indian and the United States: A documentary history.* Vol. 1. New York: Random House.

Pelton, L. (1989). *For reasons of poverty: A critical analysis of the public child welfare system in the U.S.* New York: Praeger.

Philips, L., and J. Jemerin. (1988). Changes in inpatient child psychiatry: Consequences and recommendations. *Journal of the American Academy of Child and Adolescent Psychiatry 27:* 397–403.

Platt, A. (1969). *The child savers: The invention of delinquency.* Chicago: University of Chicago Press.

Powers, R. (2002). The apocalypse of adolescence. *The Atlantic Monthly 289* (3): 58–74.

Ragg, R (2006). School uniformity. *The Ecologist 36* (9): 40–47.

Reisch, M. (1988). The uses of history in teaching social work. *Journal of Teaching in Social Work 2* (1): 3–16.

Reisch, M., and S. Wenocur. (1986). The future of community organization in social work: Social activism and the politics of profession building. *Social Service Review 72* (2): 70–91.

Saleebey, D. (Ed.) (2006). *The strengths perspective in social work practice.* 4th ed. Boston: Pearson Education.

Sarri, R., and J. Finn. (1992). Child welfare policy and practice: Rethinking the history of our certainties. *Children and Youth Services Review 14:* 219–36.

Shook, J. (2005). Contesting childhood in the U.S. justice system. *Childhood 12* (4): 461–78.

Smith, B. (1985). Business, politics, and Indian land settlement in Montana, 1881–1904. *Canadian Journal of History 20* (1): 45–64.

Stephens, S. (1995). Children and the politics of culture in "late capitalism." In S. Stephens, ed., *Children and the politics of culture,* 3–48. Princeton: Princeton University Press.

Sutton, J. (1988). *Stubborn children.* Berkeley: University of California Press.

Szasz, M. (1974). *Education and the American Indian: The road to self-determination, 1928–1973.* Albuquerque: University of New Mexico Press.

Takaki, R. (1979). *Iron cages: Race and culture in 19th century America.* New York: Knopf.
———. (1993). *A different mirror: A history of multicultural America.* Boston: Little, Brown.

Transit, R. (Ed.) (2004). *Disciplining the child via the discourse of the professions.* Springfield, Ill.: Charles C. Thomas.

Walker, T. (1980). American Indian children: Foster care and adoptions. National Institute of Education, Conference on the Educational and Occupational Needs of American Indian Women. Washington, D.C.: Government Printing Office.

Washburn, W. (Ed.) (1973). *The American Indian and the United States: A documentary history.* New York: Random House.

Weithorn, J. (1988). Mental hospitalization for troublesome youth. An analysis of sky-rocketing admission rates. *Stanford Law Review 40:* 773–838.

Zimring, F. E. (1998). *American youth violence.* New York: Oxford University Press.

Zinn, H. (1970). *The politics of history.* Boston: Beacon Press.

Missing Children | **TWO**

Representing Young People
Away from Placement

Lynn M. Nybell

On August 30, 2002, the *Detroit Free Press* featured a front-page story illustrated with a small portrait of 12-year-old boy named Prentiss under the banner headline, "State Loses Track of 302 Abused or Neglected Kids." The article tied concern about the whereabouts of Prentiss to the predicaments of the 302 young people that the newspaper came to refer to as "Michigan's missing children"— children and youth assigned to the care of the state but no longer in the foster homes or shelters to which they were assigned. The *Free Press* claimed that the state child welfare system had "lost" more than 300 of its wards. Karen Smith, a spokesperson for the state's Family Independence Agency (FIA), contested the notion that the agency had lost these children, commenting: "The vast majority of missing youths are older than fourteen and many of them are runaways from foster care. Teenage girls, especially those from homes where they were abused and neglected, often run off with boys they think they are in love with" (Kresnak 2002a:1).

The director of FIA, Doug Howard, also objected that the young people in question were not missing but were "away without legal permission" (or AWOL) instead. In a letter to the editor the following day, Howard wrote:

The state did not lose these kids. Many of the "missing" kids have walked away from their placement or been taken away without court permission. Some teenagers and parents make decisions that are contrary to agency plans and court orders designed to address the issues that brought the family to our attention. The FIA takes steps to ensure that the families abide by the plans, but it does not always happen. (Howard 2002a:12A)

These exchanges opened what would be a durable story line for children's beat reporter Jack Kresnak. The *Free Press* would publish 27 stories on "Michigan's missing children" by year's end. It also initiated years of advocacy on behalf of young people who would become known as "AWOL" foster youth in Michigan.

Before penning the August 30 story, Kresnak recognized—as the state bureaucrats did—that some portion of the children and young people did not remain in the homes, residential facilities, or shelters where they were officially placed (Kresnak 2004). Acceptance of this notion—-that young people in the care of the state sometimes leave their placements—emerged in the views expressed by FIA spokespersons and characterized the typical state response to these incidents. Before August 30, 2002, when a worker in one of these agencies identified a child or youth as "AWOL," the child's worker sometimes filed a "missing person" report with the police. The state compiled statistics on the number of these children and youth and reported the numbers to the appropriate federal funding agencies (Kresnak 2003). But after Kresnak's story and the public reaction it evoked, the circumstances of these young people became a crisis requiring immediate response. Public officials, child advocates, law enforcement agents, judges, and children themselves were mobilized to act and react to each other in new ways in response to these predicaments.

This chapter begins with a brief account of the story of "AWOL youth" in Michigan as it emerged in the *Free Press,* followed by an even briefer sketch of how the crisis in Michigan fit into a broader national concern for such children that simultaneously emerged. I argue that viewing abused and neglected young people who are away from placement as "missing children" is a relatively recent and novel development. Though inspired by an intention to protect vulnerable youth, initial reactions by the courts, the police, and the public to media reports regarding the problem of "missing children" did not resolve the problems faced by these young people, as it subjected them to greater public scrutiny, visibility, and containment. In 2003 nearly 40% of youth who ran away from placement were held in secure detention for some period of time, despite the fact that most left placement without permission on only one occasion (Sarri, Shook, and Hajski 2005; Sarri, Hajski, and Shook 2007).[1]

Consequently, I propose that an analysis of the media coverage of missing children in Wayne County reveals the possibility that viewing all young people away from placement as "missing children" runs a risk, paradoxically, of making their predicaments more difficult and their involvement in the juvenile justice system more likely. This critique, then, serves as the basis for two critical points that I discuss in my analysis. First, it underscores the need for concerted advocacy efforts on behalf of these children, particularly when they are criminalized or held to blame for running away. In Wayne County, this effort emerged through the creation and actions of the Wayne County Task Force on Children. The task force was composed of providers, lawyers, the court, foundations, advocates, and researchers whose efforts culminated in new organizational arrangements that sought to prohibit secure detention for young people away from placement and to require the development of alternatives for their care (Sarri, Hajski, and Shook 2007). Second, it raises the possibility that we should consider other ways to frame the problems faced by young people who leave placement. To prompt such reframing, I draw from an emerging scholarship that records the perspectives of young people who have been absent from foster care (Courtney et al. 2005; Finkelstein et al. 2004; Sarri, Shook, and Hajski 2005). The perspectives of these young people challenge some of the central assumptions of the "missing children" story and suggest a variety of alternative strategies to reduce their risk and resolve their dilemmas.

THE EMERGENCE OF A CRISIS

There are many reasons why observers might be concerned about the well-being and life chances of the young people who were missing from foster care in Michigan in 2002. Reviews of the cases of the 189 "missing children" in Wayne, Michigan's largest county and home of the *Free Press*, revealed that 90% of the children had been removed from distressed neighborhoods, often from impoverished homes, without sufficient food, furniture, or heat. In 70% of the cases, the parents of these children had their rights terminated, making the children permanent wards of the state (Youssef and Kresnak 2002). Many of these young people had endured an unstable and shifting set of arrangements in state care, being moved from one placement to the next (Sarri, Shook, and Hajski 2005). Furthermore, when young people in these situations left placement, as some portion did, there was reason to worry about their vulnerability to danger or exploitation.

Historically, the plight of these young people had not prompted much alarm. Moreover, a relatively lackadaisical response to older youth leaving placement was not unique to Michigan. On the contrary, a study by Courtney and Barth (1996) in California discovered that more than 20 percent of 17-year-old foster-care children exited the system by running away or otherwise refusing service; in other words, leaving was one of the principal means by which young people terminated their placements in California. Though little is known about the experiences of children who leave foster care, it appears that such exits are common enough to have been considered part of the routine operation of the system. However, in Michigan, the situation was transformed into a crisis when foster children and youth away from placement were identified as "missing children."

MAKING THE "MISSING" VISIBLE

In drawing urgent attention to the predicament of these young people, the *Free Press* drew on a widespread media and popular discourse about "missing children" that has proliferated since the 1980s—a discourse that has centered rather narrowly on spectacular cases of child abduction, despite the relative rarity of these events.[2] Though child kidnapping has been a public concern since the 1880s (Fass 1997), the term "missing children" was coined a full century later (Best 1990). Between 1979 and 1981, several cases in which children were presumably abducted by strangers received broad national publicity. These well-publicized abductions included the 1979 disappearance of 6-year-old Etan Patz, who left his parents' co-op apartment in New York City to begin the two-block walk to the school bus stop and was not seen again; and the 1982 murder of 6-year-old Adam Walsh, who disappeared from the toy department of a department store in a shopping mall in Hollywood, Florida (Best 1990; Fass 1997).

In 1984 the federal government funded the National Center for Missing and Exploited Children (NCMEC)—an agency with no formal governmental authority, but with strong links to both federal and private agencies. The NCMEC's budget now reaches nearly 50 million dollars, which the agency devotes to disseminating concern for missing and exploited children through training, community outreach, public education, and a national hotline (1–800-THE-LOST) (NCMEC 2006). NCMEC works closely with other private organizations that have been founded to address the problem of missing children, including several that grew out of the spontaneous grassroots efforts that emerged when a child disappeared (Fass 1997). NCMEC is probably most famously associated with the dissemination of photographs of "missing children" through its network of associations with media outlets, corporate sponsors, and the direct-mail company ADVO. NCMEC reports that ADVO distributes mail-cards with missing children's photographs in up to 114 million households throughout the United States each month (NCMEC 2007). Through the efforts of NCMEC and a network of related enterprises, concern for missing children has achieved extraordinary visibility, as photographs of lost children and youth have become commonplace on milk cartons, shopping bags, billboards, and public service announcements (Best 1990; Ivey 1995).

Through the 1980s, estimates of the scope of the problem were necessarily inexact as there were no established criteria for defining cases of missing children (Best 1990). However, many of those circulating claims about the problem of missing children produced large numbers that relied upon expansive definitions of the category, including youth who had left home voluntarily ("runaways"), children who were abandoned by or ejected from their families ("throwaways"), children who were removed from the custody of one parent by another in violation of a custody agreement ("parental abductions"), and children who were abducted by strangers. Best points out that the number of missing children was often estimated at 1.8 million. Though advocates pressing for attention to the problem of missing children acknowledged that a relatively small number of children were abducted by strangers, such distinctions were often lost as concern for missing children circulated.

In compliance with the 1984 Missing Children's Act that required regular incidence studies, the Justice Department published a statistical analysis of the missing children problem in 1990 and updated that analysis in 2002 (Sedlak et al. 2002). These analyses defined and categorized instances of missing children, confirming the relative rarity of stranger abduction. For example, a 2002 study found 797,500 instances in which caretakers reported children missing to the police or other agencies, all but a very small percentage of whom were recovered very quickly. A substantial portion (45%) were instances of "runaway" or "throwaway" children, and nearly as many (43%) were children "missing for benign reasons," including teenagers who were gone longer than expected. A very small percentage (involving 115 children) were classified as stereotypical stranger abductions. In the majority of those instances, children were recovered or returned (Sedlak et al. 2002).

On one hand, the differences between the expansive claims about child abductions and the more realistic numbers provided by these systematic studies are striking. On the other hand, the shocking reality that the lives of 40 individual children were lost to stranger abduction in a single year cannot be minimized. The loss of each of these lives is a nearly unfathomable tragedy. Nonetheless, as historian Paula Fass (2007) points out, the continuing conflation of profoundly disturbing instances of stranger abduction with both parental abduction and runaway youth makes the phenomenon of stranger abduction seem much more common than it is, even as it makes parental abduction and running away more profoundly disturbing than previously assumed. This conflation was apparent as the *Free Press* described foster children away from placement as "missing children," raising fearful awareness of their potential sexual exploitation and physical endangerment, and transforming a long-standing dilemma of the foster care system into a crisis.

THE SUMMER OF "MISSING CHILDREN"

It was not surprising that the predicament of Michigan's foster children surfaced as an urgent concern in August 2002, a summer when the nation was gripped with anxiety for children abducted by strangers (Smart and Smart 2003). Just prior to the initial *Free Press* report, President George W. Bush turned his attention away from building the case for war in Iraq in order to announce plans for a first White House Conference on Missing, Exploited, and Runaway Children (U.S. Department of Education 2002). The conference, sponsored by the NC-MEC and its corporate partners, was planned for September. Members of government, law enforcement representatives, corporate leaders, citizen experts, and victims' parents were among those invited to attend. Announcement of the conference gained drama and intensity occurring as it did weeks after 14-year-old Elizabeth Smart was abducted on June 6, 2002, from the bedroom in suburban Salt Lake City that she shared with her sister.

Elizabeth's plight was the subject of intense and sensationalistic media coverage from the time of her disappearance. As plans for the conference geared up, daily media attention featured press conferences with Elizabeth's parents, the massive community-wide search for the still-missing Elizabeth, and interviews with experts who speculated on developments in the case. Night after night, guests on shows such as CNN's *Larry King Live* offered expert insights into Elizabeth's disappearance. As the weeks wore on, Elizabeth's mother and father, Lois and Ed Smart, worked desperately to keep attention focused on efforts to find their missing daughter. They supplied the media with home movies of the photogenic Elizabeth as a teenager and a child. They also sponsored a website,

ElizabethSmart.com, which provided more than 20 photographs of Elizabeth. An impromptu network of related websites emerged, distributing information in preformatted flyers that could be downloaded for viewing or distribution to volunteers who participated in the expanding nationwide search effort (Smart and Smart 2003).

Thus, President Bush's statement at the fall conference gained emotional power and urgency as he appeared with Mrs. Lois Smart and the parents of other victims at his side. Bush (2002) told the assembled: "The kidnapping or murder of a child is parent's worst nightmare. Yet too many moms and dads have experienced this nightmare across America. Too many have suffered . . . when a child's life, or liberty, or innocence is taken, it is a terrible, terrible loss. And those responsible have committed a terrible crime. Our society has a duty, a solemn duty, to shield children from exploitation and danger."

The conference indexed the national prominence of the issue of "missing and exploited children" by the attendance of many high-ranking members of the administration, including Secretary of State Colin Powell and Attorney General John Ashcroft, as well as the director of the FBI, the commissioner of customs, and the secretaries of health and human services and education. Participants also included television star John Walsh, father of 6-year-old murder and abduction victim Adam Walsh, whose own show, *America's Most Wanted*, frequently featured stories of child abduction.

Despite the power-packed roster of attendees at the conference, the actions that emerged from it were narrowly focused. The president pressed for expanded cooperation between law enforcement and the media in "Amber Alert" programs, increased funding for the NCMEC, and wide dissemination of a guide for parents on "personal safety for children."

Media attention to the disappearance of Elizabeth Smart waxed and waned as the fall and then winter wore on. Then Elizabeth's story saturated the air waves again when she was discovered on March 12, 2003, in the company of two homeless adults in Salt Lake City, just a few miles from her home. In the end, John Walsh's television show was credited with disseminating a critical tip to the public that eventually led to the recovery of Elizabeth and the arrest of her abductors (Smart and Smart 2003).

STORIES OF MISSING CHILDREN

The story of Elizabeth Smart's disappearance featured the now common elements shared by high-profile stories of child abduction: a precious and blameless young victim; distraught and determined parents; a community rallied in solidarity and joined in the search for the child; and public suspicions and outrage at terrifyingly deviant individuals who perpetrate such crimes (Fass 1997; 2007). Heightened alarm for a young victim is channeled into a narrow range of options: heightened visibility, public scrutiny, and law enforcement work are the limited alternatives to which friends and family turn. The dominant media account of Elizabeth's disappearance, following a pattern of other high-profile child abductions, is a tale that affirms shared beliefs in the innocence of children and recognizes their inestimable value to their families and communities. It locates threats to children in bizarre individuals with deviant and frequently sexual urges to kidnap children and credits the media's role in rallying attention to the threats to young people.

Although the mainstream media account of Elizabeth's disappearance is the "official" tale, it is not the only interpretation of these dramatic events that circulated while she was missing. As the Smarts' recounting of their experience makes wrenchingly clear, parents and family members of abductees not only are portrayed as victims of incalculable loss but are treated as objects of suspicion and blame (Fass 1997; Smart and Smart 2003). In the context of pervasive concern about family breakdown and pathology, the family of a "missing child" is now simultaneously considered a potent source of possible threat to that victim (Fass 2007).

Submerged beneath the dominant account of Elizabeth's kidnapping and rescue are even more disturbing questions about the innocence of the young victim herself. In the tabloid press, Internet discussions, and blogs, suspicions swirled about why Elizabeth was unable to escape; why she did not identify herself to others; whether her fear for her family or a process of "brain-washing" accounts for what is construed as her docility or even complicity with her captors.[3] What I believe these counternarratives suggest is that beneath the panic and protectionism over "missing children" so evident in stranger abduction stories run strong currents of skepticism about dangerous families and suspicion about children "out of place" (Stephens 1995).

In the case of Elizabeth Smart, these alternative stories—about parents as culprits and children as culpable—lurk below the surface of the main tale of an arduous journey of "family, faith, and hope" that led to her recovery (Smart and Smart 2003). The crisis over "Michigan's missing children" allows us to examine what happens when young people who are away from placement are inserted into the protectionist discourse of "missing children." My reading of this unfolding story suggests that when young people away from placement are framed as "missing children," there is considerable danger that the anger and resentment toward young people that remains submerged in the story of the disappearance of Elizabeth Smart will surface as the central theme instead.

RESPONDING TO THE CRISIS IN MICHIGAN

Within about a month of the publication of the first article, a structure of innovative responses to "Michigan's missing children" began to emerge from the collaborative efforts of the media and a variety of public officials. For example, three weeks after the initial Kresnak article, the front page of the *Detroit Free Press* featured a mosaic design of tiny portrait photos, organized around the appeal: "Help find these kids" (Kresnak and Askari 2002a). The young faces incorporated into this design belonged to some of the foster children who were not where the state believed they should be. Inside the paper, the *Free Press* offered a two-page spread of names and photos of nearly all the children so-identified. This display was made possible because Michigan became the first state to drop legal protections of the confidentiality of foster children in order to publish the pictures, names, birthdates, and "dates of last contact" of Michigan's "missing children" on its website (www.michigan.gov/fia) (Kresnak 2002c, 2002f). Some five years after its initiation, the website had received 350,795 "hits" (or visits), generating tips leading to the location of 59 children (State of Michigan 2007).

This website, and the images and practices that emanate from it, inserted Michigan into the "missing child" discourse in the role of a parent. In mounting the website, the state turned to a newly constituted actor to resolve this newly constituted crisis—the presumably concerned, mobilized, and benevolent public. The state's new involvement of "the public" in responsibility for foster children required some new technologies—such as the website—and renewed attention to older ones, such as photography. That the state lacked photographs of nearly half of the missing children suggested that it was failing in its parental role. In the aftermath of this crisis, child welfare workers were dispatched immediately to take photographs of all 18,000 foster children in Michigan (Kresnak 2003).

These reactions were premised on the assumption that exposing the name, age, and photograph of a missing child is an act of vigilance and involvement required in such an emergency. There is very little publicly expressed doubt about whether such exposure might heighten the risks to which these young people are subjected. One adult raised in foster care described herself as "absolutely livid" about what might happen to these vulnerable children as a result of such exposure. Otherwise, a general silence ensued regarding any risk that might attend publicizing the names and identities of these young people, even after the body of one missing young woman was discovered about three weeks after her picture appeared in the paper (Kresnak 2002b:1A).

As the story of Michigan's missing children unfolded over the ensuing months, the predicaments of these children escaped or perhaps transformed the confines of the dominant "missing and exploited" children's story in several important ways. First, of course, while abduction stories usually focus on one special and unique child, the scope of this story involves dozens of young people. So, while in an occasional *Free Press* story the reader catches a glimpse of a remarkable young person in terribly challenging circumstances, this individual is quickly submerged again into stories about this problematic group with rotating membership. The lead story about Prentiss Rachal exemplifies this trend. Though concern about his whereabouts initiates the missing children crisis, we hear of him only once more, when he is discovered on September 17, outside his mother's apartment in Dallas, Texas (Kresnak 2002d).

This outcome of the Prentiss Rachal story highlights another remarkable characteristic of Michigan's missing children—specifically, the ease with which many of them can be found (Kresnak 2002e). In the wake of the website, some children were located on the rosters of local county juvenile detention centers. A more substantial number of them, like Prentiss, were found with parents and relatives. This irony—the many lost children were with their parents—is evident from the very beginning of the crisis. For example, the "reunion" picture at the center of the mosaic of missing children featured in the *Free Press* is a photograph of a handsome 5-year-old boy and his mother, who were discovered living together in Virginia.

As the stories continued to emerge in the newspaper, the *Free Press* reported that though "many relatives and guardians confirmed that the youths are unaccounted for, many also had at least some idea of where the kids were" (Kresnak and Askari 2002b:5A). In December, in preparation for a special three-part series on the "missing children" problem, *Free Press* reporters Nancy Youssef and Jack Kresnak attained access to thousands of pages of confidential juvenile court documents related to 107 of these children. They reported that in "dozens of cases" these children eluded juvenile court authorities and were shielded from the authorities by relatives (2002:1A). For example, the *Free Press* highlighted the story of 14-year-old Tiffany Jones, who called the newspaper after a reporter tried to locate her. She explained that she ran away from her grandmother's home when an FIA worker came to return her to foster care. According to the foster care records, Tiffany had been removed from her grandmother's home in May and placed in foster care, where she "screamed for twenty four hours."

She explained to the reporter "she would do whatever the state wants me to do if they put me back with my grandmother" (Schmitt 2002:10A).

Tiffany's story points to another way that accounts of these "missing and exploited children" are distinguished from stories of their most famous peers—in the degree to which these children are assigned agency in their own dilemmas, and in the way that this agency is construed as a problem. Tiffany, for example, rejected her foster placement, emphatically "saying no" to strangers she apparently perceived as threatening. But in Tiffany's case, this self-assertion is not viewed heroic. In fact, children who take such actions are viewed as out of control, or even, as we shall see, delinquent.

By October 19, 2002, two months after breaking the story, Kresnak was writing under the headline "Foster Teens Stroll Off with Ease" about two young women who ran away after being located by the police:

> The absurdity of having police spend time finding runaway foster children only to have them come and go as they please has led some to wonder what legal measures can be taken to protect such kids from their own bad judgment. Some people say that state law may have to be changed. . .
>
> A key problem in the effort to keep runaway foster children safe is that state and federal laws prohibit putting children who are wards of the court into locked-down juvenile detention facilities. (Kresnak 2002g:1A)

In response to this ongoing crisis, the media, the courts, and many of the public officials involved converged upon the necessity of two additional innovations: first, all foster children in Michigan older than 11 were given a copy of the court order assigning them to placement and a warning that running away would lead to incarceration in juvenile detention (Kresnak 2003). And second, responding to the media reports, the Third Circuit Court in Wayne County instituted an order that missing children would be located and placed in the juvenile detention center until a suitable alternative could be found. Many youth were retained for a significant period of time in the detention center or placed in another juvenile justice placement (Sarri, Hajski, and Shook 2007). Locking up children who left placement was an extraordinary response to these young people. Yet, these actions made sense to the officials who took them. Within the discursive frame of "missing children," it seemed there were few other ways to respond to young people whose predicaments were so urgent, whose level of risk was great, and whose voices in the matter were so muted.

Thus, as the media jockeyed for the rights to broadcast the "untold story" of Elizabeth Smart's joyous homecoming to her much relieved family, the journeys of Michigan's missing children had taken another turn. One *Free Press* photo of such a foster child depicts him as he is led to a police car in handcuffs after he was located at his mother's home in Detroit. The police delivered him to Wayne County Juvenile Detention Center. Another depicts a foster child on the floor of a cell, clothed in her "Property of WCJDF" jumpsuit, talking to an unseen companion through a crack in the doorway under the headline "Lockup May Be Only Option" (Kresnak 2002g).

Paradoxically, then, as the story unfolded it appeared that inserting these state wards into the protectionist discourse of "missing and exploited children" connected a substantial portion of them more closely with the juvenile justice system. Perhaps support for punitive responses to missing children was facilitated by images of young people that fit the demographics of those consigned to the status of "structurally irrelevant" in U.S. society—young and poor children of color. An image of Elizabeth Smart abducted from her suburban family broke American hearts in ways that photos of an anonymous African American teenager being led away from his mother's home in handcuffs apparently did not. Ironically, when foster children were deemed to be "missing children," frustration with and suspicion of youth and their families surface as prominent themes. On a practical level, conceiving of foster children away from placement as "missing children" evoked urgency over their predicaments, but it also tended to narrow the range of imaginable responses to their plights. The limited strategies available to respond to stranger abduction—involving law enforcement and increasingly public visibility—came to be seen as unavoidable. It required a sustained advocacy effort to insist on a broader range of alternatives.

ADVOCACY AND ALTERNATIVES

Fortunately, these troubling reactions to foster children missing from placement in Michigan did not go unchallenged. Alarmed by these developments, advocates in and outside of Michigan sought to vigorously challenge punitive responses to children away from their placement. On January 9, 2003, the Youth Law Center wrote to officials in Michigan's FIA and court system, expressing concern about the illegal secure detention of abused and neglected children in Wayne County (Youth Law Center 2003). They threatened a class-action suit unless the practice of securely detaining abused and neglected children who run from placement was discontinued (Sarri, Hajski, and Shook 2007).[4] In response to the Youth Law Center's threat to sue over these violations, the state initially argued that its practices are legal interventions into the lives of young people who willfully violate the court orders that "place" them. Nevertheless, the director of the FIA and the chief judge of the circuit court organized the Wayne County Task Force on Children, a group of agency representatives and advocates charged with addressing concerns about children missing from placement in Wayne County. This task force forwarded a raft of recommendations and activities, mainly aimed at attempting to prevent the secure detention of children who leave placement by developing alternative responses and services for these young people (Sarri, Shook, and Hajski 2005; Sarri, Hajski, and Shook 2007).

The work of the task force was aimed at changing practices and policies that transferred youth who left their placements from the child welfare to the juvenile justice system. The task force monitored outcomes for youth who left placement and promoted expanding detention alternatives, including therapeutic foster care, "fictive kin" placements, and alternative residential settings.[5] The Third Circuit Court responded with revised court practices and decisions in regard to these youth. The task force faced many barriers, and funding for important alternative programs, such as youth rights education, often fell short (Sarri, Shook, and Hajski 2005). However, after sustained effort, the task force reported dramatic results. In 2003, 149 children away from placement were placed in detention in Wayne County; by 2006, children who "AWOLed" were detained in only ten instances (Sarri, Hajski, and Shook 2007).

Nevertheless, while advocates on the task force worked devotedly to develop alternative placements and approaches to work with these young people, the *Free Press* and other Michigan papers lauded the state's more punitive actions (Kresnak 2004). Thus, advocates for children away from placement in Michigan struggled against the limited options available within the "missing children" discourse, eventually gaining very substantial success.

MICHIGAN'S MISSING FOSTER CHILDREN IN NATIONAL PERSPECTIVE

As concern about abused and neglected children missing from placement emerged as a crisis in Michigan, it surfaced in other cities and states, including, prominently, Florida. In the late spring of 2002, it was reported that Rilya Wilson, a 4-year-old foster child, had not been seen by her caregivers for well over a year—a situation that had gone unnoticed by the state (Child Welfare League of America 2004:vii). In August 2002, at the directive of Governor Jeb Bush, Florida mounted Operation SafeKids with the mission to search for and locate the 393 children under state supervision who were unaccounted for, and to recommend improvements to the state child-care system. The governor requested that the initiative be modeled after "Operation Safe," a project that called upon regional task forces to locate sex offenders and predators with outstanding warrants. The central thrust of Operation Safe Kids was to establish Regional Child Location "Strike Forces" to locate children missing from placement (Florida Department of Law Enforcement 2002).

By 2004, children missing from foster care had clearly emerged as a compelling national issue. The Child Welfare League of America (CWLA) received a grant to work in collaboration with the NCMEC to provide comprehensive guidance to child welfare and law enforcement agencies on the matter of children missing from placement (Kaplan 2004). The guidance combines recommendations for maintaining high-quality foster care programs that are consistent with CWLA standards with recommendations for responding to missing children that draw heavily on practices refined at the NCMEC (CWLA 2005). The recommendations stress close collaboration between child welfare and law enforcement agencies; increased safety and risk assessment of children perceived as at risk of being "AWOL"; the development of web-tracking systems; and efforts to involve community partners including the media and the public in efforts to retrieve missing youth.

While considering young people away from placement as "missing children" becomes a well-accepted national discourse, study of unfolding events in Wayne County alerts us to potential dangers embedded in this well-intentioned and motivated effort. As the advocates on the Wayne County Task Force demonstrate, it is essential to be highly alert to the possibility that connecting young people away from placement more closely with the law enforcement system can also accelerate a "drift" from the child welfare to juvenile justice systems (Jonson-Reid and Barth 2000). The story of "missing children" in Wayne County also raises the possibility that we should consider other ways to frame the problems faced by young people who leave placement.

HEARING YOUNG PEOPLE, EXPANDING POSSIBILITIES

What else might be done? To address this question, several researchers have interviewed young people who have gone missing. The voices of youth recorded in these interviews help point to fresh understandings and solutions of the predicaments of young people who go missing. To illustrate this point, I draw examples of the perspectives of young people who have been "AWOL" from foster care from three such studies: interviews with 42 Cook County youth who "had a history of running from care" (Courtney et al. 2005:41); interviews with

30 youth in New York City's Administration for Children's Services (ACS) who "had 'chronic' AWOL histories" (Finkelstein et al. 2004); and interviews with 15 youth drawn randomly from a population of youth 12 and older who were identified as AWOL from foster care in Wayne County (Detroit) Michigan during 2003 (Sarri, Shook, and Hajski 2005).[6]

Each of these studies is unique, yet they surface common themes. For example, each study identifies problems in placements that "push" young people to go "AWOL"; each describes the "pulls" of family and friends that help to shape these decisions; and each raises questions about the degree of containment and control that should be considered "normal" for young people in care. Each of these three themes in turn suggests a range of possible strategies to prevent or resolve difficulties for youth in foster care, thereby reducing instances of "AWOL."

Focusing on Facilities

Many young people identify problems in their placements as major factors leading to their departures. In each of the studies, young people in care disproportionately leave residential placement facilities rather than foster home placement or relative care.[7] In the Finkelstein et al. study, for example, youth portray these facilities as ones in which stealing, bullying, and fighting are common (2004:12). Heidi told interviewers in that study, "I used to leave because people were taking my stuff, I just didn't like the group home." Andrea, age 19, reported: "I'm having a lot of problems with the girls in this house. You know, one of the girls calls me Spic and stuff like that. And it is very uncomfortable when they are threatening your child, and when they are stealing your stuff, they are spitting in your food." Some interviewees in the studies described positive interactions with staff of residential group homes. For example, Courtney et al. (2005) quoted a youth who described the positive effects of relationships with staff: "And one of my staff . . . she didn't like for me to run away. That's why I didn't never run away when she was there. . . . I would leave when she was gone but she would be mad. And then I stopped running away . . . 'cause I promised her I would never run away from there no more" (50). In other disturbing stories, however, conflicts or abuse by staff was described as the trigger for the youth's departure from placement. In the Finkelstein et al. report (2004), Michael summed up his perspective on facility staff in this way: "Cause that is what my mother used to do to me. She used to always put me down and that used to make me feel bad. And half the staff say they know what it's like, but they come here with their problems. Come here, curse at kids, get mad, take out their family problems or whatever. This really ain't a good place for them to work, and that is part of the reasons that a lot of kids go AWOL" (11). The data from the research by Courtney et al. suggests that it is not rare for foster youth to encounter serious problems in placement. For example, 45% of the interviewees reported being abused or neglected in placement; 45% reported physical assault in placement; 21% of all interviewees (and 36% of the females) reported being raped or sexually assaulted in placement (Courtney et al. 2005).

Sarri, Shook, and Hajski (2005) also report that the young people described serious problems in their placements as well as in their families of origin. These authors highlight the lack of routes available to young people in placement by which to address or resolve these problems. All the youth interviewed in the Michigan study spoke about their lack of meaningful involvement in decision making affecting their lives. The youth reported that they had little or no access to workers, attorneys, court proceedings, ombudspersons, and family care review processes. Most failed to receive guidebooks or other resources that defined their rights within the system (Sarri, Shook, and Hajski 2005:38). In such a context, leaving placement is one of the few actions available to youth who seek to resolve serious problems in their placements.

Another theme that emerges across these studies is the degree to which youth who leave placement are reacting to what they perceive to be unreasonably restrictive policies and rules of the facilities where they reside. Courtney et al. (2005) stress the degree to which these restrictions conflict with normal desires for autonomy and progressively greater freedom. The study quotes a number of young people on this topic, including the following descriptions of placements: "It was like they was tying us down . . . it wasn't not life . . . we had to eat at a certain time . . . we couldn't eat they had our stuff put up. We couldn't hold our own money. They was just treating us like we was locked down . . . that mostly the reason why the kids there was running away" (60). Or, from the perspective of another youth: "You ain't got no control . . . you gotta ask to go upstairs . . . you gotta ask to go downstairs. But it's a house though, it's suppose to be our house but you gotta ask. It's crazy. You got ask to use the washroom, that's stupid . . . everybody older [here], everybody teenagers up in here, man. Why would you have to ask to use the washroom?" (53). Finkelstein et al. (2004) report being surprised by finding that so many youth reported feelings of constant boredom, created in part by such rules and restrictions, that contributed to "an overall belief that they were languishing in care" (9). They quote Denise, age 17:

> [S]ometimes I feel I am in a lock-up facility 'cause we are really not allowed to go anywhere during the week. Only on the weekends we could go home to our family

if we are allowed to or if you are on a certain amount of weeks of positive you could go on day passes and stuff. Otherwise, you can't go anywhere. Most of the time staff don't want to go outside 'cause either they are just tired or they feel there is no reason to go outside, so you can't go anywhere. We sit in here all day and do nothing. Most of the time I am sleeping if I have to be in here. (10)

Sarri, Shook, and Hajski (2005) also echo this theme, as one youth reports, "Having to go to bed at 8:30, being locked up, it doesn't make sense to take someone from an abusive home and lock them up without any family when they have done nothing" (39). Interviewees in all studies report longing for a "normal" life. For example, one youth in residential placement states: "Let me go get a job. Let me go to school. Let me do good in school. Let me take part in after school activities. Let me join the chess club and everything. I don't want people to look at me and say, 'Yeah, he's locked up, he is at [residential placement.] I don't want to be looked at like that . . . I don't want to be looked at as resident #12'" (Sarri, Shook, and Hajski 2005:39). In the context of boredom and restraint, some youthful departures from placement can be construed as an effort to move on and toward a "normal life," and to resist what appears to be unwarranted punishment or confinement.

These data on the problems with placements raise important questions about whether the problems of youth going "AWOL" can ever be resolved by focusing our responses on individual, troubled young people when important problems in residential facilities are not addressed. As Biehal and Wade suggest in a study of British facilities, AWOL incidents in their study were specifically tied to particular residential facilities. Of the 32 children's homes surveyed, two-thirds of the incidents of "going missing" occurred in 7 of the homes (Biehal and Wade 2000:214). Institutions producing higher rates of "AWOLs" were those in which senior management failed to offer clear leadership, staff morale was low, and staff appeared overwhelmed by a sense of fatalism about their ability to have an impact on the behavior of the young residents. As the authors explain: "The implication is that, whatever individual reasons young people may have for going missing, the cultures and regimes of individuals' homes are likely to be highly influential" (214).

Despite the data that reveals that particular residential facilities appear to produce high rates of AWOL incidents, few of the recommendations, guidelines, or action plans on "missing children" suggest ways to rebuild these institutions. These interviews with young people in placement suggest that far from conceding that "lockup is the only option" for abused and neglected children who leave placement, addressing the problem requires examining the conditions of the placements themselves, and offering youth viable ways to address problems and concerns that arise there.

Focusing on Family

In addition to the "push" of placement problems on these youth, researchers in each study also draw on interviews with youth to describe the powerful pull of family and friends. Many young people leaving placement—unlike the better-publicized accounts of child abductees or "runaways"—are often "running to home." Available analyses suggest that many or perhaps most of the young people who leave placement are, like Tiffany Jones, returning to friends and family.[8] The authors of the study of New York City revealed that all the children who had "AWOLed" reported that they had somewhere to go, and only two reported spending any time on the street (Finkelstein et al. 2004).

Youth returned to family to maintain contacts, address crises, or simply touch base. The following comments illustrate a few of the views expressed by young interviewees on the decision to leave placement to be with friends or family:

My main focus was to be with my family . . . and that' what I ran for. I ran to get back with my family. (Courtney et al. 2005:55)

Really, what is important to me is my family . . . They ain't the best family in the world but they do look out for me when I need it. (Courtney et al. 2005:56)

The two times I ran away . . . I was with my grandmother. I was [also] with my mother because I was frustrated. . . . They told me I couldn't see my mom or talk with her anymore, so that really frustrated me. . . . Because every time I talked to my mom and she would tell me that she loved me, I would get upset and depressed because my mom never told me that she love me. . . . My mom . . . gave up one time. And then, she just came back into my life and I couldn't see her. I was like, always want to be around my mom. (Courtney et al. 2005:55)

I miss my siblings, and I wanted to be home with them. You know, you are not home until you're home. (Finkelstein et al. 2004:14)

Like . . . I would probably run just to be with my friends, that what we probably call family . . . if you family not treating you right. . . . I mean who can you run to, your friends. They the ones that really got your back. (Courtney et al. 2005:61)

The last time I ran away . . . I went with this girl named Faith 'cause her father was in the hospital and they wasn't letting her go to a home visit or even see her father, and her father needed an operation. So I went with her to the hospital. (Finkelstein et al. 2004:17)

Expression of concern for AWOL youth typically underscores the possibility of danger that is present when young people who have been abused or neglected in the past return to family or friends. The risks that youth face when returning to their families of origin must be taken seriously. On the other hand, older foster youth recognize that they will soon be emancipated from state care. Attempting to maintain relationships or even resolve enduring relationship problems can be understood as a practical step for young people who are anxious about their upcoming independence and the prospect of "working without a net" of friends and family that are available to other youth (Shirk and Stangler 2004). Maintaining solidarity with friends can place youth in danger; it can also clearly be both a virtue and a survival strategy for youth who will soon face "independence" from the child welfare system.

In the context of contemporary society, there is widespread recognition that most young people require networks of social, emotional, and material support from well into their twenties as they work to establish themselves in jobs and relationships (Arnett 2004). The range of possible responses to youth who are AWOL expands dramatically once we acknowledge the pull of family relationships on these young people and take on board the practical needs for tangible support that loom on the life horizons of those who will soon "age out" of the child welfare system. Framed this way, preventing and resolving problems of AWOL youth involve a raft of practical policy reforms that include extending a range of benefits to youth "aging out" of foster care (Shirk and Stangler 2004).

Focusing on the Future

Finally, these three studies of AWOL youth raise questions about what our expectations should be for young people in foster placement—for example, about what level of restriction and restraint is practical or advisable. As Courtney et al. (2005) note, youth in foster care were striving for autonomy and control, wanting to feel "normal" yet valued for their individuality. Though AWOL youth are constructed as behaving in ways that are risky and illegal, youth did not view all absences as being "on the run." For example, youth who were away to help a family member, stranded on a planned visit, spending time with friends outside of placement, or returning past a deadline did not view their behavior as "running" (45). Foster youth—who frequently experienced a great deal of responsibility for themselves or others very early in life—did not view compliance with unrealistic telephone and visitation restrictions, token economies, clothing requirements, or peer restraints as "normal," fair, or healthy (Sarri, Shook, and

Hajski 2005). In at least one of these studies (Finkelstein et al. 2004), some of the youth reported as AWOL from residential facilities were between 18 and 20 years old. Interviewees in this age group frequently protested restrictions and constraints.

This does not mean, of course, that leaving placement without permission is free of risk or danger. Finkelstein et al. (2004) analyzed the narratives of young people about what happened when they left placement for indications of risk. One-third of the accounts were uneventful. For example, some youth reported that some of their "AWOLs" resulted from relatively normal occurrences of breaking curfew, leaving to help a relative, or failing to return on time from a home pass—events that they did not consider "runs." In another third of the narratives, youth reported smoking, drinking, partying, and some fighting—behaviors that are not risk free but are also not atypical for older teenagers. A few of the youth reported serious incidents of involvement with drugs, violent encounters, injury, or arrest that are consistent with fears about children "on the run."

Young people who are AWOL from placement can be seen as balancing their assessments of the degree of risk entailed in leaving against the pushes of placement problems, the pulls they feel toward family and friends, their desires for autonomy and freedom, and a variety of other factors. Assimilating our understanding of these departures to horrifying stories of stranger abduction limits our ability to make balanced or realistic responses to these complex situations.

Words matter. Describing young people who leave foster care as "missing children" makes a difference because acceptance of this powerful story shapes our response to their predicaments. The stories told by youth themselves complicate our understanding of why young people leave placement, and where they go when they do, enriching our ability to respond to their plights. Understanding the serious placement problems confronting these young people—and acknowledging their lack of sanctioned avenues to resolve them—casts doubt on simplified portrayals of their behaviors as strictly "voluntary," "willful," or "habitual." In addition, the accounts of young people returning to family and friends also challenge the assumption that punitive or damaging responses to their behavior can *necessarily* be justified by fear of the dangers and exploitations that they will face "the street." There is no question that young people in foster care (as elsewhere) require care, assistance, and guidance. But the voices of young people suggest that it is important to avoid a simplistic view of the dangers to which they are exposed when they leave placement or the safety they enjoy while they are there.

Addressing the problems of children who leave their placement requires that we build on the important work accomplished by the social work scholars cited here. We must envision an expanded research agenda that fully engages young people in the foster care system in an effort to devise pathways to their successful development. Meanwhile, we must strengthen our resistance to the sort of media sensationalism and political expediency that propels responses to young people based on simplistic or erroneous accounts of their predicaments. It requires that social-work scholars and practitioners redouble their efforts to inform public opinion rather than simply reacting to the most sensationalistic or simplistic conceptions of it. Achieving more informed and reasonable responses to young people requires that we resist a widespread contemporary tendency to hold individual children responsible for society's collective failures and substitute practices of surveillance and containment in place of guidance and care. It requires resisting the notion that our options are limited by advocating for a broad and practical agenda of program and policy reform that recognizes the humanity and agency of youth.

QUESTIONS FOR DISCUSSION

1. What are some examples of the ways that concern for "missing children" enters your everyday life? In what ways does worry about "missing children" impact your practice? What observations do you have about how such concerns have changed in your lifetime?

2. What role does the media play in shaping local social work practice? How do media images of concerns about children and youth reproduce or challenge dominant ideas about race, gender, or class? How do local practitioners engage or fail to engage productively with media images of social work practice with children and youth?

3. What lessons does the work of the Wayne County Task Force on Children in Detroit offer us? What does it suggest about the need for practitioners to critically, openly, and reflexively question their own policies and practices? What does its work suggest about the roles of research and advocacy in social work practice with children and youth?

4. How do the perspectives of young people recounted here alter or enrich your understanding of the predicaments of foster care youth who are away from their placements? What are the implications for social work practice when these perspectives are taken into account?

5. What are the political and ethical issues involved in working with young people who have left foster care "without permission"? What human rights issues are at stake? What actions would you take to draw attention to the structural factors impinging on the lives of AWOL youth and their families?

NOTES

1. Sarri, Shook, and Hajski (2005:27) report that 382 young people age 11 or over were "AWOL" in Wayne County during 2003, with 149 held in secure detention for some period of time during 2003 (4). This study also reports that 57.3% of the children had one instance of AWOL, and another 22.8 % had two (30).

2. According to the Second National Incidence Studies of Missing, Abducted, Runaway Thrownaway Children, known as NISMART-2, funded by the Department of Justice's Office of Juvenile Justice and Delinquency Prevention in 1999 there were 90 missing children whose cases were "stereotypical kidnappings," in which a stranger or slight acquaintance detained the child overnight, transported the child over 50 miles, held the child for ransom, or intended to permanently keep or kill the child. In the majority of those cases, the child was returned or recovered.

3. For example, the *National Enquirer* published stories questioning whether Elizabeth had run away from home or agreed to go with Mitchell. In a "world exclusive" that it was later forced to retract, the paper published a story under the headline "Utah Cops: Secret Diary Exposes Family Sex Ring" in July 2002.

4. As Sarri, Hajski, and Shook (2007) note, the federal Juvenile Justice and Delinquency Prevention Act (JJDPA) prohibits states receiving JJDPA funds from securely confining abused and neglected children (42 U.S. Code 533[a][12]). Michigan law also forbids the secure confinement of dependent children (M.C.L.A. 712A.15[4]).

5. "Fictive kin" were defined as "adult friends of acquaintances of the youth who are interested and willing to provide foster care for the child" (Sarri, Shook, and Hajski 2005:18).

6. The 42 interviewees in the study by Courtney et al. (2005) are described as "primarily African American (88%), evenly divided between females (52%) and males (48%), and were older teens, with 74 percent of them being between the ages of 16 and 18. Eighty percent of the youth reported that they entered DCFS [Department of Child and Family Services] care between the ages of 0 and 9 years. At the time of our interviews, 83 percent reported they had experience between three and eight placements" (41–42).

The 30 youth interviewed in the study by Finkelstein et al. were mostly girls (83%), most of whom entered care when they were over the age of 13. All were 20 years old or younger. All interviewees were under ACS care at the time of research, and all were living in congregate care facilities of various types throughout New York City and surrounding counties (2004:5–6).

In the Sarri, Shook, and Hajski research, interviewees were drawn from the larger pool of 382 AWOL youth, including mostly (85.3%) youth of color, including 56% females and 44% males (2005:26–30).

7. For example, in Sarri, Shook, and Hajski (2005:31), 54.3% of the Wayne County youth who left placement ran away from residential care or detention. The Finkelstein et al. study (2004:3) focused only on youth who ran from congregate care based on their prior research that demonstrated nearly three quarters of all such incidents are from group homes. Courtney et al. found that "many more youth run away from residential care than from foster home or home-of-relative placement, in spite of the fact that far fewer youth in Illinois reside in residential care than in either of the other two major placement settings" (2005:19).

8. For example, Finkelstein et al. report that when they asked youth in their study about destination, "Most indicated that they had a specific destination in mind prior to leaving. Very few suggested they had nowhere to go, and only three youths told us they spent at least one night on the streets during their AWOL" (2004:19). Courtney et al. also emphasize patterns of youth running to friends, family and to "touch base" with people and places important to them (2005:63).

REFERENCES

Arnett, J. J. (2004) Emerging *adulthood: The winding road from late teens through the twenties.* Oxford: Oxford University Press.

Best, J. (1990). *Threatened children: Rhetoric and concern about child-victims.* Chicago: University of Chicago Press.

Biehal, N., and J. Wade. (2000). Going missing from residential and foster care: Linking biographies and contexts. *British Journal of Social Work, 30:* 211–25.

Bush, G. W. (2002). *Remarks by the President at the White House Conference on Missing, Exploited and Runaway Children.* Accessed August 8, 2007, at http://www.whitehouse.gov/news/releases/2002/10/20021002–4.html.

Child Welfare League of America (2005). *CWLA best practice guidelines: Children missing from care.* New York: Child Welfare League of America.

Courtney, M., and R. Barth. (1996). Pathways of older adolescents out of foster care: Implications for independent living services. *Social Work, 41:* 75–83.

Courtney, M., A. Skyles, G. Miranda, A. Zinn, E. Howard, and R. Goerge. (2005). *Youth who run away from substitute care: Chapin Hall Working Paper.* Chapin Hall Center for Children at the University of Chicago.

Fass, P. (1997). *Kidnapped: Child abduction in America.* New York: Oxford University Press.

———. (2007). *Children of a new world: Society, culture and globalization.* New York: New York University Press.

Finkelstein, M., M. Wamsley, D. Currie, and D. Miranda. (2004). *Youth who chronically AWOL from foster care: Why they run, where they go, and what can be done.* New York: NYC Administration for Children's Services, Vera Institute.

Florida Department of Law Enforcement and Florida Department of Children and Families (2002). *Operation SafeKids: Results, findings & recommendations.*

Howard, D. (2002a). FIA children are not "lost." *Detroit Free Press* (August 30): 12A

———. (2002b). Statement on death of youth listed on the child locator web site. Accessed August 14, 2007 at http://www.michigan/gov/fia/ 0,1607, 7–124–5458_7691 _7752–53174-M_2002–10,00.htm.

Ivey, M. (1995). Have you seen me? Recovering the inner child in late twentieth century America. In S. Stephens, ed., *Children and the politics of culture,* 79–104. Princeton: Princeton University Press.

Jonson-Reid, M., and R. Barth, R. (2000). From placement to prison: The path from adult incarceration from child welfare supervised foster or group care. *Children and Youth Services Review* 22: 493–516.

Kaplan, C. (2004). *Children missing from care: An issue brief.* Washington, D.C.: Child Welfare League of America Press.

Kresnak, J. (2002a). State loses track of 302 abused or neglected kids. *Detroit Free Press* (August 30): 1A, 12A.

———. (2002b). Foster child is located, 310 left. *Detroit Free Press* (August 31): 1A, 11A.

———. (2002c). Photos of missing foster kids could go on state web site. *Detroit Free Press* (September 13): 1A, 7A.

———. (2002c). Lost foster child found in Dallas. *Detroit Free Press* (September 17): 1A, 5A.

———. (2002d). State knew kids weren't lost: Agency posted some as missing despite info to the contrary. *Detroit Free Press* (September 19): 1A, 10A.

———. (2002e). Director: Lost kids being found: Agency says web site is working procedures being rethought. *Detroit Free Press* (September 24): 1B, 4B.

———. (2002f). Foster teens stroll off with ease: Police feel days in searches are wasted. *Detroit Free Press* (October 19): 1A, 9A.

———. (2002g). How Michigan loses foster children: Lockup may be only option. *Detroit Free Press* (December 20): 1A, 12A.

———. (2003). Reporting holds Michigan's child welfare system accountable: At the Detroit Free Press watchdog reporter sees the impact of his stories. *Nieman Reports* (Summer 2003): 105–7.

———. (2004). Keynote address. Conference on promoting the well-being of children and youth in urban America, College of Urban, Metropolitan and Labor Affairs, Wayne State University (April 22).

Kresnak, J., and E. Askari. (2002a). Help find these kids: State is 1st to launch site with names, photos. *Detroit Free Press* (September 18): 1A, 4–5A.

Kresnak, J. & E. Askari. (2002b). Runaway finally is found—dead: Girl who fled needed lockup her family says. *Detroit Free Press* (October 9): 1A, 7A.

National Center for Missing and Exploited Children. (2006). *2006 Annual Report.* Accessed August 16, 2007, at http://www.missingkids.com/en_US/publications/NC92.pdf.

———. (2007). *NCMEC, USPS and ADVO unveil changes to the "Have you seen me?" mail program.* Accessed August 20, 2007, at http://www.missingkids.com/missing kids/servlet/NewsEventServlet?LanguageCountry = en_US= 3167.

Sarri, R., A. Hajski, and J. Shook (2007). Youth who run from placement: Organizational practices to improve services and outcomes. Ms.

Sarri, R., J. Shook, and A. Hajski. (2005). *Juveniles who run away from placement: A preliminary evaluation.* Ann Arbor: Institute for Social Research, University of Michigan.

Schmitt, B. (2002). Girl counted as lost is in hiding, says she is ok. *Detroit Free Press* (September 19): 10A.

Sedlak, A., D. Finkelhor, H. Hammer, and D. Schultz. (2002). *National Estimate of Missing Children: An Overview.* Office of Juvenile Justice and Delinquency Programs, U.S. Department of Justice.

Shirk, M., and G. Stangler. (2004). *On their own: What happens to kids when they age out of the foster care system.* Boulder: Westview Press.

Smart, E., and L. Smart. (2003). *Bringing Elizabeth home: A journey of faith and hope.* New York: Doubleday.

State of Michigan Department of Human Services. (2007). *Child locator website.* Accessed September 18, 2007, at http://www.mfia.state.mi.us/awol/.

Stephens, S. (1995). *Children and the politics of culture.* Princeton: Princeton University Press.

Youssef, N., and J. Kresnak. (2002). How Michigan loses foster children: First of three parts. *Detroit Free Press* (December 18): 1A, 8A.

Youth Law Center (2003). Letter to Ms. Nanette Bowler, Chief Judge Mary Beth Kelly and Jeriel Heard. In R. Sarri, J. Shook, and A. Hajski, *Juveniles who run away from placement: A preliminary evaluation.* Ann Arbor: Institute for Social Research, University of Michigan (January 9).

U.S. Department of Education (2002). *Secretary Paige joins President Bush to announce White House Conference on Missing, Exploited and Runaway Children.* Accessed August 20, 2007, at http://www.ed.gov/news/pressreleases/2002/08/08062002.html.

It Ain't as Simple as It Seems

THREE

Risky Youths, Morality, and
Service Markets in Schools

Linwood H. Cousins

I am sitting in Mr. Hughes's eleventh-grade English class, carrying out one day of the two years of ethnographic research that I conducted between 1992 and 1994 (Cousins 1994).[1] Mr. Hughes's classroom is located on the north side of the school that I call Community High. From this vantage point on a clear day I usually see airplanes as they arrive and take off from Newark's airport. But something else draws my attention to the world outside of school on this day. As the students and I peer out of the windows we see an automobile accident that has just occurred at an intersection near the back of the school. One of the cars is a stolen car. Several black students, including a girl who was the driver, occupy it. The students have crashed the stolen vehicle into a car driven by a black woman, a community resident whom I was told lived in a house near the back of the school. We watch the students bolt from their car and the scene of the accident before the police arrive. The word quickly got around the school that the woman was seriously injured. Someone even told me she was killed. I wasn't overly surprised. After all, I had been in the community for several months, and I knew that this kind of event was not all that uncommon. But I was still troubled, as were most of the community residents—students and adults alike.

Community High, a school of about 1,300 students at the time, is located in a predominantly black working- and middle-class community in Newark, New Jersey, that I call Village Park. Village Park had approximately 58,000 residents, and Newark had about 275,000. Like many other schools and cities, Community High and Village Park have transitioned from their early existence as working- and middle-class white and Jewish institutions to working- and middle-class black institutions, to institutions that increasingly absorb persons who are unemployed, on public assistance, and therefore troubled and troubling to others.

Changes at Community High were part of a much large shift in the nation's system of education that occurred in the context of national political and economic restructuring. As Jonathan Kozol (2005) points out, since the early 1990s we had begun to witness the rise of what he refers to as "apartheid schooling," acknowledging both intensifying patterns of resegregation in schools and the related inequalities in the facilities, teacher training, curricula, class size, and courses offered to the nation's children.[2] In the most unequal system of public education in the industrialized world (Darling-Hammond 2007), young people of color around the country were increasingly likely to attend schools with limited resources (Tatum 2007). Young people and community members all over the country struggled to respond to troubling events on the increasingly uneven terrain of such schools.

At Community High, fights among girls, fights among boys, and streetcorner drug activity by students were not uncommon. In response there were as many calls for improving morality as there were for improving race and class relations, or, more broadly, addressing the broader racial and class-based structural inequities. For example, in response to school and community problems, some school staff said key factors were single-parent families on public assistance, or children "raising themselves." Another school official said that some of these kids are "sweet" but a few are "hardcore hoodlums." Still another staff member told me, point blank, following an alleged gun incident in the school (it was more rumor than fact, and no one was injured), that "this is what happens when you take prayer out of the school."

If these people had attended several community meetings with me, they would have found much support for their beliefs from community ministers, local legislators, and parents. But they would just as easily have found opposition. Indeed, while the people I spoke to in the community and school acknowledged morality and character in the equation of school and community violence and disruption, many had difficulty excluding other factors. *Powerlessness* was mentioned most often. Some said powerlessness results from division and disorganization among blacks as a collective, and from ineffective and unreflective leadership from individual blacks.

One staff member said it was more complicated than that, stating that changing economic circumstances have left families vulnerable, in turn leaving youth vulnerable in the parts of their lives that are touched by the rising and falling prosperity of their families and community. Still another teacher was even more specific about social class relations. She linked increases in school and community violence to decreases in black middle- and working-class economic stability in Village Park, and to the elimination of several stable households due to the construction of freeways between downtown Newark and the suburbs.

Added together, the general sentiment in the school was to restore "black pride" in the school and community. This meant a host of things, but mostly race and class respectability. One key meaning was to restore behavioral and academic standards and norms largely associated by school and community members with the folk-legacy of black middle-class respectability of about 20 years earlier. And while some have thought this could be accomplished through more moral rectitude among blacks, again, others saw no way of disconnecting black violence and related problems from racially driven social, economic, and political issues of inequality, even while they believed blacks had to take more responsibility for themselves. So while there were voices calling for moral standards and character that fit with contemporary discourses of individual personal responsibility, no single voice dominated the discourse and dictated the definition of the problems or solutions.

Meanwhile, at a distance from Mr. Hughes's classroom and the community meetings in Village Park, well-recognized national figures spoke out on the issues facing urban schools. They declared, as we shall see, that the local problems like the ones at Community High were simple ones, readily resolved with moral solutions.

PURPOSE AND FOCUS

The purpose of this chapter is to examine the *framing* of social issues and problems in terms of morality and character. Framing is a powerful process. According to linguist George Lakoff, framing is part of mental structuring that shapes the way we see the world and what counts as good or bad (2004:xv). This chapter addresses the intervention of moral entrepreneurs in debates about urban schools. Moral entrepreneurs are individuals who are in the business of persuading society to make policy from particular moral viewpoints (Becker 1963). Moral entrepreneurs excel in framing.

Moral entrepreneurs, as we shall see, have a great deal to say about what is wrong with urban schools and urban school children as well as what must be done in response to these troubles. The moral views they have promulgated have successfully defined the parameters of policymaking in the context of urban schools and communities. With this in mind, the chapter attempts to conduct a dialogue regarding the relationship among youth risks, morality, and the marketing of services. I argue that simplistic moralizing about the problems of urban schools is not only powerful but potentially harmful; it is often narrow, exclusive and subjugating. It poses a threat not only to the youths, schools, and communities in question, but also to the very idea of democracy in the United States.

Certainly Community High students and community residents are in the throes of some difficult economic, social, and political circumstances. And surely there is little doubt that communities and schools like Village Park and Community High play a role in the production of these difficulties, posing risks as much as being at risk. But it is only when issues of schooling, violence, race, morality, character, and markets are placed side by side that an honest discussion can be held about changes. Moral entrepreneurs too often dominate such public processes and discourses. They reduce the rich cacophony of voices in Community High and Village Park to a solo and thereby pose a significant risk themselves by making the part—the voices of a powerful and influential few— stand for the whole. In the bargain, society gets a simple, sturdy understanding of social problems and morality to which all (but in reality mostly those with little power and cultural capital) must adhere or risk being excluded, treated, and or punished.

Robert Coles (1986) says that the politics of adults becomes the psychology of children. Indeed, adult politics become the psychology of how we "deal" with children. Embedded in this psychology are our commonsense notions of right and wrong—our sense of how to render educational and human services and achieve social justice. Debates and decisions about the education of black children in public schools have long been central to our national struggles over right and wrong. For more than a century, educational policies and programs have been at the heart of our society's institutional efforts to "improve poor people" (Katz 1995; Katznelson and Weir 1985; Tyack and Cuban 1995), to assimilate and civilize racial and ethnic groups (McCarthy and Chrichlow 1993; Spindler 1997), and, at the same time, to directly and indirectly accommodate shifting ideologies and cultural capital that keep the engines of the market place sufficiently lubricated (Apple 1982; Eckert 1989; Foley 1990; Giroux 1983; Katznelson and Weir 1985; Willis 1977).

At present, whether in school or elsewhere, public anxieties and debate center on increasing numbers of black and nonblack, troubled and troubling children and youth seen as "risky""—simultaneously constructed as both "at risk" and "posing a risk" (Stephens 1995, 1997). Our actions to address these risky youths are circumscribed by how we frame and define the problems. For example, when youth are framed as "criminals," policies and practices are then implemented that treat them as such, as seen with the proliferation of "zero-tolerance" policies in public schools. The moral entrepreneurs, key players who have excelled in this framing process, have changed from time to time, but their policy-shaping influence is ever present.

MARKETING, MORALITY, AND SOCIAL WORK

In this chapter, I argue that social workers need to develop our ability to identify moral entrepreneurs in our midst and to critically reflect upon their messages. We do well if we pause to study, or at least acknowledge, what may be inherent and irreducible complexities of morality and violence for youth who pose a risk, for those who are at risk, and for we adults who do the judging. Legislative acts and policies founded on simplistic, stigmatizing, or inaccurate assumptions shape the social services that flow from them. Therefore, as social workers we must remain vigilant about the moral assumptions that direct social policy and the effects of these assumptions on practice. The cost of not doing so is the risk of contributing to the reproduction and maintenance of social, economic, and political oppressions and inequalities in our society and beyond. Often such oppressions and inequalities are stealthily built into our therapies, interventions, programs, and procedures—activities we feel certain are necessary and fair representations of our good will, humanity, and sense of social justice. Young people labeled as "risky" too often bear the burden of this reproduction of inequality.

As social workers we need to closely examine the assumptions undergirding programs and policies in our public schools, For example, it is now common practice for public schools to have an array of social and mental health services available to students and parents (Crepeau-Hobson. Filaccio, and Gottfried 2005; National Center for Schools and Communities).[3] By 1990, no less than 500 programs had begun in schools to provide a broad array of nonacademic services related to violence, individual and family social, psychological, and health problems, and the like (Cousins Jackson, and Till 1997; Dryfoos 1994). Franklin and Allen-Meares said that "Central to the movement is the belief that the systems of care, including school systems, can be improved through *engineering new systems* [italics added] in which practitioners from various disciplines become partners to meet human needs" (1997:131). They list the terms under which such programs have evolved: "school-linked services," "comprehensive services," "full-service schools," "service integration," "wraparound services," "one-stop shopping," "co-located services," "interprofessional collaboration" (132), and, one I add to the list based on my own social work and anthropological practice, "interdisciplinary team services" (Cousins et al. 2004).

While social workers and others see an increase in school-linked services as long overdue for low-income, black, and Hispanic schools and urban communities, this increase signals complex market practices as well.[4] The well-intentioned caring, altruism, and empathy of professional human service workers and organizations coexist with the dominant political and economic interests and trends in any given moment in U.S. history. These interests and trends include, for better or worse, underlying, veiled beliefs and values about how to segregate, fix, or punish aberrant people. In light of these trends, I propose that we need to examine how such school-linked services are often at cross-purposes with the explicit social justice mission and focus of social work (Finn and Jacobson 2003; Gordon 1999). One example of this tension is the standardized expectations for parent participation that do not take into consideration employment issues that restrict the amount of time parents have to participate, or variation in parents' abilities to participate in their child's educational activities in school. In a context of simplistic moralization, parents who do not participate in school activities when they are ostensibly given the choice to do so are too easily dismissed as lacking in essential values and character. Factors that systematically disenfranchise parents and young people in such schools, however, are not examined.

As social workers, we must probe for moral questions that underlie technical solutions to the problems of young people. We must be alert to ways in which simplistic moral judgments may lead to peremptory or unnecessary exclusion or punishment of young people. We must attend to ways in which single voices suppress the democratic expression of various viewpoints on complex problems. We must be vigilant lest we surrender the hard struggle over what we collectively and morally owe young people to satisfy ourselves with engineering new technical solutions based on more narrow assumptions. To do these things, we must learn to define and recognize the characteristics of contemporary moral entrepreneurship and to make space for complex analyses.

DEFINING AND GRASPING THE MORALITY DISCOURSE

The history of intervention with young people is marked by universalizing judgments regarding morality and character based on very particular interests and narrow viewpoints. An examination of recent history helps us understand present-day discourses and practice regarding youth and risk. Let's turn then to a description of how moral entrepreneurs defined and applied morality and character to youth violence and trouble in schools and communities in the 1980s and 1990s. This discussion centers on several persons of status and influence, such as the former secretary of education, former drug czar, and current policy advocate William Bennett. As a moral entrepreneur, Bennett was a notable member of a raft of public figures who "spread their definition of the situation to politically significant groups in an attempt to persuade them to accept their perceptions and definitions of the situation, or begin to mobilize such groups into pressing for some kind of purposive social action, or create a group for such purpose" (Zimmerman 1995:61).

Along with intellectuals and advocates such as James Q. Wilson and Charles Murray, William Bennett was among the most influential scholars, public intellectuals, and policy advocates arguing for a national sense of morality and character as central to the solution of social problems, including improving education and fighting crime and violence.[5] They were the quintessential moral entrepreneurs on the public scene in the 1980s and 1990s. Their arguments pivoted on the following assertions: increases in crime, violence, and public incivility are related to a breakdown in (a) the familial and community cultivation and enforcement of "habits of virtue" (Murray 1997:19); (b) too little "moral education of the young" and "moral wealth which breeds social health" (Bennett 1995:11; Bennett, Dilulio, and Walters 1996:61); and (c) the struggle with our "moral sense," or a breakdown in restraints on social behavior in terms of "morality, enforced by individual conscience or social rebuke, and law, enforced by police and courts" (Wilson 1993:xi; 1995b, quoted in Bennett et al. 1996:27). To be sure, a "moral sense," which Wilson says drives the values beneath public perception of proliferating disorder, is "an intuitive or directly felt belief about how one ought to act when one is free to act voluntarily (that is, not under duress)" (1993, 1995a). He also says moral senses are "natural" in that they are "to some important degree innate, and they appear spontaneously amid the routine intimacies of family life" (1993:229).

Wilson, Murray, and Bennett clearly converged on what these moral values and practices are: unequivocal, reliable standards of right and wrong, noble and base, just and unjust (Bennett 1995:12; Harmon and Thomson 1996). According to Bennett and his colleagues, these values and practices "are generated by loving, capable, responsible adults who teach the young right from wrong . . . [and by] parents, guardians, relatives, friends, teachers, coaches, clergy, and others who habituate (to use a good Aristotelian word) children to feel joy at other's joy; pain at others' pain; satisfaction when you do right; remorse when you do wrong" (1996:13–14).

It may appear unreasonably stubborn or contrary to ask social workers to think critically about what appears to be "moral common sense." Yet, I suggest that this discourse frames social problems in ways that problematically narrow and distort our perceptions. In the section that follows, I illustrate three important and problematic themes of this moral discourse: (1) a conflation of morality and punishment; (2) the simplification and decontextualization of moral dilemmas; and (3) the effort to amplify and market moral messages.

Morality as Punishment

The discourse of these moral entrepreneurs conflates messages of morality with those of individual blame and punishment. Neither Murray, Wilson, nor Bennett asserts unequivocally that the virtues they commend are optimally developed in a context where people experience social, economic, and political well-being. Bennett is perhaps the most moderate of the three when he says that, for the offender and yet-to-offend, a moral sense gets reinforced as follows "by laws whose first purpose is *moral,* to punish by exacting a price for transgressing the rights of others . . . rather than [deliberating over] a liberal litany of root causes (economic poverty, lack of government funded social programs, racism) and over some conservative catechism of toughness (resort-like prisons, too few executions, too much gun control" (Bennett et al., 1996:14).

Slipping farther down the slope of "toughness on crime" and toward troubled youths, however, Murray contends that reform must begin with the young offender: "Restoring lawfulness means discarding most of the system's sympathy for the offender. A lawful system has only a minor interest in the reasons why someone commits the crime. The criminal justice system is there to punish the guilty, exonerate the innocent, and serve the interests of the law-abiding. Sympathy for the offender comes last" (1997:26).

Finally, Wilson insists that "If we try to make penalties for crime swifter and more certain, and it should turn out that deterrence does not work, then all we have done is increase the risks facing persons who commit a crime" (1975:144).

Jock Young challenges Charles Murray's analysis and policy recommendations[6] and rightly asserts that Murray frames problems of risky people and youths within a recurrent notion that "the social is simple" in explanations of the rise of crime and its root causes (Young 1997:32). Murray's notion implies that "the social world is a relatively simple structure in which rates of different social events (e.g., marriage, suicides, strikes, crimes) can be related to narrowly delineated changes in other parts of the structure" (Young 1997:32–33). Young argues, in contrast, that "the social world is a complex interactive entity in which any particular social intervention can only possibly have limited effect on other social events and where the calculation of this effect is always difficult" (33).

This peculiar mix of moral instruction and punishment leads to the conclusion about Murray that I think more or less applies to Wilson and Bennett: "[T]he essence of Murray's concerns have rather less to do with crime control than with the expansion of prison and other control systems . . . [T]he agenda for the *new century* [italics added] is about the disposal, if not elimination, of troubled and troubling people" (Rutherford 1997:48).

Morality as Simplification

The second problematic theme involves the attempt to reduce complex processes and circumstances to simplistic "truths." From the vantage point of these moral entrepreneurs, the soul of America remains embattled over a "common culture." Conservative columnist, commentator, and former professor George Will says this is the "nation's social cement," a common system of education and what Will and William Bennett call shared literary and artistic traditions, and commonly agreed upon standards of value (quoted in Graff 1992:41; see also O'Reilly 2006; Sullivan 2006). Although popular attention has recently shifted to the war in Iraq (consider the "with us or against us" public statements aimed at dissenters by President Bush and Vice President Cheney as part of garnering support for the war in Iraq), battles over a common culture continue regarding increased personal and institutional accountability in terms of welfare and education, as exemplified in the passage of "welfare reform" and the No Child Left Behind Act (Newman and Chin 2003).[7]

The general allure of discourses that simplify and reduce the complexity of morality and character regarding youth violence and education (and poverty, race, and war) is that they offer "different audiences a consistent narrative about American politics and culture" (Aldous and Dumon 1990; Bogart and Hutchison 1978; Graff 1992; Kelley 1997; Morone 1996:31; Page 1997). It is in this equation that the powerful ideology about "one nation, indivisible, with liberty and justice for all" meets another in the name of a press for a common culture of morals, character, prosperity, and—given the war in Iraq—freedom.

Clearly, youth violence in schools is a serious issue that must be addressed (Cousins 1997). And whether in a racial or class context or not, violence does tend to evoke powerful visceral responses of repulsion. This is despite the fact that violence, like morality, means too many things to too many people and is fed by an unrelenting media (Curwin 1995; Feldman 1994; Rozycki 1994). We seem, furthermore, to process these visceral responses through sociocultural channels of meanings that, in the West at least, generate emotions and beliefs based in ideas that violence, like morality, is in part natural (as Wilson said earlier about moral senses), a part of people's inner nature, soul, and spirit. In combination, such strong reactions and ambiguities have spelled trouble or lots of services, depending on how you look at it, for black and low-income communities.

But other factors must not be left out of the equation either. Not only must the subjugation of "other" voices factor in, but also how the moral entrepreneurs practice selective blindness or amnesia: they disconnect acts of "immorality" and violence from the histories of the majority in this country—whether as capitalists or legislators—or from other aspects of the sociocultural, political, and economic context of life in America (Chomsky 2003; Feldman 1994; Nagengast 1994; Newman and Chin 2003). Racism notwithstanding (Cousins 1997; Mullings 2005), one example is the indisputable role of capitalist expansion and government-funded programs in the development of "safe" middle-class suburban schools and communities at the expense of partitioning and disfranchising inner-city neighborhoods in Newark, New Jersey, Charlotte, North Carolina, and other cities across the nation (Jackson 1985; Massey and Denton 1993; Mickelson 2001; Smith 2004).

Morality and Markets

Morality involves public proclamations about how humankind should live. It entails constructed notions or beliefs about right and wrong that influence the perception and evaluation of everyday events. Moral beliefs evolve from messages and meanings implicitly conveyed in everyday talk, conversations, discourses, texts, and customary practices. Moral beliefs also evolve from explicit messages and meanings conveyed by religious, educational, economic, and political institutions that interact with the events of everyday life (Shweder and Much 1991). Character follows closely on the heels of morality and entails interpersonal patterns of virtue in terms of values, beliefs, attitudes, and lifestyles (e.g., generosity, conscientiousness, honesty, nonviolence) that fit with a received notion of right and wrong (Martin 1995).

On this much, moral entrepreneurs have been right, a position they fully capitalize, market, and exploit. But what moral entrepreneurs and others play down is the inherent tension in definitions of morality and character. Current national policy makers have shown a little more flexibility in this regard under "compassionate conservatism," but not as much as some think needs to be the case in, for example, the No Child Left Behind Act of 2001 (Darling-Hammond 2007; Dingerson, Beam, and Brown 2004). This tension is, on the one hand, about accepting morality and character as socially and culturally constructed; that morality and character have relatively unfixed meanings until meanings are assigned in terms of particular traditions; and that these meanings and traditions shape and are shaped by historical and contemporary political, social, and economic circumstances. On the other hand is the fixed, seemingly permanent and reified, sense of morality and character that moral entrepreneurs and others enunciate as natural, based in common sense and innate, and as meanings that should therefore dominate others (this "taken for granted," seemingly ordinary, and "already and always there" sense of things is what is meant by hegemony, the hegemonic rule of one set of ideas over another). Intellectuals and politicians know that meanings are constructed for better or worse, and so they treat "control over meanings" as necessary for the survival of preferred and privileged sociocultural structures and lifestyles. Although we all more or less do this to keep our culture and values alive, it is no less insidious and dangerous.

THE POLICY LEGACY OF MORAL ENTREPRENEURS

I propose that the legacy of this discourse can be identified in the legislation known as the No Child Left Behind Act (NCLB), which continues as the most recent example of moral entrepreneurship regarding schools. It is built on the assumption of providing equal, quality education to all individuals so that each can stand independently and become a contributing member of society. This is exactly what Murray, Bennett, and others, including social workers, have had in mind in servicing people — economic independence and individual responsibility. NCLB maintains the notion of the moral responsibility of individuals to become independent (i.e., black people to get off of welfare) and live responsibly by including a little-known requirement for parent involvement in schools, and it requires schools to facilitate such a relationship.[8] Interestingly, this requirement, along with well-intended actions to raise awareness in African American communities about the resources of NCLB, emphasizes alternatives to failing schools such as charter schools, school choice (means the right to transfer to

another public school), and supplemental services (NCLB update http://www
.ed.gov/nclb; Epstein 2005). This is complex because on the surface, most of
us believe that parents and communities should be involved in their children's
schooling. Yet, race and class inequalities are present in the framing and enforcement of this policy in such a way that suggests nothing much has changed.
Parents and children are provided with ostensible choices that evaporate upon
closer scrutiny. The concern with upward mobility and independence is real,
but so is the push to mainstream the poor, blacks, Hispanics, and others toward
middle American values, lifestyles, and notions of individual responsibility at
the cost of leaving behind those who do not comply quickly or well enough.
Darling-Hammond (2007) and others make just the point in their current review of NCLB.

EXPANDING OUR MORAL VISIONS

For all the reasons laid out in this chapter, it is important to apply anthropologist
Roy Rappaport's framework regarding the study and amelioration of domestic
"trouble" taking place in the United States (1993; Forman 1995).[9] His framework
captures the complexity beneath interpretations of youth violence and morality
and clarifies a pathway to more reasonably systemic resolutions. Rappaport says
that in conceptualizing "trouble," we need to be sure of at least two things: first,
that our conceptualizations are holistic or systemic, because our multitude of
troubles may be generated by a limited family of disorders, which means they
are interrelated and perhaps interdependent; and second, that we not rush to
name our troubles and thereby reify them and consequently confuse symptoms
such as substance abuse, teenage homicide, and teenage pregnancy, for example, with disorders such as poverty and so forth (297).

Consequently, by conceptualizing youth violence and disruption largely
in terms of morality and character, we may be misnaming the "trouble" and
creating additional problems. Indeed, a nonholistic and narrow definition of
violence alongside morality and character generates narrow questions that wash
away the sociocultural complexity and human plasticity that are crucial to understanding such social problems (Broughton 2003; Greenberg and Schneider
1994). Moral entrepreneurs and others would do well to legitimize, rather than
dismiss and oversimplify, the constituent components of these processes and
actions. This is about social, economic, and political structures that are mediated or acted upon by human agents or everyday people and vice versa. It is
about how the outcomes from these mediations involve people in interpersonal

and social situations largely driven by culture and society, rather than by isolated and predetermined moral and genetic propensities.

Finally, Sharon Stephens's paraphrase of Virginia Dominguez (1992) summarizes this matter and provides further direction: "[W]e should be asking much more contextually specific questions about what is being accomplished socially, politically, and discursively when different notions of culture are invoked by different groups—nation builders, minority populations, local communities, academics—to describe, analyze, argue, justify, and theorize" (1995:22).

THE "MORAL" OF THESE TROUBLES: A TENTATIVE CONCLUSION

The past is never over. In 1679 a famous call for moral reform was made on the basis of conclusions drawn by some of the most influential men in America meeting in Boston:

> The nation, they agreed, faced a terrible moral crisis: rampant substance abuse, sex (even the old taboo against naked breasts seemed to be gone), illegitimacy. Public schools were languishing, the pursuit of profits was appalling, the explosion of lawsuits completely out of hand. Worst of all, parents were doing a terrible job raising their kids—not enough discipline. "Most of the evils" that afflict our society, reported the conference, stem from "defects as to family government." (Morone 1996:30)

Critical inquiry into the interpretation of risk and youth violence can begin at the juncture at which one group says that the "powerless are morally weak in character and the powerful morally superior" or vice versa. It joins with the idea "that all people can act badly when they find themselves in personally debilitating circumstances and people who continuously live in such circumstances may act badly more frequently" (Haan, Aerts, and Cooper 1985:5).[10] The moral entrepreneurs under discussion tweak these assertions to the advantage of some citizens but the disadvantage of many others.

As such, James Morone (1996) insightfully argues that the moral crisis in question largely indicts poor people and people of color and stops at the market's edge. Left undisturbed are the following: many corporations that show no loyalty to workers who have spent a good part of their lives helping them make profits; coal mining companies, paper mills, and the like that disrespect the landscape and waterways in communities where low-income people live, thereby contributing to the perception that these residents live in such decrepit places because of their character; "payday" and mortgage lenders that prey on low-income customers by concealing high interest rates and fees; large corporations that unfairly fix market prices for their products; and crack users who get longer sentences than the professional bankers and stock brokers who steal millions of dollars (Buck 1996; Dudley 2000; Morone 1996; Smith 2004). Morone's insights are about morality too, but the kind left out of simplistic, all-encompassing stories about characterless youth in low-income and minority schools and communities.

Rappaport has proposed that consideration of systemic interdependencies must reasonably be a part of any serious diagnosis of the "trouble" of violence and related disruptions among the young. We could do much worse than to apply his framework and accomplish the holism he suggests. No less is necessary to reconfigure the kind of disorders in question—youth violence, poverty, racism, power, and their definitions.

Stephens (1995) goes in a different direction by suggesting we ask what is being accomplished by the dominant discourses of moral entrepreneurs. Silencing, exclusion, and subjugation are at least three of the socioeconomic and sociopolitical accomplishments of hegemonic moral assertions about the meanings of and solutions to youth violence. For example, silencing and exclusion of the socioeconomic and sociopolitical complexities associated with violence at Community High and Village Park assault the traditions and lifeways of nonmajority people. Silencing and exclusion, then, are part and parcel of both historical and contemporary oppression in the United States and, with the aid of moral entrepreneurs, continue as blatant acts of subjugation in the name of conserving a common culture.

However, inasmuch as the discord and heartache of the social malaise in places like Community High and Village Park are misdiagnosed, more than these schools and communities lose. Like family ideals, any intimate and honest observation of life in the United States suggests that there is a gap between the dominant morality we live *with* and the morality we symbolically live *by* (Gillis 1996, quoted in Skolnick 1997:88). And, in any case, those who do the moral policing seldom police themselves as vigorously.

Moral entrepreneurship remains alive and well. We, social workers, should be able to track the main threads running through the fabric of this chapter—public policies and services, particularly regarding risky youths in schools, that are shaped by individuals and groups that excel in framing key issues in terms of morality and character. We must keep our eyes on issues of morality and character in social policy and social work activities. Not doing so increases risks to our efforts to enhance social functioning and support social justice and equality. We must act in any number of public policy and social work practice forums (e.g., classrooms, city halls, newspaper columns, school board meetings, our therapies and counseling modalities, social support programs). We must identify, challenge, question, and otherwise expose the incomplete, narrow, and harmful logic and reasoning that mystify too many of us into lockstep formations on behalf of a common moral definition of and answer to social problems. By adding our voices to those in so-called troubled communities, we make the battle for the soul of America more inclusive of all of America.

QUESTIONS FOR DISCUSSION

1. Cousins describes moral entrepreneurs as those who are in the business of persuading society to make policy from particular moral viewpoints. Do you encounter moral entrepreneurs in your practice? What messages do they convey? To what audiences? With what effects?

2. How do moral messages about youth and school violence reflect or challenge ideologies of race, class, and gender? What are the implications for social work practice?

3. In this chapter, the author contrasts his viewpoint from the window of an eleventh-grade classroom with the viewpoint of moral entrepreneurs, such as William Bennett, who often speak out on school violence. How can social workers use our role as "witness" to enrich discussions of social problems such as school violence?

4. The author challenges us to resist "simplistic" solutions that reduce complex situations to simple moral truths. What do we gain by adding complexity to debates over school violence, for example? What would it mean to challenge simplistic solutions to this problem? In what other areas of practice with children and youth do you see the need for greater "complexity of thinking?"

5. In what ways can social workers help to amplify diverse viewpoints on subjects such as school violence? For example, how can the voices of young people, parents, and community members be entered into social work policy and practice debates?

NOTES

1. I thank the editors not only for the initiation of this project, but also for their thoughtful and insightful recommendations and revisions to this chapter. It is the better

for it. A version of this chapter was previously published as "Moral Markets for Troubling Youths: A Disruption!" *Childhood* 8 (2): 193–211.

2. See the Supreme Court decision "Parents Involved in Community Schools v. Seattle School District No. 1 et al.," decided June 28, 2007, regarding race-based school integration and the movement away from the use of race as the primary basis on which decisions are made for integrating or desegregating schools.

3. For excellent sources of data on this matter, see the Center on School, Family, and Community Partnerships at Johns Hopkins University, the National Center for Schools and Communities at Fordham University, or the Communities in Schools publicly funded initiative operating in many urban school districts.

4. In this light, the profession of social work has long struggled with the tension between being social control agents for society at large and agents of empowerment for individuals and communities.

5. As examples of their ongoing influence, Wilson received the Presidential Medal of Freedom, the highest civilian honor in the nation, in 2003; Bennett is codirector of Empower America, a string of advocacy organizations; Murray is affiliated with the American Enterprise Institute; and Gingrich is affiliated with the American Enterprise Institute and the Hoover Institution.

6. I discuss Murray's work in more detail later. But it is important to know that he is a political scientist who has played a key role in contemporary public policy advocacy regarding poverty programs and education, especially during the administration of former President Ronald Reagan (see especially Murray [1984]).

7. See also Greenwald's *Tragic Legacy* (2007) for further illumination of the logic and reasoning behind the kinds of "good versus evil" philosophies and policies driving current foreign and domestic policy in the United States.

8. See "Facts and Terms Every Parent Should Know about NCLB," available at http://www.ed.gov/nclb/overview/intro/parents/parentfacts.html.

9. The late Roy Rappaport is an American anthropologist whose writings on "diagnosing" America and the disorder of systems (1979) ring loudly in interpreting the issues under discussion.

10. These statements represent the difference between what philosophers call moral absolutism and moral relativism. Throughout this chapter, I am arguing for a moral relativism, which, according to Gilbert Harman, is "that moral right and wrong (good and bad, justice and injustice, virtue and vice, etc.) are always relative to a choice of moral framework. What is morally right in relation to one moral framework can be morally wrong in relation to a different framework. And no moral framework is objectively privileged as the one true morality" (Harman and Thomson 1996:3). Among the many directions one could travel in studying this material, again, here I have chosen simply to identify the implicit and explicit "framework" of prominent moralizers and

how their narrow and simplistic dispositions construct, reproduce, and are constructed by particular economic, political, and social processes at large within the U.S. brand of Western capitalism.

REFERENCES

Aldous, J., and W. Dumon. (1990). Family policy in the 1980s: Controversy and consensus. *Journal of Marriage and the Family 52:* 1136–51.

Apple, M. (1982). *Cultural and economic reproduction in education: Essays on class, ideology and the state.* Boston: Routledge and Kegan Paul.

Becker, H. (1963). *Outsiders: Studies in the sociology of deviance.* London: Free Press of Glencoe.

Bennett, W. (Ed.) (1995). *The moral compass: Stories of life's journey.* New York: Simon and Schuster.

Bennett, W., J. Dilulio, and J. Walters. (1996). *Body count: Moral poverty and how to win America's war against crime and drugs.* New York: Simon and Schuster.

Bogart, R., and E. R. Hutchison. (1978.) Public attitudes toward social problems: The impact of shared life experiences in the community of residence. *Social Problems 26:* 97–111.

Brenner, N., T. Simon, E. Krug, and R. Lowry. (1999). Recent trends in violence-related behaviors among high school students in the United States. *Journal of the American Medical Association 282:* 440–46.

Broughton, C. (2003). Reforming poor women: The cultural politics and practices of welfare reform. *Qualitative Sociology 26:* 35–51.

Buck, P. (1996). Sacrificing human rights on the altar of "morality": White desperation, far Right explanation, and punitive social welfare reform. *Urban Anthropology 25:* 195–210.

Burbach, H. (2000). Violence and the public schools. Accessed at http://www.people .virginia.EDU/˜rkb3b/Hal/SchoolViolence.html.

Chomsky, N. (2003). *Hegemony or survival: America's quest for global dominance.* New York: Metropolitan Books.

Coles, R. (1986). *The moral life of children.* Boston: Houghton Mifflin.

Cousins, L. H. (1994). *Community High: The complexity of race and class in a black high school and community.* Ann Arbor: University Microfilms International.

———. (1997). Toward a sociocultural context for understanding violence and disruption in black urban schools and communities. *Journal of Sociology and Social Welfare 24* (2): 41–63.

———. 2001. Moral markets for troubling youths: A disruption! *Childhood 8:* 193–212.

Cousins, L. H., Y. Hyter, L. Todman, R. Fails-Nelson, A. Bee, R. Cooper, and C. Peterson. (2004). Social and academic relationships in the lives of black children: Transdisciplinary research and practice. *Journal of Human Behavior in the Social Environment 9:* 57–82.

Cousins, L. H., K. Jackson, and M. Till. (1997). Portrait of a school-based health center: An ecosystemic perspective. *Social Work in Education 19:* 189–202.

Crepeau-Hobson, M. F., M. Filaccio, and L. Gottfried. (2005). Violence prevention after Columbine: A survey of high school mental health professionals. *Children and School 27:* 157–65.

Curwin, R. (1995). A humane approach to reducing violence in schools. *Educational Leadership 52* (5): 72–75.

Darling-Hammond, L. (2007). Evaluating "No Child Left Behind." *Nation 284* (20): 11–20.

Dingerson, L., J. Beam, and C. Brown. (2004). *26 conversations about organizing, school reform, and No Child Left Behind.* National Center for Schools and Communities, Fordham University.

Dominguez, V. (1992). Invoking culture: The messy side of cultural politics. *South Atlantic Quarterly 91:* 20–41.

Dryfoos, J. (1994). *Full-services schools: A revolution in health and social services for children, youth, and families.* San Francisco: Jossey-Bass.

Dudley, K. (2000). *Debt and dispossession: Farm loss in America's heartland.* Chicago: University of Chicago Press.

Eckert, P. (1989). *Jocks and burnouts: Social categories and identity in the high school.* New York: Teachers College Press.

Epstein, J. L. (2005). Attainable goals? The spirit and letter of the No Child Left Behind Act and parental involvement. *Sociology of Education 78:* 179–82.

Feldman, A. (1994). On cultural anesthesia: From Desert Storm to Rodney King. *American Ethnologist 21:* 404–18.

Finn, J., and M. Jacobson. (2003). *Just practice: A social justice approach to social work.* Peosta, Iowa: Eddie Bowers Publishing.

Foley, D. (1990). *Learning capitalist culture: Deep in the heart of Tejas.* Philadelphia: University of Pennsylvania Press.

Forman, S. (Ed.) (1995). *Diagnosing America: Anthropology and public engagement.* Ann Arbor: University of Michigan Press.

Franklin, C., and P. Allen-Meares. (1997). School social workers are a critical part of the link. *Social Work in Education 19:* 131–35.

Gillis, J. (1996). *A world of their own making: Myth, ritual, and the quest for family values.* New York: Basic Books.

Giroux, H. (1983). *Theory and resistance in education: A pedagogy for the opposition.* New York: Bergin and Garvey.

Gordon, E. W. (1999). *Education and justice: A view from the back of the bus*. New York: Teachers College Press.

Graff, G. (1992). *Beyond the culture wars*. New York: W. W. Norton.

Greenberg, M., and Schneider. (1994). Violence in American cities: Young black males is the answer, but what was the question? *Social Science and Medicine 39:* 179–87.

Greenwald, G. (2007). *Tragic legacy: How a good vs. evil mentality destroyed the Bush presidency*. Crown Publishing Group.

Haan, N., A. Aerts, and B. Cooper,. (1985). *On moral grounds: The search for practical morality*. New York: New York University Press.

Harman, G., and J. Thomson. (1996). *Moral relativism and moral objectivity*. Cambridge:: Blackwell.

Harrison, Faye. (1995). The persistent power of "race" in the cultural and political economy of racism. *Annual Review of Anthropology 24:* 47–74.

Hurst, H. (1994). Violent crime, fear, and public policy. *Juvenile and Family Justice Today* (Winter): 1–3.

Jackson, K. T. (1985). *Crabgrass frontier: The suburbanization of the United States*. New York: Oxford University Press.

Jenks, C. (1992). *Rethinking social policy: Race, poverty, and the underclass*. New York: HarperPerennial.

Katz, M. (1995). *Improving poor people: The welfare state, the "underclass," and urban schools as history*. Princeton: Princeton University Press.

Katznelson, I., and M. Weir. (1985). *Schooling for all: Class, race, and the decline of the democratic ideal*. New York: Basic Books.

Kelley, R.D.G. (1997). *Yo' Mama's disfunktional! Fighting the culture wars in urban America*. Boston: Beacon Press.

Kozol, J. (2005). *The shame of the nation: The restoration of apartheid schooling in America*. New York: Three Rivers Press.

Lakoff, G. (2004). *Don't think of an elephant! Know your values and frame the debate*. White River Junction, Vt.: Chelsea Green.

McCarthy, C., and W. Chrichlow. (Eds.) (1993). *Race, identity, and representation in education*. New York: Routledge.

McWhorter, J. (2000). *Losing the race: Self-sabotage in Black America*. New York: Free Press.

———. (2005). *Winning the race: Beyond the crisis in black America*. New York: Gotham Books.

Martin, M. (1995). *Everyday morality: An introduction to applied ethics*. Belmont, Calif.: Wadsworth..

Massey, D., and N. Denton, N. (1993). *American apartheid: Segregation and the making of the underclass*. Cambridge: Harvard University Press.

Mickelson, R. A. (2001). Subverting Swann: First- and second-generation segregation in the Charlotte-Mecklenburg Schools. *American Educational Research Journal 38* (2): 1–38.

Morone, J. (1996). The corrosive politics of virtue. *American Prospect 26* (May–June): 30–39.

Mullings, L. (2005). Interrogating racism: Toward an antiracist anthropology. *Annual Review of Anthropology 34:* 667–93.

Murray, C. (1984). *Losing ground: American social policy, 1950–1980.* New York: Basic Books.

———. (1997). *Does prison work?* London: IEA Health and Welfare Unit in Association with the Sunday Times London.

Nagengast, C. (1994). Violence, terror, and the crisis of the state. *Annual Review of Anthropology 23:* 109–36.

National Center for Schools and Communities (NCSC). Fordham University, New York.

Newman, K. S., and M. M. Chin. (2003). High stakes: Time poverty, testing, and the children of the working poor. *Qualitative Sociology 26:* 3–34.

O'Reilly, B. (2006). *Bill O'Reilly: Culture warrior.* New York: Broadway Books.

Page, H. (1997). "Black male" imagery and media containment of African American men. *American Anthropologist 99:* 99–111.

Rappaport, R. (1979). *Ecology, meaning and religion.* Berkeley: North Atlantic Books.

———. (1993). The anthropology of trouble. *American Anthropologist 95:* 295–303.

Rozycki, E. (1994). School violence, punishment, and justice. *Educational Horizons 72:* 86–94.

Rutherford, A. (1997). Beyond crime control. In C. Murray, ed., *Does prison work?,* 46–48. London: IEA Health and Welfare Unit in association with the Sunday Times London.

Schlosser, E. (1998). The prison-industrial complex. *The Atlantic Monthly 282* (6): 51–79.

Schwartz, I. (1989). *(In) justice for juveniles.* Boston: D. C. Heath.

Shweder, R., and N. Much. (1991). Determinations of meaning: Discourse and moral socialization. In R. Shweder, ed., *Thinking through cultures: Expeditions in cultural psychology,* 186–240. Cambridge: Harvard University Press.

Skolnick, A. (1997). State of the debate: Family values: The sequel. *The American Prospect 32* (May–June): 86–94.

Smith, S. S. (2004.) *Boom for whom? Education, desegregation, and development in Charlotte.* Albany: State University of New York Press.

Spindler, G. (Ed.) (1997). *Education and cultural process: Anthropological approaches.* Prospects Heights, Ill.: Waveland Press.

Stacey, J. (1996). *In the name of the family: Rethinking family values in the postmodern age.* Boston: Beacon Press.

Stephens, S. (1997). Capitalizing on concern: The expanding market in troubled children and troubling youth. Paper presented at the annual meeting of the American Anthropological Association, Washington, D.C. (November).

———. (Ed.). (1995). *Children and the politics of culture.* Princeton: Princeton University Press.

Sullivan, A. (2006). *The conservative soul: How we lost it, how to get it back.* New York: HarperCollins.

Tatum, B. D. (2007). *Can we talk about race? And other conversations in an era of school resegregation.* Boston: Beacon Press.

Tyack, D., and L. Cuban. (1995). *Tinkering toward Utopia: A century of public schooling reform.* Cambridge: Harvard University Press.

Willis, P. (1977). *Learning to labor: How working class kids get working class jobs.* New York: Columbia University Press.

Wilson, J. Q. (1975). *Thinking about crime.* New York: Vintage Books.

———. (1993). *The moral sense.* New York: Free Press.

———. (1995a). *On character.* Washington, D.C.: AEI Press.

———. (1995b). Crime and public policy. In James Q. Wilson and J. Petersilia, eds., *Crime,* 489–510. San Francisco: Institute for Contemporary Studies.

Young, J. (1997). Charles Murray and the American prison experiment: The dilemmas of a libertarian. In C. Murray, ed., *Does prison work?* London: IEA Health and Welfare Unit in association with the Sunday Times London.

Zimmerman, S. (1995). Understanding family policy: Theories and application. Thousand Oaks, Calif.: Sage.

"Stop the Super Jail for Kids" **FOUR**

*Youth Activism to Reclaim Childhood
in the Juvenile Justice System*

Jennifer Tilton

On a sunny afternoon in April 2001, a multiracial crowd of 150 teenagers and young adults marched in downtown Oakland to demand that the Board of Supervisors stop plans to build a "Super Jail For Kids." Months before the county supervisors had unanimously approved plans to build a new juvenile hall, expanded from 299 to 540 beds, in Dublin, a far-flung suburb of Alameda County. At first this plan attracted little attention, but that changed as youth activists began a sustained campaign. At this first protest, Latino, Southeast Asian, Tongan, black, and Jewish high school students marched alongside local college students, young teachers, and nonprofit workers toward the entrance to the offices of the Board of Supervisors. Many dressed in hip-hop styles: young men in hooded sweatshirts and sagging pants marched alongside teenage girls in tight pants flared at the ankles. The crowd slowly filed through metal detectors and past armed sheriff's deputies, sending backpacks and signs through the x-ray machines, as their chants echoed through the corridors—"Books Not Bars," Schools Not Jails," "No More Beds," and the rhythmic "Ain't No Power Like the Power of the Youth, 'Cause the Power of the Youth Don't Stop. Say What?" Older men and women with suits and briefcases stopped and stared in curiosity. We packed into the Board of Supervisors hearing, a sea of young people surrounding a row of county officials, scattered juvenile justice experts, and a few older community representatives.

This was not a standard Board of Supervisors meeting. Youth activists performed raps and spoken word poetry and told personal stories alongside more familiar calls for "alternatives to incarceration," "services," and jobs for youth. The first speaker, an organizer with Youth Force Coalition, asked for a moment of silence for people locked up in juvenile hall and then launched into a freestyle rap about prisoners behind walls, urging supervisors to put "freedom first, touch the skies, not concrete walls and metal doors." The supervisors listened with puzzled expressions on their faces, as the young audience bounced their heads in rhythm, pumped their hands in the air, and cheered for the young rapper.

The Super Jail campaign built a complex web of alliances and won a series of victories. Protestors convinced the conservative Board of Corrections to turn down $2.3 of preapproved money for the Alameda County expansion. They persuaded the two African American supervisors, Nate Miley and Keith Carson, to vote against any expansion. They forged a coalition with national juvenile justice reformers and, more surprisingly, with homeowner activists in Dublin who didn't want a juvenile jail built in their backyard. Finally, in May 2003, the Board of Supervisors voted to build a 360-bed juvenile hall at the current site. Possibly the greatest success can be stated in the words of a county staff person, who gave young people credit for getting alternatives to detention "at the forefront of the county agenda" (Ashley 2001).

This case study asks: what was the "power of the youth" in Oakland? As anthropological work on youth has shown, concepts of childhood and youth do not just vary across cultures or historical moments. The meaning of youth can only be defined relationally—and is dependent on the context of speaking (Durham 2004). High school and college students often led the combined street protests and hip hop dance parties that characterized youth activism in Oakland. Most, though not all, participants in the Super Jail campaign were relatively young, between the ages of 14 and 30. But the age of participants did not determine that activists would organize, and be recognized, as a "youth movement." Opponents of these juvenile- and criminal-justice policies could have spoken as people of color, as a working-class or a poor people's movement, as families of incarcerated youth, or as antiprison activists.

So why did they organize as "youth"? Occupying a liminal category, youth are able, even expected, to challenge authority. Certainly get-tough-on-youth-crime policies politicized many young people in California, and youth could claim a kind of moral high ground and embodied knowledge as they spoke about juvenile justice issues. Organizing as "youth," activists also explicitly linked themselves to a tradition of idealism, rebellion, and radical protest with deep roots in the Bay Area. In this case study, I will argue that the power of youth in these campaigns also came from the ways activists linked youth—and particularly "youth crime"—to childhood. Looking carefully at speeches at the Board of Supervisors protest, I show how activists used the symbolic power of childhood to criticize changes in the juvenile justice system and broader state disinvestments in children's environments.

Youth activism against the Super Jail was nurtured by a densely networked infrastructure of youth organizing efforts in Oakland. Most youth organizations in the city were direct-service providers; however, in the 1990s a core group of nonprofits developed youth organizing, advocacy, and leadership programs. The Bay Area had a number of distinctive features that encouraged youth activism, including a dense subculture of social justice activism; a network of activist-oriented underground hip hop collectives; a number of progressive organizing training centers, like the Third World Training Center and School of Unity and Liberation; and several youth media organizations that conducted research and provided training for youth activist organizations.

Many youth activist groups in Oakland organized primarily along racial or ethnic lines. Core youth activist organizations included an Asian and Pacific Islander high school activist network, an African American youth leadership organization, a multiracial group of high school students organizing against interracial violence, a street-organizing project that employed young women who had been in the juvenile justice system, and a group of Latino high school students mentored by a local labor activist that organized a series of school walkouts throughout the 1990s protesting racist school policies, demanding La Raza studies, and popularizing the slogan "Schools not Jails."

The Super Jail campaign built on a series of youth activist mobilizations that brought these diverse youth organizations together to challenge law-and-order responses to youth crime in California throughout the 1990s. In Oakland, youth activists challenged school discipline policies, proposed curfews, and loitering ordinances. Many youth-organizing groups in Oakland came together as the Kids First Coalition in the mid-1990s to write and then pass Measure K, a local resolution that mandated that 2.5% of the city's general fund be used to fund positive youth programs. The Youth Force Coalition, an umbrella youth activist organization in the Bay Area, emerged out of the Critical Resistance Conference in 1997, which brought together an older generation of activists, like Angela Davis, with youth activists to develop strategies to challenge the prison industrial complex. Finally, in 2000 youth activists led the fight against Proposition 21, a ballot initiative that increased penalties for many juvenile offenses and made it far easier to try juveniles as young as 14 as adults. Each of these campaigns directly challenged the ways particular laws and public policies "criminalized youth," but they also engaged in a much broader struggle to reshape the cultural and legal definitions of childhood.

The Youth Force Coalition and the Ella Baker Center, the two lead organizations that coordinated the Super Jail campaign, were particularly media savvy and forged close relationships with the press. We Interrupt This Message and Youth Media Council provided media strategy training for youth organizers, distributed guides to Bay Area media outlets, and developed critiques of news coverage about youth crime. Youth activists used the symbolic power of youth-led protests to gain significant media coverage that amplified the effects of any single political protest.

At the April Super Jail protest, one Asian American high school student from Oakland asked,

> What's up with the new maximum security juvenile hall? There's a secret hidden message, "You kids are bad." Have we finally given up on youth? Are bars going to teach us anything? Crime has gone down since 1996, especially youth committing crimes. What are handcuffs going to teach youth? Just because the juvenile population goes up, does that mean crime goes up? Talk about future overcrowding in juvenile hall, what about present overcrowding in schools?

To that there were loud cheers. He pointed to be audience and said, "That's right. There is your constituency. Listen to what they want to say."

Youth activists were quite conscious of the symbolic power of claims to childhood and exclusions from childhood. This high school student's speech linked juvenile hall to a maximum-security prison and highlighted the ways that the juvenile population itself had been redefined as dangerous by the state. The youth campaign against the Super Jail directly challenged representations of youth in juvenile hall as dangerous, adultlike criminals. Instead, activists consistently portrayed youth criminals as "children." At rallies, kids as young as 11 or 12 held cut-out prison bars in front of their face or carried signs with arrows pointing down that said "I could be in prison now." Even the choice of the word "kid" in the slogan "Super Jail for Kids" highlighted the incongruous juxtaposition of innocence and danger.

In rallies, youth activists chanted "Schools Not Jails, Books Not Bars" and insisted that children needed proximity to their families, not exile in juvenile halls or the far-flung system of out-of-home placements. As Van Jones, director of the Ella Baker Center, told a local reporter, "The best bed for a kid getting into trouble is a bed in his own home, not in some juvenile prison. These kids need coaches, not guards" (Glionna 2001). With this rhetoric that emphasized home, family, and recreation, activists tied incarcerated youth back to idealized childhoods and challenged the ways state policies failed to protect and nurture children at home.

The youth movement highlighted the state's role in excluding many children from the category of childhood. Most obviously, Proposition 21 and other adult transfer policies directly excluded some children under 18 from the category of childhood. Every U.S. state now allows children under 18 years old to be tried as adults, and some have no minimum age of transfer to the adult system. More broadly, youth activists suggested that representations of youth as hardened (and adultlike) criminals underlay the success of other get-tough-on-youth policies, including the zero-tolerance policies and high suspension rates that excluded many young people from remaining in school, the ultimate normative space of childhood. But these new and shifting legal boundaries of childhood remain deeply contested, as is evident in the recent 5–4 Supreme Court ruling against the juvenile death penalty.

Youth activists particularly criticized the ways state policies excluded youth of color from childhood and the protections of the juvenile justice system. The campaign against the Super Jail featured pie charts and fliers that described the overrepresentation of "youth of color" in juvenile hall and called the Super Jail "too racist" (Books Not Bars 2001). The Kids First Coalition conducted research that demonstrated that black boys were disproportionately suspended and expelled from Oakland public schools (Kids First Coalition 2000). The Proposition 21 campaign highlighted the fact that youth of color were much more likely to be defined as gang members and to be tried as adults than were white kids.[1]

Several Bay Area youth media organizations also documented how media coverage created a complex equation of crime, age, and race—criminalizing youth and racializing crime.[2] One report in particular highlighted the disproportionate representations of youth of color as criminal. Even when white youth were depicted as criminals, they were shown as children, described with terms like "innocent faces" and depicted with yearbook pictures. In contrast, minority kids were shown handcuffed, in court, framed already by the justice system (We Interrupt This Message and Youth Force, 2001a).[3]

Youth activists' claims to childhood carried cultural weight and political consequences. If youth criminals were "children," they could be defined as not fully responsible and inherently reformable. However, if children were described as "potential thugs" or superpredators, their future was already determined, and the possibilities and protections of childhood were foreclosed. These images of children of color as essentially dangerous naturalize state disinvestment in children's environments, while authorizing investment in systems of surveillance and control (HoSang 2006).

Reclaiming youth criminals as "children," youth activists were able to reclaim key elements of the modern construction of childhood that defined children under 18 as inherently reformable, vulnerable, and in need of adult protection. They used this cultural ideal of childhood to call for a broader notion of collective responsibility for children. Youth activists demanded a renewed form of adult engagement with youth and extended the notion of "family" responsibility to demand a revitalized state commitment to young people.

In a speech to the Board of Supervisors, Veronica, an 18-year-old Latina activist, carried a rosebud up to the podium and spoke in soft voice full of emotion directly to the two African American men on the board.[4]

> It is wonderful to see people of African American descent on the council and in such positions of power, but what about the other brothers? They can't get where you are because their schools aren't good. The expansion of juvenile hall is the destruction of young people souls. I see it every day. We are dying. I am dying because of what you are putting us through. Our communities are crumbling. It's a bigger picture. It's about oppression. People separate themselves out from youth. "They're rowdy." You are helping the process of killing us, Keith Carson.

Here she singled out the African American board member who had previously voted for the larger hall, and people in the audience cheered loudly. "Yes we're loud and angry. Why do you want to see our destruction? We haven't even had a chance to bloom. Stop stereotyping us, waiting for us to end up in jail sometime soon."

Veronica's speech highlighted the complex racial politics of the Super Jail campaign. Youth activists constructed a collective identity as "youth of color" affected by the "war on youth." Photos, fliers, and murals in the campaign intentionally included images of Asian, Latino, Native American, and African American young men and women joining together in solidarity against the prison industrial complex. Crackdowns on crime did affect youth across race and gender lines in Oakland, and in some neighborhoods police surveillance focused on Latino, Tongan, or Vietnamese youth. But Veronica's focus on "the other brothers" also highlighted the disproportionate affect these policies had on African American young men, who were vastly overrepresented in the local juvenile justice system. Occasionally tensions emerged within these multiracial coalitions, as youth activists or adult observers wondered whether Asian American high school boys or Latina activists could speak for youth in the system as much as African American young men (Kwon 2006).

Youth offered a flexible form of identity politics that could respond to the complexity of contemporary age and racial formations in Oakland. In California, poverty is concentrated among children and youth, and age grades are racialized. People of color are the majority of children and youth, while whites remain the majority of older people. While individual youth groups often organized along racial or ethnic lines, coming together as a "youth movement," they could craft alliances across Oakland's increasingly multiracial poor and working class.

The Super Jail campaign focused on getting the supervisors of color to change their votes. After Keith Carson agreed to support a smaller juvenile hall, youth focused on convincing the one Asian American supervisor, Alicia Lai-Bitker, to change her vote and to show solidarity with the youth of color in the juvenile justice system.[5] Activists seemed to give up on Gail Steele and Scott Haggerty, more willing to accept that the white board members would fail to identify with kids in the hall.

But Veronica's comments also hinted at the limits of racial solidarity and critiqued the ways black political incorporation had left "many brothers" behind in the city. In Oakland the chief of police was black, the county chief of probation was an African American woman, and many members of the City Council and Board of Supervisors, who consistently voted to expand policing, surveillance of youth, and other punitive policies, were people of color. Veronica explicitly argued that the infrastructure that allowed for these officials to assume positions of power was gone. She used images of the family to call for racial solidarity and to demand that the African American politicians take responsibility for the kids in the juvenile system.

Youth activists at this protest routinely shifted the focus from holding individual youth accountable to holding the state accountable for youth crime and violence. One speaker redefined the meaning of "at-risk" youth, saying, "We are at risk of police brutality, at risk of poverty, at risk of people trying to lock us up. That shit ain't right. That's not going to help us. Sorry I can't help but swear. What kind of future are you trying to build?" In a newspaper interview, Rory Caygill, the 23-year-old director of Youth Force Coalition, argued that the problem of overcrowding in juvenile hall didn't come from the actions of young people. "It's the inaction of adults to listen to creative ways to solve the problem" (Glionna 2001). Similarly, at a public hearing in July, Van Jones encouraged the supervisors to do what they asked young people to do, to stand up to peer pressure and not do the wrong thing just because someone threw money in front of them. He told the supervisors to stand up to the "peer pressure" of the powerful prison lobby (D 2001). By rhetorically stigmatizing adult behavior with language usually used to talk about problem youth, these activists shifted the focus to public policies and away from the actions of individual youth.[6]

At the April hearing, another Latina young woman, who had been on probation for five years, moving from placement to placement, criticized the failures of the system. She said:

> None of it gave me a way out. . . . In juvenile hall, there were counselors who put you down and said, "I'm glad you're here. You're paying my bills." The only reason I'm here today is that I found folks who are here [pointing to the audience] and now I'm a project director of the non-profit agency. . . . I sit here angry at all of you. You did not give me what you promised me.

This speech calls on the moral obligation adults have to nurture young people and builds on the state's role in loco parentis to argue that the state was a negligent, even abusive, parent.

Youth activists consistently argued that money spent for jails simply would not be available to invest in schools, buy books, or pay for prevention programs.[7] They developed close relationships with juvenile justice researchers and think tanks and proposed concrete alternatives to incarceration. Rachel Jackson, leader of the Books Not Bars campaign, challenged the county to live up to its rhetorical commitment to invest in "model programs" and follow "best practices." "There is a lot of agreement on what kinds of things need to happen, but where's the investments? Where's the leadership? It all ends up going back to criminal justice." She insisted, "Kids don't need to be incarcerated. They don't need public funding for their schools and recreation centers and health care and social services to be spent on prisons" (interview with author, in 2001).

The youth movement recognized the ways children remain particularly powerful symbols for political projects that aim to reconstruct a social safety net. Youth activists demanded a childhood for youth in the juvenile justice system and critiqued the ways youth of color were criminalized and excluded from the category of childhood. They also drew on notions of children and youth as dependent, vulnerable, and embedded in the family to call on a broader notion of collective responsibility for children. They extended the notion of "family" responsibility to reconstruct a vision of the state as parent and to demand that the state invest in their future.

Youth activists' claims to childhood created a quandary for supporters of the expanded juvenile hall. Supervisor Gail Steele objected to the youth movement's "sound-bite politics" and insisted that the kids in juvenile hall "are not innocent 5th graders. . . . These are deeply sick kids." But she worried that she would look like a cold-hearted bureaucrat or "ogre" when she disagreed with the youth protestors.

County officials tried to undermine the power of youth activists' claims to childhood in several ways. Some, like District Attorney Tom Orloff, emphasized youth protestors' naiveté in comparison to adult experience, "I think their basic premise is that youths should not be detained. I wish they were right, but experience has shown me otherwise" (Ashley 2001). Similarly, Supervisor Steele suggested that young people's inexperience made them bad policy makers, "You take young people who really don't have a clue about how to raise children, how difficult it is, what happens to kids, and they say, 'Close the jail. Kids belong at home.' Well I'm sorry, no they don't . . . not these kids."

Others, in contrast, worked to discredit the Super Jail campaign by casting doubt on the independence or authenticity of youth protests. An African American assistant district attorney in his early fifties told me that he thought the youth protestors were being "manipulated." Scott Haggerty insisted that the majority of activists were "adults. They're not kids." Steele and Haggerty argued that the protests were not "a spontaneous uprising of youth spurred to action by this one project," but instead the actions of "activists with an agenda they feel passionate about" (Ashley 2001).

Many of these challenges highlighted the power of the ways youth activists used childhood and youth as political identities. But these objections also point to problems with "youth" as a political identity. Youth activists had to work against the pervasive common sense that children and youth are not competent social and political actors. Opponents seemed to suggest that if "youth activists" were political activists "with an agenda," then they couldn't be seen as a "pure" voice of youth. But if they were really "youth," they were too naïve and impressionable to be good policy makers.

Youth activists put forward two very different, and potentially contradictory, images of youth in the Super Jail campaign: youth as "political actors," capable of planning and executing a political campaign, and youth as "children" who needed adult care and support. It's exactly this tension that made the Super Jail campaign powerful. By insisting that youth could be both political actors and children in need of social supports, youth activists reconstructed the concept of "the state as parent" in child-welfare and juvenile justice systems. Since the progressive era, juvenile-court systems have treated children and their families as objects of reform and in doing so often reinforced racial and class hierarchies (Gordon 1988; Platt 1977; Schlossman 1977).

Youth activists called on the state to rebuild structures and cultures of care for children and families, but they challenged the definition of children as "dependents" without the rights and voice of citizens. They challenged the juvenile justice system's narrow focus on holding individuals or families accountable, insisting instead that we hold politicians and state agencies accountable for the investments they make, or fail to make, in children. Youth activists may offer a richer concept of citizenship: instead of treating the (fictional) independent individual as the fundamental political and social unit, they offer a model of social interdependence as the ground for citizenship and for material demands on the state.

QUESTIONS FOR DISCUSSION

1. The young people described in this chapter declare that "There ain't no power like the power of youth." What is the power that is referred to in this statement? Do you see young people exercising collective power in your communities? What support exists for such efforts? What resistances arise?

2. In your experience, what connections exist between social work policy and practice and youth activism? How might social work engagement with youth activism affect policy change? In what ways might contemporary social work policy and practice be challenged and changed if social workers conceived of and engaged children and youth as competent social and political actors?

3. Tilton argues that the meaning of youth must be understood relationally, in particular contexts of speaking. What meanings do young people evoke in their efforts to "stop the Super Jail" in Oakland? What other examples can you draw from social work practice to illustrate this relational, contextualized understanding?

4. In what ways is the struggle over the meaning of "youth" connected to other struggles over race, class, and gender?

5. What visions of social activism and social justice emerge in this account? What lessons for social work practice do you take from this story?

NOTES

1. Substantial research sustains these claims. One study in Los Angeles County found that black boys were 18.4 times more likely and Latino and Asian boys, respec-

tively, 7.3 times and 4.5 times more likely to be tried as adults than white boys (Males and Macallair 2000:5).

2. As John and Jean Comaroff have noted, "In the banal theatrics of the mass media, crime becomes racialized, and race criminalized. And both, if we may be forgiven, are 'youthenized'" (2004:804).

3. These youth media organizations conducted their own research but also drew on the work of other scholars like Males (1996) and Dorfman and Schiraldi (2001).

4. The names of youth activists have been changed unless they were quoted in the press.

5. At the September 27 board meeting, Alice Lai-Bitker switched her vote, calling for a detention utilization study and exploring the possibility of fewer than 450 beds, but a week later she voted for the larger juvenile hall again (Horowitz 2001).

6. Activists were drawing on a longer tradition both in rap and in African American political thought to reverse the discourse about criminals and frame the politically powerful and the police as the real criminals (Kelley 1996).

7. The expanded juvenile hall would have cost the county 175 million dollars to build, only 33 million of which would be provided by a grant from the state. The rest of the money would have to come from the county's Emerald Fund, which activists insisted could be better used to rebuild mental health facilities or to create youth centers in communities (Horowitz 2001).

REFERENCES

Ashley, G. (2001). Poetic, idealist politics of youth activists jarring. *Contra Costa Times* (October 21).

Books Not Bars and Youth Force Coalition. (2001). *Everything you need to know about the Super Jail for Kids.* San Francisco: Books Not Bars.

Comaroff, J., and J. Comaroff. (2004). "Criminal obsessions, after Foucault: Postcoloniality, policing and the metaphysics of disorder. *Critical Inquiry 30:* 800–824.

D, Davey. (2001). Davey D's Hip Hop Corner. Political News Archive (July 25). Accessed September 2001 at http://www.daveyd.com/newsArchive.asp.

Dorfman, L., and V. Schiraldi. (2001). *Off balance: youth, race and crime in the news.* Washington, D.C.: Building Blocks for Youth.

Durham, D. (2004). Disappearing youth: Youth as a social shifter in Botswana. *American Ethnologist 31* (4): 589–605.

Glionna, J. (2001). Teens gain in fight against jail. *Los Angeles Times* (November 13). Accessed November 2001 at http://www.latimes.com.

Gordon, L. (1988). *Heroes of their own lives: The politics and history of family violence, Boston, 1880–1960*. New York: Viking.

Horowitz, D. (2001). Surprise vote for smaller juvenile hall Youth activists cheer as 2 sites, options to detention weighed. *Oakland Tribune* (September 26).

HoSang, D. (2006). Beyond policy: Ideology, race and the reimagining of youth. In P. Noguera, J. Cammarota, and S. Ginwright, eds., *Beyond resistance: Youth activism and community change*, 3–20. New York: Routledge.

Kelley, R.. (1996). Kickin' reality kickin' ballistics: Gansta rap and postindustrial Los Angeles. In R. Kelley, ed., *Race rebels: culture, politics and the black working class*. New York: Free Press.

Kids First! Coalition. (2000). *Locked out: A report on suspensions in Oakland Public Schools*. Oakland: Kids First! Coalition.

Kwon, S. A. (2006). Youth of color organizing for juvenile justice. In P. Noguera, J. Cammarota, and S. Ginwright, eds., *Beyond resistance: Youth activism and community change*, 215–28. New York: Routledge.

Males, M. (1996). *Scapegoat generation: America's war on adolescents*. Monroe, Maine: Common Courage Press.

Males, M., and D. Macallair. (2000). *The color of justice: An analysis of juvenile adult court transfers in California*. Washington, D.C.: Building Blocks for Youth.

Platt, A. M. (1977). *The child savers: The invention of delinquency*. Chicago: University of Chicago Press.

Scheper-Hughes, N., and C. Sargent. (1998). *Small wars: The cultural politics of childhood*. Berkeley: University of California Press.

Schlossman, S. L. (1977). *Love and the American delinquent: The theory and practice of "progressive" juvenile justice, 1825–1920*. Chicago: University of Chicago Press.

Stephens, S. (1995). *Children and the politics of culture*. Princeton: Princeton University Press.

We Interrupt This Message and Youth Force. (2001a). *In between the lines: How the New York Times frames youth*. Accessed May 2003 at http://www.interrupt.org/inbetw.html.

———. (2001b). *Soundbites and cellblocks: Analysis of the juvenile justice media debate and A case study of California's Proposition 21*. Accessed May 2003 at http://www.interrupt.org.

Youth Media Council. (2002). *Speaking for ourselves: A youth assessment of local news coverage*. Accessed September 2004 at http://www.youthmediacouncil.org/publications.html.

Good Mothers / Teen Mothers   **FIVE**

Claiming Rights and Responsibilities

Deborah Freedman Lustig

By having children, teen mothers seek to assume the mantle of the good mother, yet in mainstream American culture the teen mother is the antithesis of the good mother. Discourse on teen mothers is a discourse of (im)morality, blaming teen mothers for the decline of American society. As one columnist claimed, "We face a quagmire of increased unwed motherhood, burgeoning dependence on social welfare programs, spiraling criminal activity, and a consequential ballooning prison population—problems caused, like it or not, by the proliferation of inadequate parenting," which is later equated with teen parenting (Erbe 1994:A15). *People Magazine*'s cover story, "Babies Having Babies," was typical of the dominant representation of teen mothers in the U.S. media prior to the passage of the Personal Responsibility and Work Opportunity Reconciliation Act (PRWORA) of 1996, also known as welfare reform (Gleick, Reed, and Schindehette 1994).

For their comments on earlier versions of this chapter, I would like to thank Sandra Bever, Rose Glickman, Mary Grantham-Campbell, Bridget Hayden, Lawrence Hirschfeld, Deborah Jackson, David Minkus, Laura Nichols, Holly Peters-Golden, Roger Rouse, Daneet Steffens, and the editors of this volume, Janet Finn, Lynn Nybell, and Jeff Shook. For funding this research, I thank the Spencer Foundation, the Research Institute for the Study of Man; Horace Rackham College of Graduate Studies, University of Michigan; the Abigail Quigley McCarthy Center for Research on Women, College of St. Catherine; the Women's Studies Program of the Woodrow Wilson Foundation; and Sigma Xi.

Teen mothers were most often represented as either irresponsible babies incapable of making mature decisions or conniving schemers, bearing children to get on welfare or to keep their boyfriends (Dash 1989). Even sympathetic portrayals reduced teen mothers to passive, innocent victims of older men.

In this chapter, I contrast teen mothers' self-representations with public images of teen mothers in the media just prior to the passage of PRWORA, which limited welfare terms to a lifetime maximum of five years; required teen parents to live with a parent or grandparent; and limited possibilities for welfare recipients to pursue higher education. PRWORA was a drastic change from our previous entitlement system, which was based on the philosophy that the government was obligated to provide for those in need (although, among many other problems, it did not actually provide enough for families to live on). In practice and in philosophy, PRWORA led to a radically different system with less responsibility on the part of the federal government, the end of welfare as an entitlement, and temporary assistance for those who fulfilled certain requirements. With this legislation, public decision makers undermined the liberal democratic commitment to the government's responsibility for the welfare of its citizens, exemplified in the New Deal, and embraced the neoliberal belief that individual well-being is best served by the free market, not by the government (Harvey 2006).

Welfare reform had widespread public approval, yet most people knew about welfare recipients, including teen mothers, only through the media. Media representations of teen mothers, developed and elaborated in the context of an increasingly individualistic and retributive society, helped shape approval for welfare reform by portraying teen mothers as immoral and undeserving. Just as there is no unitary "mainstream," the media are not a monolithic entity: there were exceptions to these characterizations in alternative magazines such as *The Progressive* and *Ms.* (Males 1994; Woodman 1995). I draw from newspaper and magazine articles and a National Public Radio program, which convey "mainstream" views of teen mothers as childish and thoughtless, promiscuous, and selfish.[1] As I will illustrate, there were two predominant representations in the media: the Left, which portrayed teen mothers as passive victims, and the Right, which portrayed teen mothers as wanton parasites. Neither discourse engaged with teen mothers' own understandings of their circumstances and commitments, which suggest alternative policies and practices.

Most public discourse about teenage motherhood suggested that it is a social problem caused by the actions of individuals. This perspective was reflected in the popular press in the prevalence of "profiles," or mini case studies. The scant analysis in the profiles is sometimes contradicted by evidence presented in the same article. For example, one article described a young woman who had a baby in tenth grade; she graduated from high school and was attending junior college and working part time, well on her way to attaining her goal of becoming a nurse. "Marielle's decision to have a child almost guaranteed that she'd be poor. Families headed by teenage mothers are seven times more likely to be poor as other families, experts say. One reason is that most teen mothers drop out of school to raise their babies and miss the education they need to find good jobs" (Maran 1987). The mismatch between the "expert" judgment and Marielle's experience insinuates that even if some teen moms appear to be successful, they are exceptions, and that teen mothers are poor and drop out of school because they have children. The title of this article, "The New Faces of Poverty; the U.S. Economy Is Healthy, but More Americans Are Poor Than at Any Time since the 1960's," further suggests that individuals, not the economy, are to blame. In actuality, families that are headed by teen mothers are more likely to be poor mostly because teen mothers are more likely to come from poor families (Geronimus and Korenman 1992).

REPRESENTATIONS OF TEEN MOTHERS

Teen mothers in mainstream (both Right and Left) accounts are two-dimensional: they exist only as "teen mothers" and not as persons. As Gans writes in a general critique of the dangers of labeling the poor: "One of the purposes of labels is to strip labeled persons of other qualities. That a welfare recipient may be a fine mother becomes irrelevant; the label assumes that she, like all others in her category, is a bad mother, and she is given no chance to prove otherwise" (1995:12). This labeling denies teen mothers' morality and agency and their commitments to be responsible mothers. These negative depictions of teen mothers facilitated the passage of PRWORA.

In stark contrast to their public representations, my research with young mothers revealed women who were making decisions about their lives, albeit based on limited options and sometimes imperfect information. For young women in my study, having children is in itself an expression of agency as they seek to move from the status of child to that of adult. While teen mothers were commonly referred to as "children having children" or "babies having babies," the term "teen mother" includes 18- and 19-year-old women who are legal adults in our society. Scholars who observe and listen to teen mothers, regardless of their legal status as children or adults, find that for most of them, motherhood is not a consequence of uncontrolled sexuality, but the result of their desire to enter the adult world, to use their power to bear children, and to embrace the responsibilities that accompany that power (Gabriel and McAnarney 1983; Williams 1991). Ladner (1972) found that having a child was the most important marker of adult status for young African American women in the inner city. Since then, options for young poor women who don't succeed at school have become even more limited. In Kaplan's study, one teen mother revealed that "I can be a mother if I can't be anything else" (1997:181).

As Kelly (1994:10) explains, for many poor urban teenagers, motherhood "is not a deviation from but a path to approximate dominant norms." In this chapter, I will highlight the voices of school-age mothers as they articulate these dominant norms. They align themselves with mainstream morality even as they recount their decisions to have a baby as an unmarried teenager. This apparent contradiction between words and action can be seen as an example of an "aligning action." As Stokes and Hewitt explain, "members of a society facing altered circumstances but still cognizant of culture may use aligning actions to square their altered conduct with those prevailing standards" (1976:848).

To elaborate further, school-age mothers, by giving birth, engage in a behavior that they themselves often judge as wrong *in general* (they are often harsh critics of *other* teen mothers). Nevertheless, this behavior sets them on the road to a status as a mature, moral person, and they display their baby's pictures as evidence of their status as good mothers (Lustig 2004). Horowitz describes the way unwed motherhood among Latinas in the United States can serve to transform a "potentially 'loose woman' to a good mother. . . . Her past actions are reinterpreted in light of her new status as a mother" (1983:130–31). A similar process occurs among the young women I interviewed.

Public opinion of teen mothers finds so many things "wrong" with them: they are young; most of them are poor; most are unmarried; and they are constructed in the dominant discourses as "shameless." Although they are strongly identified as African American in the public eye, more and more of them are European Americans. Prior to the passage of PRWORA, teen mothers were the scapegoats, but not only for the ills of the urban poor—they were framed as both the cause of and the evidence for the moral collapse of American society. This muddled category of teen mother resonated with great force. Part of the force stems from the very fact that teen motherhood mixes up two categories: children and adults. "The teenage mother, by breaking the chronologies of the hegemonic culture, pollutes the category *child* and becomes a deviant *adult*" (Lawson 1993:105).

I do not replace the public demonization of teen mothers by canonization: teen mothers do not always act responsibly, but they do evaluate their own and others' actions and intentions according to a very high standard. While they do not always measure up to their own standards, neither do mothers or fathers of any age group. Like any other group, teen mothers vary tremendously in their level of responsibility and maturity, and, as well, any individual teen mother can change her behavior over time. In Luttrell's (2003) study of pregnant teenagers' self-representations through art and performance, she reveals their individual complexities and ambiguities. I elaborate teen mothers' discourses of rights and responsibilities in order to show that teen mothers are not "babies" but mothers—mothers who judge themselves and others according to moral principles. They apply these principles in considering childbearing, abortion, their children's fathers, their parents, school, and welfare.

METHOD

This paper is based on an ethnographic study of teen mothers and their school experiences (Lustig 1997), which includes a comparison of African American, Asian American, European American, and Latina teen mothers in an urban area of California. At the time of my research (1993–1994), base closures, plant closures, and an ongoing recession made jobs scarce, especially in the inner city. I conducted formal interviews with 78 young mothers, ranging in age from 14 to 19. I spent a school year as a participant-observer at a school program for teen mothers (School-Age Parents, or SAP).[2] I interviewed students at SAP and at other schools, and young women who had dropped out of school. When I began my research, I did not intend to investigate morality among school-age mothers; I did not ask questions about whether particular behaviors or attitudes were "right." This analytic focus developed after young mothers at school and in interviews brought up these topics and their moral implications repeatedly.

CONSIDERING MOTHERHOOD

Teen pregnancy is usually seen as an unintended consequence of sexual intercourse. The stereotypes of hormone-driven teenagers and promiscuous African Americans (Solinger 1992) coalesce into the image of the oversexed and ignorant teen mother. Writing about teen pregnancy, Faye Wattleton, former president of Planned Parenthood, claims that "[L]arge numbers of teens say they do not use contraceptives because they are 'swept away' by passion. . . . Only seventeen states and the District of Columbia mandate comprehensive sex education. As a result, many teen-agers are abysmally ignorant about their reproductive functions" (1989). Suggesting that teenage pregnancy is due to uncontrolled sexuality and ignorance, Wattleton denies teenage mothers' self-control and agency. In contrast, the young women in my study saw themselves as exercising agency and making choices, if often heavily constrained ones.

Some of my informants sought to become pregnant. Others chose not to terminate an unplanned pregnancy. Many teen mothers have had abortions, either before or after their child's birth, so their decisions to bear children should be examined in the context of alternatives. These young women struggled to weigh the practical and moral implications of their pregnancies. The two factors that influenced these young women most were the timing of the pregnancy and the quality of their relationship with the baby's father. Several of the young women terminated pregnancies when they were younger because they were not ready to have a baby. Others, pregnant shortly after the birth of one child, terminated pregnancies. It was too soon to have another child, they believed, and thus unfair to their already born child. In both these situations, the women evaluated their capacity to care for a(nother) child and found it lacking. Explaining that she would have had an abortion if she felt the circumstances weren't right to have a child, Rosa said, "Why would I bring a baby to suffer, if I wasn't going to be able to be responsible and take care of it? The baby was just going to come to suffer. Not like my daughter, thank God, she has what she needs. She doesn't suffer."

According to the moral codes of some of the young women I interviewed, abortion is an irresponsible and selfish act. By accepting the consequences of their sexuality, young mothers can demonstrate their maturity. Both in private interviews and in informal conversations in the classroom, I often heard a variant of this statement of Arlene's: "If I'm woman enough to have sex, I'm woman enough to have the baby." Similarly, Thompson describes one of her interviewees, Brenda, a successful student who got pregnant: "[She] thought of herself as the kind of girl who wouldn't have an abortion—the kind of girl who met challenges and responsibilities rather than ducked them. . . . She'd framed her hopes in terms of her responsibilities to others rather than her own rights or happiness, and she couldn't help thinking now in terms of her responsibility to the next generation" (1995:121).

Charles Murray, author of *The Bell Curve,* is one of the most outspoken of the right-wing critics of young mothers. He feels that teen mothers are incapable of caring for their children, and that they know they are incapable: "To bring a child into the world knowing that you are not intellectually, emotionally, or materially ready to care for that child is wrong" (Murray 1994).

In contrast, I found that young women engaged in a complex decision-making process when deciding when to become pregnant, carry a baby to term, terminate a pregnancy, or place their baby for adoption, including an assessment of their own readiness to be a mother. While most did not have the *material* resources to care for their children, they actively reflected on their emotional and intellectual readiness to care for a child. In response to my interview question about her family's reaction to her pregnancy, Teshay said, "If anybody was to have a baby, my mother always knew that I would be responsible, because I always kept everything in order, you know. When she would leave I was always the one in charge of everything. So I knew that I could take on the responsibility of having a baby." Like Teshay, most of the mothers had experience in taking care of others' children and based their self-evaluation on their demonstrated abilities. As Aisha said, "Well I really feel that it's not such a big deal because I raised two kids [her cousins] from birth. So I felt that I was ready to raise a baby when I had mine 'cause I already had raised two of them."

The young mothers I interviewed described adults, usually their mother, questioning them as to whether they were really ready, and they described their affirmative answers to these questions. In her interview, Yatay recounts her mother's involvement in the decision-making process:

DEBORAH: How did your mom react when you told her [you were pregnant]?

YATAY: [After I told my mom I was pregnant] she was like "Are you ready for this?" And I said, "Yeah, I'm grown" and so she had to talk to Jamal [the baby's father]. He's like, "Yeah, I'm ready." But if I could do it all over again I wish I woulda just listened to my mother, cause it's very hard. She was tellin me it's hard, and I was like "No, he's gonna help me he's gonna be there," which he was a little, but we're not married like I thought we was gonna be. . . . When I went back to Jefferson High my mom was watching her. I wasn't goin to school. I was just like ya know gettin' high or whatever and tryin' to ya know kick it [relax] with my friends, knowin I had responsibilities, but I wasn't even trippin [worrying] about my responsibilities, and when my mama found I wasn't goin to school she made me do it by myself. It was hecka hard, and I found out I can't take everything I have for granted, cause she didn't have to help me, but she did. I just took advantage of her and what she did, and so I learned my lesson. So I got out there and hustled for a job, found me a job. Then I wanted to be back in school cause I knew I had to make a better life for me and my daughter, so I just found out about SAP, then I enrolled, and I finally got day care.

Yatay and Jamal had both felt ready to take on the responsibility of a baby. Yatay was wrong about Jamal's commitment and initially wrong about her own. She is no longer involved with Jamal, a drug dealer, because she decided the relationship was not good for her. But even when Yatay was shirking her responsibilities, she was aware of them.[3]

For some young women, being a parent is a chance to start a new family and to escape an oppressive family situation. Having a child can be an act of hope for a young woman living in a desperate situation. Jacobs (1994) describes how teenage women often turn their lives around after the birth of a child, leaving behind drugs and gangs. Far from ruining her chances for a good life, motherhood may be a young woman's first step toward a good life. According to *Essence* magazine, "for teenage mothers, parenthood . . . means a premature and often traumatizing end to the relative simplicity of childhood" (DeWitt 1994). Yet many young mothers, like Gloria, never had a "simple" childhood.

> DEBORAH: Tell me about your family, when you were growing up, who lived with you?
>
> GLORIA: [My mom] had leukemia, cancer of the blood, I had all the responsibility. I was four, [my sister] was not even a year, so I took care of my sister from the time I was four years old until today. I'm still taking care of her. I raised my sister, I took care of my sister, I cooked, I was cleaning, and I learned how to do that at four years old. I was bigger than the normal four year old. I was much smarter, I could read, I could do math, I could do anything, and I've always been like that. So I did have a lot of responsibility. At that time, when I was growing up, my mom and my dad were into drugs and alcohol. They're both addicts and alcoholics, that's how I grew up. I grew up in a real abusive home, my dad was always hitting my mom, not just a slap or this or that, I mean he really beat the shit out of her. And that's how I grew up. I was the only one that could take care of either my dad, my mom, my sister or all three of them at the same time.

For Gloria, pregnancy was not "the gray cloud that immediately casts a grim shadow over a young girl's relatively carefree life" (DeWitt 1994). On the contrary, the birth of her son gave her a chance to create a new healthy family.

BABYDADDIES

Like Yatay, teen mothers may end up raising a child without the child's father, but before having children they consider not only their own maturity and responsibility, but also their partner's characteristics and the quality of the relationship.[4]

Charles Murray (1994:3–4) suggests that we should "tell young women from the outset—from childhood—that they had better choose the father of their babies very carefully, because it is next to impossible for anyone, including the state, to force a man to take on the responsibilities of fatherhood." He is implying that the large number of single mothers is evidence that young women do not choose their partners well, but I think it is more compelling evidence that most young women already know how hard it is to force a man to fulfill his responsibilities as a father. Teshay knew right from the start that she didn't want to have a baby with someone who already had a child with another woman. "I knew that I would never have kids with somebody that had kids already. Every time I would talk to a boy, I would ask if they had kids. I never wanted to deal with nobody with kids, because that's already enough for them to deal with." Carefully and rationally, she sought a man who would stay with her and their child, rejecting men who had already left their first child. Among the young women I interviewed, having a man's first baby is generally considered more prestigious, and some teen mothers look down on their peers (male and female) who have children with more than one partner. When I asked Teshay if she wanted more children, she said that she did, but only if she was still together with her daughter's father: "I don't want a whole bunch of kids by a whole bunch of different men. I hate that, ooh, I hate that. It's kind of tacky ain't it?"

But while the teen mothers in my study value a father who will care for their child(ren), who will not be drawn away by children from a different mother, they did not expect the fathers to be equal partners in child-rearing. They anticipated taking primary responsibility for their children; contributions from the father were beneficial, but not essential. They were always aware that they might have to raise their children alone. Latika's new boyfriend was helping her raise her son, but he wanted her to have *his* baby.

> He don't understand why I don't want a baby. I said, "I got a baby, it's hard enough with one, and what I look like with two?"
>
> "I'm here for this one, what makes you think I'm gonna run off and leave my own? Haven't I been helping you with this boy and blah blah, this and that."
>
> I be like, "Yeah, but still, when you gone, what I'm gonna do?"

Lanisha was also wary after her son's father left her and the baby, so she decided to have an abortion when she got pregnant by another man.

> Basically I'm afraid. I feel that if I have another baby that the babyfather end up leaving me or won't be around, and now I take care of my son by myself. I grew up

without my father and I know how it feels and I don't want to have all my kids like that. For BJ he'll probably grow up without his father. If he do see him it won't be on purpose, it'll probably be by accident. And so I don't want no more kids.

Many fathers *are* gone, and based on this reality, teen mothers make few demands on those fathers who are still around. I asked one pregnant woman if she thought the father would support the baby financially. Expressing hope, not expectation, Sharee exclaimed, "He better! I mean, he doesn't *have* to, but I think he will. He gives me money now to put in the baby's savings account."[5]

Young mothers seeking support from their children's fathers consider their ability to pay and the source of the money. In an economy with massive unemployment among young, uneducated men, especially African American men, young mothers usually could not expect much in the way of financial support from legitimate sources (Wilson 1978). Yvonne saw herself, her boyfriend, and their daughter as a family, and she was proud that he came over every day and helped with child care. But when I asked about financial assistance, she hesitated. "Well, he's still out on the streets [dealing drugs], but I'm trying to get him away from that. So I don't like to ask for anything, because I know how he's going to get the money."

While the mothers do not count on financial support, they expect some combination of financial support and child care if the father is to maintain rights to the child. Especially if the mother and father are no longer partners, the mother demands a certain (minimal) level of responsibility from the father in return for allowing him to see his child(ren). The expectations vary from mother to mother, and each young woman struggles to decide what is acceptable to her. I observed a poignant support group where several of the young women clashed over whether they should allow their children's fathers to show up after long absences to shower the children with gifts, only to leave again for an indefinite time. Drawing on their own experiences of growing up with fathers who were there with varying levels of commitment, some participants contended that any paternal involvement is preferable to none, while others countered that no father is better than an undependable, unpredictable father. Each woman was trying to figure out what would be best for her child: even as they vehemently supported their own points of view, they assessed others' experiences as potential models. In general, these young women revealed a deep critical engagement with practical and moral issues around fatherhood. These accounts suggest that instead of assuming that young mothers choose prospective fathers frivolously and blaming the mothers when their children grow up without fathers, we should teach young men from childhood what their responsibilities are and ensure that they have the skills and jobs to fulfill those responsibilities.

WELFARE

A common misperception is that welfare erodes personal responsibility: "The great problem at present is that unwed mothers on welfare, and the young men who impregnate them, are indirectly told that they do not have to be responsible for their behavior [because of welfare]" (Bethell 1993). From the point of view of young, poor mothers, welfare is a means to fulfill their responsibilities. While many of the young women resent the forms, the waiting, and the impersonal bureaucracy of the welfare system,[6] they are resigned to the paternalistic questioning, rather than humiliated by it. Especially for women who were previously on welfare as part of their own mother's "case," having a baby, moving out, and establishing their own case are signs of maturity. They do not have children in order to get on welfare, but once they have children, they want to manage their own money.

One of the provisions of PRWORA is that teen mothers cannot receive welfare unless they live in the same household with their parents or grandparents. This provision is based on the assumption that such arrangements provide the best care for mothers and babies alike. Reports from the young women in my study offer a more complicated picture. Some, like Gloria, move out of their mother's house to escape an abusive situation; others, like Iris, to escape from normal mother-daughter conflict. After Yatay moved out and proved to herself and to her mother that she could take care of herself and her daughter and do well in school, she moved back in with her mother, both for the help and for the financial savings. Yvonne had established her own welfare case, but she still lived with her mother and paid rent, despite serious ongoing arguments that led to blows.[7] She simply could not afford much of an apartment on her own. "I'm not going just because I can't stand my mother. I'm not going to move out into a squished-up studio or somebody else's house or into the streets and then have my baby in a predicament where we don't have a stable place to stay." Yvonne could not afford to pay the rent for an apartment because even a run-down one-bedroom apartment in a dangerous neighborhood cost 400 dollars a month; Aid to Families with Dependent Children (AFDC) payments were only 490 dollars a month for a woman with one child. Actually subsisting on welfare is next to impossible.

My informants feel they have the right to a roof over their heads and food on the table, and they are willing to work for it. "I'm just gonna try to look for a job because I'm not gonna depend on welfare all my life. That's nothing to depend on. It's not enough to be dependent on, especially when they cutting the checks and stuff, that's not enough to depend on to live, you know." Murray (1994) claims that "the poorer [a young woman] is, the more attractive the welfare package, and the more likely that she will think herself enabled by it to have a baby." Saying that welfare "enables" poor young women to have babies is using the language of codependency to suggest that the government is supporting young mothers / junkies in their "habit" of procreating. By the government's own calculation of poverty-level income, welfare is not enough to live on, and it is never "attractive." In a classroom discussion before the 1994 elections, the teacher pointed out that the students should be concerned since many of the candidates were threatening to cut welfare. The students responded forcefully that it didn't matter to them because they weren't going to be on welfare much longer. Many of them will stay on welfare or go on and off it, but they are not *planning* a life on welfare. Contrary to widespread popular belief that welfare "begins" with teen motherhood (Offner 1994), the evidence is that welfare dependency begins with the lack of jobs that pay a living wage and the lack of education to qualify for better-paying jobs.

SCHOOL

Young mothers experience a conflict between their current responsibilities as mothers, which often keep them out of school, and their future responsibilities, which lead them to value an education for its own sake and for the better job prospects that it brings. Staying out of school to fulfill family responsibilities is a familiar pattern to many teen mothers (Fine 1991); even before they had their own children, they often missed school to care for other family members. Rosa explained, "My mom doesn't speak really good English so when she had to take my brother to the doctors then I had to go too. He has asthma. So I had to be home a lot." Once they became mothers, they often had to miss school to keep appointments with doctors, public health programs, and welfare, each time losing a whole day because of long waits and bus transportation. Although California has a mild climate, during the rainy season school attendance dropped dramatically, as the young mothers were reluctant to take their babies out to wait for two buses in the rain. They insisted that it was not worth risking their child's health to go to school.

Before young mothers can feel comfortable about returning to school at all, they must find a reliable child care arrangement. In part because low-cost child care is frequently of poor quality, and in part because of media hype about the dangers of child care and the benefits of mothers caring for their own children, many young mothers are reluctant to send their children to a child care center, preferring to have a relative care for them. "For a mother who regards having a child as the only worthwhile thing she has ever accomplished, leaving that child with someone she does not know or trust requires a major leap of faith" (Quint, Musick, and Ladner 1994:135).

A few mothers were not ready to leave their children to go back to school after the six-week maternity leave allowed by the SAP program. Yvonne eloquently defended her decision to stay home with her baby.

> I didn't know if I wanted to leave her home with nobody, and another thing I didn't want her to get attached to nobody else. I feel that if you have a baby you should take on the responsibility yourself, you know. Now, if you get a job that's one thing, but I feel that when school comes—I don't feel that it's right to have somebody else watch your baby—they had a day care and stuff but I don't really trust that too much. And then some people have their parents or somebody at home that can help them, but I don't feel that it's their responsibility because they didn't have the child and I feel that I should be here with the child. Let me just be honest, if they didn't have independent study to offer I just wouldn't go back. Because I would rather be here and raise my child, and if I had to get my GED or if I just had to just not go back, I wouldn't because I feel that I had her, and I shouldn't burden nobody else with watching her, putting up with her, because I don't think nobody could treat her like I could.

Yvonne decided that a good mother is with her child all the time, and that this responsibility was more important than going to school. Moreover, she felt that she could care for her daughter better than anyone else could.[8]

On the other hand, for many of my respondents, becoming a mother led to a new commitment to educational achievement. Many in my study returned to or stayed in school because they wanted to be able to better provide for their children. After taking a year off after the birth of her first child, Olivia took after-school classes and went to summer school to finish high school in three years, during which time she had another baby. "I want to be prepared to have a job because I want to be able to work and have money to support my children. I don't want to depend on other people." Some young mothers see staying in school and obtaining basic skills as a sign of maturity and of being a good parent. They wanted to be able to tell their children that they graduated from high school; they wanted to be able to help their children with their homework. Demetria, age 14, explained how it felt to be one of the youngest in the SAP program: "I feel that I'm just as old as the other ones but just my number of my age [is less]. I'm mature. I know how to write, spell. I feel that for me to be so young, I'm taking care of my child, taking care of my business, doing what I got to do, *and* [staying] in school. It don't bother me."

For an assignment to write an essay defining intelligence, two students said that being a good mother was part of being intelligent. Like Demetria, they see being in school and being a mother as complementary. Being a (good) mother is a sign of maturity and intelligence. Latika wrote:

> There are many ways to define or talk about intelligence. I think intelligent people are problem solvers and good mothers. An example is a teen parent who is under 18 and is still in school and is living on their own and taking care of herself and their child. Like me, for an example; I am still in school and taking care of business. . . . The most important criteria [for defining intelligence] overall is being a good mom. . . . And just because you have a baby that doesn't make you a mother. You're not a mother until you take on your responsibility of being a mom because any female can have a baby . . . A good mom makes sure her baby comes first before any man. And her baby has everything he/she needs and she gives her baby lots of love.

"AN ANGEL OR SOMETHING"

A major reason young women have children is that they want to be responsible members of society. This desire is completely missed by their critics and those who view them as victims: "We cannot have a free society . . . unless the great majority of young people come of age having internalized norms of self-restraint, self-reliance, and commitment to a civic order" (Murray 1994). Teen mothers *have* internalized norms of self-restraint, self-reliance, and commitment to a civic order. One after another they explained how they put their children first. Olivia: "It's not whatever *I* want to do, it's whatever's right for my daughter and my new family." One after another they explained how they strive to be independent. Gloria explained:

> It's not like a big deal for us, like the way other people look at us, "Oh, you guys are so young to be doing this. Oh this that." [My boyfriend] busts his ass, he works.

I'm not on welfare, I don't get any AFDC, food stamps, I don't get none of that. He works and he takes care of me and the baby, and our son's like the biggest thing, the big deal to us. We take care of him, and then I'll start working when I get out of school."

One after another they explained how they plan to heal their families and communities. Tawina was moving to be near her family members, whom she described as pimps and prostitutes. During the interview, I asked her why she wants to move near them.

TAWINA: To help them. To help them.

DEBORAH: So you're going to be taking care of yourself and this baby and your whole family?

TAWINA: I don't know. That's how it is. I'm an angel or something. That's how I see it. Just to help them.

Tawina's commitment to the values Murray prescribes is likely to keep her in poverty, as she spreads her time and resources among her family members, like many capable young women growing up in poverty (Quint, Musick, and Ladner 1994). In Carol Stack's (1974) groundbreaking study of African American kinship networks, *All Our Kin,* she demonstrated that a complex and structured exchange of goods, services, and children made survival possible for poor families, but that the collective orientation necessary for group survival made it unlikely for individuals to escape from poverty.

Selflessness, not laziness, keeps many teen mothers in poverty. And even more than selflessness, poverty keeps teen mothers in poverty:

The very poor have used their families to cement and patch tenuous relations to survival; out of their belief in "family" they have invented networks capable of making next-to-nothing go a long way. In response, they are told that their notion of family is inadequate. It is not their notion of family that is deficient, but the relationship between household and productive resources. (Rapp 1987:234)

Teen mothers are often portrayed as teen Others, but teen mothers' values *are* "American family values." As Luker explains, "Oddly enough, the conservative dream of "family values" plays itself out in perhaps its purest form among teenage mothers in poor communities. These young mothers express a commitment to moral values over material advancement, a passionate attachment to children, and a willingness to try to sustain a family (albeit a nontraditional one) whatever the social and financial cost" (1996:164). As I described above, some teen mothers decided to have a baby as a way to embrace their moral values. In settings where they endured poverty, family discord, and limited options and resources, being a "good mother" was a commitment that many sought to fulfill. Others tried to redeem their accidental pregnancies by doing the right thing and having and raising their babies. The action of giving birth, even as a teenager, can make it possible for a young woman to live her values as a responsible, moral person.

I have emphasized that young women talk about their childbearing and rearing in deeply moral terms. Once we recognize that teen mothers can and do take responsibility for their actions, they are no longer "babies having babies." They are young women who, in the face of great adversity, are affirming their ability to nurture a child. Instead of blaming them for their children's poverty, we could provide jobs that pay a family wage, universal health care coverage, and high-quality, subsidized child care. Yet due in part to the public perception of teen mothers as parasites, PRWORA was passed, with its punitive and adversarial relationship to young mothers. As PRWORA was debated annually from 2002 until its reauthorization in 2006, the debate focused on whether the legislation had succeeded in getting people off welfare; there was much less discussion about what had happened to those who left the welfare rolls (Albelda and Withorn 2002). The state has not yet reclaimed responsibility for meeting its people's basic needs. The state's irresponsibility is made more palatable by portrayals of teen mothers as irresponsible.

While teenage mothers are not in the news so frequently today, when they are discussed, it is in the same terms as helpless children or as social parasites. A 2006 editorial in the *Toledo Blade* stated that "certainly teen mothers face well-documented hurdles as children raising children." In a 2006 government report stating that teen pregnancy, abortion, and birth rates are at their lowest ever, the authors still included the following: "The costs of teenage childbearing in the United States are substantial. . . . These costs include public assistance, health care, child welfare, and other expenses" (Ventura et al. 2006). Teenage childbearing is a cost to our society because in general teen parents live in poverty, but the report implies that the costs are due to individual behavior, not structural factors. Goodkind (this volume) explains how a focus on girls' "good" or "bad" choices obscures the social context of those choices. In a 2006 article in the *Atlanta Business Journal* on the economic savings due to the declining teen birth rate, Jane Fonda was quoted as saying, "Clearly it makes good fiscal sense, not to mention moral sense, to throw everything we've got into preventing youngsters from getting pregnant and to motivate young mothers to avoid second pregnancies." On the basis of my research with teen mothers, I would "throw everything we've got" into public education, housing, transportation, and job training that leads to family-friendly careers, not minimum-wage jobs.

Teen mothers are neither helpless victims, as public discourse on the Left asserts, nor immoral schemers, as public discourse on the Right suggests. Examining teen mothers as subjects (rather than subjects of "in-depth" coverage) reveals that young women who bear children have complex motivations, histories, and dreams. If we listen to their words and observe their actions, we hear and see responsible actors who choose to exercise their rights from a foundation of morality. In contrast to the way the mainstream marginalizes them as aberrant, immoral, or weak, teen mothers' values *are* mainstream values. By deciding to have children, they act on these values, conducting a careful moral calculus and embracing the responsibilities that accompany motherhood.

QUESTIONS FOR DISCUSSION

1. What representations of "teen mothers" do you encounter—in the popular media, professional literature, or everyday conversation? What makes these representations compelling to their audiences?

2.What notions about teen mothers are challenged in this chapter? How have these notions come to be part of professional and popular understandings? What is at stake in challenging these ideas?

3. Lustig asks us to question the dichotomy that is created in our understandings of "teen mothers" and "good mothers." What are the implications for social work practice of challenging this dichotomy?

4. How do the perspectives of the young women described in this chapter alter or enrich your understandings of their situations?

5. What new possibilities for practice with young women does this chapter inspire?

NOTES

1. Other forms of media, such as television and the movies, can also be plumbed as guides to "mainstream" understandings of teen mothers. In discussing this chapter with one of my informants, she singled out television talk shows, and especially the *Jenny Jones Show,* as particularly offensive in their portrayal of teen mothers because of the way they showcase the individual psycho-pathology of teen mothers.

2. "SAP" and all the names of young women quoted are pseudonyms.

3. Notice that her daughter was not neglected during this time but was being well cared for by her grandmother. After Yatay did return to school, she maintained straight As and a perfect attendance record.

4. African American teen mothers usually refer to their child's father as their "baby-daddy," a contraction of "baby's daddy."

5. As it happened, she chose well: he continued to support the baby, and the couple married just before the child's second birthday.

6. See Susser and Kreniske (1987) for a graphic account of the waiting and harassment involved in the welfare process.

7. The physical altercations were between Yvonne and her mother. Yvonne's baby was not hurt.

8. When her baby was about six months old, she did begin independent study at adult school.

REFERENCES

Albelda, R., and A. Withorn. (Eds.) (2002). *Lost ground: Welfare reform, poverty, and beyond.* Boston: South End Press.

Atlanta Business Chronicle (2006). Study: Teen childbearing costs in Georgia cut by declining teen birth rate (November 28). Accessed December 31, 2006, at http://sanantonio.bizjournals.com/atlanta/stories/2006/11/27/daily11.html.

Bethell, T. (1993). A girls' school in Baltimore. *American Spectator 26* (2): 17–19.

Dash, L. (1989). *When children want children: The urban crisis of teenage childbearing.* New York: William Morrow.

DeWitt, K. (1994). Teen moms who beat the odds. *Essence 25* (4): 53–55.

Erbe, B. (1994). Reinventing parenting. *Oakland Tribune* (August 26): A15.

Fine, M. (1991). *Framing dropouts.* Albany: State University of New York Press.

Gabriel, A., and E. McAnarney. (1983). Parenthood in two subcultures: White middle-class couples and black, low-income adolescents. *Adolescence 8* (71): 595–608.

Gans, H. J. (1995). *The war against the poor: The underclass and antipoverty policy.* New York: Basic Books.

Geronimus, A., and S. Korenman. (1992). The socioeconomic consequences of teen childbearing reconsidered. *Quarterly Journal of Economics 107* (4): 1187–1214.

Gleick, E., S. Reed, and S. Schindehette. (1994). The baby trap (babies having babies). *People* (October 24): 38–56.

Harvey, D. (2006). *A brief history of neoliberalism.* Oxford: Oxford University Press.

Horowitz, R. (1983). *Honor and the American dream: Culture and identity in a Chicano community.* New Brunswick, N.J.: Rutgers University Press.

Jacobs, J. (1994). Gender, race, class, and the trend toward early motherhood. *Journal of Contemporary Ethnography 22* (4): 442–62

Kaplan, E. B. (1997). *Not our kind of girl: Unraveling the myths of black teenage motherhood.* Berkeley: University of California Press.

Kelly, M.P.F. (1994). *Towanda's triumph: Social and cultural capital in the urban ghetto.* Baltimore: Institute for Policy Studies, Johns Hopkins University, Occasional Paper No. 16.

Ladner, J. (1972). *Tomorrow's tomorrow.* Garden City, N.Y.: Anchor Books.

Lawson, A. (1993). Multiple fractures: The cultural construction of teenage sexuality and pregnancy. In A. Lawson and D. Rhode, eds., *Politics of pregnancy: Adolescent sexuality and public policy.* New Haven: Yale University Press.

Luker, K. (1996). *Dubious conceptions: The politics of teenage pregnancy.* Cambridge: Harvard University Press.

Lustig, D.F. (1997). In and out of school: School-age mothers in urban California negotiate parenthood, gender, class, and race/ethnicity. Ph.D. dissertation, University of Michigan.

———. (2004). Baby pictures: Family, consumerism, and exchange among teen mothers in the USA. *Childhood 11* (2):175–93.

Luttrell, W. (2003). *Pregnant bodies, fertile minds: Gender, race, and the schooling of pregnant teens.* New York: Routledge.

Males, M. (1994). In defense of teenaged mothers. *Progressive 58* (8): 22–23.

Maran, M. (1987). The new faces of poverty; the U.S. economy is healthy, but more Americans are poor than at any time since the 1960s." *Scholastic Update 119:* 6–9.

Murray, C. (1994). What to do about welfare. *Commentary 98* (6): 26–34.

Offner, P. (1994). Target the kids: A welfare reform proposal. *New Republic 210* (4): 9–11.

Quint, J., and J. Musick, with J. Ladner. (1994). *Lives of promise, lives of pain.* New York: Manpower Demonstration Research Corporation.

Rapp, R. (1987). Urban kinship in contemporary America: Families, classes, and ideology. In L. Mullings, ed., *Cities of the United States: Studies in urban anthropology.* New York: Columbia University Press.

Solinger, R. (1992). *Wake up little Susie: Single pregnancy and race before Roe v. Wade.* New York: Routledge.

Stack, C. (1974). *All our kin: Strategies for survival in a Black community.* New York: Harper and Row.

Stokes, R., and J. P. Hewitt. (1976). Aligning actions. *American Sociological Review 41:* 838–49.

Susser, I., and J. Kreniske. (1987). The welfare trap: A public policy for deprivation. In L. Mullings, ed., *Cities of the United States: Studies in urban anthropology,* 51–68. New York: Columbia University Press.

Sylvester, K. (1995). Talk of the Nation, National Public Radio (January 31).

Thompson, S. (1995). *Going all the way: Teenage girls' tales of sex, romance, and pregnancy.* New York: Hill and Wang.

Toledo Blade. (2006). Bemusing baby boom (November 30). Accessed December 31, 2006, at http://toledoblade.com/apps/pbcs.dll/article?AID = /20061130/OPINION 02/611300305/-1/OPINION.

Ventura S. J., J. C. Abma, W. D. Mosher, and S. K. Henshaw. (2006). Recent trends in teenage pregnancy in the United States, 1990–2002. Health E-stats. Hyattsville, Md: National Center for Health Statistics.

Wattleton, F. (1989). Teen-age pregnancy: The case for national action. *Nation 249* (4): 138–41.

Williams, C. (1991). *Black teenage mothers.* Lexington, Mass.: Lexington Books.

Wilson, W. J. (1978). *Declining significance of race.* Chicago: University of Chicago Press.

Woodman, S. (1995). How teen pregnancy has become a political football. *Ms 5* (4): 90–92.

SIX

The Well-Being of Children and the Question of Attachment

Kerrie Ghenie and Charlie Wellenstein

We have witnessed a growing preoccupation among social workers and child-serving agencies with the problem of childhood attachment and the treatment of attachment disorders. More and more, it seemed, young children in the foster care system were the subject of assessments and interventions that focused on their abilities to attach—to establish enduring bonds of emotional connection and trust to a primary caregiver. Over the past decade in Montana we have observed the increasing use of a diagnosis of "Reactive Attachment Disorder" and a concomitant trend toward "attachment interventions" in out-patient therapy, foster care, group homes, and residential care wherein children (ages 3–12) are the subjects of highly structured and, at times, unorthodox treatments, which have included bottle feedings, holdings, and tethering to a staff person designated as a primary parent figure. As child welfare educators and practitioners, we were both puzzled and concerned. We hold a deep appreciation for the experience of parent-child bonding, and we understand the significance of supportive, safe, and loving relations and environments for healthy child devel-

We are indebted to Janet L. Finn for helping to create and shape our work. Her intellectual and editorial contributions, constructive criticism, guidance, and patience have made this chapter a reality. Janet is a model for best practice at all levels of practice.

opment. But something else seemed to be at work here. It seemed that, rather than bolstering the material, social, and emotional support of children in the context of their family and community, practitioners had taken a more narrow view—one that located the disorder in the child and framed intervention as a child-fixing package of technologies and tactics that would render him or her able to "attach" and thus succeed in a new family. As we looked to the literature, it seemed that we were witnessing not merely a local aberration but a broader trend, wherein children in foster care are seen to be "at risk" for a diagnosis of attachment disorder, and thus further at risk for diagnoses of deeper pathologies in adulthood (see Barth et al. 2005 for a critique). These highly individualized forms of intervention seem to be stripped of the larger context that shapes both public policy and the lives of children and families, predominantly poor and minority, who are implicated in the child welfare system.

This chapter represents our effort to think through the complex terrain of attachment in relationship to the welfare of children and families and the practice of social work therein. We turn to history as a tool for helping us understand present policies and practices. We explore the emergence of notions of "attachment" and "permanency" and their complex relationship to concepts of childhood and the "best interests" of children. We consider the ways in which these concepts shape and are shaped by child welfare policies and practices, paying particular attention to shifting policies and practices in the last half of the twentieth century. Additionally, we consider the competing values of child well-being and rights, parental rights, and government intervention.

At the turn of the twenty-first century, we find the child welfare system in an interesting yet somewhat concerning state. In 1996 the passage of the Adoption and Safe Families Act established that our national goals for children in the child welfare system are safety, permanency, and well-being. While laudable in theory, meeting these goals places competing demands on social workers and parents by simultaneously shortening the time period in which parents can make changes required to regain custody of their children and requiring "concurrent planning" whereby the social worker must be pursuing an alternative permanent placement, in the event that the birth parents are not able to regain custody. We suggest that current constructions of "permanency" and the "best interests" of the child are premised on a reductionist view of attachment, which overemphasizes a single primary attachment and fails to take the larger familial, social, cultural, historical, political, and economic contexts of a child's life into account. We contend that this narrow perspective can lead to "infant determinism"—the notion that "failings" of early childhood will inevitably result in poor outcomes for adulthood—and the reproduction of racial and class-based inequalities. We argue instead for a context-rich view of attachment and a meaningful, integrated appreciation of the practice of permanency that recognize the multiple possibilities and capacities for human bonding throughout the life course.

A RETROSPECTIVE VIEW OF CHILDREN'S WELL-BEING AND ATTACHMENT

Let us start with a brief look at ways in which notions about children, well-being, and attachment have shifted over time. During the colonial period in the United States, high child and adult mortality rates and the difficult nature of daily survival contributed to a stolid sense of practicality in parent-child relations. Children were generally viewed as miniature adults and parental property, and parental authority was honored with little outside interference (Hacsi 1996; Maza 2001). Many families counted on the contributions and labors of children for subsistence. Attachment in this context implied a sense of family and community interdependence necessary for survival. A formal child welfare system did not exist. If the system of familial or community care broke down, children were sent to poor houses or workhouses or given for indenture; their attachment to home and family was not a concern.

The mid-1800s saw a shift toward a greater preoccupation with the well-being of children, especially the children of newly arriving immigrants and the poor (see Finn, this volume; Nelson 1995). Charity organizations sought to "save" poor children by detaching them from their families of origin and the corrupting potential of urban life and attaching them to rural, Christian families to receive moral and work-related training. Thus, "other" people's children were readily separated from their emotional attachments to family, home, community, and culture and thrust into ties characterized more by servitude than sentimentality. Child-savers were less preoccupied with the emotional well-being of these children than with their potential for future risk or productivity.

The late nineteenth century saw not only a preoccupation with the children of the poor but also the emergence of a middle class in which the labor of women and children was not required for family survival. As McGowan describes, this "permitted upper-income citizens to turn their attention to educational and developmental needs of their own children, as well as those of the orphaned, poor and delinquent" (2005:12). The quality of the maternal-child relationship was recognized (Grossberg 2002), and, among the middle and upper classes, a view of children as economically valuable was replaced by a view of children as emotionally priceless (Zelizer 1994). Working-class parents, who often relied upon their children's financial contributions to maintain the household, could literally not afford such a sentimental view.

Concurrently we saw a shift toward saving children not only from poverty but also from cruelty, as states developed legal statutes to address child abuse and courts authorized anticruelty societies to remove children from abusive and neglectful homes (Hutchison and Charlesworth 2000:580). Further, "[W]hat we now know as foster care took root in the last two decades of the 19th century when some child protection organizations began to pay families to take in homeless children so the children would not have to work" (Price 2005:357). These practices suggest that the space and sentimental value of childhood itself were coming to be officially recognized. They also point to the belief that children's emotional and physical needs could be met in a substitute home setting.

Early twentieth-century child welfare policies reflected the growing acceptance of childhood as a distinct stage of development in need of protection, regardless of social class. The turn of the century saw the beginning of federal government involvement in child welfare and a move toward interventions that focused on children's attachment to birth family and respect for parental rights. In 1909 the first White House Conference on Children brought national attention to "the plight of destitute families, agency problems with the boarding out of children, and the importance of home care" (Karger and Stoesz 2006:392). The conference focused on the need for family rehabilitation rather than child removal and led the federal government to develop the United States Children's Bureau in 1912 to conduct research, collect and exchange information with states, and educate the public about child welfare issues (CQ Researcher 2005; Grossberg 2002; Karger and Stoesz 2006; Mather, Lager, and Harris 2007). States began to develop compulsory education laws, child labor laws, and juvenile courts that shaped notions of childhood as a protected category. Further, the establishment of the mother's pension, which offered financial assistance to widowed and other "worthy" poor mothers, signaled that the value of the mother-child bond crossed class lines. The passage of the Social Security Act of 1935 authorized federal financial assistance to impoverished families through the Aid to Dependent Children Program and to states to protect and care for homeless, dependent, neglected, and potentially delinquent children. Foster care, the preferred placement option, was seen as a temporary intervention while child welfare agencies provided services to parents with the goal of family reunification.

THEORIZING ATTACHMENT

In the post–World War II era, rapid growth in research on children's emotional needs regarding parental attachment sparked discussion of children's need for "permanency"—the continuity of an emotional relationship with a parent figure. It also prompted change in child welfare policy and service delivery. In the 1940s, research began regarding the role of child-parent attachment in child well-being, which prompted a focus on the quality of children's emotional relationships in relation to their overall health. Robertson and Bowlby (1952), in observing the effects that short-term separation from parents had on children in a London hospital, documented that children go through phases of separation and loss during a hospital stay without their mothers (these studies operated from an implicit assumption that mothers were "naturally" the primary caretakers, and thus the term "parent" was equated with "mother."). These phases include protest, despair, and denial/detachment, which impact the child's level of trust. In 1952 Bowlby reported to the World Health Organization that to ensure mental health, infants and young children need a relationship with their mother, or a permanent mother substitute, that is continuous, loving, and mutually satisfying. He noted that maternal deprivation occurs when the mother or permanent mother substitute is unable to give the child loving care, and that a child is deprived when removed from his or her mother's care for any reason. Bowlby (1969) found that children who were separated from their mother in the second or third year of life often suffered severe distress. He concluded that the disruption of the continuity of the parent-child bond had serious consequences for the child (Lindsey 2004:37). Making specific reference to the difference between maternal bonds of attachment and those of a substitute, Bowlby noted, "Deprivation will be relatively mild if he is then looked after by someone with whom he has already learned to know and trust, but it may be considerable if the foster-mother, even though loving, is a stranger" (1952:12). According to Bowlby, partial deprivation may result in child anxiety, excessive need for love, and feelings of revenge, guilt, and depression, which can lead to neurosis and instability of character. Complete deprivation, such as that which occurs in institutional settings, has far greater effects on character development and may fully preclude the child from developing relationships with others. This was groundbreaking work, and Bowlby, Robertson, and others continued to study attachment and develop comprehensive theories and treatment approaches (Ainsworth 1967; Ainsworth et al. 1978; Harlow 1958, 1959; Harlow and Harlow 1966) . Their research laid the groundwork for the permanency planning movement in child welfare, which, within a decade, would actively advocate for all children to "have a sense of permanency in their life" (Lindsey 2004:37).

Building on the insights of attachment theory, Maas and Engler's (1959) study of children in foster care revealed concerns regarding the lack of permanency for children in out-of-home care. They expressed concern regarding "foster care drift"—a term used to describe children spending long, indeterminate periods of time in foster care without a plan for their future—and regarding the practice of termination of the parent-child relationship without providing children with a permanent alternative. Echoing concerns expressed by child welfare advocates of the Progressive Era that children should not be removed from their families "for reasons of poverty," Maas and Engler argued that poor health, low income, poor housing, and marital breakup were major contributors to foster care placement. They recommended that communities provide a wide range of prevention services to families to address these varied needs and enable children to remain with their parents. From their perspective, attachment went beyond the mother-child bond to a sense of belonging and well-being in family and community.

The 1960s and early 1970s saw another shift in policy and practice from an emphasis on poverty to an emphasis on cruelty, reminiscent of the late 1800s. In 1962 Dr. Henry Kempe identified the Battered Child Syndrome, which established that many childhood injuries were the result of physical abuse by parents or other caretakers and provided the medical community with information to help identify signs of possible child abuse (Kempe et al. 1962). It also focused public attention on child abuse and neglect and helped lead to the passage of child abuse reporting and investigation legislation in the mid-1970s. As Lindsey (2004) describes, this shift in policy and practice resulted in a move toward a narrow focus on investigation and protection and away from a broader emphasis on child well-being. With this shift came a decreased emphasis on the preservation of the family and the material support needed to sustain familial and community attachments.

In 1973 Goldstein et al. put forth their position that the "best interests of the child" should serve as the paramount standard regarding removal and placement of children (Goldstein et al. 1973, 1979, 1986). They proposed three guidelines when making decisions about the placement of children. First, children need nurturing relationships, and, in particular, one "continuous and unconditional relationship" with an adult who is capable of becoming the child's parent. Second, the "child's sense of time" should be taken into account. The child's developmental age needs to be a determinant to minimize psychological harm by delays in placement. Thus, the younger the child, the more urgent the need for a permanent plan to ensure continuity of care. Third, they acknowledged that the state has a limited role in terms of intervention in family life and a limited scope in terms of prediction and monitoring of outcomes. That is, the child welfare system may have substantive knowledge about what is "best" for children, but only limited authority to interfere with parenting practices. In effect, their work championed the significance of parent-child attachment at the same time that it cautioned against removal of children from their parents in the hopes of finding a "better" attachment.

By the early 1970s, attachment, permanency, and battered child syndrome were central concerns in child welfare, and addressing them posed complicated and contradictory problems for policy makers and practitioners alike. Policy makers worked to create structures and mandates to address the varied and complex emotional and physical needs of children. These policies sought to strengthen governmental involvement with families and raised further concerns regarding children's rights vs. parental rights. This blurred the line of parental autonomy and allowed for greater government intrusion in families to ensure the safety of children. The child welfare system determined the limits of parental autonomy, the minimal standard of parenting, and the criteria and protocol for removal of children from their home. These mandates often conflicted with the need for one primary attachment brought forth by Bowlby, Ainsworth, Harlow, and the "Best Interests" proponents.

The Child Abuse Prevention Treatment Act of 1974 (CAPTA), the first major piece of federal legislation to address child abuse and neglect, provided federal funds to states for passing mandatory reporting laws for child abuse and neglect, allowed grants for the prevention and treatment of child abuse and neglect, funded demonstration projects, and added physical abuse, emotional neglect, and sexual exploitation as reportable offenses. "Before the decade ended, all 50 states passed laws requiring doctors, teachers, and other child-care professionals to report suspected abuse" (Price 2005:358). Thereafter, the number of reports of child abuse and neglect grew exponentially (Shireman 2003). "The number of children in foster care had risen from 177,000 in 1961 to more than 500,000 in 1979" (Jansson 2008:491), and length of stay in foster care, foster care drift, lack of efforts to reunite families or place children with adoptive families, and an overrepresentation of minority children in the foster care system were symptoms of a system in crisis. The child welfare system itself was relentlessly detaching children from families without the resources or wherewithal to support children in retaining or re-establishing the emotional bonds needed for healthy development.

By 1978, in states with large Native American populations, 25–35% percent of Native American children had been removed from their family and placed in culturally inappropriate settings (Jones 1995). A practice of forced detachment, which began with the Indian boarding schools and continued into the late 1960s through the Indian Adoption Project of the Child Welfare League of America, appeared to be repeating itself within the foster care system. Tribal leaders and members advocated for federal legislation to protect their familial, tribal, and cultural rights, which led to the passage of the Indian Child Welfare Act (ICWA) in 1978. Recognizing the fundamental importance of a child's right to connect not only to family but also to culture, community, and place, ICWA established specific guidelines for child removal, placement, and family reunification. It also established tribal jurisdiction for all cases involving American Indian children, and the right for tribes to intervene in state court proceedings. It upheld American Indian tribal and family rights to determine culturally appropriate permanency and attachment for their children. In effect, ICWA represents a profound challenge to narrowly conceived notions of attachment and child welfare.

In a broader return to attachment and permanency concerns, a new focus in federal legislation emerged in the 1980s, which emphasized family preservation and reunification. The Adoption Assistance and Child Welfare Act (AACWA) of 1980 was intended to reduce the number of children entering foster care, reduce the length of time spent in foster care, and find permanent placements for children who could not return home. It created title IV-E of the Social Security Act, the main source of federal assistance for child welfare, and provided the first federal procedural rules for child welfare case management, permanency planning, and foster care placement reviews. It required states to make reasonable efforts to prevent the removal of children from their families, and reasonable efforts for family reunification once placement occurred. It further mandated that courts review open child welfare cases on a regular basis and placed importance on permanency planning, which included subsidizing adoption for children with special needs. AACWA represented a key moment of convergence in child welfare policy wherein those concerned with family values or cost-effective intervention found common cause with those concerned with the needs of children to be with their parents and those advocating for the rights of children and families living in poverty.

Initially following the passage of AACWA, foster care rates decreased; however, due to many social, political, and economic factors in the 1980s and early 1990s (including economic downturn, higher numbers of single and teenage parents, concern over drug-addicted parents and babies, increasing hostility toward provision of public welfare, and increased incarceration rates), foster care rates began to rise again. Foster care caseloads, which had dropped to fewer than 300,000 in 1986, soared to nearly 500,000 again by 1995 (Price 2005:358). What is of key interest here is that the intent of the legislation was to support family preservation and reunification. The outcomes, however, suggest a trend in the opposite direction, one moving away from the attachment of children to their birth families, especially among poor and minority families. Some argue that confusion regarding the "reasonable efforts" provision of the Adoption Assistance and Child Welfare Act added to the length of time many children spent in foster care. Numerous child welfare workers and court personnel did not know the extent to which reunification services must be provided under the reasonable efforts provision and therefore allowed services to go on indefinitely. According to Testa and Miller, this "perpetuated the malpractice of allowing children to spend too many years detached from their biological parents while preventing them from forming new attachments to their foster homes"(2005:409). This, coupled with a lack of adoptive homes for eligible children, saw a large number of children "aging out" of the foster care system each year without adequate preparation to transition to adulthood and with few family or adult attachments to help them (Mather, Lager, and Harris 2007; Nixon 2005; Shireman 2003). Additionally, due to broader economic shifts, the number of households in which both parents worked contributed to a critical shortage of foster homes. "Thus, by the late 1980's, with permanency planning beset with multiple problems, foster care was an unreliable way of serving many of the most endangered children in the United States" (Karger and Stoesz 2006:403).

It is important to attend to this broader social and political climate that heavily impacted the child welfare system. This was a time in which the public welfare system was under widespread political attack, evidenced by a growing hostility toward the poor, the unemployed, and, especially, single mothers. The Reagan era "crystallized and intensified the long standing conservative tradition of demonizing poor people, their families, and their communities—along with the government systems designed to assist them" (Albelda and Withorn 2002:1). Poor single mothers were viewed as the cause of the national economic decline while welfare was seen as a failure, and calls were made for ending it as an entitlement (Hays 2003). This marked the beginning of a shift in American policy and practice toward retrenchment—funding cuts for social welfare programs that targeted the poor, devolving responsibility from the federal government to state governments, and privatization of social welfare services. These trends shaped the context of child welfare policy and practice in complicated ways. On the one hand, policy makers wanted to encourage the preservation and reunification of families; on the other hand, social supports for poor families were being eroded, and particular *kinds* of families, especially those headed by single women of color, were being blamed for a host of social ills.

In an attempt to reverse the concerning trends of increasing numbers of children in care, lack of permanent plans, and a shortage of foster care resources, the federal government enacted several pieces of legislation. The 1986 Independent Living Initiative appropriated limited funds to states to help adolescents develop skills to transition successfully from foster care to independence. The 1993 Family Preservation and Support Services Act provided federal funds to states for family preservation and support services for families at risk due to substance abuse, community violence, poverty, and homelessness to prevent foster care placements. The Multiethnic Placement Act (MEPA) of 1994 attempted to decrease the length of time children spent in foster care awaiting adoption by eliminating discrimination based on race, color, or national origin of the child or the prospective parent. MEPA was amended through the Interethnic Adoption Provision of 1996 (IAP), which removed potentially misleading language in the act and reconfirmed that discrimination would not be tolerated (Heifetz Hollinger 1998). It did not, however, address the reasons why minority children are overrepresented in the foster care system, nor did it increase the number of minority adoptive parents (Roberts 2006). MEPA and IAP attempted to make the child welfare system color blind; moreover, they failed to acknowledge and address the prevalence of institutional racism, the root cause of the overrepresentation of minority children in the system. Once again we see both a systemic disregard for the context of poverty in which families of color are overrepresented and a disregard for the attachment of children of color not only to family, but also to community and cultural identity.

THE CURRENT U.S. CHILD WELFARE SYSTEM

The early and mid-1990s saw public backlash against U.S. social welfare policies that served children and impoverished families. As described earlier, this was part of a broader neoliberal shift toward devolution, privatization, and the blaming of the poor and of welfare for "causing" poverty. In the 1980s and early 1990s, the Aid to Families with Dependent Children (AFDC) program and its recipients drew heavy and cruel criticism. The prevailing arguments against AFDC were that it fostered dependency, laziness, and a culture of poverty that attached people to public assistance for life and followed generational patterns — children raised on welfare would raise their children on welfare (Hays 2003).

Criticism of the child welfare system was strong as well. Despite previous policy and practice attempts to decrease the number of children in foster care, by the mid-1990s the foster care rate remained steady, near 500,000. Public criticism echoed that of the past several decades: the high number of children in foster care, the length of foster care placements, foster care drift, overrepresentation of minority children, and a lack of permanency planning for children in foster care. The child welfare system was also criticized as being biased toward family preservation at the expense of child safety and well-being. Questions continued about the emotional toll long-term foster care had on children, and fear of attachment problems and resulting mental health concerns became part of popular discourse. Attachment treatment programs and practices were being developed and began to see regular use in mainstream practice. Ironically, this emphasis on individualized, privatized technologies and interventions of attachment occurred at the same time as the radical *detachment* of the state from its social welfare responsibilities to its most vulnerable citizens.

Strong calls for reform to AFDC, child welfare policies, and the foster care system were well supported by congressional conservatives and saw less than expected opposition from congressional moderates and liberals. What resulted, the Personal Responsibility, Work Opportunity Reconciliation Act of 1996 (PRWORA), ended welfare as an entitlement program and limited cash benefits to five years over the course of a parent's lifetime. The passage of the Adoption and Safe Families Act of 1997 (ASFA) made the most significant changes to the child welfare system since the enactment of the Adoption Assistance and Child Welfare Act of 1980 and had sweeping implications for children's rights, parental rights and responsibilities, and the right of the government to intercede in family. According to the U.S. Department of Health and Human Services, "This legislation, passed by congress with overwhelming bipartisan support, represents an important landmark in federal child welfare law. It establishes unequivocally that our national goals for children in the child welfare system are safety, permanency and well-being" (U.S. Department of Public Health and Human Services, Administration for Children and Families 1998). In effect, however, this legislation has dovetailed with PRWORA to limit time and resources available to parents in the system to maintain or restore bonds of attachment with their children.

Let us take a closer look at ASFA. This act dictates that child safety is paramount, and key provisions show consideration for a child's sense of time regarding permanency needs. ASFA allows time-limited family preservation services, including funding for family reunification, adoption promotion and support activities, postadoption assistance, and substance abuse treatment. It clarifies that reasonable efforts for placement prevention and family reunification are not required when aggravated circumstances exist, shortens the time frame for making permanency decisions, and allows for concurrent planning for adoption or other permanent placement while providing reasonable efforts to reunite the family. The court must now approve a permanency plan by the time a child has been in foster care for 12 months (or 30 days for aggravated circumstances), and states are compelled to initiate court proceedings to terminate parental rights to free a child for adoption if that child has been in foster care 15 of the last 22 months, unless compelling reasons to the contrary exist. ASFA promotes adoption of children in care through adoption incentive payments, and it requires a national review system to hold states accountable for achieving permanency outcomes for children.

Upon closer examination, it appears that ASFA sets up a new set of problems regarding attachment. First, the act affirms the commitment to a specific vision of birth family (i.e., maternal attachment); second, it is built on disregard and impatience with birth families who cannot meet this standard; and third, it was passed in a context in which welfare laws insisted that all families dedicate their labors to the market. As Roberts argues, "The overlap of ASFA and the 1996 federal welfare adjustment law marked the first time in US history that the federal government mandated that states protect children from abuse and neglect with no corresponding mandate to provide basic economic support to poor families" (2006:53). In addition the broader retrenchment of the welfare state resulted in reduced funds for mental health services, substance abuse treatment, housing supports, health care, and child care—the very supports so desperately needed by families involved in the child welfare system (meanwhile incarceration rates and federal dollars for corrections soar). Since poverty plays a significant role in child neglect and foster care placements, retracting the financial safety net that was AFDC removes a critical prevention component. It further begs the question: What value does society place on impoverished families in the United States? Without providing comprehensive social welfare policies and services to address the complex nature of poverty, it seems unlikely that welfare reform will significantly reduce the number of people living in poverty, nor will it decrease the number of children entering the foster care system due to neglect. This, in conjunction with ASFA's mandates for timely permanency plans for children, leaves one to wonder if we are entering a new era of child saving. Are we once again allowing for the detachment of children from impoverished families and promoting attachment with families approved by the child welfare system? Are children being denied attachment to their families of origin "for reasons of poverty"? Color-blind policies, shortened time frames, privatized services, and lack of state support for poor families have made for a "perfect storm." Welfare reform is pushing mothers into the workforce with no concern about the welfare of young children, in complete contradiction to attachment principles, but the child welfare system is silent on the impact of these market forces on children and families.

Stein notes, "ASFA is best understood as part of the political reform agenda that began when the 104th congress passed the PRWORA" (2003:670). ASFA was passed on the heels of welfare reform, a time when concern for personal responsibility was a priority, and represents the confluence of welfare and child welfare policies, privatization and marketization of social services, and the individualization of intervention that work against meaningful attachments. Both policies share the common value that the state should not "reward" single mothers or parents using illicit drugs through economic support. ASFA overhauled the time line for parents to reunify with their children but failed to address the larger systemic problems that undermine timely service provision and reunification. As Stein explains, time lines for case reviews and termination are complicated by the expansive work that must be negotiated and completed among various government, legal, and private systems and service providers, all of whom have differing philosophies, values, and requirements. ASFA does not address the difficult interplay among courts, Child Protective Service workers, and private services providers; poorly trained court and CPS workers; heavy CPS caseloads and court calendars; and high worker turnover rates in the child welfare system—all of which contribute to the protracted nature of the child welfare system.

ASFA represents an attempt to address the needs of children in out-of-home care and has been successful in drawing attention to the important fact that children need safety and stability. However, like previous child protection policies, it is reactionary and limited in focus to children and families in relation to abuse and neglect. It will not decrease the incidence of child abuse and neglect in the United States. It does not address the numerous social, political, and economic conditions, such as poverty, racism, discrimination, poor housing, poor health, and lack of community supports, that contribute to child abuse and neglect. It also does not address or prevent the psychological, emotional, and interpersonal conditions of parents and families that contribute to abuse and neglect. Since the implementation of AFSA, foster care rates have remained steady. In fiscal year 1998, 560,000 children were served by the foster care system. As of 2005, an estimated 513,000 children were in foster care (U.S. Department of Public Health and Human Services 2006). It seems that children, rather than adults (parents, case workers, court personnel, policy makers, community members) have to bear the brunt of situations that are out of their control. Why can't we, as a society, develop comprehensive, family-centered policies and services that minimize the impact on children?

In sum, the current web of social policies (AFSA, PRWORA, and IPA) purportedly developed to address poverty, child abuse and neglect, and racism has focused reform on individual families and children while ignoring larger social, political, and systemic influences. This plays out in child welfare through a focus on attachment to the zenith. We contend that this narrowly defined emphasis on attachment has come at the expense of ignoring the cultural and economic impacts that occur within the child's community. As policy and practice move further toward individual technologies of treatment, the structural conditions affecting the lives of poor families, particularly poor families of color and their children, continue to go unacknowledged and unaddressed.

REFLECTING ON ATTACHMENT

In this section we return to a consideration of attachment in relationship to theory, diagnostic categories, and intervention strategies. As discussed earlier, there is significant research on the importance a positive parent-child attachment that is applied to foster care. Most notable are the theoretical underpinnings that are well described in the works of Bowlby (1969) and Ainsworth et al. (1978). More recently, other studies, including Stein (2005), propose that a secure attachment may prevent a foster care placement breakdown, and the American Academy of Pediatrics states that "Having at least one adult which is devoted and loves a child unconditionally is key to helping a child overcome the stress and trauma of abuse and neglect" (2000:1147). Theories of attachment have been influential in the development of ASFA's goals of permanency, safety, and well-being. These goals are well intended and purport to honor children's rights to grow in a consistent, safe, nurturing environment. However, we find ourselves puzzling over fundamental questions. The decreased time frames for reunification and increased focus on adoption under current policy are intended to move children through the child welfare system in timely manner; it seems, though, that children's voices and experiences regarding family, forms of attachment, and permanency get lost in the process. Children are required to detach from their previous attachments (family, home, neighborhood, school, community, and cultural context) and reattach elsewhere. We question whether this is healthy or even fully possible. Meanwhile, their parents are expected to attach themselves to the marketplace. Poor parents are expected to leave their children in the care of others and seek work, with no guarantee of earning a living wage. Parents involved in the child welfare system are expected to "improve" with limited support for personal change and virtual neglect of the structural circumstances of their lives. They are blamed and judged by a narrowly calibrated scale of attachment. Additionally, it seems that the current focus on attachment as a key component of permanency and mental health has been unevenly focused on children in the child welfare system. Separation of children and parents outside the child welfare system occurs regularly without concern. Such separation may even be deemed a marker of status and a pathway to privilege. For example, children of the privileged classes are often sent to boarding schools to "prepare them for power" both in terms of educational opportunity and in terms of building capital in social networks. Promising child athletes may be sent to live with coaches or with substitute "sport" families, some at a very young age, to enhance their competitive chances. Concerns about their capacity for attachment are not raised. Do we somehow sanction a level of detachment by and from parents of the more privileged classes when there appears to be some other type of gain?

We also call for critical reflection on the race- and class-based implications of ASFA and its relationship to belief and practices regarding attachment. A 2006 synthesis of the research of disproportionality in child welfare conducted by the Casey Family Program found that a majority of children in the foster care system are from families that receive or qualify for public assistance. The study also found "race as one of the determinants of decisions at the stages of reporting, investigation, substantiation, placement and exit from foster care" (Hill 2006) This results in children of color being removed more often, receiving fewer services, experiencing lower reunification rates, and remaining in foster care longer than their white counterparts. As social workers we have an ethical obligation to question and challenge policies and practices that systematically disadvantage poor children and children of color in such profound ways.

We turn now to consideration of the use of attachment in diagnosis and treatment of the troubles of children in foster care. There is a current trend to use attachment theory as a base for clinical diagnosis and related treatment approaches for foster children. We see three key problems with the current application of attachment theory. First, attachment theory has been used to locate the problem in the child (through a diagnosis of Reactive Attachment Disorder, or RAD). This focus moves away from the broader contexts and conditions that play a key role in healthy child development. Second, we contend that a singular emphasis on attachment lends to infant determinism. This not only predicts a disastrous lifetime outcome for a child but also moves policy makers from promoting proactive family- and child-friendly legislation. Third, attachment theory has been translated into practice through treatment approaches that seem questionable, in particular through the diagnosis and treatment of RAD.

The mandate of "permanency" under current legislation may have fueled both the focus on attachment as a quick fix answer to children who have been maltreated and the increase in the diagnosis and corresponding treatment of RAD. According to the *Diagnostic and Statistical Manual of Mental Disorders,* RAD is marked by "disturbed and developmentally inappropriate social related- ness in most contexts before age 5 years and is associated with gross pathological care" (American Psychiatric Association 2000:127). The diagnosis is divided into two subtypes, both marked by problems in social relationships. Children with the *inhibited* type show an inability to form relationships due to being extremely withdrawn. Children with the *disinhibited* type show an "indiscriminate socia- bility or a lack of selectivity in the choice of attachment figures" (128).

Several researchers have found problems with the RAD diagnosis. For example, Hanson and Spratt (2000) express concern that children are over- diagnosed based on a history of abuse and neglect. Zilberstein argues that there is a disconnect between attachment theory and the RAD diagnosis. She states that RAD "contrasts with the conception of attachment fostered by attachment theory and common usage. Attachment involves the mutual and trusting rela- tionship of a child with a primary caretaker, but this relationship is not specifi- cally targeted in the diagnostic manual. Recognition of this reciprocal event is important" (2006:56).

This pursuit of a diagnosis appears to block professionals and caregiv- ers from a focus on the nature and potential of reciprocal relationships in the child's life. In focusing on the child as the locus of the problem, professionals fail to look beyond individual pathologies and see possible gaps in services and community risk factors or to see relational possibilities in the child's life. How- ever, biological parents, foster parents, and caseworkers alike may find comfort in knowing there is a diagnosis—a way to name and frame a child's troubles— and thus a prescribed path toward intervention and possible cure.

Barth et al. (2005) suggest that foster and adoptive parents pursue attach- ment therapies for fear that if their foster children are not engaged in attach- ment treatment there may be a tendency for their children to move toward sociopathy. However, there is no evidence to confirm that children with attach- ment issues grow up to prey on society. Barth et al. also note that attachment treatment places the blame on prior caregivers, thus relieving the current fos- ter parents of any responsibility to change their method of parenting or attend in different ways to the foster child's social world. Chaffin et al. point out that "proponents of attachment therapies commonly assert that their therapies, and their therapies alone, are effective for children with attachment disorders and more traditional treatments are either ineffective or harmful" (2006:78). The authors also suggest that parents tend to believe in the predictive power of RAD and attachment-based treatments. Thus, it seems as if there is a significant gap between our theoretical models of human attachment and the assumptions that guide diagnosis and treatment of other people's children. To summarize somewhat boldly, it seems that larger issues of poverty, racism, social exclusion, and violence become reduced to blaming of birth parents who fail the test of proper parent-child bonding. Through diagnosis and treatment of their children in care, the problem is further reduced to one located in the "detached" child, who has one therapeutic shot at connection before being written off as a future sociopath.

PRACTICE IMPLICATIONS

We believe that practitioners, especially social workers, are remiss when they fail to view attachment as broadly conceived. Once a child enters the child welfare system, there is more than the parent-child relationship at work. Practitioners too often turn a blind eye to the political, historical, sociological, cultural, and economic forces that profoundly impact a child's life circumstance and chances. The result of this singular focus is a reductionist, "context stripping" view of attachment that tends to blame parents and children, especially poor and minority parents and children, for their problems (Saleebey 2006). Thus we end with the problem being personalized and depoliticized and located in the body of the child or in the mother-child relationship. Poor mothers are blamed for their failure to simultaneously attach to the labor market and to their children; with the tearing of the social safety net, they become relegated to the ranks of the disposable poor. The child may have a chance, if he or she can "reattach." But a child's failure to do so means failure of treatment and absolves the professionals involved of any larger responsibility. The child is then labeled "at risk" of becoming a "risky" youth or adult. It seems that the seduction of labels and of the marketplace of expertise trumps a long, hard look at the problematic context of children's lives and the structural violence wrought by poverty, inequality, and racism. Thus we need "complexity thinking" with regard to attachment (Adams, Dominelli, and Payne 2005:6–7). We need to name and address the questions of infrastructure that leave parent-child attachments vulnerable. We need to challenge the lack of environmental safeguards. We need to examine the interacting and amplifying effect of social policies impacting families, the poor, and people of color. We need to claim an ethical stance as social workers and challenge the detachment of social welfare policies and practices from a moral and social obligation to the poor, vulnerable, and excluded. We need to address institutional racism and challenge the racializing of attachment and color-blind policies.

Although laudable, when permanency is defined only in terms of attachment there are bound to be shortcomings. This suggests there is only one type of successful relationship for a child in the child welfare system. We propose that lasting relationships should also be expanded to and nurtured in the child's broader community and across the child's life course. With whom beyond immediate family has the child formed significant relationships? How are these relationships important not only in the child's current circumstances but also as the child moves toward adulthood? How might these ties be identified and supported? This requires that social workers do social work—understanding the child in the environment and looking for and encouraging attachments that can occur within that environment.

As social workers, we need to critically reflect on the role of classism in shaping our assumptions about children, families, and attachment. We seldom speak directly to class relations or our beliefs regarding the effect of class on attachment and success in adulthood. We have rarely, if ever, seen poverty noted as a primary factor in the attachment in a foster child's life. But we know from our practice experience that it is present. Conversely, ask any child welfare worker when the last time middle- or upper-class parents were investigated and lost custody for failing to attach to their child and the likely response is never. We need to seriously examine the role of class and classism in shaping the lives of children and the decisions of professionals with considerable power over those lives.

Further, the child welfare system's own lack of environmental safeguards continues to plague social workers and the children and families with whom they work. When there are no stated commitments or allocated resources to respond to the structural, environmental problems confronting families and children in the system, social workers look to a lottery system that includes attachment as an answer. Thus, they pursue the perfect winning combination of a potential parent who has all the perfect attributes and can bond with the child. (A refrain commonly heard at child placement meetings is "This placement will work if we can find just the right parent.") The odds of a winning match in this drawing are dismal. Yet social workers continue to be forced to play while there is little or no acknowledgment that this is a losing game. In addition, policy makers continue to advertise this attachment lottery as the best possible plan. However as Kagan states, "It is far more expensive to improve the housing, education, and health of approximately one million children living in poverty in

America today than to urge their mothers to kiss, talk to and play with them more" (1998:91).

We suggest viewing attachment as a worthy goal but not a singular outcome measure. We agree with the proponents of attachment: children need loving and nurturing caregivers. However, attachment is a platitude plagued with problems. What is needed for each child is a comprehensive plan on the micro, mezzo, and macro levels that looks beyond this singular and possibly unachievable outcome. The search for attachment does not get children, parents, or caseworkers to the needed answers to overcome child abuse and neglect histories nor improve the outcomes for the children in foster care. (For a thoughtful view of child placement, we suggest reading Whittaker and Mallucio's [2002] reflections.)

We also suggest that when attachment difficulty is brought forth as a primary issue for child welfare, social workers should consider the following:

1. Every attempt should be made to avoid infant determinism. This view condemns maltreated children to a path littered with negative assumptions and dismal outcomes, and it does not allow for seeing a child as a person with strengths or as resilient. Moreover, the policy ramifications of infant determinism must be recognized. As Gladwell cautions, "infant determinism doesn't just encourage the wrong kind of policy, ultimately it undermines the basis of social policy. Why bother spending money trying to help older children or adults if the patterns of a lifetime are already, irremediably in place?" (2000:86).

2. We acknowledge that children in the foster care system have behavioral problems. We also acknowledge that there is significant importance in a parent-child bond. However, the diagnosis of Reactive Attachment Disorder comes with a stigma similar to that attached to adults who are given the diagnosis of personality disorder. Therefore, considering the gravity of this diagnosis, we suggest that children have the right to a second opinion. Chaffin et al. suggest caution about the "allure of rare disorders in child maltreatment" (2006:86). According to the *Diagnostic and Statistical Manual IV R* (American Psychiatric Association 2000:129), the prevalence of RAD "is uncommon." Further, Chaffin et al. argue that professionals engaged in making these assessment must have "expertise in differential diagnosis and child development" to ensure an accurate diagnosis and possible treatment. In addition, Chaffin et al. note that "claims of exclusive treatment [i.e., attachment treatment is the only means to successful outcome] should never be made," and benefits of attachment treatments should not be claimed without scientific evidence. Finally, we view some attachment treatment as "unorthodox" and advise those who practice in this area to seriously consider the ethical implications of such practices (see Reamer 2006).

3. Workers should consider how attachment is tied into issues of race and class. The workers may see a problem as existing in the parent-child relationship, whereas it may actually be an issue of lack of progressive policy. As Roberts points out in her book, *Shattered Bonds: The Color of Child Welfare*, "the ingredients for a strong child welfare program are clear and simple. First, reduce family poverty by increasing the minimum wage, instituting a guaranteed income, and enacting aggressive job polices; second, establish a system of national health insurance that covers everyone; third, provide high quality subsidized child care, preschool education and parental leaves for all families. Increasing the supply of affordable housing is also critical" (2002:268).

4. We encourage social workers to look at the outcomes of youth who age out of the foster care system (Courtney and Hughes 2003; Pecora et al. 2006; Shirk and Strangler 2004). What are the significant changes that need to occur in foster children's lives to ameliorate the familial, economic, and social barriers that the youth will face upon reaching adulthood? Child welfare workers cannot enforce familial attachments, but they can have an impact on the child's education and health by maintaining those community attachments throughout the search and procurement of a permanent placement. For example, as Stein notes, "young people who have had several placements can achieve educational success if they remain in the same school—and this meant that they were able to maintain friendships and have contacts with helpful teachers" (2006:429).

5. Finally, we encourage workers to avoid seeing factors in a vacuum, and instead embrace social work's mission and guiding principles. Child welfare works best when the system is seen as integrated. A positive child–adult attachment can help a child in a disorganized neighborhood; a strong community can mediate the effects of poor parenting and child maltreatment; and a major investment in child- and family-friendly social policy acts not only as a shield from risk but as a fulcrum toward positive lifetime outcomes. Our current increasing trend to use attachment theory and treatment as a singular mechanism of intervention does not move us toward success.

QUESTIONS FOR DISCUSSION

1. To what extent do notions of "attachment" affect your life and your practice? Who speaks or writes about these concepts? To what audiences? To what effect? How do concepts of attachment, both implicit and explicit, shape your practice with children and youth?

2. What repercussions do you see in your own practice from the intersection of AFSA (which demands that children are protected from abuse and neglect) and PRWORA, the 1996 federal welfare act (which demands that caretakers participate fully in the labor market)?

3. What factors contribute to making "attachment" such a significant construct in child welfare practice at this particular historical juncture?

4. What aspects of the current social structure make reciprocal relationships between children and their caregivers especially vulnerable? What are the race- and class-based dimensions of this vulnerability?

5. Ghenie and Wellenstein suggest that we resist stripping away the context of children's problems to the point that "attachment disorder" is a diagnosis that belongs to an individual child. In your work, what actions have you taken to help place a child's predicament in a larger social context? What steps can you imagine taking?

REFERENCES

Adams, R., L. Dominelli, and M. Mayne. (2005). *Social work futures: Crossing boundaries and transforming practice.* New York: Palgrave Macmillan.

Adoption and Safe Families Act of 1997. P.L. 105–89

Ainsworth, M. D. (1967). *Infancy in Uganda: Infant care and the growth of love.* Baltimore: Johns Hopkins University Press.

Ainsworth, M. D., M. C. Blehar, E. Waters, and S. Wall. (1978). *Patterns of attachment: Psychological study of the strange situation.* Hillsdale, N.J.: Lawrence Erlbaum.

Albelda, R., and A. Withorn. (2002). Introduction. In R. Albelda and A. Withorn, eds. *Lost ground: Welfare reform, poverty and beyond,* 1–7. Cambridge, Mass.: South End Press.

American Psychiatric Association (2000). *Diagnostic and statistical manual of mental disorders.* 4th edition revised. Washington, D.C.: American Psychiatric Association.

Barth, R. B., T. M. Crea, K. John, J. Thoburns, and D. Quinton. (2005). Beyond attachment theory and therapy: Towards sensitive and evidence-based interventions with foster and adoptive families in distress. *Child and Family Social Work* 10: 257–68.

Bowlby, J. (1952). *Maternal care and mental health.* Geneva: World Health Organization, World Health Organization Monograph Series No. 2.

———. (1969). *Attachment and loss.* New York: Basic Books.

———. (1988). *A secure base: Parent-child attachment and healthy human development.* New York: Basic Books.

Chaffin, M., R. Hanson, B. Saunders, T. Nichols, D. Barnett, C. Zeanah, L. Berliner, B. Egeland, E. Newman, T. Lyon, E. LeTourneau, and C. Miller-Perrin. (2006). Report on the APSAC Task Force on attachment therapy, Reactive Attachment Disorder, and attachment problems. *Child Maltreatment* 11 (10): 76–89.

Courtney, M., and D. Hughes. (2003). *The transition to adulthood for youth "aging out" of the foster care system.* Chicago: Chapin Hall Center for Children at the University of Chicago.

Gladwell, M. (2000). Baby steps. *New Yorker,* January 10: 80–87.

Goldstein, J., A. Freud, A. Solnit, and S. Goldstein. (1973). *Beyond the best interests of the child.* New York: Free Press.

———. (1979). *Before the best interests of the child.* New York: Free Press.

———. (1986). *In the best interests of the child.* New York: Free Press.

Goldstein, J., A. Solnit, S. Goldstein, and A. Freud. (1996). *The best interests of the child, the least detrimental alternative.* New York: Free Press.

Grossberg, M. (2002). Changing conceptions of child welfare in the United States, 1820–1935. In M. K. Rosenheim, F. E. Zimring, D. S. Tanenhaus, and B. Dohrn, eds., *A Century of Juvenile Justice.* Chicago: University of Chicago Press.

Hacsi, T. (1996) From indenture to family foster care: A brief history of child placing. In E. P. Smith and L. A. Merkel-Holguin, eds., *A history of child welfare,* 155–73. New Brunswick, N.J.: Transaction Publishers.

Hanson, R., and E. Spratt. (2000). Reactive Attachment Disorder: What we know about the disorder and implications for treatment. *Child Maltreatment* 5 (2): 137–45.

Harlow, H. F. (1958). The nature of love. *American Psychologist, 13:* 673–85.

———. (1959). The development of affectional patterns in monkeys. In B.M Foss, ed., *Determinants of infant behavior.* London: Methuen.

Harlow, H. F., and M. K. Harlow. (1966). Social deprivation in monkeys. In M. L. Haimowitz and N. R. Haimowitz, eds., *Human Development.* New York: Thomas Y. Crowell.

Hays, S. (2003). *Flat broke with children: Women in the age of welfare reform.* New York: Oxford University Press.

Heifetz Hollinger, J., and American Bar Association on Children and the Law National Resource Center on Legal and Court Issues. (1998). *A guide to the multiethnic placement act of 1994 as amended by the interethnic adoption provisions of 1996.* Washington, D.C.: American Bar Association, Administration for Children and Families Monograph 90cw1087/01.

Hill, R. (2006). Synthesis of research on disproportionality in child welfare: An update. Seattle: Casey Family Program.

Hutchison, E. D., and L. W. Charlesworth. (2000). Securing the welfare of children: Policies past, present, and future. *Families in Society, 81* (6): 576–85.

Jansson, B. S. (2008). *Becoming an effective policy advocate: From policy practice to social justice.* 5th edition. Pacific Grove, Calif.: Thompson Brooks/Cole.

Jones, B. J. (1995). *The Indian Child Welfare Act handbook: A legal guide to the custody and adoption of Native American children.* Chicago: Section of Family Law, American Bar Association.

Kagan, J. (1998). *Three seductive ideas.* Cambridge: Harvard University Press.

Karger, H. J., and D. Stoesz. (2006). *American social welfare policy: A pluralist approach.* 5th edition. Boston: Pearson Education.

Kempe, C. H., F. N. Silverman, B. F. Steele, W. Droegemiller, and H. K. Silver. (1962). The battered child syndrome. *Journal of the American Medical Association 181:* 17–24.

Lindsey, D. (2004). *The welfare of children.* 2nd edition. New York: Oxford University Press.

McGowan, B. G. (2005). Historical evolution of child welfare services. In G. P. Mallon and P. McCartt Hess, eds., *Child welfare for the 21st century: A handbook of practices, policies and programs,* 10–45. New York: Columbia University Press.

Mass, H., and R. Engler. (1959). *Children in need of parents.* New York: Columbia University Press.

Mather, J., P. B. Lager, and N. J. Harris. (2007). *Child welfare: Policies and best practice.* Pacific Grove, Calif.: Thompson Brooks/Cole.

Maza, P. L. (2001). Confronting the dilemmas of child welfare: Past, present and future. In S. L. Hofferth and T. J. Owens, eds., *Children at the millennium: Where have we come from, where are we going?,* 303–23. New York: JAI.

Nelson, K. (1995). The child welfare response to youth violence and homelessness in the nineteenth century. In E. P. Smith and L. Merkel-Holguin, eds., *Child welfare: Journal of policy, practice and program,* 56–70. Washington, D.C.: Child Welfare League of America.

Nixon, R. (2005). Promoting youth development and independent living services for youth in foster care. In G. P. Mallon and P. McCartt Hess, eds., *Child welfare for the 21st century: A handbook of practices, policies and programs,* 573–95. New York: Columbia University Press.

Pecora, P. J., R. C. Kessler, K. O'Brien, C. Roller White, J. Williams, E. Hiripi, D. English, J. White, and M. A. Herrick. (2006). Education and employment outcomes of adults formerly placed in foster care: Results from the Northwest Foster Care Alumni Study. *Children and Youth Services Review, 28* (12): 1459–81.

Price, T. (2005). Child welfare reform. *CQ Researcher 15* (15): 345–68.

Reamer, F. G. (2006). Nontraditional and unorthodox interventions in social work: Ethical and legal implications. *Families and Society 87* (2), 191–97.

Roberts, D. (2002). *Shattered bonds: The color of child welfare.* New York: Basic Books.

————. (2006). Adoption myths and racial realities in the United States. In J. J. Trenka, J. C. Oparah, and S. Y. Shin, eds., *Outsiders within: Writing on transracial adoption,* 49–58. Cambridge, Mass.: South End Press.

Robertson, J., and J. Bowlby. (1952). Responses of young children to separation from their mothers. *Courrier Centre Internationale Enfance 2:* 131–42.

Saleebey, D. (Ed.) (2006). The strengths perspective in social work practice. 4th edition. Boston: Pearson Education.

Shireman, J. (2003). *Critical issues in child welfare.* New York: Columbia University Press.

Shirk, M., and G. Stangler. (2004). *On their own: What happens to kids when they age out of the foster care system.* New York: Basic Books.

Stahmner, A. C., L. K. Leslie, M. Hurlburt, R. Barth, M. Bruce Webb, J. Landsverk, and J. Zhang. (2005). Developmental and behavioral needs and services use for young children in child welfare. *Pediatrics* 116 (4): 891–900.

Stein, M. (2005). Young people aging out of care: The poverty of theory. *Children and Youth Services Review 28:* 422–34.

Stein, T. J. (2003). The Adoption and Safe Families Act: How Congress overlooks available data and ignores systemic obstacles in the pursuit of political goals. *Children and Youth Services Review 25* (9): 669–82.

Testa, M. F., and J. Miller. (2005). Evolution of private guardianship as a child welfare resource. In G. P. Mallon and P. McCartt Hess, eds., *Child welfare for the 21st century: A handbook of practices, policies and programs,* 405–22. New York: Columbia University Press.

U.S. Department of Health and Human Services, Administration for Children and Families, Administration on Children, Youth and Families, Children's Bureau. (1998). Program Instruction. Accessed June 8, 2006, at http://www.acf.hhs.gov/programs/cb/laws_policies/policy/pi/pi9802.htm.

Whittaker, J. K. , and A. N. Maluccio. (2002). Rethinking "child placement"; a reflective essay. *Social Services Review 3:* 109–34.

Zelizer, V. A. (1994). *Pricing the priceless child: The changing social value of children.* Princeton: Princeton University Press.

Zilberstein, K. (2006). Clarifying core characteristics of attachment disorders: A review of current research and theory. *American Journal of Orthopyschiatry 76* (1): 55–64.

Contexts and Settings | **PART II**

Childhood by Geography | **SEVEN**

Toward a Framework of Rights,
Responsibilities, and Entitlements

Jeffrey J. Shook

A consistent finding in the literature on decisions to treat juveniles as adults in the justice systems is that decision making varies substantially both across and within states (Shook 2005). Variation across states, at least in part, is the result of legislative differences regarding the jurisdiction of the juvenile court and mechanisms that exist to transfer juveniles to and sentence juveniles in the criminal justice system. These differences reflect the vague, conflicting, and inconsistent definitions of the category of "juvenile" employed by states to signify whether an individual "belongs" in the juvenile or the criminal court. Within-state variation is largely the result of differences in the interpretation of these "definitions" and the determination whether an individual "fits" into a particular legislatively defined category. Making this determination requires legal actors to engage in the active process of constructing and employing meanings regarding whether a youth has "crossed the line into adulthood." Because the categories of "juvenile" and "adult" are neither well defined nor static, and decision-making processes are subject to the influence of broader competitions over resources, power, norms, values, and ideology, the process of constructing and employing these meanings produces substantial variation across both time and space (see Bishop et al. 1989; Bishop and Frazier 1991; Singer 1996).

This type of variation has produced what I have termed in previous work "childhood by geography" (Shook 2005). Inherent in this concept is the idea proposed earlier in the book that childhood is a socially constructed category, not some universal or immutable set of characteristics, and that one's inclusion in this category (for justice system purposes) is dependent, at least in part, upon where one lives. This concept is also consistent with the broader theme woven together throughout this book that contestations and negotiations over the categorical significance and cultural parameters of childhood are ongoing across multiple sites and locations, conducted with and within a variety of symbols, beliefs, and institutions, and involve a variety of actors (including children) representing a diverse array of interests, values, and resources. As documented in previous chapters, the results of these contests and negotiations are not merely symbolic but have very real and substantial consequences for the experiences and representations of children and youth. This is particularly true with regard to treating juveniles as adults in the justice systems.

There has been, however, fairly little critical assessment of the idea of "childhood by geography" (but see Bishop 2004; Shook 2005). It is an important issue, though, because the decision to treat a juvenile as an adult reflects contests and negotiations over the category of "childhood" that occur at an important boundary, the point where and when an individual is deemed to be subject to the full retributive power of the state.[1] Because of the substantial consequences that attach to the outcomes of these contests and negotiations, the variation encompassed in the idea of childhood by geography underscores the inherent inequality and injustice in determinations regarding whether a juvenile should be and is subject to this power. Thus, the goal of the chapter is to assess the concept of childhood by geography and to use this assessment to build a framework that seeks to more fairly and equitably balance the rights, responsibilities, and entitlements of children and youth.

The chapter begins with a brief review of changes in waiver legislation and findings regarding decision making in order to establish a foundation regarding what I mean by the concept of "childhood by geography." This includes a discussion of the different definitions of the category of "juvenile," the processes through which youth are transferred to the criminal court, and the factors that influence these decisions. After establishing this foundation, I move to assess this concept in relation to discourses of citizenship. Citizenship is an emerging, although largely undefined, discourse in scholarship on childhood. I argue that it is particularly important in debates over whether juveniles should be treated as adults because it involves the principle that individuals are endowed with specific rights and that the endowment of those rights requires the attachment

of specific responsibilities. Treating juveniles as adults for justice system purposes, however, subjects a juvenile to the responsibilities of "full" citizenship
without the accompanying rights of full citizenship, revealing tremendous inconsistencies and contradictions in how we treat and regard children and youth
(Shook 2005).

Based on this critique, I then turn to discuss these inconsistencies and contradictions in relation to principles of law. In the United States, the law and legal
system are predicated on notions of fairness and equality. Thus, I examine the
question of whether and how these inconsistencies and contradictions either
violate or are justified by the law. Following this discussion, I turn to various
discourses and perspectives that have been used to address, critique, and support policies and decisions to treat juveniles as adults. In particular, I am interested in drawing from these discourses to move toward a framework that seeks
to more equitably balance considerations of rights, responsibilities, and entitlements in order to address the issue of childhood by geography.

CHILDHOOD BY GEOGRAPHY

The proliferation of legislation over the last several decades that has eased the
process of treating juveniles as adults and transformed the boundary between
the juvenile and criminal justice systems is well documented (Bishop 2000; Fagan and Zimring 2000; Feld 1999; Shook 2005; Torbet et al. 1996; Torbet and Szymanski 1998; Zimring 1998). There are two general outcomes of these legislative
changes that bear mention. First, they have lowered the minimum age at which
a juvenile is eligible to or must be treated as an adult, expanded the number
and type of offenses for which a juvenile may be treated as an adult, and shifted
criteria toward more offense-based characteristics, effectively reconstructing
the boundary between the categories of "juvenile" and "adult" by allowing or
requiring a broader population of youth to be labeled as adults. Second, they
have restructured the mechanisms that have served to police this boundary by
shifting power from judges to prosecutors and enacting alternative procedures
that allow juveniles to be treated as adults in the juvenile court. The net effect of
these changes has been to make this new boundary more porous by establishing
mechanisms that are less likely to serve as barriers to sending juveniles to the
adult criminal court or otherwise treating them as adults.[2]

Assessments of these legislative changes have resulted in a general narrative describing the juvenile court as an increasingly punitive institution as documented, in part, by the changing boundary between the juvenile and criminal

justice systems. While these assessments are important, this general narrative neglects the reality that the juvenile justice system in the United States is not a monolithic entity but consists of many different state and local systems (Tanenhaus 2002). In fact, not all of the legislative changes fit neatly into this narrative, as states have varied tremendously with regard to the type and degree of legislative change. This fact underscores the reality that definitions of the category of "juvenile" vary dramatically across states with regard to the age at which a juvenile may or must be treated as an adult, the offenses for which a juvenile may or must be treated as an adult, and the characteristics and processes that determine whether a juvenile may or must be treated as an adult.[3] What exists, then, is a situation where an individual defined as a juvenile in one state (or court) is not necessarily defined as a juvenile in another state (or court).

This reality is problematic, particularly in light of research on the consequences of treating juveniles as adults. Youth transferred to the adult system are disproportionately youth of color and poor youth and are often sentenced to adult prisons where the conditions of confinement differ considerably from juvenile institutions with regard to the programs and services youth receive, and where youth are at increased risk for abuse (Bishop 2000). Youth tried as adults emerge from the justice system with a criminal conviction that limits employment and other possibilities. Transferred youth are also more likely to recidivate, recidivate faster, and commit more serious offenses when they do recidivate, thereby increasing instead of reducing the risk to public safety (see Redding 2003). In large part, these consequences raise the possibility that variation across and within states belies the purposes for which these laws were passed and indicates a need for more regulation over decision-making processes to better ensure that the "right" juveniles as being treated as adults.

At the same time, these legislative changes reveal a fundamental shift in the categories of childhood and adolescence. While youth have been tried in the adult system since the inception of the juvenile court, the legislative changes of the last several decades have demonstrated an increased willingness to treat juveniles as adults and have challenged ideas regarding the nature of the categories of childhood and adolescence. In particular, they have rejected the notion that differences between children and adults require protected, separate, and dedicated spaces to address the needs and behaviors of children. As I briefly detail in the following pages, however, there remains tremendous ambiguity and ambivalence regarding the cultural parameters and significance of these categories, resulting in substantial variation in legal definitions and determinations regarding who deserves this protected space.

Legislative Differences in the Category of Juvenile

To understand legislative differences in the definition of the category of "juvenile," it is useful to begin with an example—the case of a 15-year-old charged with armed robbery. In Indiana, this youth is automatically excluded from the jurisdiction of the juvenile court and considered to be an adult. The same 15-year-old charged in Pennsylvania is automatically excluded from the juvenile court only if he or she committed the offense with a gun or was previously adjudicated delinquent for the same offense. Otherwise, he or she may only be transferred following a hearing and judicial determination (although there is a presumption that he or she should be transferred). In Michigan, this 15-year-old may be retained in the juvenile court, tried as an adult in the juvenile court, or tried as an adult in the criminal court based on the discretion of the prosecutor's office. The same 15-year-old in Ohio may be transferred based on the discretion of a judge following a hearing and consideration of specific criteria. In New Mexico, this youth would be retained in the juvenile court under a "youthful offender" category where he or she is subject to juvenile or adult sanctions. In Pennsylvania, the criminal court may send the 15-year-old back to the juvenile court following a hearing or keep the youth in the criminal court and sentence him or her as an adult upon conviction. Upon conviction in the criminal court for any offense in Ohio and Indiana, the youth must be sentenced as an adult, but if the youth is convicted of a lesser included offense in the criminal court in Michigan, he or she may be sentenced as a juvenile or may receive a juvenile, blended, or adult sentence if designated as an adult in the juvenile court.

As this example highlights, there are significant differences across states with regard to whether and how youth are treated as adults. Although this particular youth *may* be treated as an adult in each state, he or she is subject to markedly different outcomes and / or decision-making processes and procedures based on the state in which he or she committed the offense. In some states, this youth is automatically excluded from the juvenile court based on a legislative decision that specific characteristics (e.g., age and offense) preclude membership in the category of juvenile. In other states, he or she is initially presumed to be a juvenile and has the right to a due process hearing before the decision to treat him or her as an adult is made. In some states, conviction requires an adult sentence, whereas in others the court has a variety of options including a juvenile, adult, or blended sentence. Some states have even developed special categories (e.g., youthful offender) that carry their own specific procedures and range of potential outcomes. The net result of this legislative arrangement is that the same youth is or can be labeled differently, and that geography is a key factor in explaining these differences.

As is evident from this example, a major area of difference across states with regard to the definition of the category of juvenile is the stipulation of whether a particular youth *may* or *must* be treated as an adult. Some transfer mechanisms are discretionary in nature because they specify a group of youth who may be transferred to the criminal court and locate discretion in an individual (judge or prosecutor) to make the determination (see Shook [2005] for a more explicit discussion of different transfer mechanisms). Other provisions automatically require a juvenile to be treated as an adult by excluding certain groups of youth from the jurisdiction of the juvenile court. Thus, in Ohio the 15-year-old in the example above is presumed to be a juvenile, whereas in Indiana this youth is automatically an adult. Within this structure, states also differ with regard to the range of offenses for which a youth *may* or *must* be treated as an adult. For example, states that automatically exclude youth from the juvenile court typically do so for a relatively narrow list of violent and serious offenses. These lists vary substantially, however, representing a patchwork of different offenses and offense characteristics. In Illinois, youth aged 15 or older and charged with a violation of the substance or weapon offense acts within 1,000 feet of a school or public housing development are automatically considered to be adults, while most other states with exclusion laws do not automatically exclude youth charged with substance or weapon offenses. Variation across states with regard to the offenses for which a juvenile is eligible to be treated as an adult are not limited to exclusionary systems as there is also a tremendous amount of variation in discretionary systems. In many respects, the patchwork of offenses and offense characteristics existing in these laws reveals the tremendous ambiguity surrounding the cultural category of childhood and reflects fundamental differences in the willingness of states to protect traditional boundaries between the categories of juvenile and adult.

This ambiguity is also reflected in legislative differences regarding the age at which juveniles can be treated as adults, as states differ widely on this matter. In certain respects, age differences are fairly straightforward—states employ different minimum ages at which a youth can be treated as an adult. Some states (28) set a minimum age at which a juvenile may be treated as an adult, typically ranging from 10 to 17 years old (Griffin, Torbet, and Szymanski 1998). At the same time, many states (23) do not specify a minimum age, allowing juveniles at any age to be treated and sentenced as adults. The issue is more complicated, however, because age differences are often based on specific offenses and characteristics. For example, all juveniles charged with murder in Pennsylvania are automatically labeled as adults, whereas juveniles charged with any other crime must be at least 14 to be transferred. In Michigan, a juvenile charged with any felony offense may be tried and sentenced as an adult at any age. In Ohio, the minimum age at which a juvenile may be tried as an adult is 14 regardless of offense. Similar to differences in the offenses that make a youth eligible to be treated as an adult, differences in the age at which a juvenile may or must be treated as an adult reflect substantial ambiguity and uncertainty regarding the cultural category of childhood.

The purpose of this brief discussion was to use a few examples to illustrate the tremendous inconsistencies and contradictions in how states define the category of juvenile. As is obvious, legislative differences in the category of juvenile are quite complex and are often dependent on subsequent decisions and decision-making processes. This discussion, however, was intended to illustrate the reality that young people in the United States are increasingly required or eligible to be labeled as adults for justice system purposes and that whether or not they are labeled as adults is dependent, at least in part, on where they live. In the next section, I further highlight the importance of geography in these determinations.

Differences in Decisions to Treat a Juvenile as an Adult

The concept of "childhood by geography" refers not only to legislative differences, but also to the fact that decisions to treat juveniles as adults vary tremendously *within* states. This type of variation is the result of differences in the determination of whether a juvenile "fits" into a legislatively defined category. While this type of variation is clearly a product of discretionary systems, it also exists within exclusionary systems (Singer 1996) and is a result of the fact that decisions to treat juveniles as adults occur across a variety of decision-making points. An example of within-state variation at one decision-making point can be found in research I conducted with Rosemary Sarri in Michigan (2004). In this study, we examined four counties and found that these counties varied substantially with regard to the types of mechanisms they used to treat juveniles as adults and the type of youth they treated as adults. For example, one county utilized only the state's prosecutorial discretion transfer provision to send violent offenders to the criminal court. Further, this county utilized Michigan's designation provision as an alternative to transfer, limiting the number of youth it transferred and committed to adult prisons. The other counties regularly transferred youth through both the judicial and prosecutorial discretion provisions, and all used the designation provision in different ways—one rarely used it, one increasingly used it as an alternative to transfer, and one used it to widen the net of juveniles that were treated as adults. There was also variation over time with regard to how these counties used the transfer and designation provisions, illustrating the importance of both time and space in understanding these determinations.

Similar to other work on decisions to treat juveniles as adults (Bishop et al. 1989; Bishop and Frazier 1991; Singer 1996), we attributed this variation to a variety of contextual and organizational factors (Shook and Sarri 2004). For example, in Michigan a county must pay half the cost of sending a youth to a juvenile correctional facility (whereas it pays nothing to commit a youth to the adult prison system). Because of the high cost of these facilities, one county in our study directly attributed the increase in judicial transfers to the fact that it could not afford to pay the costs of placing these youth in juvenile facilities. Another example of one of these factors is the willingness of other actors to challenge these decisions. In one court, judges and defense attorneys were very likely to challenge transferred cases both formally and informally. These challenges were significant because prosecutors were aware of them and sought to limit them in their decision-making practices.

It is important to point out that variation in decisions to treat juveniles as adults not only occurs at the initial decision making point but is also produced during the subsequent case-processing phase. As mentioned previously, criminal court sentencing options pertaining to juveniles differ across states. Differences in sentencing options are important because they shape the degree to which the juvenile / adult label is contested and negotiated at later decision-making points. While this research generally shows that youth receive more severe sentences in the criminal compared to the juvenile court, it also shows that many youth receive relatively lenient sentences (e.g., probation) in the criminal court (Redding 2003). This has led some scholars to argue that the juvenile justice process, at least in part, is reproduced in the criminal court (Kupchick 2003; Singer, Fagan, and Liberman 2000). These findings suggest that while the decision to label a juvenile as an adult is important and sets in action a specific case-processing trajectory, this label is not necessarily static but instead is fluid and subject to contestation and negotiation in the criminal court as well. These contests and negotiations are influenced by a variety of factors, including the law, the organization of the court with regard to processing juvenile offenders, the willingness of legal actors to challenge the "adult" label, and the types of cases that enter the criminal court.

In sum, this section expanded the idea of "childhood by geography" by moving beyond differences in the legislatively defined categories of "juvenile" to include an understanding of variation in determinations regarding whether a juvenile "fits" into this category. As the discussion reveals, "place" or "space" is a central component in the production of the cultural category of childhood. The decision to treat a juvenile as an adult requires legal actors to actively construct and employ meanings of childhood. Because there is a tremendous amount of ambiguity and uncertainty surrounding this category, legal actors must draw from a variety of different organizing fields of knowledge in order to determine whether specific offense and offender characteristics indicate that a juvenile has crossed the line into adulthood. As I argued previously, these organizing fields of knowledge are likely to be as representative of "place" as they are of the individual or knowledge pertaining to the developmental state of the individual, raising important questions regarding the equity and fairness of decision making given differences in the consequences affixed to the "adult" or "juvenile" label. In the next section, I examine this idea in relation to emerging discourses of citizenship.

Citizenship

In many respects, the process of treating a juvenile as an adult expresses a fairly liberal construction of the competency, responsibility, and capacity of children and youth through the explicit determination that these youth are equally as culpable, competent, and responsible as adults. This is in direct contrast to most areas of law and policy that construct children and youth as fairly incompetent and incapable by restricting their ability to participate in social and political processes. Legal and policy regulations prohibit youth from consuming alcohol, smoking, driving, voting, entering into contracts, serving on juries, and controlling their own sexual and reproductive freedom. Further, although children and youth do possess some substantive legal rights (e.g., speech), these rights are not equal to those of adults and are subject to greater restriction. In large part, differences in the legal construction of children and youth reproduce social and cultural norms and practices that similarly construct youth as less capable, competent, and responsible, thereby excluding or regulating their participation in many aspects of civic, social, cultural, and political life.

It is quite clear from this brief discussion that while treating juveniles as adults in the justice system subjects them to the full responsibility of citizenship, children and youth do not receive the benefits of full citizenship in the United States with regard to political or social processes. For example, they may lose the right to vote (felony disenfranchisement) before ever gaining it. This example is particularly important because the right to vote is the primary means through which individuals can participate in the laws that establish and regulate justice system processes. Discourses of citizenship are increasingly emerging in scholarship on children and youth, largely flowing from the United Nations Convention on the Rights of the Child (CRC). This document has been read by many as extending a form of "citizenship" to children through its provision of rights, privileges, and protections (Invernizzi and Milne 2005). While not necessarily extending "full" citizenship to children and youth (Milne 2005), it endows them with specific rights and protections not otherwise available and raises a multitude of questions regarding the extent and effects of this form of citizenship.

My interest in invoking notions of "citizenship" in this context, however, is much narrower than the broad scope of inquiry these questions suggest. I am not necessarily interested in arguing for an extension of "full" citizenship to children and youth, or in discussing the specific form of citizenship inherent in the CRC or other emerging discourses. Instead, I am interested in the contradictions apparent between the denial of full citizenship for equal participation in society and the reality that treating juveniles as adults explicitly labels them as full citizens for retributive purposes. The nature of punishment presupposes the idea of good and bad citizens (Milne 2005). Those who are good citizens continue to receive all the rights attached to this status, while those who deviate from the status of good citizen can experience restrictions on their rights. This understanding is consistent with scholarship that argues that the U.S. criminal justice system is based on a retributive theory of punishment, whereby laws represent a social contract among citizens to control their individual desires and interests in order to produce a "mutually respecting community of citizens" (Young 1994:38–39). An offender has thus violated this contract and deserves to be punished, yet this approach is based on the notion of a society of equals (Murphy 1979, as cited in Young 1994). "A retributive justification only works morally to legitimate punishment if those subject to punishment are indeed equal citizens who receive the social benefits which oblige them to obey the rules in return" (Young 1994:39).

Because treating a juvenile as an adult is largely about retribution—"do adult crime and receive adult time"—the reality that juveniles are not equal citizens raises important moral and philosophical questions. Given that young people in the United States do not enjoy the rights of full citizenship, largely because they are viewed as incompetent or incapable actors, is it fair and just to hold them to the responsibilities of full citizenship? If so, for what reasons and how should the decision-making process be organized and regulated? These questions require attention to the moral and philosophical inconsistencies and contradictions inherent in the practice of treating juveniles as adults. They also require consideration of the reality of the experiences of childhood for a large population of children and youth. In the United States, children and youth are not guaranteed basic entitlements and supports that will help them become "successful" adults. For example, poverty rates among children are extremely high in the United States, particularly for children of color, and symbolize the problematic conditions in which many individuals experience their "childhood." Further, educational disparities continue to persist despite the continued, and growing, recognition of the importance of education for a number of life outcomes.

Although approaches like the CRC seek to address these gaps by providing access to entitlements and supports, the United States is one of only two countries that have not ratified the convention. Because the proliferation of legislation that has eased the process of treating juveniles as adults was largely reactionary in nature, the experiences of childhood faced by many children were not considered, and the approach to violent, serious, and chronic juvenile crime largely centered on retributive policies and practices. When viewed in this light, addressing the inequalities and unfairness inherent in the reality of childhood by geography is even more essential because of the arbitrariness of these policies and practices. Thus, there is a need to return to questions of rights, responsibilities, and entitlements in rethinking policy and practices toward children and youth, particularly those that seek to punish youth in a manner similar to adults. In the next section, I examine childhood by geography in relation to fundamental legal principles in order to further justify the need for this framework.

CHILDHOOD BY GEOGRAPHY AND THE LAW

Despite the inherent inconsistencies and contradictions that exist in the concept of childhood by geography and notions of citizenship, these realities are largely justified in U.S. law. A primary justification for "childhood by geography" is the principle of federalism. Federalism refers to the relationship and authority divided among different levels of government. In the United States, the Constitution grants specific powers to the federal government. The Tenth Amendment expressly states that "The powers not delegated to the United States by the Constitution, nor prohibited by it to the States, are reserved to the States respectively, or to the people." This clause establishes the federalist form of government practiced in the United States, where power is shared between the federal and state governments. In areas where power is not explicitly granted to the federal government through the Constitution, the federal government has two primary mechanisms to influence state policy and practice. The first is by attaching funding to the requirement that a state follow federal legislation and regulations. The second is through a broad interpretation of the Commerce Clause granting Congress the power to regulate interstate commerce.

Federalism is important, then, because it establishes the authority of states to regulate many areas of social life, including the power to punish. Thus, states have substantial power to create, organize, and regulate criminal and juvenile justice systems by establishing jurisdictional boundaries, requiring specific procedures and processes, and mandating punishments. The reality of "childhood by geography," then, is justified, in large part, by the inherent power of states established through the federalist form of government. This power is not absolute, however, as it is constrained by federal and state constitutions. For example, specific amendments included in the Bill of Rights have been interpreted as limiting the power of the state to search homes and automobiles, to require the appointment of an attorney, and to provide restrictions on executions. These are rights endowed to individuals and provide specific protections in interactions with state actors or institutions. Outside of these limited protections, states have broad authority to regulate and administer their criminal and juvenile justice systems. The reality of this arrangement is that these systems are allowed to and do vary substantially.

Important in this discussion is the fact that children and youth do not have a "substantive" right to be treated as a "juvenile." Substantive or fundamental rights are derived from state and federal constitutions and may only be infringed upon by the state in limited situations. Examples of substantive or fundamental rights include the right to free speech or to vote provided specifically by the Constitution, or the right to privacy derived from the Supreme Court's interpretation of the Fourteenth Amendment's Due Process Clause. The U.S. Constitution, however, does not grant a right to be treated as a "juvenile" because the juvenile justice system is a statutory creation. Similarly, most state constitutions do not grant a right to be treated as a juvenile. Thus, states may establish and regulate the boundaries between the juvenile and criminal justice systems with little legal justification or regulation. In essence, they are free to define the category of juvenile and decide what characteristics make one deserving of this label.

Although the previous discussion provides a justification for variation in the category of juvenile across states, it does not address within state variation or the fact that states prescribe different rights responsibilities and privileges based on age. The former issue is important because while legal justifications clearly exist for variation across states, within-state variation seemingly offends notions of fairness and equality because it means that the same law is being applied differently. Challenges on this basis—equal-protection challenges—are limited in their effect because "age" is not a protected category, and classifications based on age are subject to only a minimum level of review. While there have been some differences in how courts have dealt with this issue, equal-protection arguments have generally failed to overturn transfer statutes.[4] The same principle justifies the inconsistencies and contradictions in the rights, responsibilities, and privileges of children and youth. Because age is not a protected category, the state may create classifications based on age as long as they are "reasonably related to legitimate state interests." Given that children and youth are socially and culturally constructed as being incompetent and incapable, it is not surprising that the state can easily regulate the degree to which they may be denied the full privileges and rights of adulthood. Further, because review pertains to the specific regulation and state interest, courts do not often necessarily engage in a more systematic review of the contradictions and inconsistencies in the allotment of rights, responsibilities, and entitlements.

Juvenile Death Penalty

The recent Supreme Court decision regarding the death penalty for juveniles is instructive for understanding legal issues surrounding the punishment of children.[5] This case was based on fairly narrow legal grounds—the Eighth Amendment's Cruel and Unusual Punishment Clause—and does not directly apply to the issue of "childhood by geography." The Court's analysis, however, extended beyond the Eighth Amendment's "evolving standards of decency" test and included the Court's own judgment regarding the execution of children. The Court based its abolition of the death penalty for juveniles, in part, on developmental psychology research and emerging research regarding brain development. In particular, the Court held that this research justified differential treatment for children and youth based on the idea that juveniles are less culpable than adults.

Interestingly, the Court also based its decision on notions of citizenship and international law. Arguing that children and youth are denied many of the rights of citizenship, the Court held that they should not be subject to the full retributive power of the state. Further, the Court reasoned that although international law, particularly human rights standards and the Convention on the Rights of the Child, does not directly apply in the United States, it can provide some guidance in examining the issue of the juvenile death penalty. In particular, the Court relied on the fact that the full weight of international law and opinion is against the execution of juveniles. Although this case applied directly to the death penalty, the arguments furthered by the Court provide some basis for extending human rights and citizenship arguments in considering the broader issue of "childhood by geography."

TOWARD A FRAMEWORK OF RIGHTS, RESPONSIBILITIES, AND ENTITLEMENTS

As mentioned previously, there has been relatively little critical assessment of the reality that geography plays such a significant role in decisions to treat juveniles as adults. This lack of attention is problematic for several reasons. First, tremendous consequences attach to this decision, including long prison sentences, increased risk of harm, lack of access to necessary programs and services, the negative impact of a criminal record, and higher rates of recidivism, to name a few. Given these consequences, the prominent role that characteristics of "place" play in the decision raise important questions regarding both the fairness and efficiency of existing decision-making processes and thus require a re-examination of these policies and practices. Second, despite the inherent unfairness of childhood by geography, it is largely justified by the law. Although there is tremendous ambiguity and ambivalence surrounding childhood—and a primary theme of this text is that it has undergone a significant transformation in light of changing political, economic, and cultural conditions—childhood remains an important, and many would argue essential, cultural category. Thus, while there is a need for a vigorous debate regarding the parameters and significance of the cultural category of childhood, there remains a need to recognize this category in the law and provide necessary protections to guard against the relative arbitrariness in decisions to treat juveniles as adults.

Third, the reality that youth can be treated as adults, and that decisions to do so are substantially influenced by a variety of political, economic, cultural, organizational, and contextual contingencies, is inconsistent with existing social, legal, and cultural regulations that limit the extent to which young people are allowed to participate as full citizens in society. The contradictions and unfairness existing in this arrangement are substantial and undercut the very legitimacy of this practice. Consequently, there is a need to assess these considerations in both policy and decision-making processes. Because the proliferation of legislative changes that eased the process of treating juveniles as adults was largely retributive in nature, many of these issues were not considered. Addressing them, then, requires a willingness to engage in debates and discussions regarding the issue of treating juveniles as adults and the recognition that these debates must be grounded in empirical knowledge on transfer, child and adolescent development, brain development, treatment and rehabilitation programs, conditions of confinement, the law, and legal and decision-making processes.

At the same time, it is important to recognize that these are not merely empirical questions, but also involve moral or philosophical considerations that require attention to meaning, power, history, context, and possibility (see Finn, this volume). Consequently, there is a need for the development of a framework that seeks to balance considerations of rights, responsibilities, and entitlements to provide guidance for the creation of policies and practices that increase the likelihood that youth are treated equitably and fairly. In the remainder of this chapter, I discuss discourses on the issue of treating juveniles as adults, drawing on the strengths and limitations of these perspectives in an attempt to move toward a framework that seeks to balance considerations of rights, responsibilities, and entitlements.

Discourses of Rights, Responsibilities, and Entitlements

One of the dominant discourses arguing against prevailing trends to treat juveniles as adults is what I refer to as the "child-savers" discourse. This discourse is grounded in a long tradition of child advocacy in the United States, as well as traditional notions of the characteristics of children and youth. It centers on the widely varying and sometimes destructive conditions surrounding youth and the way that society has chosen to support and control them. A key attribute of this discourse is that children and youth are often painted as "victims" of broader failures in the social system, and their behavior is largely attributed to these failures and not to their own agency. Thus, children and youth are portrayed as objects, not as subjects engaged in the construction of the social world. An extension of the child-savers discourse points to how youth in the contemporary United States are being scapegoated for many of society's problems (Males 1999). This position argues that children and adolescents are not only the victims of society's neglect, but also blamed for the country's problems.

Despite its resonance with traditional notions of childhood, one of the key limitations of the child-savers discourse is its focus on children and youth as objects (e.g., passive, dependent, victims). This limitation is significant because it enables what I term the "superpredator" discourse. Similar to the child-savers discourse, the superpredator discourse grounds understandings of childhood in traditional notions of "innocence" and "passivity" and asserts that individuals who commit violent and serious crimes are not acting like "children" but instead are exhibiting agency and, therefore, "adult" characteristics. A key difference here is that these behaviors are not explained through failures of the broader social system, but through the idea that they reveal that the individual is something "other" than a child. Because the child is often defined in relation to the adult, the conclusion is that these individuals should be treated as adults. Consequently, this discourse resonates with many people because it allows society to retain traditional ideals about the nature of childhood and further reinforces these ideas through policies and practices that treat juveniles as adults.

Although producing different consequences, these discourses share a major weakness—that they are grounded in notions of the child as an object. Taken to their extreme, violent and serious crime become something that is either not the "fault" of the individual or identifies the individual as something other than a child. Thus, scholars have sought additional perspectives to provide guidance on the issue of treating juveniles as adults. One important discourse finds its roots in developmental psychology and is based on the idea that childhood and adolescence is a period when individuals are in the process of going through specific stages that include physical, biological, cognitive, motor, and moral development. Because they have not completed these stages, measurable differences should exist between children and adults, and these differences should guide how we treat juveniles. An important part of this perspective is that as children age they become less distinguishable from adults and, consequently, should be subject to higher degrees of punishment and accountability. Advocates of this perspective thus feel that it can be used to inform juvenile and criminal justice policies.

The developmental discourse has been advanced by emerging research on adolescent brain development. The key findings from this research have shown that the brain continues to develop throughout late adolescence and into early adulthood. In particular, it posits that the main area of development occurs in the prefrontal cortex, the part of the brain that controls decision making and impulse control (Goldberg 2001). These findings are consistent with research that has found that adolescents are highly susceptible to peer influences and exhibit poor planning and judgment skills. In large part, this research supports contentions that youth are less culpable or blameworthy than adults and therefore should be punished less severely than adults.

Although this perspective provides useful evidence regarding child and adolescent development, it is not without its limitations in informing policy and practice. Some of these limitations stem from the difficulties of measuring and articulating differences between "children" and "adults" that can be used to reliably inform policy and practice. More important, however, these limitations stem from the reality that this approach does not account for the socially constructed nature of childhood and adolescence and the contradictions and inconsistencies inherent in the representations and experiences of children and youth.

Zimring (1982) sought to deal with some of these dilemmas through his conception of adolescence as a "learner's permit." Informed by developmental psychology, he argues that adolescence is a period of "learning" and that there is a need to balance rights, responsibilities, and entitlements both to protect youth and to give them an opportunity to gain needed experiences. For example, he argues that the age of full criminal responsibility should be pushed back so that youth are not held fully responsible for the mistakes that they make during this process of learning. Further, he argues that youth should be given more opportunities to make their own choices and provided with necessary supports such as access to education and training. Because this approach is considered unrealistic in the current political and social environments, Zimring (2000) argues for the necessity of waiver and asserts that it should be used only when the level of punishment in the adult system is greater than that available in the juvenile justice system.

Given the realities of the current political and cultural environment, another perspective asserts that the only way to fully protect children and youth is to provide them with the "rights" of adulthood. Similar to the "child-savers" discourse, the rights-based discourse starts from the premise that children are failed by the existing social system. Instead of locating the solution in the protection of youth, however, this discourse asserts that children and youth will only be protected if they are endowed with rights equal to those of adults. Advocates of the rights-based discourse extend their arguments beyond the justice systems to endow a broader set of rights in interactions with a variety of actors and institutions, including parents. Despite the fact that this discourse addresses issues of citizenship, and, at least in some respects, the reality of childhood by geography, it has largely been dismissed by scholars who recognize the need to create a protected space for children and youth.

A final perspective relevant to this discussion is the human rights discourse. As discussed previously, the human rights discourse draws from international conventions and standards to delineate a set of rights, entitlements, and responsibilities for children and youth that fills the gap left by many social, cultural, and legal systems. In many ways, this perspective draws from a variety of the other discourses. While it is not without criticism, the human rights discourse serves as an important foundation for recognizing and advancing the interests of children and youth and a useful analytical tool to assess the experiences of youth. For example, Sarri and Shook (2005) used this perspective to examine juvenile justice administration and found many instances where the system was violating or falling short of human rights standards and conventions. Although it offers a great deal of promise in addressing broader issues of rights, responsibilities, and entitlements, the human rights discourse does not fully address the issue of childhood by geography and, as discussed previously, does not necessarily define young people as full citizens. Thus, there remains a need to develop a framework to guide policy and practice.

Rethinking Rights, Responsibilities, and Entitlements

The task of developing a "framework" that balances considerations of rights, responsibilities, and entitlements is a substantial one. This chapter has, at the very least, achieved the more modest goal of critically analyzing the reality of "childhood by geography" and promoting debate, discussion, and action toward developing and enacting such a framework. The purpose of such a framework would be to guide policy and practice with regard to treating juveniles as adults. The need for such a framework is clear, I assert, because of the need to both protect and re-envision the cultural category of childhood. In large part, the outline for such a framework already exists in the various discourses I referred to in the previous section. I now draw on these discourses to delineate this outline in the remainder of the chapter.

This framework must begin with a consideration of rights. Childhood, despite its social and cultural significance, carries very few distinct or special rights. Instead, the various meanings attributed to this category have justified the denial of rights and privileges, not their extension. Consequently, a starting point in developing a framework is the need to articulate specific rights. Although controversial, given the experiences of many children in the United States it is a necessary endeavor. A substantial amount of this work has been done by the Convention on the Rights of the Child. The CRC has extended rights to children and youth and designated responsibilities to states that address issues such as needs, culture, health, education, and welfare.

The CRC also addresses justice system processes with regard to children, and while it does not specifically grant the right to be treated as a "juvenile," it has been read in conjunction with other international standards and rules to provide this right (Sarri and Shook 2005). This is an important starting point because, as discussed previously, children do not have the substantive right to be treated as juveniles under U.S. law. Recognizing and extending this right is central to a framework balancing the rights, responsibilities, and entitlements of children and youth because it would grant the juvenile court jurisdiction over a young person, create a presumption that this person belongs in the juvenile court, and require certain processes and procedures to be followed to transfer this person to the criminal court. Extending this right would begin to address the issue of childhood by geography by requiring that youth be, at least initially, defined as juveniles for justice system purposes.

A primary justification for extending this right is the notion of citizenship raised earlier. Given that young people are not granted legal or social rights to full citizenship, there is substantial justification that they should retain the right to be treated as juveniles in the justice systems and that this right should be vigorously protected. Another justification for extending this right is that it is consistent with the bulk of empirical knowledge pertaining to the issue of treating juveniles as adults, which shows that these policies and practices have substantial consequences for youth, the public, and the justice systems. In addition, research on adolescent development and, in particular, emerging research on adolescent brain development is also consistent with this position, thereby providing substantial justification for extending this right.

While a strong case can be made for recognizing and extending the right to be treated as a juvenile, important questions remain regarding what processes will exist, if any, for transferring juveniles to the criminal court. Although he has argued to limit waiver, Zimring (2000) has made a case regarding the "punitive necessity" of waiver. Further, as Bergmann (this volume) notes, a focus on rights can lead to unintended consequences. Consequently, there is a need to consider the extent to which juveniles can be transferred to the criminal justice system and the processes that will be put in place to protect against arbitrary and capricious decisions.

Although this is a debate and discussion that requires space well beyond that allotted to this chapter, I offer some recommendations in this direction. One is that the articulation of the "right" to be treated as a juvenile must be meaningful and requires a stringent standard and system of review. The purpose of transfer must also be well articulated and limited in scope in order to guide decision making, and standards need to be well defined. The decision-making process must be well regulated, granting discretion to a "neutral" actor, and take into consideration a sufficient amount of information regarding the individual, not just the act. Further, the right to be treated as a juvenile should extend to the age of 18, as this age is consistent with the vast majority of states, principles of citizenship, and the Supreme Court's decision in *Roper v. Simmons.*

The next consideration in developing such a framework involves responsibilities. The idea of responsibility has several dimensions—the responsibility of the individual juvenile in the commission of the act and the responsibility of society for the care and upbringing of children and youth. Zimring's (2000) argument that transfer should be limited to situations where the punishment available in the criminal court exceeds that available in the juvenile court neglects an important principle underlying the juvenile court—the idea that juveniles are less culpable or responsible than adults, and, therefore, that they are deserving of less punishment. As noted previously, this principle was recently reaffirmed in the *Roper* decision based on its consideration of various arguments regarding the culpability of youth. Assessments of responsibility, then, require attention to this principle and the articulation of guidelines detailing the range and limits of punishment for young people. These guidelines must consider research on adolescent development and brain development and reflect the reality that legal and social regulations largely prohibit youth from full participation in society based on the premise that they are not considered competent or responsible enough for the privileges of full citizenship.

Using these guidelines, assessments of responsibility can better balance the degree of punishment available in the juvenile and criminal justice systems. Such assessments should reflect the fact that the juvenile court does provide significant punishments for youth. In fact, legislative changes over the last several decades have not only eased the process through which juveniles can be treated as adults but have increased the type and degree of punishment that juvenile courts can enact. Thus, many nontransferred youth are subject to sanctions that are similar to, if not more restrictive in some cases than, those available in the criminal court. At the same time, it should also reflect the fact that there are marked differences between the juvenile and criminal justice systems, differences that, according to research on recidivism, appear to have an important bearing on the subsequent behavior of young people.

Assessments of responsibility should also reflect a second dimension—the responsibility of society for the care of children and youth. This aspect of responsibility is consistent with the last component of this framework—entitlements. Because children and youth are largely considered to be dependent on others for their care and support, their behavior and development must be viewed in conjunction with the degree that society has actually assumed and fulfilled this role. It is clear, however, that many children have been failed by society and have not received the necessary care, support, and protection. Consequently, attention must be paid to how society has fulfilled its role in providing sufficient care in assessments of responsibility. This requires attention to issues regarding the entitlements, or rights, provided to children and youth. As mentioned previously, the CRC has provided a substantial list of entitlements and rights that includes issues such as housing, health care, nutrition, and education. U.S. ratification of the CRC would begin the process of building and strengthening this list so that decisions to treat juveniles as adults focus not only on the responsibility of the individual youth, but also on the extent to which society upheld its responsibility for caring for the particular youth in question.

Eliminating variation in discretionary systems is a nearly impossible task. The goal of this chapter was to problematize the tremendous variation that exists in determinations to treat juveniles as adults and to argue that this variation is especially troubling in light of the need to create a protected space for children and youth. In moving toward a framework of rights, responsibilities, and entitlements, my aim was to begin a discussion regarding how this variation—essentially childhood by geography—can be reduced. I offer this framework as a starting point for a more vigorous and nuanced discussion that considers the empirical, as well as moral and philosophical, basis for these policies and practices.

QUESTIONS FOR DISCUSSION

1. What knowledge do you have of the ways that childhood varies by geography? What accounts for your knowledge (or lack of knowledge) of this variation? Should the social work profession challenge variation in the idea of childhood by geography? Why or why not?

2. Is citizenship an important consideration in thinking about the rights, responsibilities, and entitlements of children and youth? Why or why not? What does it mean to include considerations of citizenship in discussions of policy and practice?

3. What are the pros and cons of bright line rules (e.g., all youth under a certain age must be treated as a juvenile) compared to discretionary systems (e.g., individuals make case-by-case determinations regarding who should be treated as a juvenile)? Can discretionary systems be developed that will limit the variation identified in this chapter? If so, how?

4. Should childhood represent a protected space, as suggested in this chapter? If so, what should this space look like? Who should be included in it? Should it include violent and serious juvenile offenders?

5. Do you agree that there is a need for a "framework" that seeks to limit "childhood by geography"? What else needs to be added to this "framework" so that it truly balances the rights, responsibilities, and entitlements of children and youth?

NOTES

1. In 2005 the U.S. Supreme Court held that juveniles could not be executed. Thus, youth are no longer subject to the full retributive powers of the state. They are, however, still subject to very long prison sentences, including life without the opportunity for parole.

2. Bishop (2000) provides an extensive discussion of the consequences of these legislative changes. Specifically, she argues that there has been an increase in the number of juveniles treated as adults, especially when viewed in light of decreases in violent and serious juvenile crime.

3. Definitions in the category of juvenile not only pertain to transfer but also involve the upper age of jurisdiction for the juvenile court. While 37 states and the District of Columbia allow juvenile court jurisdiction until age 18, 10 states limit juvenile court jurisdiction to individuals under the age of 17, and 3 limit it to individuals under the age of 16. Connecticut recently based legislation that will extend juvenile court jurisdiction to age 18. This legislation will go into effect in 2010.

4. See Frost Clausel and Bonnie (2000) for a discussion of appellate cases regarding juvenile waiver.

5. *Roper v. Simmons*, 543 U.S. 551 (2005).

REFERENCES

Bishop, D. M. (2000). Juvenile offenders in the adult criminal justice system." In M. Tonry, ed., *Crime and Justice: A Review of Research.* Chicago: University of Chicago Press.

———. (2004). Injustice and irrationality in contemporary youth policy. *Criminology and Public Policy 3:* 633–44.

Bishop, D. M., and C. E. Frazier. (1991). Transfer of juveniles to criminal court: A case study and analysis of prosecutorial waiver. *Notre Dame Journal of Law, Ethics and Public Policy 5:* 281–302.

Bishop, D. M., C. E. Frazier, and J. C. Henretta. (1989). Prosecutorial waiver: Case study of a questionable reform. *Crime and Delinquency 35:* 179–201.

Fagan, J., and F. E. Zimring (2000). *The changing borders of juvenile justice: Transfer of adolescents to the criminal court.* Chicago: University of Chicago Press.

Feld, B. C. (1999). *Bad kids: Race and the transformation of the juvenile court.* New York: Oxford University Press.

Frost Clausel, L. E., and R. J. Bonnie. (2000.) Juvenile justice on appeal. In J. Fagan and F. E. Zimring, eds., *The changing borders of juvenile justice: Transfer of adolescents to the criminal court.* Chicago: University of Chicago Press.

Goldberg, E. (2001). *The executive brain: Frontal lobes and the civilized mind.* Oxford: Oxford University Press.

Griffin, P., P. Torbet, and L. Szymanski. (1998). Trying juveniles as adults in criminal court: An analysis of state transfer provisions. Washington, D.C.: U.S. Department of Justice, Office of Juvenile Justice and Delinquency Prevention.

Invernizzi, A., and B. Milne. (2005). Children's citizenship: A new discourse? *Journal of Social Sciences 9:* 1–6.

Kupchik, A. (2003). Prosecuting juveniles in criminal court: Juvenile or criminal justice? *Social Problems 50:* 439–60.

Males, M.A. (1999). *Framing youth: 10 myths about the next generation.* Monroe, Maine: Common Courage Press.

Milne, B. (2005). Is "participation" as it is described by the United Nations Convention on the Rights of the Child (UNCRC) the key to children's citizenship? *Journal of Social Sciences 9:* 31–42.

Redding, R. (2003). The effects of adjudicating and sentencing juveniles as adults: Research and policy implications. *Youth Violence and Juvenile Justice 1:* 128–55.

Sarri, R.C., and J. J. Shook. (2005). Juvenile justice in the United States: Adherence to human rights conventions. In L. Majka and M. Ensalaco, eds., *Children's Human Rights: Progress and Challenges.* Rowman and Littlefield.

Shook, J.J. (2005). Contesting childhood in the U.S. justice system: The transfer of juveniles to the adult criminal court. *Childhood: A Global Journal of Child Research 12:* 461–78.

Shook, J.J., and R. C. Sarri. (2004). *Treating juveniles as adults.* Report prepared for the Workgroup on Juvenile Waiver. Ann Arbor, Mich.: Institute for Social Research.

Singer, S.I. (1996). *Recriminalizing delinquency: Violent juvenile crime and juvenile justice reform.* Cambridge: Cambridge University Press.

Singer, S.I., J. Fagan, and A. Liberman. (2000). The reproduction of juvenile justice: A case study of New York's juvenile offender law. In J. Fagan and F.E. Zimring, eds., *The changing borders of juvenile justice: Transfer of adolescents to the criminal court.* Chicago: University of Chicago Press.

Tanenhaus, D.S. (2002). The evolution of juvenile courts in the early twentieth century: Beyond the myth of immaculate conception. In M.K. Rosenheim, F.E. Zimring, D.S. Tanenhaus, and B. Dohrn, eds., *A century of juvenile justice.* Chicago: University of Chicago Press.

Torbet, P., R. Gable, H. Hurst, I. Montgomery, L. Szymanski, and D. Thomas. (1996). *State response to serious and violent juvenile crime: Research report.* Washington, D.C.: U.S. Department of Justice, Office of Juvenile Justice and Delinquency Prevention.

Torbet, P., and L. Szymanski, L. (1998). *State legislative responses to violent juvenile crime:*

1996–97 update. Washington, D.C.: U.S. Department of Justice, Office of Juvenile Justice and Delinquency Prevention.

Young, I. M. (1994). Punishment, treatment, empowerment: Three approaches to policy for pregnant addicts. *Feminist Studies 20* (1): 33–57.

Zimring, F.E. (1982). *The changing legal world of adolescence.* New York: Free Press.

———. (1998). *American youth violence.* New York: Oxford University Press.

———. (2000.) The punitive necessity of waiver. In J. Fagan and F.E. Zimring, eds., *The changing borders of juvenile justice: Transfer of adolescents to the criminal court.* Chicago: University of Chicago Press.

From "Youth Home" to
"Juvenile Detention"

EIGHT

Constructing Disciplined Children in Detroit

Luke Bergmann

In June 1996 Wayne County's executive officer, Ed McNamera, attended the cer-
emonial groundbreaking for construction of a new Juvenile Detention Facility
in downtown Detroit. The event was accompanied by the usual accoutrements:
a vacant lot, loosened dirt, hard hats, ribbons, scissors, and not a small dose of
congratulatory rhetoric. Any public works project of this magnitude, after all,
would require considerable and coordinated political and organizational work.
And indeed, it was an event long in the making, and marked the conclusion of
years of wrangling among multiple municipal, corporate, and residential fac-
tions within Wayne County and the Detroit metropolitan area.

Of course, it is hardly unusual for any major building venture to become
mired in a swirl of competing interests and logistical conflicts. At stake here,
however, were not just concerns over building dimensions and easements. In
this case, at the heart of negotiations of the proposed building project, and influencing decisions about its location, dimensions, and function, were key concerns
around which this volume is oriented: the cultural nature of childhood and adulthood, and their relationship to the welfare state and governmental apparatuses.

When he took the microphone to talk to the assembled stakeholders and
members of the press, Mr. McNamera declared that the new facility for housing

young people suspected of criminal offense would be a "symbol of rehabilita-tion." This was a loaded notion, the multiple meanings of which the county executive may have been scarcely aware. His remark seemed to reference both the rehabilitation of kids who are locked up and the rehabilitation of the city's profoundly dilapidated downtown. Perhaps most important, his comment was evocative of the county's efforts to rehabilitate its credibility as a governing body capable of taking appropriate care of children. An additional question would remain: what kind of care (or supervision or surveillance) should this be?

Embedded in decisions about the construction of the new facility—from its location to its architectural design—were conflicting cultural frames of refer-ence concerning the nature of childhood. Indeed, in a climate shaped by shifting political and cultural sensibilities about crime and punishment, as sentencing guidelines have changed and prosecutors and judges have been given (and are exercising) greater discretion in sentencing youth to the adult criminal justice system, distinctions between childhood and adulthood have attained particular urgency: Do people of a certain age merit treatment that is distinctly different than that offered to those who are older? What is it about the nature of child-hood that should afford children a different standard of care? Do young people have a special capacity for rehabilitation; should they be seen as particularly de-serving of rehabilitation?

In institutional practice, questions about the nature of childhood turn on whether the juvenile justice system should be distinct from or more closely coupled with the adult criminal justice system. Thus, in the juvenile justice system—and throughout the case study I present here—there are two compet-ing institutional frames: one oriented around the "detention" of juveniles and the other around the "treatment" of at-risk youth.

This, of course, mirrors the defining (and ever-unresolved) tension in American corrections between punishment and rehabilitation,[1] but it also re-flects a fundamental lack of clarity about the nature of childhood in contempo-rary cultural politics. It is not just that there are opposed ideologies that support "treating" or "detaining" children, and that map onto conventional political di-chotomies. Rather, discourses about the care and disciplining of children reflect deep cultural ambivalences about childhood as a cultural category and about the nature of agency, responsibility, and citizenship for young people. "Treat-ment" and "detention" are ideal ends of an ideological pole along which most political actors lie somewhere in the middle, moving in one direction or another depending upon shifting circumstances and contexts.

In the case of contemporary trends in juvenile justice, already profound tensions between treatment and detention are made more complex as they are refracted through recent emphases on the "rights of the child."[2] Particularly confounding is the manner in which an emerging discourse about the rights of children might be taken to support *both* increased treatment *and* more regulated detention for young people in the juvenile and criminal justice systems.

On one hand, if we expand the rights of citizenship for youth, we should be particularly attentive to special protections for them and to their opportunities for rehabilitation. On the other hand, the same ideological emphasis might be used to support more regulated and mechanistic treatment in justice system contexts. The regimentation and standardization of supervision, after all, would be rational tactics to guard against abuses and infringements upon the rights of young people. Indeed, the establishment of broadly conceived and standardized actionable rights for children is critically important for lawyers and policy makers in their efforts to improve the circumstances of young people under state supervision. At the same time, the standardization of care that this entails would represent a move away from the contingency-based orientation that has been at the heart of the juvenile justice system. The handling of children might then be guided less by an ethics of case-specific nurturance than by an ethics of population management and procedural equity.

So even in cases where there may be wide agreement to provide and maintain greater rights for the young, such an orientation has unclear institutional ramifications. Indeed, in the day-to-day practices of the juvenile justice system, as lawyers, judges, and other officials of the juvenile and criminal courts make decisions about how to designate young people in various circumstances and of various ages as either *juveniles* or *adults,* they are constantly maneuvering around and negotiating questions concerning the rights and responsibilities of children.

These negotiations are one of the front lines on which categorical distinctions between childhood and adulthood are socially produced, and their significance extends beyond their immediate consequences for young people facing criminal charges. Childhood and adulthood are cultural categories—like race, gender, and class—and their negotiation as institutional labels in justice system contexts engages and shapes widely held cultural assumptions. In the case that I present here, we see how key cultural concepts operate in governmental politics, in the geography of the city, and in the local community. Beyond this, we see how cultural meanings are encoded in physical settings, so that such places attain the character of what sociologists and philosophers have called "social spaces."[3] The juvenile detention facility is not only a site for the creation and re-creation of cultural understandings of childhood, but itself becomes a space invested with social meaning; as a building, its mortar and bricks constitute an important cultural object.

This chapter is based on historical and ethnographic research that I conducted over a two-year period between 1999 and 2001. Archival research consisted of reviews of news coverage of juvenile detention, court records, transcripts of zoning commission meetings, and notes from meeting participants that I acquired from the participants themselves. While doing fieldwork, I visited the Wayne County Juvenile Detention Facility most days of each week. I conducted both formal audiotaped interviews and informal conversations with young people who were locked up at the detention facility, as well as administrative and frontline staff.

TREATING, DETAINING, AND CONSTRUCTING CHILDREN: DILEMMAS IN DETROIT

Trouble at the Youth Home

In a social context characterized by conflicting ideas about the nature of childhood, the rights of children, and tensions between treatment and detention in the juvenile justice system, Wayne County's Juvenile Detention Facility emerged as a key institution, and the framing of its troubled history became critical to debates about how justice should be carried out for young people in the future.

The public record of problems at the Wayne County Youth Home—as it was officially known until 1994—recedes back into the 1960s, but there was a marked proliferation of civic and public dissatisfaction with the facility beginning in the early 1980s. In July 1981 an anonymous complaint was made to the Department of Social Services (DSS) suggesting that the facility was neither well maintained nor kept clean, and later that year the DSS made an on-site visit to the Youth Home. A letter sent from the DSS to Judge Gladys Barsamian, who was the presiding judge with the Juvenile Division of the Wayne County Probate Court, summarizes the response of the investigators: "The on-site investigation revealed that generally the Youth Home facilities are in deplorable conditions related to cleanliness, and the health and safety of residents." The report of the on-site investigator detailed numerous problems with the facility, including dirty toilets, "filthy floors," and insufficient maintenance staff.

A follow-up report, issued in late December of the same year, offers further details regarding poor conditions in the Youth Home and improper handling of inmates there.[4] Inmates from both the boys' and girls' units reported to the investigators that they were often the subjects of verbal abuse: "Boys are called 'punks,' and 'faggot,' and girls were referred to as 'tramps' along with other derogatory remarks." The report also notes that boys reported being allowed to fight on their units. The report concludes that "in general, it is evident that there is no monitoring of disciplinary measures used by staff."

For the following decade, the Youth Home failed to meet Department of Social Services standards. In 1988, amid further reports about licensing difficulties and consistent overcrowding, Wayne County voters passed a $2.5 million annual millage either to renovate the Youth Home or to build another one. But by the end of the decade, no work had been done.

Through the early 1990s, with still no progress toward a reduction in overcrowding, there was a steadily increasing cascade of negative press regarding the institution. Along with this was a proliferating sense of disquiet within civic bureaucracies and the community about the capacity of the facility's administration ever to pull the Youth Home into shape. In the summer of 1992, one of the elevators used to transport inmates to the top floors of the six-story wing malfunctioned and plunged three stories. The same summer, the state Department of Social Services withdrew its operating approval of the facility. Then, in March 1993, an abuse investigator and staff trainer at the Youth Home was fired after he had refused to conceal allegations concerning the sexual abuse of teenage girls at the Youth Home. This, in turn, led to a messy eruption of press coverage around questions of sexual abuse at the institution, and the perhaps more ominous possibility of a systematic, ruthless, and high-level administrative effort to cover up any wrongdoing.[5]

A few months later, clamoring complaints in the popular press and among youth and parent groups had provoked various efforts to initiate some sort of change in the administrative structure that had led the Youth Home to its much publicized dismal state.[6] As the Youth Home had come to a point of crisis, county administrators knew that some action would need to be taken. The question was what to do, and informed by what understanding of the nature of childhood? Should the county be guided by an imperative to emphasize "treatment" or "detention" for children in the county facility?

Finding The Fix: Strategies for "Rehabilitation"

The corrective plan with the most political support behind it, the one favored by then acting director of the facility Ron Lockett, called for the shrinking of the current Youth Home. Whether through the razing of the old building or its reduction in size, Lockett hoped to fashion a more tractable institution. Toward this end, he planned to follow a growing national trend: reduce Youth Home admissions to only young people who had committed violent or significant property crimes. Before the end of 1993, County Executive McNamara announced a plan to reduce the juvenile population from 215 to 146, and to establish a "Work and Learn Institute" to offer incarcerated kids job training and counseling programs. The thrust of the plan was to create two tracks for juvenile offenders. While less grave cases would be diverted to community programs during the disposition of their charges, those facing serious cases would be locked up. Attended by a wave of hopeful publicity, the announcement was framed by its proponents as a possible end to the long history of problems at the Youth Home.

Perhaps unsurprisingly, however, the next year saw no movement toward any of these possibilities. An impatient editorial in the *Detroit Free Press,* "Youth Home: Disgraceful Conditions Demand a Solution Now," called on county officials to "[f]ix the problems at the youth home. Do it now. Do it right." Instead, a new crisis emerged.

In March 1994, having received a formidable litany of complaints and grievances against the Youth Home, the Civil Rights Division of the U.S. Justice Department launched a preliminary inquiry into the possibility that a full investigation into rights violations at the facility would be warranted.[7] Probably the most egregious allegation involved a staff member against whom at least five previous abuse cases had been substantiated by the DSS. The DSS concluded that he had beaten up a 16-year-old boy in front of other employees, leaving the adolescent with a concussion. Though the DSS recommended that the abusive worker be moved, he was still on the job at the time of the complaint filing.[8]

The Justice Department gave the county 49 days to reach a set of "minimal standards," at which time the facility would again be investigated. The county signed onto this "consent decree" under threat of immediate lawsuit. It was obligated to meet all requirements spelled out by the Department of Justice within the allotted time or again face a lawsuit.

One of the major stipulations of the consent decree settlement required that the physical facility be renovated to meet basic DSS standards. This made old questions—which had been entertained by Youth Home administrators and city officials for several years already—suddenly very pressing. Should the county spend what would doubtless be millions of dollars renovating an old, and perhaps hopelessly dated, building, or should it devote probably more money to building an entirely new facility?

In the wake of the complaints filed with the federal government in late 1993, a *Free Press* reported asked Lockett to reflect on the problems that line staff had been having with kids in the facility.

> Understaffing has forced excessive overtime demands that can leave staff members with "frayed nerves," especially when they are forced to defend themselves from attacks or break up fights among youths. . . . "Youth Home" is a misnomer—it's filled with juvenile offenders. . . . At various times, rapists and murderers are here. Youth Home sounds like it's Spencer Tracy's Boystown. This is a juvenile *jail.* (March 2, 1994)[9]

Indeed, it was at Lockett's provocation that from 1994 onward in all official and juridical records, the name of the institution was changed from "Youth Home" to "Juvenile Detention Facility." And though one need not be a socio-linguist to spot the implications of the difference, a brief review of the language is instructive.

The significance of the shift from "Home" to "Detention Facility" may be self-evident. Perhaps most importantly, the construction of the institution as a "home" recalls old legacies in juvenile justice, where "boy's homes" or "youth houses" (or any number of other similar permutations) were established to deal with young people who were in some manner delinquent, and where the line between state paternalism and state punition remained blurred. "Detention" is an entirely different entity, drawing on distinct historical legacies and associated with institutional expediency in the contemporary configuration of the justice system.[10]

With the rise of a neoliberal interest in the ordered socializing of children,[11] the social category "youth" has become associated with the attribution of expanded agency to young people, both as a means of describing their political participation (their agency as citizens, market consumers, and class actors) and as a means of referencing their "risk" to ordered public culture and private institutions. We celebrate "youth empowerment" at the same time that we fret over our "reckless youth." In either case, "youth" refers not simply to individual young people, but rather to collective cultural formations. "Youth" indicates the arrangement of young people into enterprising subcultural groups and has tended to index their possession of a generative, if unsettling and disorderly, power.[12]

Meanwhile, "juvenile" is a more explicitly biological category; it is associated with the natural sciences and is not so suggestive of the cultural agency of children. "Juvenile" is a more individuating term. Thus, its incorporation into state taxonomies reflects the expansion of *biopower* ("Numerous and diverse techniques for achieving the subjugations of bodies and the control of populations") through contemporary society.[13] We do not speak of "juvenile culture" the way we do of "youth culture," but the phrase "juvenile delinquent," situating the disorder of individual young people in the context of the institutional and political order of the state, is of course quite familiar.[14] As a category implying the state ordering of young people, then, the term *juvenile* carries greater disciplinary weight.

Lockett's emphasis on the dangerousness of the inmate population there and on the seriousness of their crimes (noting that they are rapists and murderers, for example), and his hopes to separate young offenders who would be treated more like adults, was well served by his reframing of the institution: from a *home* for *youth* to a *detention facility* for *juveniles*.[15]

In the constant push and pull between emphases on treatment and detention, and in light of the remarkable hullabaloo in the press over abuses of kids in the Youth Home, Lockett's effort to track "serious" juvenile offenders into an institutional setting more reminiscent of adult detention facilities is strikingly ironic. For the push to reform the county's handling of young offenders (and the more general "rehabilitation" of the Youth Home, in the county executive's words) was clearly motivated by a public outcry over the mistreatment of *children*, in particular. The Youth Home's handling of children was framed as a kind of child abuse—an infringement upon the rights of children—and evocations of the vulnerability of children to such abuses richly laced discourse proclaiming the need for institutional reform. But as they unfolded, changes to the detention facility only solidified institutional categories and settings that would diminish important distinctions between how children and adults should be disciplined.

Not long after the Justice Department issued the consent decree, and in spite of Lockett's success in complying with its recommendations, the Wayne County Department of Youth Services made a change at the top of the institution. While the installation of Leonard Dixon (who was recruited from Dade County, Florida) as facility director did not send the Feds running back to Washington, D.C., Dixon clearly made some strides in tightening the detention facility's theretofore loosely run ship.

Most of the initial reforms that came under his tenure, however, were less revolutionary than procedural. While Dixon had talked a lot about developing rehabilitative programs when he first arrived, the most significant of his early interventions did not involve new programs for incarcerated kids. Nor did these involve structural reorganizations of facility personnel, beyond complying with requirements that there be more staff on hand. Rather, Dixon's main emphasis was on changing the workplace climate at the facility, from one where detention staff felt at great liberty to act with discretion in handling inmates, to one where they would act according to rigid institutional prescription.

Indeed, Dixon's call for facility staff to get in line—"to get with the program," as he would say—was loud and blunt. Nearly 5 years later, when I spoke with him in the conference room attached to his darkly hued and lavishly appointed office in the new detention facility, decorated with commendations and memorabilia from his days in Dade County, he talked about his early period at the facility with a still fresh and nearly defensive determination.

> I mean, the place was in just terrible shape. When you walked in, you could smell the urine. And not only was the facility over crowded, they were treating kids like shit. But, you know, they didn't know any better. I mean, people thought, these kids are locked up, who cares about mental care. . . . At the time there was a 1–30 ratio of staff people to residents. Now there is a ratio of at least 1 to 10. That's the regulation, we have to have a minimum of 1 to 10. . . . And one of the most important things that we did was to get rid of some of the supervisors who weren't doing their jobs. You know, people are resistant to changing when they been doing things the same way for a long time.

Dixon's concern that the staff people were not attentive to the "mental care" of inmates at the facility, it should be noted, was befuddling when considered in the context of his larger agenda, which he was at pains to articulate during the initial stages of his tenure. For Dixon was not just bearing down on uncontrolled staff people who were acting with rash neglect for the facility's policies. Rather, his handling of the staff was part of a broader trend at the facility that moved precisely away from "treatment" and toward a more expedient version of "detention." This set up a complex dynamic. On the one hand, the facility was being reformed, made more just, more sound—made purportedly better for children according to the most recent estimations of what a "humane childhood" should be.[16] On the other hand, and simultaneously, Dixon was pushing for the facility to become more rigid, more militaristic—less concerned with responding to the peculiar needs and concerns of children, and more concerned with defining itself in the narrowest sense as a place where young people should be detained and not interfered with, where staff people are explicitly directed not to be attentive to "mental care."

Dixon was not especially reflective about the complexity of these simultaneous and possibly contradictory trends. In his view, the problem with disobedient staff became conflated with the larger distinction between "treatment" and "detention." Consequently, it was not entirely surprising that staff people did not see his efforts to curtail their involvement with the kids in such a generous light.[17]

On one of my first days of fieldwork at the Youth Home, I had a chance encounter with one of the most senior line staff there. He had worked at the facility for over 20 years and was able to talk credibly about the changes that had taken place over the last couple of decades, and to voice, in particular, the concerns of line staff. He said that he longed for the days when staff people there could "actually take care of the kids." He said, "You know, before Dixon we didn't have to wear these uniforms, looking like corrections officers . . . and we were allowed to have meaningful interactions with the youth in here, to treat them like family, not so impersonally. . . . Before, you felt like you could really help. Now all you are is a guard."[18]

Building a New Vision: Envisioning a New Building

After debating their options for a couple of years, administrators with Wayne County had decided by June 1996 to respond to the federal government's concerns about the crumbling physical structure of the Detention Facility by constructing an entirely new building. At the official groundbreaking, Ed McNamara, with neither an apparent understanding of its double entendre nor an appropriate sense of irony, called the new building "a symbol of rehabilitation." For while the new building was clearly a symbol, if not simply a gauge, of Wayne County's efforts to rehabilitate its much maligned image, the plan for the facility was sending mixed messages regarding its interest in rehabilitating kids who would be incarcerated there.[19] Indeed, the cultural meanings associated with the physical characteristics of the new building and (more contentiously) the lot where it would be built were central in the continuing debates over the tension to emphasize either "treatment" or "detention" for juvenile offenders in Detroit.

Certainly the most complicated element of the plan for the new facility— and that which elicited the greatest concern among both residents of the city and inmates of the old Youth Home—was the proposed location. The groundbreaking ceremony where McNamara declared his hopes for rehabilitation took place in a vacant lot about one and a half miles from the old Youth Home. The lot, which had been the site of the Old Receiving Hospital, was on the eastern edge of downtown Detroit, right across the street from the county jail. Wayne County bought the parcel of land from the city for much below the market value. But the county's decision to locate the building there was not just an economic one, nor even one born of administrative convenience. Indeed, it was not a coincidence that as the state was shifting its laws to facilitate the sentencing of younger and younger children to the adult criminal justice system, the Juvenile Detention Facility would move *away* from the Juvenile Court and land smack dab in the middle of the adult "criminal justice complex" in Detroit, right across the street from where more and more young people would likely be in court. One cannot help but see the move into the adult criminal justice complex as supporting the general trend toward "detention" represented by the establishment of a smaller facility. Otherwise, with ample land near the Juvenile Court, why wouldn't the county detain younger offenders close by?

Surprisingly, debate did not emerge around the proposed location until residents of the neighborhood caught word of the county's plan to build. Nearly a year before the 1996 groundbreaking ceremony, in the late summer of 1995, as Wayne County was preparing to purchase the lot on St. Antoine Street and was initiating hearings to gain zoning clearance from the City Planning Commission, residents of the downtown areas proximate to the building site were already gearing up for a struggle against the planned facility. The Lafayette-Elmwood Association (LEA) and the East Lafayette Community Action Council (ELCAC) are neighborhood organizations composed of residents and business owners located around the Lafayette Park area. For the past few decades, while vast tracts of the city have fallen into disrepair and many of the grand old homes adjacent to downtown have been abandoned, the Lafayette neighborhood has thrived, and it is currently one of the most desirable in the downtown vicinity. The high-rise apartments that were built after urban-renewal tear-downs in the 1950s and 1960s have been consistently occupied and well maintained, and they are a manicured oasis for many middle-income people of various races and ethnicities.[20]

Through the late summer and fall of 1995, residents of the Lafayette area, most of whom were members of the neighborhood organizations, attended and spoke at multiple hearings, repeatedly outlining the nature of their concerns and pleading with the city and county to change their plans and rescind their agreement to construct the facility downtown. There were two central thrusts of the neighborhood protest. First, neighborhood residents expressed worry that a Juvenile Detention Facility would bring undesirable social elements into the neighborhood. These elements were imagined to be not only the incarcerated kids themselves, of course, but their families and friends. In a letter sent to

Mayor Archer and members of the City Council, organizers of ELCAC summa-
rized the foundations of this concern:

> Wayne County made this proposal in total disregard of the surrounding neighbor-
> hood. . . . There are recreational facilities and over 10 schools in the neighborhood. . . .
> The Parkwycke Tower Apartments are immediately adjacent to the proposed site.
> Approximately one hundred and forty families live in that building, including sen-
> ior citizens, and families with small children who must walk to school.

Glenn Weisfeld, an active member of ELCAC, reported to the City Council his
concerns about the sorts of people that a detention facility would attract: "These
are gangbangers . . . they will molest and intimidate people. People won't want
to shop there."[21]

Second, residents of Lafayette park argued that they already were bearing
most of the criminal justice load in the city, and that they should not have to
shoulder responsibility for housing more incarcerated people. For officials from
the county and city, the logic supporting the construction of a new juvenile jail
within urban space that was already associated with various criminal justice uses
seemed unassailable. After all, they might reasonably suppose, the juvenile jail
isn't going to look any more menacing than, or demand significantly more real
estate than is occupied by, the adjacent jails and law-enforcement offices already
in the area. But as a letter from ELCAC to the City Council succinctly put it:
"Our neighborhood has two jails adjacent to the Murphy Hall of Justice. Adding this project will create the impression that the Detroit center city is more
suitable for those accused and convicted of crime than for commercial and
residential development." As concerns about the property value and quality of
life implications of a downtown jail increased, the rallying cry among neighborhood residents became, as publicly posted fliers and petition notices made clear,
"SAY NO!!! To a PRISON in our NEIGHBORHOOD." At their local meetings,
and at hearings with city officials, neighbors would hand out small slips of paper
with a bright red hash mark covering the neologism "Jailtown."

As a last resort, residents of the area filed suit under the auspices of ELCAC
against the city and county for conspiring to build a penal institution within
a range of residential buildings in clear violation of state zoning statutes. The
filing of this suit and its defense elicited some of the strangest double-speak
around the nature of the new Juvenile Detention Facility. In short, the city and
county argued that the new building would not represent a violation of zoning
laws because it would not be a *penal facility*. In legal briefs filed on the county's behalf, it maintained that the new Juvenile Detention Facility would not be

a jail, but rather a "residential care facility." This, of course, rubs awkwardly against the county's concurrent talk about the good sense inherent in locating the detention facility in the celebrated "criminal justice complex" because people charged with crimes would be detained there.[22] Why, if the facility is primarily a "care facility," would it be especially appropriately located in a "criminal justice complex"?

The county's decision to move the detention facility downtown for the sake of institutional coherence, and its simultaneous insistence that the facility is not a "jail" but a "care facility," demonstrates as well as anything the tension and confusion that surrounds the county's interest in and understanding of juvenile justice. But more than this, the county's double-speak in the zoning hearing shows the extent to which, and startling ease with which, the social category "juvenile" and categorical distinctions between juveniles and adults may be subject to institutional intervention and manipulation.

In the midst of the ambitious infrastructural changes undertaken by the county, shifting understandings of childhood were especially resonant for those who worked and lived in the new facility—staff and inmates alike.

Early in November of 1999, all of the kids at the old Youth Home building were herded into vans and driven the mile and a half to the brand-new Juvenile Detention Facility, right across the narrow street from the towering Wayne County Jail. With the move to the new facility, the tension between adult and juvenile institutions and their respective meanings and mutual fluidity became heightened. For many of the kids incarcerated there, the move to the criminal justice complex was eerily reminiscent of other early morning visits downtown for hearings in one of the adult courts there.

It is hardly surprising, then, that with this tracing of their tracks to adult court, young detainees' sense of proximity to the complex of adult facilities in their new digs was especially acute. And suspicion was running high among the kids that the decision to move them close to the adult courthouses and jails was a reflection of the increasing likelihood that they themselves would soon end up within one or more of them. While movement between the Juvenile Detention Facility and the county jail would still require a ride in a locked van (albeit a very short one), their new proximity seemed to have a real effect on senses of vulnerability to "adult time" among the incarcerated kids there. And just in case some had not taken note of this likelihood, staff at the Juvenile Detention Facility were quick to point it out.

On the third day that the new facility had been open, a young African American woman was assigned to the lead position on one of the units where older kids were housed. After the inmates there had eaten lunch, she endeavored to establish some rapport with them. A portly woman of a little over 5 feet, the unit leader turned the television off and strode to the front of the room. She introduced herself to the group, most of whom were already familiar with her from previous episodes in the facility. "I respect you," she said. "I really do. I feel for you all. I have kids of my own, so I know how hard it can be. And I know my kids would have a hard time up in here. But let me say: just like I respect you, you need to respect me too." She continued with a preacher's enthusiasm: "You all need to understand where you are. You aren't in any day care center any more. Look at this place," she said, waving her short arms around the room, and looking up at the barred second tier walkway over her head. "You know what's right across the street from you now?" she asked, referring to the adult county jail on the other side of the narrow street. "That's the real thing right there. . . . Right next door, and you need to understand that, cuz they are setting you up in here. I'll tell you, you don't even know it, but they are *setting you up* in here. They're just getting you ready to go across the street." The kids on the unit again all nodded appreciatively. "I'm just being real," she said. "I'm just being for real."

The heightened sense of vulnerability that young people at the new Juvenile Detention Facility felt to the adult criminal justice system was reflected in the euphemism for it inspired by the facility's new location. At the old Youth Home, young inmates' references to the adult system were often clumsy and uncertain, and they usually involved the name of a particular courthouse or institution, "Frank Murphy" (the Frank Murphy Hall of Justice), or "the 36th" (36th District Court). At the new facility, all institutional complexity was reduced to the phrase "across the street." Conversations among kids and staff people there were often abuzz with invocations of "across the street," what might be happening there, who might be heading over there from the new facility. And where the move from the old Youth Home to one of the adult facilities had been a dreaded possibility for many young people facing transfer to adult court, there was some reassurance, however deluded or misguided, in the adult system's physical and socio-spatial distance. In contrast, a move "across the street" for those locked up in the new facility seemed both foreboding and easy—only a few steps away.

As the unit leader's arm-waving gesture toward the new techniques and technologies of surveillance would suggest, the physical dimensions and features of the new building reinforced this sense of proximity. From the street, the new facility and the adult Wayne County Jail strike an almost comically deliberate semiotic contrast. Where the jail is a 12-story monolithic concrete rectangle with narrow slit windows, the new Juvenile Detention Facility is low slung and sprawling, faced in mottled brown ceramic tiles. From the outside, the windows are large and square, with pleasant turquoise hued hanging blinds. The waiting area is lined with enormous street-level picture windows and is carpeted and equipped with comfortable blue chairs. There are house plants in the corners.

But from the inside, behind the buzzing red steel doors that lead out of the waiting area and into the heart of the building, the contrast between the two spaces is much less obvious. The two-tiered units at the new Juvenile Detention Facility are designed according to adult correctional facility specifications. Each unit is equipped with multiple cameras, and all the doors are controlled by officers in a central room lined with television monitors. No one can go anywhere in the facility without the knowledge and permission of this shadowy surveillance team. From the individual cell-rooms, the windows, so generous appearing from the street, are opaque and too high to look out of in any case. While the new Juvenile Detention Facility is equipped with an impressive gymnasium, the only access to fresh air for young people locked up there is on the roof, in a small brick enclosed cell, covered on top with a perforated sheet of metal. It all amounts to a far cry from the old Youth Home, where the kids played outside in an expansive yard and looked out from their units through big, clear windows.

With the construction of their new building, administrators at Wayne County hoped to "rehabilitate" the county's image as a competent agency, putting years of bad publicity about abusive supervision and dilapidated infrastructure in the old Youth Home behind them. But, as the discourse surrounding and social space constituting the new Wayne County Juvenile Detention Facility would suggest—where phrases like "care facility" and "criminal justice complex" slip smoothly past one another, and where windows that appear inviting from the outside are inaccessible from within—the county's commitment to the active rehabilitation of children under their care was less clear.

We live during a period in which there are profound unresolved tensions around the nature of childhood. Across the globe, this is evident in concerns over the participation of young people in physical labor, the recruitment of them into warring armies, and uncertainty about their status as political citizens. Questions concerning the social constitution of childhood—its categorical parameters, meanings, entitlements, and responsibilities—are being actively negotiated throughout the world in day-to-day practices and through formal institutional procedure.

In the United States, questions about the nature of childhood are most actively negotiated in the handling of children designated as "juvenile offenders." Here, questions about childhood rights may compel both more rehabilitative

and more regimented, and therefore punitive, handling. In institutional practice, ideological confusion about the nature of childhood, and the instrumental-
ity of punitive state measures, is awkwardly reduced to and hidden in a simple
binary frame: treatment vs. detention. Ultimately, this opposition has led to a
system of tracking childhood offenders into two groups. One group is made up
of young people who are "treated" as children and diverted toward community
treatment settings and therapeutic programs, and the other group includes children for whom adultlike "detention" is deemed more appropriate. As I noted
above, the rhetoric describing the trend toward detention in Detroit emerged
around a push to restructure the Youth Home as a smaller facility, reserved for
only more serious cases. In Detroit, county administrators favored handling the
chronic overcrowding at the Youth Home through the distillation of the population to those who had committed only violent crimes, or the most serious
property crimes. Other young people (those charged with status offenses, or less
serious, nonviolent crimes) would be diverted to community programs. This facility reduction was proposed, very explicitly, as a reform measure and sounded
notes that were familiar to and resonated with progressive supporters of the juvenile justice system. But in its situation of the Youth Home as a marker that
distinguished those who would benefit from or are deserving of rehabilitation
from those who are imagined to have a less supple character, who are a different
order of person, less amenable to the salutary intervention—care, rehabilitation, nurturance—this tendency runs counter to the principles on which the
juvenile justice system is based. Foremost among these is the notion that there
are discernible and codifiable social categorical distinctions between children
and adults. In legal discourse, this distinction is expressed through questions
about judgment. Children, the reasoning goes, merit the sympathy and care of
the state, as opposed to its punitive rage, because they do not have the judgment of adults. Moreover, crimes that they commit cannot be used to measure
whether they are adults or children. Rather, such a logic suggests that children
who commit more serious crimes are *more* in need of rehabilitation. But the
rhetoric accompanying and justifying the shrinking of the Youth Home, emphasizing the dangerousness of young offenders, seems to buy into an entirely
different, even antithetical, logic.

Of course, it should not be surprising that in an institutional and ideological
context characterized by such deep ambivalence about the nature of childhood,
the county's belabored plans to track young people into two discrete categories
has not worked out according to design. As with the old Youth Home, the new
high-security Juvenile Detention Facility now not only houses the "most serious

offenders" but has become, by default, an overbuilt warehouse for many young people charged with minor "status offenses" and children who are wards of the state and simply waiting for safe placement in the community.

The case study presented here demonstrates that uncertainties about the nature of childhood, and efforts to frame it as either categorically distinct from or bearing a more contingent relationship to adulthood, are reflected not only in legal discourse, but through the physical institutions, structures, and spaces where the state actually encounters and manages young people. Childhood is a remarkably fluid category, and individual actors may change its legal parameters with the rapping of a gavel. In Detroit, ambiguousness about the nature of childhood has been built into the physical structure and social spatial location of the Juvenile Detention Facility; it has been captured and is embodied in steel, bricks, and glass, buzzing doors and swiveling surveillance cameras.

QUESTIONS FOR DISCUSSION

1. Bergmann argues that cultural meanings of categories such as "childhood" are embedded in bricks and mortar. Consider a particular structure designed for use by young people in your community. What notions of children and youth are evident in the design of this structure?

2. In your community, is there contestation over issues of physical space for children—in schools, detention centers, recreation programs, mental health treatment programs, gymnasiums, parking lots, malls? What issues are at stake? Who are the contesting parties? Who are the audiences for this struggle?

3. What can we learn from this account about how the relationships between the adult criminal justice system and the juvenile justice system are being reconfigured? What are the consequences for young people?

4. What are the various ways that young people have been characterized in social service programs (for example, as youth, juvenile, criminal, child, student, resident, patient, client, participant)? How does each characterization vary? How does each notion reconstruct the role of helping professionals?

5. Compare Bergmann's account of building a Juvenile Detention Center in Detroit with Tilton's account of efforts to "Stop the Superjail for Kids" in Oakland. What similarities and differences do you note in these accounts? What more would you like to know about the effort to build detention centers in these communities? What are the implications for practice embedded in each story?

NOTES

1. For a thorough treatment of this tension, see Garland (1993).

2. Indeed, since the codification of universal rights of the child through the United Nations Convention on the Rights of the Child (still not ratified by the United States), this debate has been characterized by a shifting balance between enumerations of special rights, which all children below a certain age should be afforded, and the simultaneous recognition of local cultural and political contingencies, which might allow for or encourage roles and practices for children that are more "adult" according to normative western conventions. See Stephens (1995).

3. Pierre Bourdieu (1984), Henri Lefebvre (1991), Michel DeCerteau (1984), David Harvey (1990), in addition to many others, have written about the construction of "social spaces."

4. The report describes the conditions in nearly every room in the facility. The entry for room 14 of Unit 2N is typical: "Floor corners are filthy, very strong urine odor in room; upon examination of the bed urine-soaked linen was found under the blanket and folded at foot of bed." Many of the rooms were found to have "dirty toilets" and "filthy floors." Nearly half of the rooms are described as having "foul odors." The description of room 104 in the school reads: "Torn drapes, wires exposed in bathroom light switch, floor dirty." Invoking the Youth Home's policy forbidding "inhumane or improper treatment" and an explicit prohibition against "standing a child for more than an hour," the report indicates that several inmates at the facility reported being made to "stand track" (standing without moving or talking): "For use of profanity, for flatulence, for talking while watching T.V. They may stand track for up to 2 hours for these 'infractions.' Residents reported in one instance a youth was made to stand track nude. The youth was standing for twenty minutes while staff called him 'faggot.'"

5. Concerns about these abuses, along with other eyebrow-raising concerns at the Youth Home, were detailed in several *Detroit Free Press* articles that ran during the summer of 1993. A front-page story recapitulated the case, followed by one involving the beating of a boy with a belt and broomstick, and another on a lawsuit filed by the family of a 13-year-old runaway who was beaten up by several older youth while he was incarcerated there. Headlined "Troubles Plague Crumbling Youth Home," the article begins with a note of sympathy for Ron Lockett, who had a month earlier taken over as executive director there:

> Lockett . . . can't say he didn't know what he was getting into. Before taking charge of the
> 33-year-old institution on July 4, Lockett was director of the overseeing agency, Wayne
> County Youth Services, and as such was well acquainted with the home's list of troubles:
> The heating, plumbing and ventilation are broken, chunks of concrete periodically rain

down from the crumbling shell of the six-story building. Chronic overcrowding routinely leaves 20 or 25 troubled or potentially dangerous youths crammed into units built for 18 people, putting added stress on a staff that already is weary of mandatory overtime and abuse investigations from the state. At any given time, more than 10 percent of the 230 or so boys and girls in the youth home are on a suicide watch, tying up more workers. (*Detroit Free Press*, August 16, 1993)

6. The *Metro Times*, an alternative weekly paper with a wide circulation throughout the city and suburbs, ran a cover story about the Youth Home. Underneath a picture of a young man sitting slouched and disconsolate in a dingy Youth Home hallway reads the headline: "Who Cares: Tough Time in the Wayne County Youth Home." The *Metro Times* article describes the deplorable physical state of the facility and mentions problems with chronic overcrowding, especially as it leads to overworked, and thus physically and mentally compromised, employees.

7. The *Free Press* covered this story on its front page: "Twenty years after a judge ordered Wayne County to provide a safe, clean environment at the Youth Home, and six years after county voters agreed to tax themselves $2.5 million a year to build a new youth facility, the six-story institution on the edge of downtown Detroit is still a bulging mess." According to the *Free Press*, the division was responding to four sorts of complaints: "Allegations of physical and sexual abuse of young people by staff members, with repeat offenders staying on the job. Chronic overcrowding, understaffing and lack of training. Failure to provide basic necessities for juveniles, such as beds, adequate heating and cooling, nutritious meals and telephone access. [And] allegations that the Detroit Police Department has not investigated complaints from Youth Home residents about illegal activity at the institution" (*Detroit Free Press*, March 2, 1994).

8. Meanwhile, another worker who had been promoted to a different job with the county had 27 abuse cases filed against him over the course of seven years. While at the commencement of the inquiry, county officials assured the press that the complaints were unfounded and likely the work of rabble-rousing staff and ungrateful parents, the list of deficiencies found by the Department of Justice in their investigation fills nearly 14 single-spaced typed pages. In the report that they produced in late December 1994, the investigators separate their findings into three categories: operational, medical and mental health, and environmental. In addition to numerous procedural problems and inadequate services and support, the most alarming and scandalous of the findings are those having to do with abusive staff people, and the administration's failure to properly discipline these staff and/or fire them. The report states that "[s]everal examples illustrate the severity of the problem at WCJDF. First, one direct care worker who was found guilty of hitting a child in the head with a chair and on another occasion stripped and paraded a naked youth in clear view of his peers was terminated and subsequently rein-

stated to his position at the facility. . . . A current employee was found to have physically abused a juvenile and to have forced the youth to urinate on himself." As had previous developments, the public release of the report provoked quite a bit of noise in the press. The *Detroit News* ("Feds Hit Youth Home Abuse") published a lead article that opened: "Hundreds of troubled youths at the Wayne County Juvenile Detention Facility are in immediate danger from violent jailers, contaminated food, overcrowding and roach- and rodent-infested food, the U.S. Justice Department has said."

The *Free Press* also published a long article focusing on the work that the facility would need to do to comply with all of the remedial requests made by the federal government.

9. See Garland (1990), Rothman (1980), and others on the development of detention as a punitive measure.

10. See Ortner (1992). In particular, the following passage: "And finally, there is the language itself. Middle class are 'teenagers,' 'adolescents,' 'young persons,' all terms that emphasize stages of development along an age continuum, and indeed one that is continuous with that of their parents, who are older, but not Other. The term 'youth,' on the other hand, is reserved for the lower classes (as the Cultural Studies people use it too). Although it too is an age term, it is a collective noun. While teenagers or adolescents are individual persons of a particular age range, youth has the ring of a tribe, an Other. And while the term "teenagers," coded as middle class, has a certain innocence about it, the term "youth," coded as lower class, is faintly ominous" (4).

11. For more on the nature of youth as a subcultural category, see multiple studies from the "Birmingham School," including Willis (1977) and Hebdige (1979).

12. Foucault (1990:140).

13. As Sharon Stephens (1995) suggests: "In an earlier period of modern society, non-compliant children could be categorized as 'going through a stage' (as Prout and James [1990] note, 'a biological explanation for a breakdown in social relationships') or, in more extreme cases, as 'juvenile delinquents,' in need of social correction and rehabilitation."

14. Indeed, an alternate plan proposed by Lockett called for the housing of this class of charged juveniles at an adult jail in neighboring Hamtramck.

15. This had recently been made especially explicit with the United Nations Convention on the Rights of the Child.

16. Staff people understood the Dixon administration as almost single-mindedly oppressive of them. Fueling this may have been Dixon's transparently anti-union orientation, and his obvious resistance to the legacy and strength of union support in Detroit. As he said: "I would say that the union piece is destroying this town. It's almost like with the car industry, where the unions are driving good businesses and good industry out of the city. We need to move from an industrial model to one where we say 'it's everybody's job to do a good job.'" And with a strong union behind the line workers at the facility,

Dixon's efforts to replace many of them and restructure their responsibilities were met with considerable and effectively organized acrimony.

17. Most staff at the Detention Facility found his administration fundamentally unjust; staff people did not see Dixon's changes as merely an effort to reduce abuse, but to exert a power-mongering control over them.

18. Foucault's work is instructive here. In his formulation, processes of *governmentality* unify keepers and kept, guards and inmates, in expansive webs of power relations, so that any increase of disciplinary techniques exercised against staff at the facility will impact both guards and inmates alike. See Foucault (1991).

19. Two articles from the *Free Press* Op-Ed page illustrate this. "Juveniles Must Be Kept Apart from Adults" and "Wayne County Breaks Ground for Rehabilitation" (June 26, 1996) appeared right on top of one another, and both reflect different sides of this "mixed message." One supports the idea that juveniles need to be kept separate, and the other supports a facility that will move them physically and procedurally closer to the adult criminal justice system.

20. The most well-to-do residents of the area tend to live either in the relative luxury of 1300 Lafayette, one of the most exclusive high-rise buildings in the city, or in the sprawling complex of Mies Van der Rohe–designed condominiums that line the western edge of the meadowlike Lafayette Park. The condominium complex, one of the city's few modernist landmarks, is all glass and white brick, arranged in balanced squares and rectangles, and surrounded by annual gardens and flowering trees that seem always to be undergoing some intensive maintenance by a green-clad army of professional gardeners. The preponderance of the most active members of ELCAC live in these condominiums, and they formed the core of a vigorous protest of the county's plans to build a new detention facility in their environs. They were joined by residents of a lower-income apartment building immediately across the street from the proposed site, for whom the impact of a new detention facility would likely be the greatest.

21. Quote from Jane Slaughter, "NIMBY's or not?" *Metro Times*, December 6, 1995. This group of neighbors seemed to have an objection to kids in the neighborhood generally, as expressed through their fight against the opening of a charter school in the old Lafayette Clinic Building. The intersection of St. Antoine and Monroe streets, where the facility would be built, forms the northeast corner of one of downtown Detroit's few viable tourist districts. While the Eastern Market area to the east of downtown is more active and interesting, and Mexican Town in southeastern Detroit is both much larger and a genuine ethnic community offering visitors a taste of "real" cultural otherness, "Greektown," as the three-block stretch of Monroe street is known, has been far and away the most famous destination for out-of-towners and day–tripping suburbanites over the years. Greektown is a short strip of restaurants, bakeries, and bars, most of which are run by Greek ex-pats, that specialize in Greek fare. Certainly much of

what sustains these businesses are the many customers from the sheriff's office, which is a half-block away, the police department headquarters, a block away, and the district courthouses and county jails, which are bunched together and fill a couple of blocks north of Greektown. But for area residents, the proximity of Greektown and what the city calls the "criminal justice complex" is much less harmonious.

22. Wayne County Circuit Court, Case No. 96–629973, *East Lafayette Community Council v. City of Detroit and County of Wayne.*

REFERENCES

Ainsworth, Janet. (1997). Achieving the promise of justice for juveniles: A call for the abolition of juvenile court. In Anne McGillivray, ed., *Governing Childhood.* Aldershot: Dartmouth University Press.

Bourdieu, Pierre. (1984). *Distinction: A social critique of the judgment of taste.* Cambridge: Harvard University Press.

Certaue, Michael de. (1984). *The practice of everyday life.* Berkeley: University of California Press.

Cicourel, Aaron. (1968). *The social organization of juvenile justice.* New York: John Wiley.

Coronil, Fernando. (1997). *The magical state: Nature, money and modernity in Venezuela.* Chicago: University of Chicago Press.

Foucault, Michel. (1990). *The history of sexuality.* Vol. 1. New York: Vintage Books.

———. (1991). "Governmentality." In Burchell, Gordon, and Miller, eds., *The Foucault effect: Studies in governmentality.* Chicago: University of Chicago Press.

Garland, David. (1990). *Punishment and modern society: A study in social theory.* Oxford: Clarendon Press.

Halloway, S., and G. Valentine. (2000). *Children's geographies.* New York: Routledge.

Harvey, David. (1990). *The condition of postmodernity.* Oxford: Oxford University Press.

Hebdige, Dick. (1979). *Subculture:The meaning of style.* London: Methuen.

James, Allison, and Alan Prout. (1990). *Constructing and reconstructing childhood.* London: Falmer Press.

Lefebvre, Henri. (1991). *The production of social space.* Oxford: Blackwell.

Ortner, Sherry. (1992). Resistance and class reproduction among middle class youth. CSST Working Paper no. 71, University of Michigan.

Rothman, David J. (1980). *Conscience and convenience: The asylum and its alternatives in progressive America.* Boston: Little Brown.

Stephens, Sharon. (1995). *Children and the politics of culture.* Princeton: Princeton University Press.

Willis, Paul. (1977). *Learning to labor.* New York: Columbia University Press.

NINE

Educating All Our Children

Ruth Zweifler

"No child will be left behind, not one single child."

—George W. Bush, 2001

In 1975 I was among a group of citizens in Michigan who came together to establish the lay advocacy program that has become the Student Advocacy Center of Michigan (SAC/MI,) the only organization in the state offering lay advocacy support to children in both regular and special education. Our efforts to assure equity and excellence in education focus particularly on policies and practices harmful to those children historically least well served by our public schools: children of color and those who are poor or are in need of special services.

Advocacy for individual children is the heart of our work. Children in regular education programs are among our least protected citizens. When schools fail to nurture these children, there is little or no recourse for them or their families. SAC/MI endeavors to give voice to these children and to assure that their interests are represented in efforts to correct academic or disciplinary problems. This remains the priority mission because it is through the experiences of the

This chapter is a product of staff, board, and volunteers at the Student Advocacy Center who have worked together through the years to turn quality education for all children from promise to reality. I close with gratitude and in loving memory of Marcene Root, Jerome Strong, and Emma and Albert Wheeler. We also thank Maureen Bishop and the students at the *Michigan Journal of Race and Law* for their support in preparation of an earlier version of this article.

individual children we represent that we identify the gap between the rhetoric and the reality of delivering quality education to all children.

This mission is particularly important given dramatic recent changes in policies and practices regarding the exclusion of children from schools. From the 1950s through the 1990s, educators and policy makers sought ways to extend effective education to more and more inclusive populations of children. Although the efforts left much to be desired—conversations about how to reduce absenteeism or dropout rates rarely included the students who were the objects of concern—the goal was honored in both policy discussions and individual student conferences. In the early 1990s, however, a number of school districts began installing policies centered on concepts of "zero tolerance," replacing the emphasis on inclusion with a sense of righteousness about removing children who might be dangerous or detrimental to the school environment. "Zero-tolerance" policies include a variety of school disciplinary practices that mandate automatic suspension and/or expulsion from school for offenses perceived to be a threat to the safety of other children, school employees, or the school community itself (Skiba and Peterson 1999). In 1994 zero tolerance achieved national policy status when President Clinton signed the Gun-Free School Zones Act (GFSA) into law.[1] In Michigan, the Mandatory Expulsion Act of 1995, enacted in the wake of the GFSA, amended the Michigan School Code of 1976. This act serves as the basis of the state's zero-tolerance policy.[2] It was marketed as a way to stop dangerous "punks," older adolescents with guns, from threatening schools. Instead of netting sharks, the law and its attendant policies and practices ensnare minnows—young children who are frightened, sometimes thoughtless, rarely dangerous, but now clearly endangered.

While zero-tolerance laws originally focused on truly dangerous and criminal behaviors, such as gun possession, some states like Michigan extended these laws to include possession of other types of weapons, as well as the possession or use of drugs (Skiba 2000). School districts also quickly expanded the policies even further to include infractions that pose no safety concern, such as "disobeying [school] rules," "insubordination," and "disruption" (Advancement Project and Harvard Civil Rights Project 2000). The list of offenses that trigger zero-tolerance responses continues to grow. Additionally, many school districts invoke the language of zero tolerance and expel children for violating school rules when the zero-tolerance policies do not extend to the behavior punished. Actions that were once considered relatively harmless childhood pranks now result in expulsion and often criminal or juvenile delinquency charges. For example, aspirin, Midol, and even Certs have been treated as drugs, and paper clips, nail files, and scissors have been considered weapons (Advancement Project and

Harvard Civil Rights Project 2000). Once snared, regardless of the offense, the student is likely to be treated as if he or she has violated the weapons law and will receive all the harsh penalties that accompany a charge of possessing a gun, including permanent expulsion and referral to the courts.

My work at SAC/MI has provided me with sobering insights into the changes that have taken place in the educational system, particularly with regard to disciplinary policies and practices. In this chapter, I use these experiences as a lens through which to critically engage with the development and consequences of zero-tolerance policies and to serve as a starting point to envision more promising directions for those entrusted with nurturing our youth. I also ground my experiences in an extensive review of the literature regarding the consequences of these policies.

FOUR STORIES

The four stories that follow are from the case files of students who came to the attention of the Student Advocacy Center because of their alleged violations of Michigan's Mandatory Expulsion Act. These students come from four different Michigan counties in different parts of the state and represent urban, rural, and suburban districts. These stories are not exceptions but are typical of the types of cases we represent and the children whose access to education is interrupted or permanently closed when they are ejected from schools under the provisions of zero-tolerance policies and practices.

John

In November 2001 John, a Caucasian eighth grader, was taunted by a classmate who wanted to know what he was carrying in his duffle bag. John finally replied, "What do you think I have, a bomb?" John was sent to the office. No alarm was sounded, nor was the building evacuated. A school administrator (not a trained police bomb expert) later searched his duffle bag and locker. No bomb was found. Nevertheless, John was expelled from school without a hearing.

Mary

Mary is an African American eighth grader who has been regularly threatened and harassed by members of another family in her neighborhood. After a particularly serious altercation in May 2002, her mother called the school to report her concerns about Mary's safety as well as her ability to respond appropriately. Mary's principal questioned her and found that she was carrying a knife because she was feeling so unsafe. She readily gave the knife to the principal, who then suspended her and requested an evaluation to see if Mary qualified for special education services. The Multidisciplinary Evaluation Team (MET) found a history of possible depression and school phobia. Mary's academic testing indicated a student with considerable ability and potential; however, her schoolwork was inconsistent and did not rise to her potential. The MET found that it did not know Mary well enough to determine whether she was eligible for special education as she was relatively new to the district. It recommended a follow-up review in three to four months but found her ineligible for services at that time. The district immediately recommended permanent expulsion for violation of the Mandatory Expulsion Act.

Mark

In June, as school was drawing to a close, Mark, an African American sixth grader with a history of behavioral problems, had a very bad day. He was involved in two fights, one during school and one immediately after. There were no weapons and no injuries. The superintendent of his school district sent a letter to his parents informing them that Mark was expelled from the district and that there was no appeal of this decision.

Ellen

Ellen is a Caucasian third grader at an elementary school in a rural county. Ellen reported a bomb threat written on the bathroom wall and was interrogated by the police, who demanded a handwriting sample. Subsequently another message appeared: "There is a bomb in here." Ellen told the police that she had written the second message but not the first. She alleges that the police told her that she could not go home unless she confessed to both incidents. Juvenile Court found Ellen "not guilty" of the first incident and placed her on probation for the second. Ellen was expelled from school in March 2002.

Advocates from SAC/MI intervened in each of these cases—sometimes successfully, sometimes less so—to try to assure that these students' educational, social, and emotional needs were met. Concern for the predicaments of children like these must not be left to one small nonprofit agency. All of us who are responsible for the well-being of our children must commit ourselves to assuring children's rights to education.

AN OVERVIEW OF ZERO TOLERANCE

In 1954 *Brown v. Board of Education* heralded equal educational opportunities for children of color.[3] This landmark decision ended legalized segregation and recognized the education system as an important site for ensuring racial equality and integration. In the mid-1970s, state and federal laws mandated educational services for children with disabilities.[4] Despite continuing inequalities in the educational system and problems surrounding the implementation of policies and practices of inclusion, these reforms, at the very least, signaled a commitment to universal public education for all children.

But in the 1980s, as political decisions based on the assumption of personal responsibility and "Just say 'No'" grew ever more frequent, the complementary commitment to socially responsible policies and actions withered. Then passage of the Gun-Free School Zones Act in 1994 mapped the way along a very different path. Justified as a means to protect both children and teachers by removing "dangerous" children from schools, GFSA was consistent with a broader transformation in policies and practices toward children and youth that focused on exclusion. In particular, it required any state receiving Elementary and Secondary Education Act funds to enact a law requiring that children possessing firearms face an expulsion of at least one calendar year. GFSA does provide exceptions to this mandate. For example, the law states that "Such State law *shall* allow the chief administering officer of a local educational agency to modify the expulsion . . . on a case-by-case basis." Most states, however, do not provide for case-by-case consideration, instead retaining the rigid mandatory expulsion provisions of GFSA. Other notable provisions contained in GFSA include the requirement that each state provide a "description of the circumstances surrounding any expulsion," including the name of the school, the number of students expelled and the type of firearms concerned when a violation requiring an expulsion takes place. GFSA also requires an educational agency to have a policy requiring that any student who has brought a firearm or weapon to school be referred to the criminal justice or juvenile delinquency system.

In addition to complying with the requirements of GFSA, state legislatures and local school districts over the last decade have enacted and adopted a wide variety of zero-tolerance laws, policies, and informal practices that have swept uncounted numbers of our most vulnerable and needy children into the streets, where they remain uneducated, underserved, and unsupervised. In large part, GFSA has served as a springboard for these policies and practices, and its ambiguity has substantially compounded these effects. For example, while the term "firearm" is explicitly and carefully defined, the term "weapon" is not defined anywhere in the statute. Furthermore, even though GFSA explicitly mentions firearms, *not weapons*, when mandating a student's expulsion, the inclusion of the term "weapon" in the referral requirement has led many states to enact laws, and many school boards to enact rules, that similarly apply the one-year expulsion to any "weapon," thereby increasing GFSA's reach (Advancement Project and Harvard Civil Rights Project 2000). States and local school districts have broadened zero tolerance even further beyond weapons, including drugs and alcohol, and in some instances fighting or homework completion (Modzeleski 2000).

Given the reach of zero-tolerance policies and practices, it is important to consider the extent to which states provide due process rights to students subject to expulsion and suitable educational alternatives for children and youth who are expelled. State laws vary widely in terms of the degree to which they protect rights of students accused of violating zero-tolerance provisions. Rubin (2004) surveyed all states for inclusion of student protection clauses in their school codes. Clauses protecting the rights of students ranged from clear definitions of firearms and weapons to due process protections, from provision of alternative education during exclusions to incentives for prevention programs. In most states these protections and alternatives are extremely limited or minimal. For example, if a child in Michigan, of any age, is expelled for a mandatory offense, the student is excluded from any school in the state unless the program is sight-and-sound separated from any other educational program. Michigan also places extra burdens on the families of expelled students who bear the responsibility for securing alternative education, although such programs are few and far between and are under no obligation to accept a student. Michigan parents are also expected to take the responsibility for petitioning for reinstatement, whereas other states put this onus on school districts. These severe burdens ultimately result in disproportionate effects upon children of color, poor children, and children who may be eligible for special education. There is no obligation for any agency to provide services, support, or supervision for these troubled and/or troubling children.

The trend to exclude a broad range of children and youth from schools, to provide insufficient due process protections, and to provide minimal alternatives for children after they are expelled raises numerous questions and concerns. Which children are most affected by these policies and practices? If, indeed, children expelled from school are dangerous, why do we, as a society, not seek to provide the necessary programs and services to assist them? If, indeed, they are not dangerous, why are they not in school? Is it only the children directly affected who are harmed by these policies, or do the policies have a broader reach into our schools and communities? What is our societal obligation to nurture and educate children and youth? I examine these questions, to the extent possible, in the remainder of this chapter.

UNDERMINING THE VISION OF UNIVERSAL EDUCATION: WHO IS EXCLUDED?

Universal education is not only a moral commitment to our youth but an essential element of a socially and economically healthy society. Yet, as the following quote illustrates, poor record keeping within the public system denies acknowledgment of the growing numbers of children for whom the door to education is closed.

> I am writing to inquire whether you are aware of any recent reports detailing suspensions and expulsions in Michigan. I am updating a report on Zero Tolerance that Michigan's Children created several years ago. The report relied on the 2001–02 School Safety Practices Report from the Center for Education Performance and Information. However, we were hoping to obtain more recent information. I contacted the State Board of Education, but they do not have specific data regarding the length and number of expulsions by offense, grade level, gender, or ethnicity. (Query to SAC/MI, April 2007)

This example is important because it symbolizes the lack of data collected and maintained by the very state agencies charged with administering zero-tolerance policies and practices. Although both federal and state laws require school districts to provide expulsion data, there are few enforcement or oversight mechanisms that force the schools to accurately track and report data. Without these mechanisms, state and local authorities have not collected the data necessary to make informed judgments about the consequences of zero-tolerance policies and practices. The reluctance to collect and report this information is compounded by the requirements of No Child Left Behind, the Bush administration's signature education program, that penalize schools with high rates of disciplinary problems. The lack of accurate and comprehensive data about who is barred from educational services limits understandings of the consequences of these policies and precludes wise policy planning. In large part, it also indicates a general lack of interest in the children who are so impacted, a result that is not surprising given the characteristics of the children who are most affected by zero-tolerance policies and practices.

Despite the limitations of official data sources, researchers have revealed some important trends. Every study that has been completed has determined that these policies have radically increased the number of expulsions (First 2000). Several studies have revealed that zero-tolerance policies primarily affect young children in sixth through ninth grades (Polakow-Suransky 1999). All existing studies show that zero-tolerance policies disproportionately affect children of color (First 2000), and many find that they have disproportionately affected children and youth with special needs (Polakow-Suransky 1999). Other studies indicate that many youth expelled through these policies and practices end up in the justice systems in what is referred to as the "school-to-prison pipeline" (Advancement Project 2005; Civil Rights Project and Institute on Race and Justice at Northeastern University 2003). At the same time, studies have shown that proactive disciplinary practices, as differentiated from reactive policies and practices associated with zero tolerance, reduce incidents of undesirable behavior (Skiba 2000). I expand on many of these points throughout the rest of the chapter to further demonstrate the consequences of these policies.

Impact on Children of Color

> Asked why an elementary school principal reacted so differently towards two children who had behaved in similar ways he replied, "I know that he will resume as soon as I leave but when I tell Billy [a Caucasian child] to stop he does so. Robert [an African American child], on the other hand, stands there and asks, 'Why' when I chastise him."

Although zero-tolerance policies do not explicitly target children and youth of color, studies consistently indicate a disparate impact upon racial minorities (Skiba et al. 2002; Townsend 2000). These policies can be applied in extremely subjective ways that are often influenced by racial prejudice (Keleher 2000). For example,

> An African-American high school student in . . . Rhode Island offered to help his teacher dislodge a stuck diskette from his classroom's computer. But when he pulled out his keychain knife to help release the disk, he fell afoul of . . . "zero tolerance" rules, which mandate automatic exclusion for any student who brings a "weapon" to school. . . . On the other hand, a white student in . . . Vermont was neither suspended nor expelled when he explained that he'd brought a loaded shotgun to school because it was hunting season. (Keleher 2000:2)

In every school district examined, scholars and policy makers have found significant racial disparities in student suspensions and expulsions, with African American and Latino students much more likely to be suspended or expelled than their white counterparts. In some areas, African Americans are suspended or expelled at twice their proportion of the school population, while in other locations Latinos are expelled up to four times their proportion of the school population (Keleher 2000). This disproportionate representation of African Americans in the expulsion rates is not due to socioeconomic status. Studies that have accounted for this possibility by controlling the poverty level have still found that race makes a significant contribution to rates of school suspension (Skiba 2000; Urban Institute 1999).

According to Skiba (2000), the primary source of racial disproportionality is the vast differences in the number of times that students are sent to the office by classroom teachers. Once the student is referred to the main office, there are no significant differences between white and black students in mean number of days per suspension; however, African American students are nearly twice as likely to be referred to the office as white students. There are also differences in the types of incidents that result in a referral, with African American students disproportionately sent to the office for behavior such as loitering, disrespect, excessive noise, threat, and the ambiguous category called "conduct interference." White students are typically referred for more explicit behavior, such as smoking, endangering, obscene language, vandalism, and drugs/alcohol. The categories that result in suspensions for African American students are typically more subjective, and it has been hypothesized that the "disproportionate discipline of African-American students may be due in part to a misrepresentation of differences in the behavior of black and white students that are essentially culturally biased" (Skiba 2000:2).

While the life chances of all expelled students are affected, the effects are even more significant on families without the economic resources to pursue alternatives, including disproportionate numbers of minority children. Since more minorities are excluded from educational services, zero-tolerance laws support a culture that perpetuates a system of racial and ethnic disparities in education attainment. A lack of education prevents entry into many avenues of employment. This, in turn, leads to behaviors that reflect anger and despair and may portend future encounters with the penal system. For example, in Michigan, there are more young African American men in prison than there are in college (Justice Policy Institute 2002). This appalling fact severely affects not only the individuals in question, but also the African American community and the society as a whole.

Impact on Children with Special Education Needs

> An eight-year-old boy with a recognized learning disability was denied his role in
> the school play, a part he had worked very hard to master, because of misbehavior
> on the playground. When he cried and muttered angry words he was excluded from
> school altogether. Then there was the 12-year-old girl who, left alone in an unat-
> tended special education classroom with four male students, pointed a pair of blunt
> scissors at them and told them to leave her alone. She was expelled for possession of
> a dangerous weapon.

An analysis of the records of expelled students who came to the attention of
SAC/MI in the 1999–2000 school year revealed that many of the students who
were expelled should have been screened for special education services eligibility
long before the triggering incident (Edmonds-Cady 2002). The most common
risk factors were indications of emotional problems (17%), previous trauma
(15%), diagnosis of ADHD (15%), participation in private counseling or therapy treatment (13%), and depression (11%). While Michigan does not explicitly
track how many expelled students had been certified as needing special education services, the SAC/MI study found that 71% of the students in the study
either were special education certified, were receiving protections under the
IDEA, or had identifiable risk factors prior to the expulsion incident. Students
with emotional disorders (depression, bipolar disorder, etc.) are at particular
risk as they are often expelled for behaviors symptomatic of their disability, such
as explosive behavior, aggression, and impaired judgment. Students eligible for
special education as emotionally impaired comprise about 8% of all special education students but 26% of school removals greater than 10 days among special
education students. These students were not expelled for violent acts. Rather,
they were expelled for writing, verbalizing, exhibiting signs of fear and anger,
or just poor judgments, which is particularly problematic given that the fear
and anger they were expressing may have been directly linked to the lack of accommodations and support provided to them in the first place (Edmonds-Cady
2002).

Some school boards refuse to diagnose or test students for disabilities, even
when the symptoms that should have alerted school officials are present. Fifty-
two percent of the children in the center's study had exhibited one or more risk
factors but had never been referred for evaluation. Only 1% of the general student body has been found eligible as "emotionally impaired" at any one time,
though experts claim that 20% of U.S. children and adolescents have at least
one diagnosable mental health disorder, with about 11% suffering from serious

emotional disturbance (Demytteare et al. 2004). The failure to properly identify students with special needs or to provide the necessary academic support for eligible students results in students being penalized academically and punished for behaviors that could and should have been averted by positive, supportive behavior plans.

A student who is eligible for special education services is guaranteed a free, appropriate public education (FAPE) regardless of disciplinary status. For those students who have been expelled under a zero-tolerance policy, such services, when delivered at all, most often provide two to four hours a week in an isolated location. Even the casual observer would find this inadequate. While it sounds as if these children are better off than students expelled without these services, the services provided are strikingly inadequate. Children in need of special education require, by definition, *more* services than the average student, not less. Yet expelled students receive only a fraction of the services available to average in-school students. Also, these students miss the socialization that only a school or classroom can offer.

Impact Upon Children in Early Adolescence

> "In elementary school they [students] are children, in middle school they are young adults and in high school they are adults!"
>
> —Middle school principal

Is he right? Are middle school and high school students functioning at the same level as adults? That assertion occurred during a conference to determine the consequences for a 12-year-old boy who rode his friend's bicycle to the neighboring elementary school and abandoned it there. The principal labeled the act a "felony." The presence of an advocate was critical to the decision to allow the student to remain in school.

Every expulsion study of students by age and grade identifies early adolescence as the period when students are most likely to receive school exclusion penalties. Zero-tolerance policies are expecting children in this age group to think and behave in an adult manner. The policies further require that students recognize and act in their own best interest, commensurate with competent adults, navigating a confusing and legalistic system of disciplinary policies and procedures (Pitts 2005).

Paradoxically, these policies have taken hold just as a raft of new scientific studies produced added evidence of adolescent immaturity (Geidd et al. 1999; Yurgelun-Todd 2007). Recent research studies have revealed that while the brain is 85% developed by mass by the time a child is 5 years of age, the brain continues to evolve well into adulthood. Specifically, the prefrontal cortex (the part of the brain responsible for planning, judgment, and control of emotional responses) is in the process of maturation during the adolescent years and is not yet fully equipped to control emotions or make good judgments, leading to more risk-taking behavior. In addition, adolescents were not able to interpret facial expressions accurately, misidentifying fear 100% of the time when emotion shown was shock or anger. This misidentification is due to the prefrontal cortex not yet interacting with the emotional part of the brain as it does in adults and can lead adolescents to react more aggressively toward other people.

The American Psychological Association (APA) disseminated a lengthy review of the intent and consequences of zero-tolerance policies (American Psychological Association 2006). In a section of the report addressing the developmental appropriateness of zero-tolerance policies, the APA reported:

> Particularly before the age of 15, adolescents appear to display psychological immaturity in at least four areas: poor resistance to peer influence, attitudes toward and perception of risk, future orientation, and impulse control. The case for psychological immaturity during adolescence is also supported by evidence from developmental neuroscience indicating that the brain structure of adolescents is less well developed than previously thought. Developmental neuroscientists believe that if a particular structure of the brain is still immature, then the functions that it governs will also show immaturity; that is, adolescents may be expected to take greater risks and reason less adequately about the consequences of their behavior. Finally, a growing body of developmental research indicates that certain characteristics of secondary schools often are at odds with the developmental challenges of adolescence, which include the need for close peer relationships, autonomy, support from adults other than one's parents, identity negotiation, and academic self-sufficiency.

Research on adolescent brain development has played an important role in debates regarding the culpability of young people and their capacity to stand trial (Juvenile Justice Center 2004). It is ironic that while vigorous debates about the implications of this research are conducted by those involved with the juvenile justice systems, there has been little conversation among educators—individuals responsible for the healthy development of our youth—about these issues. Instead of representing a space focused on positive youth development, the educational system continues to rely on punishment and control to the detriment of both children and the institution. Alternatives to expulsion, including redirection of unwanted or unacceptable behaviors, would be more beneficial than expulsion, which may lead to dire consequences, especially for children who may have no other resources for education. For example, Michigan has a well-conceived but underused program called the Michigan Positive Behavior Support Initiative (PBS), which advocates responding to children by first assessing the child's personal and social milieu. It requires planning that includes both expectations and goals for the student, but also ways in which the adults will modify the environment and interactions. PBS offers a detailed map of a new and promising journey for our children and those who teach them (Michigan Department of Education 2000).

Impact on the School Community

> The School Board members and their advisors sit above us on leather chairs while we [parents and child] sit below on folding chairs, confused and intimidated.
>
> —A parent

> My son is fearful and bewildered. His friend, Jimmie, is a good kid, yet he was expelled when he was 14 for receiving an unsolicited email. Now my son wonders what he might do that could bring such a punishment.
>
> —Testimony to a state commission

> My classmate didn't act out so no one paid him any attention until he committed suicide. Then everyone went to his funeral and cried.
>
> —A student

The emphasis on punishment and repression impacts the whole school population, including staff and "good students," as well as those unfortunate enough to be caught in the net of zero-tolerance policies. In the summer of 2000, 50 high school students from 50 different school districts in Michigan attended a seminar I conducted on zero tolerance. Students spoke of the oppressive climate permeating their schools. They expressed deep concern for their fellow students as well as anxiety about the way youth in general are perceived. Punitive laws legitimize a poisonous climate of fear and suspicion on the part of both staff and students. With the proliferation of these stringent laws, the general public believes that there must be a problem, and the fear of violence is reinforced. There is no forum for young people to examine concerns and identify strategies to make schools safe and nurturing places for all students, and no method of calculating the damages that zero-tolerance policies inflict on other students and faculty.

I have conducted focus groups that include both those students who are highly successful and those who struggle to get through school. In those groups, participants readily agree that they can identify the students who "can" and those who "can't" get away with frowned-upon behaviors. While students attend their required government classes and learn the values of inclusion, fairness, and justice that we profess for our civic life, they are keenly aware that those same values are often not practiced in their schools. In a study on the development of legal socialization, Alex Piquero and colleagues (2005) look at the interactions that may influence the development of either recognition of legal legitimacy or cynicism toward the law and authority. That study refers back to an earlier study by Tom Tyler (1990) on perceptions of legal legitimacy:

> First, legitimacy had an independent influence on compliance. . . . Second, using contact with legal authorities as an intervening variable, Tyler found that procedural justice influenced subsequent perceptions of legitimacy even after controlling for prior perceived legitimacy suggesting that perceived procedural fairness is an important antecedent to legitimacy. (Piquero et al. 2005:109)

The emphasis on rules and standards of behavior for the students, juxtaposed with the absence of perceived fairness in administration of those standards, would seem to provide a culture of profound cynicism about the way their world really works.

Zero-tolerance policies exemplify this problem because the severity of penalties and consequences of permanent expulsion from school services are not accompanied by stringent due process protections to ensure proper use of zero-tolerance laws. It is interesting to note that clear federal and state protections exist for many classes of individuals. For example, the Civil Rights of Institutionalized Persons Act (CRIPA) protects incarcerated adults and juveniles. Teachers and school administrators have specific due process avenues. Yet students in general public education programs are protected only by the general right to due process contained in the 1975 U.S. Supreme Court decision *Goss v. Lopez*, in which "the Court made it clear that '[l]onger suspensions or expulsions for the remainder of the school term, or permanently, may require more formal procedures.'"[5] However, the opinion does not specify what these "formal procedures" might be. This lack of clear due process protections leads to casual and capricious decisions to expel. There is no requirement for vigorous scrutiny of evidence before making the life-affecting decision to expel a student. School administrators fail to assess individual acts for intent or potential danger. School district personnel act as investigator, prosecutor, judge, and jury for students accused of violations of zero-tolerance policies.

The failure to observe stringent rules of evidence or to consider the intent of actions leaves students distrustful of the adults to whom they should look for support and guidance. This distrust can have deadly consequences. In the April 22, 2007, CBS *60 Minutes* segment on the massacre at Virginia Tech, "The Mind of an Assassin," narrator Scott Pelley reports, "In 81% of school shootings they studied, other kids knew in advance and said nothing." Psychologist William Pollack of Harvard Medical School gave *60 Minutes* an advance look at his interviews with the kids who knew but didn't tell adults, stating: "Well, think about it from their point of view, you're afraid to tell them because, one, you're afraid you'll get in trouble. Two, you're afraid your name will get out and people will hurt you and, *three, you're afraid that the person you talk about won't get help, but, will somehow be harmed or adjudicated. So you keep your mouth shut*" (emphasis added).

The Consequences of Long-Term Expulsion: The Absence of Alternatives

Data about student status, postexpulsion, is rarely forthcoming. We know that alternative education programs are not readily available. A number of issues remain unclear: how long expelled students are out of school; when or whether expelled students are ever reinstated in their home district; and whether they are able to enroll in a new district or in an alternative setting.

Home schooling is not realistic for a poor, ill-educated, or overworked parent. Access to private alternatives—or to another public school district—is highly questionable even if the school is willing to admit the expelled student. Children expelled under the weapons law are barred from all public schools in Michigan. When a child is expelled for a violation of local school rules and is therefore not barred from all public schools in the state, he or she is nevertheless rarely permitted to enroll in another district. Furthermore, prohibitive fees, transportation, and age requirements usually present insurmountable barriers for even the most determined families.

Many studies of what is called the school-to-prison pipeline spell out the chilling consequences of these policies on the larger community. "Out-of-school youth are more likely than in-school youth to engage in risky behavior that endanger others and drain public resources. . . . Research has . . . found a strong correlation between expulsion and dropping out (Advancement Project and Harvard Civil Rights Project) which puts these students at future risk of unemployment, low-wage jobs, public assistance, health problems, drug use, criminal conduct and incarceration" (Rumberger 2001). This latter outcome is a particularly troubling public cost, but one that has been documented in Michigan. In a nonrandom sample of 204 young women in three types of juvenile justice settings, 74% had been suspended and 20% expelled (Sarri et al. 2003). These consequences strongly question policies and practices that prioritize exclusion over concerted efforts to ensure that sufficient resources are directed to the healthy development of children and youth.

RECOMMENDATIONS

Based on this discussion, as well as my years of experience in this field, I strongly believe that it is possible to assure safe, well-disciplined schools while still guaranteeing that even our most troubled or troubling children will be provided with the intellectual and social skills to become active, productive members of our society. The following recommendations, either individually or, preferably, as a package, hold the promise of achieving that goal:

1. *Guarantee all children an appropriate public education.* Either through legislation or through constitutional amendment, assure that all children, regardless of disciplinary or other status, have access to a free, appropriate public education.

2. *Collect and analyze accurate data.* Although we know the general profile of children likely to be caught in the zero-tolerance web, many states have no way to assess the magnitude and consequences of these policies. Basic information should include (1) demographic data, such as race / ethnicity, gender, free / reduced lunch status, special education eligibility, grade level, and assessment test scores; (2) exclusions by length of time the student is out of school; (3) clearer and more specific definitions and reporting of violations; and (4) descriptive information about the status of the student (e.g., not in school, detention or juvenile court jurisdiction, alternative placement, special education plan). Complete and accurate data are essential to assess the impact of zero-tolerance policies, and, though often ignored, the law does require such collection and reporting.

3. *Codify due process protections.* New York State offers a model for such protections: "No pupil may be suspended for a period in excess of five school days unless such a pupil and the person in parental relation to such a pupil shall have had an opportunity for a fair hearing, upon reasonable notice, at which such pupil shall have the right to representation by counsel, with the right to question

witnesses against such pupil and to present witnesses and other evidence on his behalf. . . . A record of the hearing shall be maintained. . . . A[n administrator] shall have the authority to modify this suspension on a case-by-case basis."[6] If we continue to rely on exclusion as a primary disciplinary mechanism, it is essential that we ensure that procedures are in place to protect against arbitrary decision making.

4. *Implement clear standards for alternative education.* Once the need for an alternative educational program for a particular student is established, an accessible, appropriate program with needed supports should be provided. Elements of such a model program would include instructional hours at least equivalent to mainstream programs; transportation, when not located at the neighborhood building; opportunities to complete and receive credits; and an opportunity to transfer back to the home school after alternative conditions are met. With support from the Charles Stewart Mott Foundation, the National Youth Employment Coalition's Working Group on Effective Practices in Community-Based and Alternative Education has developed a comprehensive education tool that can be used to identify effective practices and develop tools to improve educational practices for vulnerable youth (Thakur 2004).

5. *Address the obvious disparate impact on children of color.* The continuing shame of racially disparate punishments must be challenged. In addition to establishing proactive, child-centered disciplinary programs, suspensions/expulsions should be monitored for disparate impact on vulnerable populations and an audit conducted when necessary.

6. *Proactively identify children with disabilities and children exhibiting risk indicators.* Disturbing behaviors and/or failure to make academic progress should signal the need to evaluate and determine eligibility for special education services. Nevertheless, these children are often ignored or dismissed as troublemakers or kids who just do not care. Federal regulations of the Individuals with Disabilities Education Act of 1997 require districts to implement Child Find, the process by which children are initially identified and evaluated for special education services. In a letter dated April 23, 2001, the Michigan Poverty Law Program submitted a Model Child Find Provision for Michigan Regulations. It included sections on Target Populations, Methods of Identifying Children, Public Awareness, and Administration. Implementation of such recommendations would go a long way to assure that children who need special supports will receive them.

7. *Provide treatment for substance abuse.* The current practice of expelling students for possession or use of illegal substances is shortsighted at best. These

young people need access to treatment and education or they will eventually join the growing number of prisoners incarcerated for substance abuse crimes, at great cost to society.

8. *Address bullying behaviors.* Considerable attention has been paid recently to the corrosive effects of bullying behavior on the victims. Too often, schools have dismissed reports about such torment as "he said, she said" events, leaving children to solve the problems as best they can, sometimes with devastating consequences as many of the school shooters have been identified as such victims. Recent bills in the Michigan legislature seek to correct this situation (S.B. 1156, H.B. 5616). The danger, given past practices, is that a new target population, "bullies," may be identified for expulsion. Rather, this new sensitivity must be employed to understand and redirect the bully while protecting the victim.

In winter, you wear a coat, and it keeps you warm. The knife made me feel safe.

Saying she didn't want to get in trouble, the 12-year-old had turned in a knife to her counselor. She was immediately referred for permanent expulsion. At the hearing she was asked why she had the knife. The above quote was her response. No one asked her why she felt unsafe or how they might help her to feel safe. A vigorous public school system serving all children well is essential to a robust democracy. The long evolution from the earliest elite colonial academies to a public school system that has moved from asking "Who should be educated?" to "How shall we best educate all?" is regressing. The goal is no longer to assure that all young people will receive a free, individualized, and equitable education and become full participating members of their communities.

Many of the laws and customs established to make our society work, to make it orderly and safe, do not actually do so. They certainly do not assure a society where each member is equally able to achieve his or her aspirations. Beyond contributing to the resistance to reducing the achievement gap, exclusions from the classroom and/or the school correlate to dropout numbers and carve a path to incarceration, as has been well documented through the Harvard Civil Rights Project's voluminous information on the "school-to-prison pipeline."

For more than 30 years, I have spoken with troubled youth both individually and in groups. Invariably, when asked what adults can do to be supportive, they reply, "Talk to us. Talk to *me*." There is a hunger for attention and recognition. A study reported in *Science* magazine found that students who wrote for fifteen minutes—one time, at the beginning of the semester—about their most important values showed remarkable end-of-semester grade improvement (Wilson 2006). More than money or fancy materials, attention must be paid!

To identify a child as dangerous or to say that a child "scares me" is often enough to remove that child from all educational and support services. The recommendations above offer an alternative approach—one that will move to assure safe, appropriate learning environments for all of our children. Eliminating zero-tolerance laws—policies and practices that perpetuate suspicion and fear toward vulnerable children—would be the most effective means to achieve the goal of equal education. Laws to protect against violence are firmly in the criminal code and should be kept in that milieu. Removing these explicit statutes from the school code and concentrating on prevention and support are more hopeful means of achieving the safe, productive school environment that we wish for all of our children.

QUESTIONS FOR DISCUSSION

1. How do school discipline policies impact children in your life and practice?

2. What has made zero-tolerance policies so compelling to educators, social workers, and the public at this particular historical juncture?

3. What notions of childhood are embedded in zero-tolerance policies? How do these notions intersect with ideas about race, gender, class, or disability?

4. Consider the four stories that Zweifler recounts in this chapter. What alternatives to suspension or expulsion could be considered in these instances?

5. What lessons does Zweifler offer us for practice in regard to school discipline policies?

NOTES

1. Gun-Free School Zones Act of 1990, pub. L. no. 101–647, 104 Stat. 4844 (codified in scattered sections of 12, 18, 20, 21, 28, 31, 46, U.S.C.).

2. Michigan Compiled Laws 380.1310 and 1311.

3. *Brown v. Board of Education,* 347 U.S. 483 (1954).

4. Individuals with Disabilities Education Act (IDEA), 20 U.S.C. (1994).

5. *Goss v. Lopez,* 419 U.S. 565 (1975).

6. N.Y. Education Law 3214 (2001).

REFERENCES

Advancement Project. (2005). *Education on lockdown: The schoolhouse to jailhouse track.* (March). Accessed August 1, 2007, at http://www.advancementproject.org/publications/opportunity-to-learn.php.

Advancement Project and Harvard Civil Rights Project. (2000). *Opportunities suspended: The devastating consequences of zero tolerance and school discipline.* (June). Accessed June 1, 2007, at http://www.advancementproject.org/reports/opsusp.pdf.

American Psychological Association. (2006). Zero tolerance policies can have unintended effects, APA report finds. *APA Online: Monitor on Psychology 37* (9): 7.

Civil Rights Project and Institute on Race and Justice at Northeastern University. (2003). *School to prison pipeline: Charting intervention strategies of prevention and support for minority children.* (May). Accessed July 7, 2007, at http://civilrightsproject.ucla.edu/convenings/.

Demytteare, K., R. Bruffaerts, J. Posada-Villa, I. Gasquet, V. Kovess, J. P. Lepine et al. (2004). Prevalence, severity, and unmet need for treatment of mental disorders in the World Health Organization World Mental Health Surveys. *Journal of the American Medical Association 291:* 2582–90.

Edmonds-Cady, C. (2002). *The children left behind—our students "at-risk."* Ann Arbor: Student Advocacy Center of Michigan.

First, J. (2000). Executive Director, the National Coalition of Advocates for Students. *Testimony before the U.S. Commission on Civil Rights.* (February 18). Archived at the Student Advocacy Center, Ann Arbor.

Geidd, J. N., J. Blumenthal, N. O. Jeffries, F. X. Castellanos, L. Hong, A. Zijdenbos, T. Pauls, A. C. Evans, and J. L. Rapoport. (1999) Brain development during childhood and adolescence: A longitudinal MRI study. *Nature Neuroscience 2:* 861–63.

Grisso, T., and L. Steinberg. (2003). *The MacArthur juvenile adjudicative competency study.* Accessed August 30, 2007, at http://www.nicic.org/Library/018908.

Justice Policy Institute. (2002). *Cellblocks or classrooms? The funding of higher education and corrections and its impact on African American men.* http://www.justicepolicy.org/coc.pdf.

Juvenile Justice Center. (2004). *Adolescence, brain development and legal culpability.* Washington, D.C.: American Bar Association. Accessed August 29, 2007, at http://www.abanet.org/crimjust/juvjus/Adolescence.pdf.

Keleher, T. (2000). Program Director, Applied Research Center, Racial Disparities Related to School Zero Tolerance Policies. *Testimony before the U.S. Commission on Civil Rights.* (February 18). Archived at the Student Advocacy Center, Ann Arbor.

Michigan Department of Education, Office of Special Education and Early Intervention Services. (2000). *Positive behavior support for ALL Michigan students: Creat-*

ing environments that assure learning (executive summary). (September). State of Michigan.

Modzeleski, W. (2000). *Briefing on the civil rights implications of zero tolerance policies in schools.* Address to the U.S. Commission on Civil Rights. (February 18).

Piquero, A. R., J. Fagan, E. P. Mulvey, L. Steinberg, and C. Odgers. (2005). Criminology: Developmental trajectories of legal socialization among serious adolescent offenders. *Journal of Criminal Law and Criminology 96:* 267–98.

Pitts, M. (2005). *Adolescent brain development: A review.* Ann Arbor: Student Advocacy Center of Michigan.

Polakow-Suranski, S. (1999). *Access denied: Mandatory expulsion requirement and the erosion of educational opportunity in Michigan.* Ann Arbor: Student Advocacy Center of Michigan.

Rubin, D. (2004). *Statutory protections in state codes.* Ann Arbor: Student Advocacy Center of Michigan.

Rumberger, R. (2001). Why students drop out of school and what can be done. Paper presented at the conference on Dropouts in America: How severe is the problem? What do we know about intervention and prevention? (January). Harvard University.

Sarri, R., M. Ruffolo, S. Goodkind, C. Albertson, and J. Allen. (2003). *Youth in transition: A comparative study of adolescent girls in community-based and residential programs.* Ann Arbor: Institute for Social Research, University of Michigan.

Skiba, R. J. (2000). *Zero tolerance, zero evidence: A critical analysis of school disciplinary practice.* Research review submitted to the U.S. Commission on Civil Rights. (February 9).

Skiba, R., R. S. Michael, A. Nardo, and R. Peterson (2002). The color of disciplines: Sources of racial and gender disproportionality in school punishment. *Urban Review 34:* 317–42.

Skiba, R. J., and R. L. Peterson. (1999). The dark side of zero tolerance: Can punishment lead to safe schools? *Phi Delta Kappan 80,* 372–77.

Stone-Palmquist, P. (2005). *Nowhere to go: The devastating journey of youth expelled from Michigan schools.* Ann Arbor: Student Advocacy Center of Michigan.

Thakur, M. (Ed.) (2004). NYEC EDNetTool. 2nd edition. Washington, D.C.: National Youth Employment Coalition. Accessed April 25, 2008, at http://www.nyec.org/pn_tools/prodreg.cfm.

Townsend, B. (2000). Disproportionate discipline of African American children and youth: Culturally-responsive strategies for reducing school suspensions and expulsions. *Exceptional Children 66:* 381–91.

Tyler, T. R. (1990). *Why people obey the law.* New Haven: Yale University Press.

Urban Institute. (1999). *Snapshots of America's families II: Children's behavior and well-*

being, 3. Accessed August 1, 2007, at http://www.urban.orgn/content/Research/ SAF/Snapshots/1999Results/children'sBehaviorsandWellBeing/Behavior.htm.

Wilson, T. D. (2006). The power of social psychological interventions. *Science 313* (September 1): 1251–52.

Yurgelun-Todd, D. (2007). Emotional and cognitive changes during adolescence. *Current Opinion in Neurobiology 17* (2): 251–57.

TEN

Constructing Ability and Disability Among Preschoolers in the Crestview Head Start Program

Patricia A. Jessup

> She [Rachel] got to where she'd pull herself up and then
> to where she'd scoot a little bit. . . . I think she's settled,
> calmed down quite a bit for the most part. But she's a lot
> more mobile and around and into things. . . .
> She responds to her name.
>
> —Ms. King, Head Start teacher

> I am highly biased for the rights of Rachel. I mean for Rachel
> to be bombarded with all the stimuli that could occur in
> with, let's say we have 18 children or 19, where it's difficult to
> have a corner of quiet. I wonder what we're doing with her
> rights versus Rachel's needing to be scheduled and needing
> to have a very structured situation and a very quiet situation,
> and maybe being held and rocked.
>
> —Ms. Jones, special education director

Within educational settings, perceptions of students are shaped by constructions of ability and disability, as well as by prevalent perspectives on children and childhood. These constructions influence educational policies, practices,

This chapter is based on my dissertation research that was completed under the guidance of Dr. Sally Lubeck. Prior to undertaking research in the Crestview Head Start Program, I had explored issues related to children with disabilities in three other Head Start programs in my work with Dr. Lubeck on her research project entitled "The Social Contexts of Head Start."

and discourse and have real consequences for children's education, even in the early years.

In a larger research project that I draw on here, I investigated the interplay of these policies, practices, and discourses in the lives of young children in one Head Start program, Crestview Head Start (CHS).[1] In this chapter, I illustrate the ways that differing perspectives and discourses of disability affect where and how specific children like Rachel are educated. I describe the ways in which Crestview Head Start shaped an inclusive discourse about children with disabilities[2]—a discourse that helped to reinforce existing program policies and practices and allowed Rachel to be an integral member of the Head Start classroom. I examine the ways that this discourse stood in contrast to the exclusive and categorical language used when these same children were subsequently placed in public school kindergarten. In kindergarten, inclusion was not accepted practice, which resulted in Rachel being placed in a separate classroom for children with severe disabilities. By bringing to light the assumptions regarding disability that shaped these practices, I provide a lens for considering how constructions of ability and disability are playing out in other settings.

When I use the concept of "discourse," I reference a "mode of action" that is both "shaped and constrained by social structures" and "socially constitutive" (Fairclough 1992:64). In my study, the discourse about children with disabilities is supported by various routinized social practices, for example, federal legislation, the policies and practices of CHS, and perspectives of disability in society at large and in education. The categorizing and deficit language used in federal legislation, shaped by prevalent perspectives on disabilities, in turn, shapes the language and practices related to children with disabilities in educational settings.

In this chapter, I illustrate the ways that the identities of children with disabilities are constructed in discourse, and, in turn, how these constructions influence children's inclusion in or exclusion from regular education settings. In both CHS and kindergarten, the discourse about children with disabilities— shaped by policies and practices—served to constitute children with disabilities in particular ways. And in both, there appeared to be an alignment of policies, practices, and discourse. In CHS this alignment led to inclusion of all; in kindergarten, to exclusion of many children with disabilities from regular education classrooms.

CRESTVIEW HEAD START

Driving toward CHS, one sees rolling fields of corn and soybeans. A steady stream of cars is interspersed with trucks pulling oversized loads of prefabricated housing along the north/south highway that dissects the region. Numerous lakes dot the landscape, and along a secondary road an occasional Amish carriage suddenly comes into view. These sights are emblematic of the midwestern region served by the CHS program.

CHS is one of the initial Head Start summer programs developed in response to the 1965 federal Head Start initiative, the keystone of President Lyndon Johnson's War on Poverty. Head Start is a comprehensive program for preschool children of families living in poverty. Mr. Miller, the executive director, has directed the CHS program since 1965 when he was asked to apply for a summer Head Start grant. CHS has grown since that first summer and is now a "full-year" (school-year) program serving 167 children.

Along with the growth in numbers of children and geographic area served, CHS has also expanded its work with children with disabilities. As of 1972, all Head Start programs were mandated to have 10% of their enrollment slots for children with disabilities (U.S. Department of Health, Education, and Welfare 1973). In the early years of CHS, there were no other programs available for children with disabilities in the area. Later, local school districts began providing equipment and some services, such as a preschool special education class, and these services continued to develop with the passage of P.L. 94–142 in 1974.[3]

P.L. 94–142, now known as the Individuals with Disabilities Education Act (IDEA), mandated education for all children with disabilities beginning at age 5. This legislation encourages inclusion through its mandate that all children with disabilities receive a "free appropriate public education," and that this education, to the greatest extent possible, be with peers without disabilities. However, it also establishes a separate special education system and allows for segregation of children with disabilities in separate classrooms and facilities. The 1986 amendment to IDEA (P.L. 99–457) lowered the mandated age for the provision of services to age 3, with implementation mandated by the 1991–92 school year.

To comply with this mandate, the local multicounty special education agency in the midwestern region of my study asked CHS to serve young children with disabilities. Under this arrangement, children who were receiving early intervention (0–3) services from the special education agency would also, from age 3 until entrance to kindergarten, receive special education services within the CHS program. Separate preschool special education classrooms that had been established in the local area were disbanded. The identified young children were assigned to one of five CHS classrooms based on where they lived. Thus the numbers of children with disabilities within any classroom varied from year to year. The types and severity of disabilities represented by the children also varied, but regardless of the type or severity of disability, all children with disabilities were included in CHS from age 3 until they entered kindergarten.

Federal Head Start Performance Standards encourage the inclusion of all children with disabilities in Head Start programs and specifically promote the recruitment of children with severe disabilities, thus opening the door of Head Start to all children with disabilities. But local implementers of policy mandates actively shape policy by the interpretations and choices they make in their local situation. Consequently, variation exists from place to place as to whether and how the boundary between regular and special education is crossed. CHS used the opportunities provided by federal and state policies to implement a wide range of program policies that encouraged and supported the inclusion of children with disabilities in CHS. Mr. Miller, the executive director, believed in including children with disabilities in the regular education classroom, and through his many years as an educator he had seen inclusion work "very, very well." His view was shared by the CHS director and education / disabilities coordinator, and accepted by the CHS teachers and the families they served.

I found the CHS program to be unique in its provision of services to children with disabilities. I had explored issues related to children with disabilities in three other Head Start programs in my work with Dr. Sally Lubeck on her research project entitled "The Social Contexts of Head Start" (Lubeck et al. 2003). Each of those Head Start sites fulfilled its mandate to have 10% of its enrollment slots filled by children with disabilities, but each did so in a different way, and none included children who were considered to have severe disabilities. These decisions reveal varying interpretations of federal policies and different understandings of disabilities.

CONCEPTIONS OF DISABILITY

Although accepted in this local situation, inclusion, a term with numerous meanings and usages, is controversial in the field of education. Inclusion contains the assumption that all children, regardless of the severity of their disability, should be in regular education programs in their neighborhood schools with necessary supports provided in those classrooms. Although many arguments can be made for the value of inclusion for children with disabilities (e.g., socializing with age peers without disabilities, hearing "normally" developing speech, being a member of a classroom community), numerous concerns also have been raised regarding inclusion. The inclusion issue has been debated frequently. Bailey et al. describe the varying positions as follows:

> For some the arguments in support of inclusion are so strong as to conclude that segregated services are not acceptable under any circumstances. For others, inclusion is considered highly desirable for most children, but may not be the best choice in some situations. Still others view inclusion as an excuse not to provide the special services a child with a disability really needs. (1998:30)

These varying views of inclusion are influenced by assumptions held about disabilities and form part of the context shaping educational practices for children with disabilities, including at CHS. Differing assumptions about disability underlie decisions about education disability classifications, discourse, and educational placement, and these differing assumptions have emerged strongly in the debates over inclusion. Special education has been dominated by a medical model of disability, or what Priestley (1998:209) calls a "preoccupation with impairment" in which children's bodies and minds are measured against "physical and cognitive norms." The social model, based on a social constructionist perspective, casts a distinctive light on these issues and illuminates how children come to be constituted, through discourse and other social practices, as disabled and in need of special education services.

Medical Model

Emphasis in the medical arena is on the etiology of the disorder, diagnosis of symptoms, and treatment or rehabilitation to restore "normal" functioning. Such a focus has led to numerous advances by medical researchers, resulting in the prevention of certain disorders and interventions to lessen the effects of others. The medical perspective on disability, however, is problematic. Numerous scholars (e.g., Barnes, Mercer, and Shakespeare 1999; Gartner and Lipsky 1990; Hahn 1997; Ingstad and Whyte 1995; Linton 1998; Mitchell and Snyder 1997; Oliver 1996; Rioux 1994; Wendell 1996) have written about the medical model of disability and its impact on individuals with disabilities. From a medical perspective, a disability is viewed as a sickness or a "pathological impairment, or a physical or mental inability to perform so-called normal tasks" (Hahn 1997:317). These descriptions locate the problem in the individual and focus on deficits of the individual. Fulcher (1989:27) notes that the medical view is based on a "natural science discourse and thus on a *correspondence* theory of meaning," by which objects are assumed to "essentially correspond with the term used to describe them." Consequently, within a medical discourse, individuals with disabilities are seen as particular disabilities rather than as whole persons.

In the medical framework, terms such as childhood and disability have been seen as fixed, definable categories—once categorized, an individual is thus located in "distinct domains of social life" (Stephens 1995:7). A person's disability is seen as something that can be objectively assessed "as a technical issue" (Fulcher 1989:27) for which professionals need only to find the appropriate rehabilitation, educational program, or therapeutic intervention. Once assessed and categorized, plans can be made, for example, for appropriate schooling, living arrangements, and treatment of the child with disabilities based on age, disability classification, and other essentialized characteristics.

The dominant discourse within special education locates disability in the individual. Thus, difficulties in behavior or learning within the classroom potentially can be construed as a result of the child's disability, that is, "disability explains school failure" (Gelzheiser 1990:44). Ferguson and Ferguson (1998:305) state, "it is this reliance on a pathological definition of difference, and a service response that either remediates or at least ameliorates, that has defined special education and the relationship between special and general education." Often this results in attention being turned toward special services and diverted away from accommodations and instructional strategies that could benefit the child in the regular education classroom.

Social Model

The social model of disability locates disability external to the person and recognizes the socially constructed aspect of disability. Disability is viewed as "a consequence of the interaction between individuals and the environment" (Hahn 1997:315). Disability is placed in context and is theorized in "similarly complex ways to the way race, class, and gender have been theorized" (Davis 1997:3). Within the social model, the individual is not lost. However, the focus is not on the individual's deficits but on the individual's experiences within the wider context of family and society, including institutional and policy contexts. Significant in this approach are the emphases on the changing nature of disability over time and the wide range of barriers in society, such as physical, attitudinal, and policy barriers.

The social model also encompasses multiple influences on the construction of disability. Legislation, institutions, media representations (see Barnes 1994; Hahn 1989; Mitchell and Snyder 1997; Thomson 1997), language (see Corbett

1996; Corker and French 1999), and other everyday practices (see Armstrong and Barton 1999; Gething 1992) are all part of the construction of disability, and these constructions are intimately tied to the treatment of people with disabilities.

From a social model perspective, a child's biological condition cannot be separated from the ways in which children with disabilities are talked about, the network of educational practices in which these children are immersed, nor the social, cultural, historical, political, and economic context in which policies and practices are developed and implemented. This is not to disregard the dominant medical perspective but to suggest that the impact of the medical view on children with disabilities and their education be carefully reconsidered. The social model provides a means to take another look and to illuminate taken-for-granted assumptions. From this perspective, the focus in education moves from the deficits of the child to needed environmental and instructional modifications. Classroom practices, as well as the educational policies that shape those practices, need to be considered.

In addition, major consideration is given to the role of language in the environment, as language is considered "as a system by which reality is actively and collectively constructed" (Sampson 1998:23). Or, as stated by Jaworski and Coupland (1999:3), discourse is "language use relative to social, political and cultural formations—it is language reflecting social order but also language shaping social order, and shaping individuals' interactions with society." The significance of the particular language used comes from how it functions within social relationships.

Consider, for example, *disability* and *special*, terms that are ever present in the field of *special* education. Neither term is neutral. Linton (1998:30) describes the prefix *dis* as connoting separation and creating "a barrier, cleaving in two ability and its absence, its opposite. Disability is the 'not' condition, the repudiation of ability." *Special* can be used to indicate a positive or better than ordinary person or situation, such as a hero or a wedding. It also can be used to designate difference, for example, Special Olympics as separate from the Olympic Games. But, "when the term 'special' is applied to disabled people, it emphasizes their relative powerlessness rather then conferring them with honour and dignity" (Corbett 1996:49). Educators frequently, and euphemistically, use the term special when difference and powerlessness are intended rather than "better than ordinary." Children with disabilities, already somewhat powerless by virtue of their age, often have little power over decisions regarding their education or the location of that education.

Disability and *special* are commonly used in everyday and professional language, as well as being instantiated in federal legislation and guidelines. Special education labels for children with disabilities are institutionalized in federal and state education mandates and in the Head Start Performance Standards. Because of the pervasiveness of these classifications and the lengthy history of their use, it is not surprising to hear educators employ them when talking about children with disabilities. It is important, though, to consider how these terms are utilized and their impact on children, as language is "not just used to name things but, more importantly to work out how to behave toward people" (Hartley 1982:1; cited in Saunders and Goddard 2001). Additionally "entrenched attitudes" are absorbed by speakers through language (Saunders and Goddard 2001).

Assumptions about disabilities influence and are influenced by policies, practices, and discourse, all of which are intertwined at many levels in the construction and experience of disability, and work in relationship with one another to constitute children with disabilities in particular ways. Looking at these areas, and their interrelationships, provides a way to consider how children are constructed as able or disabled, and, in turn, constituted as includable or not in regular education settings, and to see the inclusion of children with disabilities in the CHS program "as both constrained by social structures" and an active part of the process of production that potentially transforms or sustains social structures (Chouliaraki and Fairclough 1999:1). In this chapter, I provide only a brief overview of the role of policy and classroom practice before focusing on the role of discourse in shaping, changing, and sustaining constructions of disability.

CLASSROOM PRACTICES

Of the five classrooms operated by CHS, I focused my research in Mrs. King's classroom where seven children who had been identified as having a disability prior to age 3 were enrolled. Four were included in the morning session and 3 in the afternoon. These children represented a broad array of the disability categories specified in federal legislation and included children considered to have "severe" as well as "mild" disabilities. During the 1999–2000 school year, I was a participant observer in the classroom. This classroom provided an opportunity to see the inclusion of children with "severe" as well as "mild" disabilities enacted on a daily basis.

Ms. King was in her third year of teaching. She was certified to teach children from birth through grade 3 but was not specially certified to work with children with disabilities. Her training had been in early childhood education (ECE) rather than early childhood special education (ECSE). Although there is considerable overlap between ECE and ESCE, the latter tends to locate disability in the individual and operate from the perspective that intentional interventions are needed to develop skills and to address specific objectives for individual children (Odom and McEvoy 1990; Wolery and Wilbers 1994). In contrast, ECE at the time focused more on a developmentally appropriate approach with an emphasis on free play and creative exploration. The educational philosophy and curriculum of CHS fit with this ECE approach and focused on children developing at their own pace in an appropriate environment. This approach supported having children at varying places in their development in the same classroom and supported Ms. King in creating space for each child.

Ms. King included the children with disabilities in all activities and within these activities addressed the development of each child. She was flexible, sensitive to the varying needs of children, aware of children's need for independence, and willing to work with children with disabilities—attributes that contributed to a positive and inclusive atmosphere for all children in her classroom. It was an environment that allowed for mobility and exploration by all children while maintaining a balance between safety, availability of materials, and monitoring. Ms. King provided opportunities for social interaction across the day. Some children with disabilities did not interact extensively or intensively, but all increased their level of interaction to some degree over the course of the year.

Attending to each child and making accommodations in every part of the day required Ms. King to be cognizant of the needs of each child and, with the help of her assistants, to engage in intentional practices aimed at involving all children in every aspect of the program. Over the course of the year, the children, to varying degrees and in spite of numerous challenges, became a part of this classroom community.

LANGUAGE USAGE IN CRESTVIEW HEAD START

Although federal and local policies set the stage for inclusion at CHS, Ms. King's willingness to be adaptable and attentive to individual children provided a space for children with disabilities to grow and change in a classroom with their peers. Both policies and practice shaped, and were shaped by, the language related to disability at CHS. I examine this dialectic relationship below because it reveals the importance of language in understanding the experiences and representations of children and the reality that these experiences and representations vary tremendously across time and space.

Language Usage in the Classroom

Ms. King generally did not use disability labels or special education categories in her talk about the children in her classroom.[4] Her comments about individual children with disabilities usually focused on specific incidents, classroom accommodations, or progress a child was making, similar to those she made about any of the children in her classes. She focused on the child's behavior without reference to his or her specific disability or special education label. In Ms. King's talk, the absence of classificatory and special education language is noteworthy, and it was unexpected based on my prior experiences in other Head Start and K-12 settings. For example, in one site during three interviews with the Head Start disability coordinator and a special education supervisor, 35 different terms were used to refer to children with disabilities. These included special education categories, medical diagnoses, and general terms such as "not high functioning," "real different," and "delays."

A series of examples is illustrative of the language Ms. King used in relation to children in her class.

I may do a fifteen-minute circle time. They're there for two minutes and then we build up that time. Now Jorge can sit longer than Christy, depends [on] what we're doing.

Sometimes I'm so frustrated with him [Jorge] I've just about had it. But then the next second he's turning around and talking to me in complete sentences with a sense of humor and having a good time, and he couldn't do that before.

Before he [Matthew] couldn't put sentences together. He could tell you words but he couldn't put his thoughts together.

Socially I've seen a lot [of change]. She [Katie] used to stay to herself. . . . Her attention span has gotten longer, . . . I think she's learned to speak up and talk when she doesn't hear something.

I think she's [Rachel] settled, calmed down quite a bit for the most part. But she's a lot more mobile and around and into things. . . . She responds to her name.

I think her [Carrie] whole thing is getting an exposure to kids. Something she's not had before and getting her to do something, or try something, trying.

The checklist gives you an idea of some of the things and concepts that you can look through and see. Okay, it will say [certain children] didn't do good kicking the ball. Then outside playing you're able to observe when they're able to do it, and [when] you're out there you might be kicking with them. And that's how we do it more on a conscious level, like today when Charlie counted. I had to go and write that down . . . that he's able to count to 20.

I went through to see how many letters these kids knew and most of mine that were going on [to kindergarten], . . . knew at least 16 letters and have come a long way. Even like with Carrie, she now can make a C, an H, and a Y.

In these excerpts Ms. King, in a matter-of-fact manner, described children's behavior in the classroom and how she viewed changes in the children. Her comments were individualized and implied what behaviors she expected or valued for each child. For example, when discussing changes, her comments are based on modifications she felt individual children should make, for example, that Jorge and Christy sit in circle time, Jorge and Matthew communicate in sentences, Katie be more assertive, Rachel be more mobile and more "settled," Carrie attempt new things, and children learn the letters and numbers. These were her judgments, as the teacher, regarding what each child should do. Ms. King referred both to behaviors that concerned her and to ones that she valued. From her talk one would not easily know that Katie, Jorge, Matthew, Christy, and Rachel were the children who were labeled as having disabilities and that Carrie and Charlie were not, as there was no use of labels or direct reference to their disability aside from comments about Rachel's mobility.

The types of descriptions are similar for all children; they are descriptions of children's behavior, what they like to do, improvements they have made, and skills they are learning. When Ms. King mentioned difficult behaviors, they were generally followed with comments about how she, as the teacher, was dealing with them or her frustration if things were not changing. In her discussion of children's behavior, Ms. King did not reinforce differences between the children with and without disabilities in her classroom but noted the areas of progress and difficulty for each child.

The language Ms. King used creates a picture of all children within the classroom being her responsibility, of Ms. King taking children where they were and helping them develop skills and knowledge that they needed, and of all the children being includable in her classroom. The children were at very different places along the developmental spectrum: some could not talk or walk, while others were academically beyond what is generally expected for their age. Nonetheless, Ms. King focused on their behavior and talked in a similar way about all children and her work with them.

It is worthwhile considering why Ms. King seldom used special education labels. I would suggest three reasons: (1) the philosophy of the Crestview Head Start program, (2) the focus of Head Start on assessment of behavior, and (3) the lack of purpose for labels in this setting. The philosophy of CHS was "that all children can learn the necessary skills to succeed, to learn at their own rate and to learn self-confidence" (Crestview Head Start 1999:1). At CHS *all children* included those with disabilities. This belief that all children can learn influences the language that is used by CHS personnel.

The emphasis in Head Start generally, and at CHS specifically, on individuation also appeared to influence Ms. King's language. In many of the excerpts, Ms. King's evaluation or assessment of individual children was evident. Making assessments was reinforced by program expectations that she complete checklists regarding each child's skills in various areas. The purposes of these assessments, for children with and without disabilities, were to reveal skills that had been mastered and ones that needed further development, and to help Ms. King know where to focus her attention with each child. Individuation encouraged a focus on skills and behaviors of all children and thus helped shape Ms. King's language.

The inclusion of all children with disabilities in CHS left no reason for Ms. King to talk about children with disabilities in terms of their identified disabilities. Labels had little impact on life in the CHS classroom; labeled or not, "they're all going to be part of the class."[5] With no decisions to be made about placement, Ms. King focused on the children, their progress in her classroom, and different interventions, not different classrooms. As a consequence, categorizing language was not needed.

This alignment of policy, classroom practices, and expected and expressed language at CHS coalesced to support the inclusion of children with disabilities. This is not to say that everything at CHS was perfectly implemented or that deficit language never appeared. But program policies, Ms. King's classroom practices, and the language used by Ms. King and other staff all served to support the inclusion of children with disabilities.

Language Usage Related to Kindergarten

For children with disabilities, the process for entering kindergarten was complex and placement outcomes varied. There were five children with disabilities in the CHS classroom who were moving on to kindergarten the next fall. Four of these children were going to the same school district and would have been in the same elementary school if inclusion was the accepted practice. However, it was not. This district operated a half-day, every-day kindergarten program and a full-day, every-other-day kindergarten. Additionally, special education kindergarten categories were subdivided so that classrooms existed for each of the classifications of mild, moderate, and severe and profound disabilities.

Thus, kindergarten placement decisions were negotiated for each child. This decision-making process included a report on the child's progress at CHS, observations in the CHS classroom by potential kindergarten teachers, whether regular or special, and, as deemed appropriate, the school psychologist, and speech, occupational, and physical therapists. In the spring an Individualized Education Program (IEP) meeting was held for each child, and their kindergarten placement was reviewed and approved.[6]

There was a shift in Ms. King's discourse when talk turned to kindergarten. Her discourse changed as the structure changed. For kindergarten, she drew on the special education discourse of labels and categories. Ms. King explained that some children with disabilities, based on what they can and cannot do, would not be included in regular kindergarten classes as they had been in CHS. Assessments of children's skills and behavior that Ms. King used to guide her work in the classroom now served another purpose. The children must show to what degree they "can do" whatever it is that is necessary to get into regular kindergarten; a kindergarten that was organized to accept, for the most part, only children who would not need additional assistance. For example, Ms. King noted that Katie would "make it" to regular kindergarten. And she expected that Matthew might. "We think he's [Matthew] going to make it for regular kindergarten. . . . [We're] pushing real hard. I think a lot's going to depend on his reevaluation." In contrast, Ms. King was unsure about Sandy's placement, "but supposedly there's a mild classroom somewhere, and somewhere there's a moderate classroom."

These comments contain three different kindergarten outcomes. There was no question that Katie was "going to make it" to regular kindergarten. Constructed as individual achievement based on the child's effort, along with adults' "hoping" and "pushing," placement was not so certain for Matthew. The CHS personnel saw a need to advocate on his behalf and to do this based on Matthew's improvement in areas such as following directions and matching patterns. The focus was on what Matthew could and could not do to be accepted in a regular kindergarten classroom, not on ways to accommodate him there. For Sandy, the option of placement in a regular kindergarten was not part of this discussion. Ms. King assumed that she would have a special education placement. Under the system that existed, Ms. King recognized that the only question was which class, the "mild" or the "moderate" classroom. The regular classroom is not assured, but an "opportunity" that is only for some.

In discussing Matthew, Ms. King indicated that his parents and the CHS staff were both "pushing for regular kindergarten." "Pushing" implies that there is some force they are pushing against. In this case they are not pushing against the opinion of one or two professionals but against an entire school system that operates on the assumption that separate classrooms are necessary for children with disabilities, including children like Matthew. The district did not expect regular kindergarten teachers to accommodate the broad range of children included at CHS.

School districts, with a range of classrooms for children with disabilities, reinforce the view that not all children can "make it" in the regular classroom even with support services. As a result, the Head Start children with disabilities were subject to evaluation of their behavior and skills to make the "best" match with available programs. And, as was seen with Matthew, this might involve conflicting assessments of what is "best."

Each of the four children from CHS was placed in a different kindergarten program. Katie was placed in the regular full-day kindergarten but attended every day rather than every other day. Matthew was enrolled in the regular kindergarten classroom for the morning and a special education kindergarten for children with mild disabilities in the afternoon. Sandy was placed in a class for those with moderate mental handicaps, a classroom that was located in her home district but not in her home school. Rachel was placed in the classroom for those with severe and profound disabilities that was located in another county and required a lengthy bus ride. Clearly, for children with disabilities, entrance into a regular kindergarten was a hurdle, insurmountable for some, rather than an open door.

Although there was an increase in Ms. King's use of special education language when discussing the transition to kindergarten, she still did not use it extensively. In contrast, among special education personnel, categorical language was pervasive. In the following discussion I draw on interviews with Ms. Jones, the special education director of the district to which Katie, Matthew, Sandy, and Rachel were going for kindergarten, to illustrate her use of language related to (1) children's levels of functioning, (2) children's rights, and (3) the needs of individual children.

Level of Functioning

Ms. Jones used the terminology of special education and related evaluative and classificatory terms. Words such as *hearing impaired, mild range, severe profound, moderate child, borderline, functional disabilities, lower functioning,* and *autistic* appeared throughout the interview. In response to a question regarding the criteria teachers and other observers use to decide on the placement recommendation for an individual child, Ms. Jones replied:

> Whether it can function in the size of the group they would be in. We look at group size, you look at the learning criteria, or what the main criteria is for the child. Is the purpose socialization mainly if they're lower functioning children in your kindergarten level? Are their rights being handled and the rights of other children? . . . I guess I have extreme difficulties if a child is functioning emotionally, intellectually, socially more than two years below the mean of a classroom.

Ms. Jones begins by objectifying the child as "it," and questions whether "it" can function as expected in a particular size of class. She draws on a common assumption in special education that certain children cannot function with large numbers of children, and thus a separate small class is preferred over accommodations within the regular education classroom. An example of this appeared in her comments about Rachel, who was placed in the severe and profound classroom for kindergarten. In the following excerpt, Ms. Jones appeared to make assumptions about Rachel based on that categorization.

> I am highly biased for the rights of Rachel. I mean for Rachel to be bombarded with all the stimuli that could occur in with, let's say we have 18 children or 19, where it's difficult to have a corner of quiet. I wonder what we're doing with her rights versus Rachel's needing to be scheduled and needing to have a very structured situation and a very quiet situation, and maybe being held and rocked.

Ms. Jones described Rachel as needing a situation in which stimulation is limited and the classroom is very quiet and structured. This statement surprised me since I had been observing Rachel's participation in a CHS classroom where she actively explored the room and seemed to enjoy and benefit from the stimulation and activities of 12–15 other children. The Head Start classroom and the regular kindergarten classroom might be quite different, but the contrast between what I had seen Rachel do in Head Start and what Ms. Jones was describing for her left me wondering if Ms. Jones defined Rachel on the basis of the "severe and profound" label and assumed that any and all children in this category needed quiet and structure. If so, such assumptions potentially could decrease Ms. Jones's ability to see inclusion as an option.

Ms. Jones also suggested some criteria on which placement decisions are based. One is the child's level of functioning—emotionally, intellectually, and socially—in relation to other students in the class. Children found to be "more than two years below the mean" are not considered appropriate for regular kindergarten. The use of such language and approach accentuates the differences between children and defines some children as *too* different to be included in regular education.

Ms. Jones expanded on this view. She mentioned the difficulties with having a broad range of abilities represented in the kindergarten classroom. To one side she placed the child who is "functioning at a two-year level" and to the other kindergarten children "reading at the sixth-grade level." "You expect a spectrum out of kindergarten children, a broad range," but "it's a massive span and you have to balance that out."

It probably would be easier to teach a similar group of children or accommodate the kindergartner who is reading at the sixth-grade level rather than the child who is "functioning at a two-year level." However, for a child that is too different in one way, namely, considerably below grade level, exclusion is acceptable in order to "balance" the classroom. Yet a child too different in another direction, that is, considerably above grade level, can remain. Increasing the teacher's ability to deal with a broader range of students becomes less important when certain children can be removed. Thus, traditional teacher education practices and school district sorting practices can militate against the inclusion of all children with disabilities into the "regular" classroom.

Children's Rights

In her comments, Ms. Jones introduced the language of rights. She said she was "highly biased for the rights of Rachel" and contrasted Rachel's right to inclusion with her need for structure and quiet. In the following excerpt, Ms. Jones again uses the word "rights" and raises the issue of the impact of children with disabilities on the other children in the regular classroom. She asked, "Are their rights [those of the children with disabilities] being handled and the rights of the other children?" She emphasized this point when explaining Sandy's placement. "Sandy should not impinge the *rights* of other children, but I would be very sensitive to Sandy's *rights* and her development and what she's learning and the language she's picking up [italics added]."

The word "rights" is invested with power and infers justness and correctness. A person with rights has a claim to access some thing or privilege. Children with disabilities, for example, have a right to a free appropriate education. Ms. Jones implies that these children also have a "right" to exclusion from the regular education classroom based on what it is considered "appropriate."

Ms. Jones's feeling about the rights of children involved the rights of both children with disabilities and those without disabilities in the classroom. Implicit in her statements is a conflict between the rights of children with disabilities and the rights of other children; that is, that potentially within one classroom the rights of all cannot be met. On one hand, it might be the child with disabilities whose rights are being met to the detriment of others in the class, as was mentioned with the possibility of Sandy impinging on the rights of others. In other situations, it is the rights of other children that come before those of the child with disabilities. Not proposed were teaching and accommodations that could allow all into the classroom, for example, Sandy learning to refrain from interfering with others as she did in the CHS classroom. Realistically there will always be competing rights within classrooms, but teachers can be prepared to work with and accommodate children who vary considerably on the developmental spectrum.

Individual Children's Needs

Ms. Jones recognized the importance of meeting the needs of individual children. However, she primarily discussed meeting needs through various "appropriate" placement options or "tailor-made programs," such as the one that allows Katie to attend kindergarten every day. Classroom modifications were commonplace at CHS. In kindergarten, however, the emphasis is on having multiple programs so a specific child has the "correct" placement match rather than addressing needs within the regular education classroom. The implication is that a range of programs is necessary as not all are capable of being included in regular education.

Various topics emerged in Ms. Jones's talk about children with disabilities in relation to kindergarten—disability categories, levels of functioning, and the need to address children's rights and needs. Throughout, language sustained the exclusion of children with disabilities from the regular education classroom.

Ms. Jones, as well as Ms. King when the conversation turned to kindergarten, was influenced in her language use by the structure of a continuum of placements, and the societal and educational assumptions about individuals with disabilities that lie beneath that system. The existence of a range of placements required that decisions be made about children in relation to the available options. In turn, the purpose of particular classrooms focused attention on how each child "fit" with the specified classroom purpose. The institutionalized practice of a continuum of placements shaped the language that was used, and the continued use of this language also perpetuated a particular perspective on children with disabilities and their education and thus served to maintain the continuum of placements.

Skidmore (2002:120) provides a model of pedagogical discourse that I find relevant. He contrasts a "discourse of inclusion" with a "discourse of deviance." I would suggest that the former was dominant at CHS and the latter in the kindergarten situation. According to Skidmore, a discourse of inclusion is premised on the following: (1) "every student has an open-ended potential for learning," (2) educational failure stems from an "insufficiently responsive presentation of the curriculum," (3) the school response to learning difficulties should focus on reform of curriculum and development of pedagogy, (4) teaching expertise focuses on the "active participation of all students in the learning process," and (5) a "common curriculum" should be used with all students. CHS, with its emphasis on the development of all children, the need to consider changes in teaching and activities, the involvement of all children, and the use, aside from time spent on individual goals, of a common curriculum, appears to be closely aligned with the premises of a "discourse of inclusion."

In contrast, the "discourse of deviance" is based on the following assumptions: (1) "a hierarchy of student ability on which students can be placed," (2) education failure is due to student deficits, (3) the school response to learning difficulties is to "remediate the weaknesses" of individual students, (4) teacher expertise is centered in the "possession of specialist" knowledge, and (5) an "alternative curriculum" is to be used with the less able (120). The assignment of children to a range of kindergarten placements appears consistent with these assumptions.

Focused on what children could do and might learn, the inclusive program at CHS shaped an inclusive discourse about children with disabilities. The continuum of placements at kindergarten shaped a different discourse—one that emphasized difference and required categorical language to slot children into particular types of classrooms based on the extent of their perceived abilities. In each, the discourse was influenced and constrained by particular policy interpretations and implementations. Discourse, in turn, helped to maintain the existing structures as it served to constitute children with disabilities in ways that reinforced each program's policies and practices.

A child's education cannot be separated from the ways in which children with disabilities are talked about, the network of educational practices in which these children are immersed, and the social, cultural, historical, political, and economic context in which policies and practices are developed and implemented. Because decisions to include or not include children with disabilities in regular education have consequences for children, it is important to make visible the assumptions and processes underlying these decisions. The issues and processes highlighted in this study provide a way to look at work with children with disabilities in other settings and locate points of intervention for increasing the inclusiveness of these settings. As Skidmore (2002:129) maintains, "*the combined development of all is the condition of the full development of each*" [italics in original].

QUESTIONS FOR DISCUSSION

1. What are the dominant constructions of disability in the settings where you practice? How do they intersect with ideas about gender, race, and class? What do these constructions of disability mean for your practice?

2. How have conceptions of disability changed over time in your own life and work? What are the impacts of these changes on young people?

3. In what ways is the language of "rights" used in the settings in which you work? Who is interpreting the "rights" of young children and/or children with disabilities? Who benefits most from the particular interpretation? Who benefits the least or is victimized by this interpretation?

4. Consider how federal and state mandates, and local interpretation and implementation of those mandates, influence the provision of services to children generally, and in particular to children with disabilities.

5. How can you make space for all children within the settings in which you work? How can you make space for all children to have a say in what is "best" for them? What perspectives on childhood and disability would be most inclusive of all children in educational and other settings?

NOTES

1. Pseudonyms are used for the location, program, and individuals in this chapter.

2. In this chapter I use the term "children with disabilities" to refer to those children who have been labeled as having a disability. Even though disability is a term that labels and marginalizes certain people and directs attention to deficits rather than abilities, many in the disability community have chosen to use "disability" as a descriptor as it is a convenient "marker of identity" (Linton 1998:12). .

3. Originally titled the Education for all Handicapped Children Act (P.L. 94–142), this legislation was renamed the Individuals with Disabilities Education Act (IDEA) in 1990.

4. For purposes of this discussion, I am drawing only on the language used by the CHS teacher and not including similar examples from interviews with Ms. Davis, the education/disabilities coordinator, and Mr. Miller, the executive director, both of whom supported the inclusion of all children with disabilities in the CHS classrooms.

5. This comment was made by Ms. Davis, the education/disabilities coordinator.

6. By law, parents are to have a voice in this decision process. From my observations, however, it appeared that the professional staff made the placement decisions prior to the IEP. At the IEP meeting, parents were expected to approve the placement decision and give input into details of that placement, for example, logistics of transportation or how many days the child would be in the specified kindergarten each week.

REFERENCES

Armstrong, F., and L. Barton. (Eds.) (1999). *Disability, human rights and education: Cross-cultural perspectives.* Buckingham, U.K.: Open University Press.

Bailey, D.B.J., R. A. McWilliam, V. Buysse, and P. W. Wesley. (1998). Inclusion in the context of competing values in early childhood education. *Early Childhood Research Quarterly* 13 (1): 27–47.

Barnes, C. (1994). Images of disability. In S. French, ed., *On equal terms: Working with disabled people,* 35–46. Oxford: Butterworth-Heinemann.

Barnes, C., G. Mercer, and T. Shakespeare. (1999). *Exploring disability: A sociological introduction.* Cambridge: Polity Press.

Chouliaraki, L., and N. Fairclough. (1999). *Discourse in late modernity: Rethinking critical discourse analysis.* Edinburgh: Edinburgh University Press.

Corbett, J. (1996). *Bad-mouthing: The language of special needs.* London: Falmer Press.

Corker, M., and S. French. (1999). Reclaiming discourse in disability studies. In M. Corker and S. French, eds., *Disability discourse,* 1–11. Buckingham, U.K.: Open University Press.

Crestview Head Start. (1999). *Parent handbook.* Crestview: Crestview Head Start.

Davis, L. J. (Ed.) (1997). *The disabilities studies reader.* New York: Routledge.

Fairclough, N. (1992). *Discourse and social change.* Cambridge: Polity Press.

Ferguson, P. M., and D. L. Ferguson. (1998). The future of inclusive educational practice: Constructive tension and the potential for reflective reform. *Childhood Education* 74 (5): 302–20.

Fulcher, G. (1989). *Disabling policies? A comparative approach to education policy and disability.* London: Falmer Press.

Gartner, A., and D. K. Lipsky. (1990). New conceptualizations for special education. In S. B. Sigmon, ed., *Critical voices on special education,* 175–82. Albany: State University of New York Press.

Gelzheiser, L. M. (1990). Reducing the number of students identified as learning disabled: A question of practice, philosophy, or policy? In S. B. Sigmon, ed., *Critical voices on special education*, 43–50. Albany: State University of New York Press.

Gething, L. (1992). *Person to person: A guide for professionals working with people with disabilities*. 2nd edition. Baltimore: Brookes.

Hahn, H. (1989). Disability and the reproduction of bodily images: The dynamics of human appearances. In J. Wolch and M. Dear, eds., *The power of geography: How territory shapes social life*, 370–88. Boston: Unwin Hyman.

———. (1997). New trends in disability studies: Implications for educational policy. In D. K. Lipsky and A. Gartner, eds., *Inclusion and school reform: Transforming America's classrooms*, 315–28. Baltimore: Paul H. Brookes.

Ingstad, B., and S. R. Whyte. (Eds.) (1995). *Disability and culture*. Berkeley: University of California Press.

Jaworski, A., and N. Coupland. (1999). Introduction: Perspectives on discourse analysis. In A. Jaworski and N. Coupland, eds., *The discourse reader*, 1–44. London: Routledge.

Linton, S. (1998). *Claiming disability: Knowledge and identity*. New York: New York University Press.

Lubeck, S., P. A. Jessup, M. deVries, and J. Post. (2001). The role of culture in program improvement. *Early Childhood Research Quarterly 16*: 499–523.

Mitchell, D. T., and S. L. Snyder. (1997). Introduction: Disability studies and the double bind of representation. In D. T. Mitchell and S. L. Snyder, eds., *The body and physical disability: Discourses of disability*, 1–31. Ann Arbor: University of Michigan Press.

Odom, S. L., and M. A. McEvoy. (1990). Mainstreaming at the preschool level: Potential barriers and tasks for the field. *Topics in Early Childhood Special Education 10* (2): 48–61.

Oliver, M. (1996). *Understanding disability: From theory to practice*. London: Macmillan.

Priestley, M. (1998). Childhood disability and disabled childhoods: Agendas for research. *Childhood 5* (2): 207–23.

Rioux, M. H. (1994). New research directions and paradigms: Disability is not measles. In M. H. Rioux and M. Bach, eds., *Disability is not measles: New research paradigms in disability*, 1–7. North York, Ont.: L'Institut Roeher Institute.

Sampson, E. E. (1998). Life as an embodied art: The second stage—beyond constructionism. In B. M. Bayer and J. Shotter, eds., *Reconstructing the psychological subject: Bodies, practices and technologies*, 21–32. London: Sage.

Saunders, B. J., and C. Goddard. (2001). The textual abuse of childhood in the English-speaking world: The contribution of language to the denial of children's rights. *Childhood 8* (4): 443–62.

Skidmore, D. (2002). A theoretical model of pedagogical discourse. *Disability, Culture and Education* 1 (2): 119–31.

Stephens, S. (1995). Children and the politics of culture in "Late Capitalism." In S. Stephens, ed., *Children and the politics of culture*, 3–51. Princeton: Princeton University Press.

Thomson, R. G. (1997). *Extraordinary bodies: Figuring physical disability in American culture and literature.* New York: Columbia University Press.

U.S. Department of Health, Education, and Welfare. (1973). *Head Start services to handicapped children: First annual report of the U.S. Department of Health, Education, and Welfare to the Congress of the United States on services provided to handicapped children in Project Head Start* (congressional report). Washington, D.C.: U.S. Department of Health, Education, and Welfare.

Wendell, S. (1996). *The rejected body: Feminist philosophical reflections on disability.* New York: Routledge.

Wolery, M., and J. S. Wilbers. (Eds.) (1994). *Including children with special needs in early childhood programs.* Washington, D.C.: National Association for the Education of Young Children.

Children and Youth in a Medicalized World | **ELEVEN**

Young People's Agency in
Mental Health Treatment

Ben Stride-Darnley

My Mad Plan

When I am <u>Mad</u> [picture of unhappy face with smoke coming out of ears], I can take time out [picture of little boy/person saying "I can handle this!!"]:

1. At my <u>desk</u> [picture of desk],

2. At a <u>table</u> [picture of table],

3. At the <u>couch</u> [picture of couch].

I will stop [road Stop Sign] and <u>think</u> [picture of a bright light bulb] before I act. I will keep my <u>hands</u> [picture of hands] and <u>feet</u> [picture of feet] to myself. I will make choices that help me and others.

Signature _____

Teacher _____Guardian _____

This is a copy of "My Mad Plan." It is designed as a contract between client-student,[1] teacher, and guardian, and it incorporates pictures to help clarify the wording, making it more age / skill level appropriate (unfortunately I have had to describe the pictures). It is a key tool of staff in guiding young people at Northern Ontario Service (NOS), a child mental health assessment and treatment service, toward better self-controlled behavior, the lack of which is one of the causal factors that contribute to their attending NOS. The guardian signature assists in consistency between home and educational settings, which staff noted during interviews as a key feature of successful assessment and therapy. The "safe spaces" of desk, table, and couch are preidentified to assist young people in removing themselves from stressors (such as school / therapeutic work, adults, or other young people), thus giving them space and time to control their emotions and physical response to stressors. It is one of many strands of therapeutic activity highly influenced by Cognitive Behavioral Therapy (CBT), and it supports group and individual sessions aimed at self-recognition of a variety of emotional states and how best to deal with the more negative ones. "My Mad Plan" along with pictures of various good and bad emotions are posted in numerous formats around the classrooms, and the plan is repeatedly described during daily activity by staff at key quiet times, such as registration, as well as during "loud times," when the plan needs to be put into action.

One such instance occurred when the NOS group was transitioning from math to language, midway through the morning session. Johnny wanted to continue his work on long subtraction.[2] He had been struggling with it all week but was doing particularly well on this occasion. He wanted to postpone his least favorite lesson, language, until after lunch, which is when group (therapeutic) work was scheduled. This point of tension between the child's wishes and the requirements of routine led to a battle between Johnny, on one side, and the teacher and child and youth workers, on the other. Johnny was angry, vocal, and defiant. When staff members invoked the Mad Plan, Johnny sought to challenge the protocol and demanded that he be able to go to the carpeted area of the class—not one of the predesignated safe spaces. Eventually, after some disruption, Johnny

I wish to thank all of the child, adolescent, and staff research participants, without whom this chapter would not be possible. I also thank Marsha Newby (child and youth worker), Dean Huyck (teacher), and Don Buchanan (coordinator, Child and Youth Health Partnership) for their ongoing support, as well as their constructive criticism of this chapter and other reports; Hamilton Health Sciences, Hamilton-Wentworth District School Board, and the *Northern Ontario Service* for their cooperation; and Wayne Warry and readers for their constructive criticism of earlier drafts. My research was funded through McMaster University Graduate Research Scholarships and Bursaries, and through a Graduate Award (#GA011205–013) from the Provincial Centre of Excellence for Child and Youth Mental Health (CoE) at CHEO. The views contained herein are those of the author and may not be similarly shared by the CoE. Any errors herein are entirely the author's.

conceded and went to the couch, where he was praised for his achievements at math but was reminded that language and spelling were just as important. Through a process of negotiation, it was decided that the language class would not be all reading and writing, but time would also be allocated to the word game Boggle, which Johnny and the other the client-students enjoyed greatly.

I suggest that these events are very much framed by adult terms and conditions. Johnny wanted to continue his clear successes and avoid future difficulties. He attempted to achieve this by acting in ways that defied adult controls over appropriate behavior and activities. Because staff wanted to maintain the daily routine, Johnny was effectively able to act with *agency* and negotiate the content of the second half of the morning's programming. Even though the outcome was not to continue with math, which was Johnny's initial desire, Johnny was able to negotiate less lesson time and more game time. By using the Boggle game, staff members were able to continue educational activities while the client-students practiced their spelling, and Johnny was able to gain by having fewer "book lessons." The scenario is also framed by adults on a second level— that of the Mad Plan itself. While its content and language suggest that the decision-making power is with the young person—"to make good choices" and head to the safe space of desk, table, or couch—these are predetermined by the contract and staff. Even if the young person would find the carpet or sitting up against a wall a more calming space to think and consider how best to proceed, as Johnny's efforts illustrated, it was the staff rather than the client-student who made that determination.

It should also be noted that these conditions are not necessarily as the staff would wish. For example, this particular site of the NOS had recently changed the school location in which it was based so that, as one staff member reported, "in effect, the burden is shared across the city's elementary schools" (interview, March 2006). In the new location, the NOS site had been allocated two classrooms (usually divided into a main or education room and a quite or therapy room). However, the second room was down the corridor past four or five other "regular" school classrooms, even though the next-door class room was being used as storage prior to school enlargement in the following academic year. This distance made going to a safe and quiet space exceptionally difficult at times of high stress or noise, when the Mad Plan might most need to be implemented, such as when Johnny was most disruptive. In the instance of Johnny practicing a certain level of agency, staff agency was also limited and framed by institutional and policy conditions. In interviews with the staff at this site, the majority stated they often felt unable to remove the "noise makers" because of the distance between the two rooms, which reduced the effectiveness of the Mad Plan.

[handwritten annotation: reframing agency to "confined agency"]

AGENCY DEFINED AND EXPLORED

The concept of *agency* is key to this chapter and therefore needs further definition and explanation before we move onto additional ethnographic examples. For the purposes of this chapter, agency should not be considered to be a
service or program, but an individual's or a groups' capacity to make decisions,
act, and interact with other people in a socially competent way (Bourdieu 1999,
1998, 1977; Giddens 1982). Ahearn's (2001) exemplary article explores the various definitions and uses of agency, so I will not repeat all of the debates here. I
do, however, consider Ahearn's (2001:112) "provisional definition of agency" as
"refer[ring] to the socio-culturally mediated capacity to act" to be a particularly
useful definition in light of the discussions that follow. Ahearn, as an anthropologist, advocates for an understanding of the cross-cultural specificity in definitions and use of agency. This means that cultural forms of agency, albeit societal
or institutional, are greatly influenced by the particular contexts (cultural, historical, political economic) in which agency is performed (Ahearn 2001:113).

It is important to clarify and examine agency as a concept because it has
undergone considerable shifts in understandings within research and policy
literatures in terms of both what it is and who has it. The work of childhood
research "forefathers" such as Piaget (1962) and Erikson (1963) has highly influenced psychological and social science theories on childhood and adolescence
as life stages and understandings of the young people who exist within these
categories. These early endeavors broadly saw children as empty vessels totally
influenced by the actions of adults who educated them, both formally and socially. Within this understanding, young people lack agency of any kind, and
this largely remains society's view of children and youth (Boggin 1998; Bucholtz
2002; Hockey and James 2003; Lee 1999; Wolf 2002). Recent scholarly literature
has questioned this "top-down" model of childhood, adolescence, and young
people in two ways: first, some scholarly work has attempted to "historicize"
childhood as a social category by presenting it as a defined life stage with a recent genesis and specific cultural context (Cannella 2002; Colón and Colón 2001;
Harkness 1996; Hendrick 2003; Seifert 2000; Thorne 2004). Second, some scholarly work has focused on the social worlds of young people and their capacity
to act within these social worlds (Alanen 1994; Göncü et al. 1999; Holloway and
Valentine 2003; James, Jenks, and Prout 2001; James and Prout 1997; Prout and
Hallet 2003; Valentine, Skelton, and Chambers 1998; Wyness 2000, 2006). Both
of these more recent approaches question the lack of young people's agency—
the former implicitly, the latter more explicitly.

In this chapter, I question the totality of both the lack of agency attributed to children and youth by earlier positions and the full agency of recent scholarly research of childhood and adolescence as life stages. Instead, using examples such as "My Mad Plan" and the following case studies, I argue for the concept of *confined agency*. That is to say, within adult designated localities, such as schools or children's services, young people's social action and cultural (re)production are framed, but not necessarily dictated by, the homogenizing influences determined by adults (Lee 2001; Nybell 2001; Pike 2003; Rasmussen 2004). This recent shift in historical and cultural understanding of agency, or agentive capacity, as a characteristic ascribed to children and youth has become of interest to practitioners, especially in relation to how it might affect services, policy, and daily practice (Foley et al. 2003; Prout 2000; Shook 2005; Stephens 1995). Moreover, wherever possible some of this more recent research has moved toward directly incorporating young people's perspectives (Christensen and James, 2001; Delgado 2006, Mason and Fallon 2001; Roberts 2003; Stride-Darnley and Buchanan 2005) rather than purely taking adult views and recollections of their childhoods (Chaput-Walker 1991; Lahelma 2002; Musgrave 2002). I too follow this more recent approach (Stride-Darnley 2007b). In doing so, I explore and examine simplistic, essentialized notions of childhood and adolescence and begin to elucidate why such essentialism is problematic for both those within the categories and those offering services designed for them (Frankenburg, Robinson, and Delahooke 2000).

Although this chapter was conceived and largely written prior to Vandenbroek and Bouverne-de Bie's recent examination of agency and educational norms through textual examinations of childhood, parenthood, and day care, I see parallels between their call for a "recontextualizing of children's agency" (2005:139) and my proposal of confined agency as a suitable heuristic device with which to better understand the lives of children and adolescents associated with medical mental health settings and, by an extension, welfare or school settings. I present evidence that focuses on one research site where agency is nearly always contested within academic and policy literature (a service for younger children), and one where agency is less contested (a service for youth). I argue that the ethnographic evidence suggests that both "younger" and "older" young people access agency and perform with it, but that agency is mediated and confined by the contextual and cultural frames of the services, and, by extension, the staff. I do not consider this proposed rethinking as being a definitive or authoritative "final" conception. Rather, I hope that it can be a launchpad for discussion and consideration.

THE STUDY

I carried out more than eighteen months of ethnographic fieldwork, which is cultural anthropology's key methodology, with young people who were attending day assessment and treatment mental health programs, and this chapter gives illustrative examples from two sites (Stride-Darnley [2007a] provides detailed explanation of the variety of qualitative methodologies and analytical processes used in my fieldwork). The first site, which for the purpose of this study I shall call the Northern Ontario Service, is in a city of more than 100,000 people in northern Ontario, Canada. This site's services are partially funded through provincial (equivalent of state) Ministry of Children and Youth and Ministry of Education, with some connections with local hospital and medical community services. The children accessing services are between 5 and 12, but during my fieldwork most were between 7 and 12 years old. Usually 80% of the children are male, although during my research as many as 93% were male. NOS is designed as short-term segregation incorporating assessment and treatment services for a range of presenting behaviors, including but not limited to significant levels of impaired learning, impaired self-control, and impaired social performance when compared with their peers. It would not be atypical for client-students to be diagnosed with attention deficit/hyperactivity disorder (AD/HD), oppositional defiant disorder (ODD), and at times obsessive compulsive disorder (OCD) in conjunction with severe learning impairments during their assessment process with NOS. First contact with NOS generally occurs because the children's behavioral difficulties are so severe that the children cannot function in their "home schools." Although these services are physically located within two "regular" elementary schools, they are separate from the main school's activities and regulations. For example, neither staff nor children are answerable to the school principal for disciplinary matters, and, unlike the other classes, NOS students do not have to attend school assemblies. Onsite staff consisted of two child and youth workers and one special education teacher, with visits from registered nurses, a psychometrist, and other mental health professionals working with the NOS.

The second site, Cornerstone Youth Service, is in southern Ontario, Canada, and is part of Hamilton Health Sciences (HHS) Integrated Child and Youth Mental Health Portfolio. This site offers day-treatment services using the Therapeutic Community Model to adolescents aged 13–18, who present a range of internalizing psychiatric diagnoses with about 80% comorbidity. Diagnoses include, but are not limited to, mood disorders, anxiety disorders (including specific disorders such as post-traumatic stress disorder, school refusal, and obsessive compulsive disorder), Tourette's Syndrome, Asperger's Syndrome, schizophrenia, eating disorders, and drug and alcohol abuse. Most client-students at Cornerstone have impaired self-image, and all have histories of substantial nonschool attendance. Usually 55–60% of clients are female. The clients served by Cornerstone lack both the social and coping skills required to deal with their mental health problems (Stride-Darnley and Buchanan 2005). Staff described the service as a "last-resort safety net" for students who could not cope with regular high school, and as "stepping stone" back to good mental health and a "more normal life" (interviews, April 2005–May 2006). Onsite staff consisted of six child and youth workers, a psychometrist, a social worker, two teachers, and a child psychiatrist (the clinical director). Cornerstone's funding is predominantly through Health monies, with funding for education programming being derived through section 20 of the Ontario Education Act of 1994. Cornerstone is physically independent of all other HHS hospitals as it rents two floors of a downtown building that is relatively anonymous for a psychiatry facility (the only Cornerstone sign is located on a quiet side road at the entrance to the parking lot). During the fieldwork period, the hospital was able to rent the remaining two floors, and so this anonymity and relative independence has begun to change. One of the processes of the therapeutic programs at Cornerstone is to "shift [the] locus of control so they're actually in the driver's seat in terms of their treatment" (interview, April 2005), whereas at NOS the therapeutic processes were aimed at encouraging understanding of emotions and achieving "good decisions" and "good behaviors" (interview, March 2006). During interviews, nearly all Cornerstone staff stated or implied these as goals or accomplishments of their service. This "relocation of control" is especially important for reducing the impact of behaviors, and reactions to situations, that might previously have led to either removal from the class setting (in the case of NOS children) or self-withdrawal resulting from high anxiety (in the case of Cornerstone adolescents).

Both services used "evidence-based" cognitive behavioral therapy to encourage the young people to learn how to recognize the physical and emotional feelings associated at times of "bad" reactions, and to stop and think prior to acting on those feelings. Such "relocation of control" could be considered as the service's and staff's attempt to increase or improve their client-students agentive capacity. However, I suggest that because relocation of control takes place through a medicalized process of assessment and treatment, it is semantically parallel to encouraging confined agency. To explore this assertion, I present four further ethnographic examples. First, I will discuss the use of "free" time and computer time at NOS. These times in particular are used by adults as a reward for children's good work and behavior as well as being one arena where staff hope that "good choices" are made ("good choices" being a demonstration that therapeutic lessons have been learned). I will then turn to use transportation to Cornerstone and the process of scheduling and timetabling as illustration of teen confined agency within their medicalized setting.

Confined Agency and "Free" Time at NOS

During interviews with the children at NOS, they all described how important having choices was to their daily routines at school. This leads me to ask an important question: if the children describe and carry out choice, are we witnessing the expression and performance of agency and competency? The ethnographic evidence is that the answer is a partial yes—the children at NOS do access and perform agency, but the access to and performance of agency is framed and confined by their social and institutional setting. Here I present illustrative examples of events and discussions about recess, which is probably the biggest portion of "free" time in schools in North America. Most often children have to go outside for this time, which is motivated in part by the need of adults to have a break from the children as well as a need for children burn off some energy. During my time as a classroom volunteer, recess was often used as a reward, but this does not necessarily motivate students to do their best. We can see from the interview transcript with Simon below that adult assumptions (both mine and the system's) do not necessarily guarantee full understandings of children's behavior.[3]

> I: What you like best about being here and what you like least about being here?
>
> R: (P6) The best thing about being here is I have the choice to go in or out because at Williams [old home school] they say if you don't have no detention you go out but if you have a detention you stay in.
>
> I: And you're getting lots of detentions at Chapman.
>
> R: No.
>
> I: OK.
>
> R: But that's why I always go outside—but I don't want to (P3) so I'd hit kids and get to stay indoors (P3) and the least I like is work.

This appeared to contradict my observations of outside recesses from earlier in the week, which Simon had appeared to enjoy. So I asked a follow-up question:

ɪ: So um when you're outside do you like playing by yourself or do you like playing with other kids?

ʀ: Other people.

ɪ: (P3) And do you miss that when you are here, because recess when we go out there aren't any other kids out there?

ʀ: No I like it when it's just me and another person.

ɪ: You're happy with that?

ʀ: Yup I am happy with two players, I don't like lots of people.

Midway through the first exchange, I had presumed that Simon, who had extreme behavioral difficulties (and was later assessed to have an ODD diagnosis), had received so many detentions so often that extra resources from the NOS were sought by the home school and by Simon's parents. I had presumed that Simon's detentions for school-yard violence were a reflection of his medical diagnosis and resulted in a negative consequence (losing his free time). I was wrong. Because detentions require students to stay indoors at recess, I had not even imagined that Simon would purposefully seek out a detention so he could stay indoors. At his home school, Simon had worked hard—exercising agency—to get detentions. At NOS, where having a choice to go outside or not depended on responding to behavioral cues and working well, Simon would regularly comply with requests, thereby earning the right to choose. The second exchange explains some of Simon's reasoning for wanting to stay in at his home school but go outside at NOS: "I like it when it's just me and another person" and "I don't like lots of people." Big crowds of children were not an issue at this NOS site because their recess was at a different time from the rest of the school—a decision by NOS staff taken specifically to avoid violent confrontations. To me, Simon's actions—lacking self-control, getting detentions, and losing free time—initially appeared to demonstrate a lack of competence. However, it seems that Simon was expressing his agency, albeit in socially negative ways.

At one site, I was encouraged to head outside at recess with the client-students, who quickly found out that I had never played hockey (field hockey just did not cut it) and could not skate. These Canadian children where astounded. They were shocked that I had grown up in a place (England) that did not get cold enough for lots of snow in the winter. Not skating seemed to be paired with my strange accent. As we were transitioning to an outside recess, Johnny said to a staff member, "Don't worry about him—it's just Ben. He sounds funny because he's from abroad. He's friendly but he's never played hockey though. I thinks [sic] he's from France." My "being foreign" and lacking hockey experience meant that I was designated the goaltender by Josh, another client-student. And if I excelled at this position in their eyes, I could, at the next recess, attempt to play another position and take a few shots on goal. Now let me be clear. We were not playing ice hockey proper. We were in our outside boots and bundled up suitably for an early March recess. We were using plastic hockey sticks and a ball with holes in (to prevent it from gaining too much speed and hurting anyone). The imagined space was a rink, though, marked out by the school building on one side and the kindergarten's play space on the other. We practiced our passing and had to pretend coming to a two-foot halt as though we were on ice (it being fairly chilly, there actually was some residual ice from small puddles on the tarmac). While the children got to choose the content (going outside over staying indoors, hockey over soccer, for example) and what the rules of their hockey game were (number of passes before shooting, making me a net minder), the decisions regarding where it took place, with what equipment (despite Josh's complaints), and in what time and space were all made by adults (probably rightly so). This example is illustrative of a confined agency. At the scale of the children's lives, they had a significant level of autonomy and decision-making capacity for this recess—indeed, some children opted to stay indoors and play card or board games. The hockey example, with usual "control" over an adult witnessed through my positioning, participation, and education by the young people at NOS, was a source of pride for Josh at least. He spoke animatedly to Ms. Clair, the class teacher, about my skills and how he had made the right choice to put me in goal; my saves challenged him to really aim properly and shoot well. It is apparent that the young people's decision-making capacity motivated them to participate and behave at NOS at times when they had to decide whether to present good decisions and behaviors, such as during times when the Mad Plan might need to be implemented, making *free time* a part of the ongoing therapeutic processes. However, I would suggest that a nuanced interpretation of these children's agency, witnessed in their autonomy and decision-making capacities, is very much framed or confined by the options staff had made available.

Computer Time at One NOS Site

At one of the two NOS sites, the school has a bank of eight or so Internet-ready computers in the library, and staff make use of "computer time" as a considerable motivational reward. Each day, "credits" could be earned through good work or effort, as well as behavior that followed the Mad Plan or other CBT

processes. If credits were earned, then the next morning, as the first activity after roll call, client-students could go down to the library for up to 20 minutes of
computer time. They could choose from a considerable range of online freeware
games that were not only educational but fun. Client-students could not access
computer time without having handed in homework or without having a good
report from home. The homework usually entailed completing unfinished math
or language exercises from that day's classes. The actual time with computers
was carefully monitored by the client-students themselves. To ensure they got
their 20 minutes, they checked the library clock and confirmed with a child and
youth worker (CYW) the time they entered the library. Staff generally described
computer time as helping to motivate the client-students, and one member of
staff said it helped to "very quickly switch on their brains, so they could start
thinking and not just acting" (interview, March 2006). In many respects, computer time is much like an extra period of free time—the young people had
control over the content the games, but not over the format or the rules that
structured their control. Below I explore one flashpoint in more detail.

One morning Daniel, a 7-year-old male client-student, had not completed
any of his homework, but before the teacher had a chance to ensure it had all
been finished, he snuck downstairs with the rest his classmates and the CYWs.
Daniel was unusually quiet in the walk downstairs. He continued to be quiet
while sitting at the computer, until the teacher arrived a few minutes later. Daniel almost immediately became very upset, to the level of disturbing the others'
computer time, complaining that he just was "not able to finish the work, not
had time at home, and anyway it was too difficult." The teacher was adamant
that the previous day he had been doing well on the assignment even if he had
been a little slow. In fact, Daniel only had three more sums, and the teacher argued he could easily get them done and still have time for the computers. Daniel
moved to a table, a "good" choice, but gradually became so wrapped in the time
he was losing and how unfair it was that he eventually lost all of that day's computer time and still had one more sum to do. The teacher and the CYWs, who
usually reinforced successes rather than failures verbally, suggested to Daniel
that his loss was a direct result of his actions and not theirs, and he should not
blame them for it. He had decided not to complete his very brief homework, and
he had decided to hide this from the teacher. Once caught, he had not quickly
done the sums, and therefore *he* had lost an enjoyable reward. All of the potential was his; he just had to make good decisions. The rest of Daniel's day was
fairly unsuccessful academically, and he had to take a relatively large amount of
homework home. He did, however, regain control of his behavior and by lunch-

time had ceased to be disruptive. His good choices in this arena were praised on numerous occasions both in direct conversations between the staff and Daniel and as an example to the whole group at the end of the day. His choice to move to a desk when he was frustrated in the library was noted as a particularly good action. The next morning his homework was completed and he had computer time.

I interpret this flashpoint as a prime example of the NOS therapeutic aims in action. During this illustrative example, we see an attempt to retrain a young person so that when frustrations arise, he has options other than defiance and violence—options that show the young people that they have control over their actions or, in my words, that they have *agency.* Through repeated examples—throughout the daily routines and through specific therapeutic times—the client-students at NOS are reminded that they have options and are in control of making their own choices. While Daniel's progress was not a steady linear improvement from this point forward, gains were small and ongoing. The bonus of computer time with its choices and enjoyment clearly worked to encourage good participation and behaviors. Yet it is a fairly structured reward, which required a good day, followed by a good night, rounded off with the completion of homework. And the actual computer time itself had specific parameters. As most of the client-students did not have access to home computers, the reward was motivational enough to genuinely encourage compliance with all of these structures. These structures help frame the young people's agency within the context of this NOS site, where their agency is being directed to a certain confined form—away from having agency to make "poor" decisions and toward having agency to make "good" decisions.

These ethnographic illustrations of free time and computer time at NOS are important examples of confined agency because play has traditionally been associated with children's worlds (Göncü et al. 1999; James, Jenks, and Prout 2001; Piaget 1962). Staff use both negative and (more frequently) positive examples of children's agentive actions at recess, such as choosing to "flare up" or making "good decisions," as part of the ongoing therapeutic process. The ethnographic evidence suggests that while the children attending NOS are making choices and learning about choosing how to behave, these choices are very much framed both by adults making options available (caliber of hockey equipment, access to computers, etc.) and by adults delivering cognitive behavioral therapies in which the young people participate. In the next two case studies I present data from Cornerstone that suggest that confined agency also influences the daily practices and performance of teens.

Transportation, Self-Performance, and Confined Agency

The primary medical theory or discourse at Cornerstone is the Therapeutic Community Model, which posits that a community in and of itself can be therapeutic, and that the atmosphere of a therapeutic site becomes therapeutic (Kennard 2004). This means that, on a daily basis, members of the community all have a responsibility for creating and maintaining the community's calm, caring, and supportive atmosphere. The Therapeutic Community Model has become known in Canada as best practice for programs dealing with vulnerable client-student populations (Bloom et al. 2003). An implication of the Therapeutic Community Model is that client-students have as much control as possible over their interaction with others as well as their programming. Indeed, after referral and an initial tour, the decisions to attend a formal "intake" interview and then, if space is available, to join and attend Cornerstone lies entirely with the client-students. Staff see the process of choosing to attend the intake interview, and choosing to be part of the therapeutic community (with its responsibilities), as a demonstration of "opting in" to the community and the beginning of a client-student's therapeutic recovery. In terms of this chapter's theoretical discussions, the model enables a significant reduction of the *confined* elements of young people's confined agency.

Yet a broader understanding of the context of daily routines at Cornerstone suggests that client-students' agency is not so clearly unconfined. Part of the medicalized intake process includes an assessment of transport needs to get to the service. At both NOS and Cornerstone, some client-students are transported to and from the sites by taxi. This is in part because the services cover a wide geographical area, in part because client-students' behavioral difficulties make long journeys on buses with lots of children nearly impossible (in the case of the NOS), and in part because regular early morning commitment to getting into a taxi reduces the hurdle of making a journey on a public transit or on a school bus (in the case of the Cornerstone adolescents). At Cornerstone, taxis are justified by staff as increasing the likelihood of successful attendance, participation in the therapeutic community, and thereby opportunities for successful participation in the various therapeutic programs. Over half of the client-students come to Cornerstone by taxi, and the remainder either walk or get rides from parents, guardians, or siblings.

My participant observations from September 2005 to June 2006 included informal conversations with client-students about their taxi rides. These conversations developed out of client-student comments about having to share the taxis with students who attend "regular" high schools downtown. Cornerstone client-students all complained that they regularly had to wait for the other students. They also commented that they had the longest days of any of the taxi riders, which seemed "tedious" and a "little unfair." While they got picked up from home first and dropped off at Cornerstone first each morning, this situation was reversed in the afternoons—they got home last. This arrangement was negotiated to ensure a certain level of confidentially for the client-students. As part of the conversations we held, client-students addressed how they justify Cornerstone to the other three kids with whom they share the cab. While they get the taxi and choose to attend the psychiatric day treatment program, all 12 client-students said they described Cornerstone as an "alter-ed" (alternative education) program, or a special school; none said they described it as a psychiatric facility. Ironically, their taxis are paid for by the local school board, not the hospital, because the client-students will be completing some high school classes each day, and the local schools cannot meet these kids' educational (or mental health) needs. Client-students gave reasons of confidentiality and desire to seem "normal" and "fit in" for giving partial truths to the other taxi riders (Stride-Darnley 2007b).

Although this may not seem too significant an issue, the ethnographic "flashpoint" of the client-students' external performance toward the other taxi riders and their attempts to limit the stigmatizing impacts of their mental ill-health are an interesting site for exploring understandings of agency. The Cornerstone teens all demonstrated agency in order to attend the day treatment program. They had made the "big decision" to get help with their psychiatric problems and were acting with agency by getting the taxi on a (nearly always) daily basis, thereby using resources available to help them increase the likelihood of successful attendance and therapy. Here we see agency in opposition to the confining elements that are part of their mental illness, rather than adult-designed and adult-designated places, spaces, and activities, as discussed above in the NOS case. Indeed, some staff suggested during interviews that Cornerstone's therapeutic processes teach client-students how to live with their circumstances—to have agency within a confined context. Yet through the client-students' denial of Cornerstone being a primarily psychiatric facility, we witness two further processes. We see them acting with agency by claiming their right to confidentiality, but we also see the content of their agency being confined by societal expectations. These teens call on the marginal (but still less stigmatizing than a psychiatric hospital) space of an alternative or special education site, which in reality is a partial truth. The client-students are trying to limit the social stigmatizing impact of having a mental illness—this is agency that is simultaneously confined and exercised. Moreover, that these teens *have* to get a taxi reflects the societal and monetary pressures on services for teens with mental health difficulties and diagnoses. Taxi rides are necessary because there is neither the political will nor the resources (even in the relatively rich setting of Canada) for services to be locally situated. Rather, the single intensive service is in a central downtown location purportedly accessible to all. This illustrative example suggests that even for a population presumed to have more agency than their younger counterparts (within an essentialized age-based understanding of life-stages), there are still daily negotiations and contestations of performance, which I suggest forms confined agency.

Scheduling and Timetabling at Cornerstone

One of the roles that a teacher at Cornerstone has taken on is to track attendance for each programming session (two before and two after the lunch hour). Usually, two or three therapeutic programming options run concurrently in addition to an English/humanities and a math/science class. During a weekly staff meeting, the lead child and youth worker raised a concern over attendance. The collated statistics showed that too large a percentage of client-student hours were in the two classes, which apparently meant that not enough client-student time was being spent in therapeutic programming. The lead CYW suggested that hospital administrators would not fund a "special ed school" with some medical practices, but it would continue to fund a day treatment program with educational elements. Views were sought about how to remedy these uneven statistics. Staff noted that many of those who attended regularly—those well on the way to therapeutic recovery—were preparing to return to a "normal" high school and had committed to getting various high school credits while still at Cornerstone. This meant their need for, and attendance in, therapeutic programming was considerably diminished, although they did diligently attend their scheduled therapeutic programs. Staff also commented that the incoming client-students—who were most at need for participating in the therapeutic community and programming, those at the nadir of their mental ill-health— were scheduled for a greater proportion of therapeutic programming, but were also least likely to attend. So the statistics were accurate but did not reflect the variety of readiness to attend and participate.

I raised the issue of how each client-student's schedule was organized with staff and client-students during interviews. All responded by stating it was usual for one of the first meetings between client-student and tutor/CYW to focus on organizing the weekly schedule. Client-students and staff expressed the importance of picking the programming elements they felt confident would enable short-term successes—most often the nonacademic / nonclassroom-based activities such as crafts, photography, ceramics, woodworking, hiking, bowling, YMCA, or relaxation. The client-students described their scheduling choices as just that—*their* choices—and some even used the variations in the "relocation of control" metaphor to describe this first step. Staff, on the other hand, described how they could push the client-student toward certain programs either as a recognition of the client-student's specific clinical diagnoses or, at times, because a particular program was at capacity: "Obviously, they get a lot of control, a lot of choice, but ultimately its up to us to get them into the programs that are best for them" (interview, April 2006). Schedules were regularly discussed at the weekly individual sessions between client-students and their tutor / CYW in order to assess progress and successes, as well as deal with difficulties. Many CYWs, in interviews, spoke of "directing" the schedule, especially at the end of a semester or when therapeutic progress had been accomplished, in order to keep client-students moving: "Cornerstone is a stepping stone, not a long-term facility," and we "don't want them too comfortable, too reliant" (interviews, 2006).

Here we again see ironic tensions surrounding the therapeutic work at Cornerstone and other mental health services like it. On the one hand, staff want client-students to take control of, attend, and benefit from the programming offered. On the other hand, staff have to negotiate these choices within the contexts of individual therapeutic needs as well as the confines of space and availability, thereby reducing the amount of real control client-students have. Having increased control or agency over participation is an expressed key element in the young person's therapeutic recovery—through these experiences it is hoped that they, as client-students, are no longer disabled by their mental ill-health. Furthermore, it is hoped that by making the decisions, having agency to do so, client-students commit to an individually tailored schedule and begin their "investment" in Cornerstone, and, in turn, become more likely to attend regularly and thereby gain from the therapy. Like the choices over free time in the NOS setting, Cornerstone's client-students' expression of agency, I suggest, is a good example of confined agency: the choices made were clearly directed by the adults' expertise and knowledge, whose framing is, in turn, under surveillance by senior hospital administrators.

There has been a distinct gender imbalance in my presentation of young people's voices and in the ethnographic vignettes explored above. Apart from staff perspectives, very few female voices have been presented. This is especially the case for the ethnographic evidence from NOS. During fieldwork at NOS, there was only one girl out of fifteen or so client-students, and staff recollected in interviews that in the preceding three years just three girls had attended NOS (interviews, 2006). To assure the girl's anonymity and confidentiality, I presented all the young NOS voices as male. Such a male focus is perhaps to be expected, as relatively few girls present the clinical levels of behavioral disorders that NOS best serves through day programming (Brochin and Horvath 1996; Frankel and Feinberg 2002). I have no concrete conclusions on what this imbalance means in terms of cultural expectations for behavior, mental ill-health, and psychiatric disorders, and how these areas relate to young people's competencies and agency. I do, however, interpret this imbalance as being symptomatic of a cultural and societal bias in the limits of acceptable behaviors and who is most likely to breach these limits, thereby needing additional support. This imbalance generates three initial questions that warrant additional research: Are we missing the agency of girls who are perhaps quietly disruptive, noncompliant, and underachieving academically? Are young boys in fact expressing unacceptable forms of agency when they exhibit behavioral levels that meet with *DSM-IV-R* diagnostic criteria? Does the classroom structure itself contribute to these male-oriented biases?

In my introduction, I presented a simplistic view of young people's agency within an understanding of childhood and adolescence, in which their capacity to act as individuals within institutional settings is often called into question. This questioning occurs for at least three reasons. First, young people are automatically seen as vulnerable and incapacitated (Finn and Nybell 2001). Second, agency is deferred to adults because they are the people who provide services to children and youth, and because young people in many circumstances cannot care for themselves (Backe-Hansen 2003). Third, young people are often described as either not knowing how to behave or not being able to behave within these settings (Crosson-Tower 1998; Downs et al. 2000), and indeed part of the *DSM-IV-R* symptom descriptors for various behavioral and mental health disorders are made in comparison to peers' performance within specific settings (American Psychiatric Association 2000). However, I have argued that young people do have agency, and that we should begin to think about complex and plural childhoods and adolescences, rather than singular or essentialized childhood or adolescence. Through my utilization of illustrative case studies I have explored how confined agency takes place in two mental health services in Canada. Rasmussen (2004:155) highlights the design and designation by adults of (often institutional) places for children. It is perhaps the adult design of these medicalized institutions in conjunction with their social location that contributes most to the confining and framing of the young people's agency. I assert that in each of the case studies, young people's agency is directed by adult, societal, or institutional frames. Through My Mad Plan, free time, and computer time, we witness various motivations interacting with choices and desires, where even "successes" all are framed by adult and institutional constraints: the bonus of computer time, with its choices and enjoyment used to encourage good participation and behaviors, is an option at only one NOS site. At Cornerstone the taxi rides are, at the same time, a supportive frame that increase client-students' ability to act with agency and participate in therapy and a point of friction that generates stresses that the therapeutic context is meant to alleviate. Scheduling "choices" are an expression of agency that encourage successful therapeutic participation but are negotiated to reflect staff knowledge and institutional parameters. It should be noted that adult actions and their agency are also framed in part by the young people's agency and in part by restrictions made by policy or institutional requirements. In these contexts, confined agency is an ongoing and multilayered interaction and dialogue.

In closing, I present a brief section of David's interview transcript, which I suggest epitomizes confined agency at NOS:

ı: Do you think there's anything really important I should know about this place?

ʀ: (P6) That the teachers give us lots of maths and language?

ı: (P3) Is that a good thing or a bad thing?

ʀ: So, so, we hate working but they make us, cos they're adults.

ı: OK.

ʀ: And we're, we're not adults.

In this relatively simple response, David acknowledges both his status within a social category and that this status dictates a limit to choices in what he can do at NOS. Perhaps this is to be expected. After all, the quote above comes from a (mere) 8-year-old, who is (in the classic view of childhood and children) supposed to do as he is told when at school and needs to learn the skills of reading writing and arithmetic. I am not suggesting that this is not the case. Rather, through this fairly astute quote, David demonstrates competent understanding of the social stratification between adults and children within the NOS's medicalized setting. We would do well to remember that children's agency can still be demonstrated in these settings, especially as part of therapeutic activities.

— So how do you change this?

QUESTIONS FOR DISCUSSION

1. Stride-Darnley examines assumptions of the cognitive behavioral theories that help to shape practice with young people at two mental health agencies in Canada. What theories about children and youth are prevalent in your work? What assumptions about children and children's agency are embedded in these frameworks?

2. Many contemporary interventions with children and youth stress terms that emerge in this chapter, such as "making decisions," "having options," or executing "good choices." Why might preoccupations with children's choices be so prevalent at this particular historical, political, and cultural moment?

3. What notions about childhood emerge in "My Mad Plan"? What notions of children's agency or confined agency does it contain?

4. The author identifies some spaces and times in which children are able to exercise greater agency (e.g., playing hockey at recess). In your work with children, where do you observe spaces and times that afford children greater agency?

5. What would it mean to consider the ways in which children and youth "coconstruct" social work practice, albeit from confined positions of limited power? What new ideas or practices might emerge from considering children and youth as agents in "making up" social services?

NOTES

1. I have chosen to use the term "client-student" as an attempt to be conciliatory toward both the senior medical professionals, who see clients as clients (or patients), and the youth, who see and describe themselves as students. See Stride-Darnley (2007b) for further discussion of this negotiated presentation.

2. All individual names are pseudonyms, and all child or youth examples are based on accumulations from fieldwork situations, interviews, and conversations. No individual child or youth is identifiable. However, institutional names for one site have been given at the request of staff and administrators. All participants were made aware of this format as part of the free and informed consent/assent processes.

3. All of my interviews were transcribed verbatim, with the following notations: I =

interviewer; R = respondent; and P3 = pause for count of 3. Italics for a word or portion of a word indicates a volume increase for that word or part of the word.

REFERENCES

Ahearn, L. M. (2001). Language and agency. *Annual Review of Anthropology 30:* 109–37.

Alanen, L. (1994). Gender and generation: Feminism and the "child question." In J. Qvortrup, M. Ardy, G. Sgritta, and H. Wintersberger, eds., *Childhood matters: Social theory, practice and politics,* 27–42. Aldershot, England: Avebury.

American Psychiatric Association. (2000). *Diagnostic and statistical manual of mental disorders: 4th Edition—Text Revision (DSM-IV-TR).* Washington, D.C.: American Psychiatric Association.

Backe-Hansen, E. (2003). The social construction of competence and problem behaviour among children. In C. Hallett and A. Prout, eds., *Hearing the voices of children: Social policy for a new century,* 177–91. London: Routledge.

Bloom, S. L., M. Bennington-Davis, B. Farragher, D. McCorkle, K. Nice-Martini, and K. Wellbank. (2003). Multiple opportunities for creating sanctuary. *Psychiatric Quarterly 74* (2): 172–90.

Boggin, B. (1998). Evolutionary and biological aspects of childhood. In C. Panter-Brick, ed., *Biosocial perspectives on children.* Cambridge: Cambridge University Press.

Bourdieu, P. (1977 [1972]). *Outline of a theory of practice.* Translated by Richard Nice. Cambridge: Cambridge University Press.

———. (1998 [1994]). *Practical reason: On the theory of action.* Stanford: Stanford University Press.

———. (1999). Scattered Remarks. *European Journal of Social Theory 2* (3): 334–40.

Brochin, H. A., and J. A. Horvath. (1996). Attention deficit/hyperactivity disorder. In G. M. Blau and T. P. Gullotta, eds., *Adolescent dysfunctional behavior: Causes, interventions and prevention,* 37–60. London: SAGE Publications.

Bucholtz, M. (2002) Youth and cultural practice. *Annual Review of Anthropology 31:* 525–52.

Cannella, G. S. (2002). Global perspectives, cultural studies, and the construction of a postmodern childhood studies. In G. S. Cannella and J. L. Kincheloe, eds., *Kidworld: Childhood studies, global perspectives, and education,* 3–18. New York: Peter Lang.

Chaput-Walker, F. (1991). The hard times of childhood and children's strategies for dealing with them. In F. Chaput-Walker, ed., *Studying the social worlds of children: Sociological readings,* 216–34. London: Falmer Press.

Christensen, P., and A. James. (2001). What are schools for? The temporal experience of children's learning in northern England. In L. Alanen and B. Mayall, eds., *Conceptualizing child-adult relations,* 70–85. London: Routledge.

Colón, A. R., and P. A. Colón. (2001). *A History of children: A socio-cultural survey across millennia.* London: Greenwood Press.

Crosson-Tower, C. (1998) *Exploring child welfare: A practice perspective.* 3rd edition. Boston: Allyn and Bacon.

Delgado, M. (2006). *Designs and methods for youth-led research.* London: SAGE Publications.

Downs, S. W., E. Moore, E. J. McFadden, S. E. Michaud, and I. Costin. (2000). *Child welfare and family services: Policies and practices.* 6th edition. Boston: Pearson.

Engalbert, A. (1994). Worlds of childhood: Differentiated but different. Implications for social policy. In J. Qvortrup, M. Ardy, G. Sgritta, and H. Wintersberger, eds., *Childhood matters: Social theory, practice and politics,* 285–98. Aldershot, England: Avebury.

Erikson, E. (1963). Childhood and society. 2nd edition. New York: W. W. Norton.

Finn, J., and L. Nybell. (2001). Capitalising on concern: The making of troubled children and troubling youth in late capitalism. *Childhood* 8 (2): 139–45.

Foley, P., N. Parton, J. Roche, and S. Tucker. (2003). Contradictory and convergent trends in law and policy affecting children in England. In C. Hallett and A. Prout, eds., *Hearing the voices of children: Social policy for a new century,* 106–20. London: Routledge.

Frankel F., and D. Feinberg. (2002). Social problems associated with ADHD vs. ODD in children referred for friendship problems. *Child Psychiatry and Human Development* 33 (2): 125–46.

Frankenberg, R., I. Robinson, and A. Delahooke. (2000). Countering essentialism in behavioural social science: The example of "the vulnerable child" ethnographically examined. *Sociological Review 48* (4): 586–611.

Giddens, A. (1982). *Profiles and critiques in social theory.* Berkeley: University of California Press.

Göncü, A., U. Tuermer, J. Jain, and D. Johnson. (1999). Children's play as cultural activity. In A. Göncü, ed., *Children's engagement in the world: Sociocultural perspectives,* 148–70. Cambridge: Cambridge University Press

Harkness, S. (1996). Anthropological images of childhood. In C. P. Hwang, M. Lamb, and I. E. Sigel, eds., *Images of Childhood.* Mahwah, N.J.: Lawrence Erlbraum Associates.

Hendrick, H. (2003). The child as a social actor in historical sources: Problems of identification and interpretation. In P. Christensen and A. James, eds., *Research with children: Perspectives and practices,* 36–61. London: Falmer Press.

Hockey, J., and A. James. (2003). *Social identities across the life course.* Basingstoke: Palgrave-Macmillan.

Holloway, S. L., and G. Valentine. (2003). *Cyberkids: Children in the information age.* London: Routledge-Farmer.

James, A., C. Jenks, and A. Prout. (2001 [1990]). *Theorizing childhood.* Cambridge: Polity Press.

James, A., and A. Prout. (1997). *Constructing and reconstructing childhood: Contemporary issues in the sociological study of childhood.* London: Falmer Press.

Jenks, C. (2005). A new death of childhood. *Childhood* 12 (1): 5–8.

Kennard, D. (2004). The therapeutic community as an adaptable treatment modality across different settings. *Psychiatric Quarterly* 75 (3): 293–307.

Lahelma, E. (2002). School is for meeting friends: Secondary school as lived and remembered. *British Journal of Sociology of Education* 23 (3): 367–81.

Lee, N. (1999). The challenge of childhood: Distributions of childhood's ambiguity in adult institutions. *Childhood* 6 (4): 455–74.

———. (2001). Children in their place: Home school and media. In N. Lee, *Childhood and society: Growing up in an age of uncertainty,* 70–86. Buckingham: Open University Press.

Mason, J, and J. Falloon. (2001). Some Sydney children define abuse: Implications for agency in childhood. In L. Alanen and B. Mayall, eds., *Conceptualizing child-adult relations,* 99–113. London: Routledge.

Musgrave, S. (2002). *Friendship in the lives of teen girls.* Toronto: Annick Press.

Nybell, L. (2001). Meltdowns and containments: Constructions of children at risk as complex systems. *Childhood* 8 (2): 213–30.

Piaget, J. (1962). *Play, dreams and imitation in childhood.* New York: W. W. Norton.

Pike, L.T. (2003). The adjustment of Australian children growing up in single-parent families as measured by their competence and self-esteem. *Childhood* 10 (2): 181–200.

Prout, A. (2000). Researching children as social actors: An introduction to the Children 5–16 Programme. *Children and Society* 16: 67–76.

Prout, A., and C. Hallett. (2003). Introduction. In C. Hallett and A. Prout, eds., *Hearing the voices of children: Social policy for a new century,* 1–9. London: Routledge.

Rasmussen, K. (2004). Places for children—children's places. *Childhood* 11 (2): 155–73.

Roberts, H. (2003). Children's participation in policy matters. In C. Hallett and A. Prout, eds., *Hearing the voices of children: Social policy for a new century,* 26–37. London: Routledge.

Seifert, K. L. (2000). Uniformity and diversity in everyday views of the child. In S. Harkness, C. Raeff, and C. M. Super, eds., *Variability in the social construction of the child (New Directions for Child and Adolescent Development* 87 (Spring): 75–92). San Francisco: Jossey-Bass.

Shook, Jeffery J. (2005). Contesting childhood in the U.S. justice system: The transfer of juveniles to adult criminal court. *Childhood* 12 (4): 461–78.

Stephens, S. (1995).Introduction: Children and the politics of culture in "late capital-ism." In S. Stephens, ed., *Children and the politics of culture,* 3–48. Princeton: Prin-ceton University Press.

Stride-Darnley, B. (2007a). Differing orders of data: Using qualitative and quantitative methodologies to investigate the role of arts at a day treatment program for young people with psychiatric and emotional difficulties. Ms.

———. (2007b). Sites of re-enculturation: Habitus, hexis corporeal and further anthro-pological interpretations of a Canadian mental health service for youth. Ms.

Stride-Darnley, B., and D. Buchanan. (2005). The importance of arts in a day treatment program for adolescents with mental health problems. Applied Research Report for Ontario Ministry of Culture and Recreation / Children's Mental Health Ontario.

Thorne, B. (2004). Theorising age and other differences. *Childhood* 11 (4): 403–8.

Valentine, G., T. Skelton, and D. Chambers. (1998). Cool places: An introduction to youth and youth culture. In T. Skelton and G. Valentine, eds., *Cool places: Geogra-phies of youth culture,* 1–34. London: Routledge.

Vandenbroek, M., and M. Bouverne-de Bie. (2005). Children's agency and educational norms: A tensed negotiation. *Childhood* 13 (1): 127–43.

Wolf, A. (2002). *Does education matter? Myths about education and economic growth.* London: Penguin.

Wyness, M. (2000). *Contesting childhood.* London: Falmer Press.

———. (2006). *Childhood and society: An introduction to the sociology of childhood.* Bas-ingstoke, U.K.: Palgrave / Macmillan.

TWELVE

*Children and Youth in
Community-Based Reform*

Lynn M. Nybell

Over the last two decades, social work practice has become increasingly preoccupied with identifying and measuring levels of risk to which young people are exposed. In the context of social, economic, and political change in the lives of young people, social work scholars have suggested that research on risk and resilience can offer guidance for the design and delivery of social programs (Fraser 2004:2). Frameworks of risk and resilience are now so broadly accepted that the Council on Social Work Education accreditation standards mandate that all social work students acquire knowledge about the impact of exposure to risk factors on human behavior (Council on Social Work Education 2001).[1]

Risk-focused models are applied to a wide range of youthful behaviors—"failing in school, getting in trouble with the courts, using illicit drugs, engaging in unprotected sex, joining gangs, getting shot, or attempting or committing suicide," to cite just a few examples (Fraser 2004:3). It is argued that risk factors can be broadly defined to include "any influence that increases the possibility

I would like to acknowledge the people I met in the town I call Stockton for their openness to my study and their trust in my judgment. I particularly thank the social worker I call Blair Thompson. My efforts on this project were supported in part by a sabbatical leave award from Eastern Michigan University.

of harm, contributes to a more serious state or maintains a problem condition" (Coie et al. 1993). However, the impact of risk factors can be offset by the presence of protective factors, or, "those positive internal and external resources that contribute to adaptive outcomes in the presence of risk" (Fraser 2004:5). Proponents of these models argue that since risk and protective factors correlate with the emergence of youthful dysfunction, early intervention into those factors is likely to reduce the negative outcomes with which they are associated. Social work scholars have promoted "prevention science," which uses assessments of risk in individual young people or among populations of youth before selecting interventions from a roster of empirically tested interventions (Fraser and Galinsky 2004; Hawkins and Catalano 2005).

Within the profession of social work, the risk-factor paradigm has been received as intuitively appealing and logical—a new kind of "common sense" in social work with children and youth. The appeal of the paradigm is rooted in both its "humanistic intention" to prevent danger and harm to young people and its "economic intention" to carefully channel resources to interventions based on their costs and benefits to communities and the nation (Kelly 2001). In addition, it is difficult to dispute any movement so highly self-conscious of the need to apply empirical evidence to the development of policy and practice with young people. Perhaps because of these multiple appeals, models of risk and protection have proliferated largely unchallenged within the social work literature on children and youth (Sharland 2006).[2]

Meanwhile, critical scholars—often outside of the U.S. profession of social work—have begun to question whether risk assessments do not passively report levels of risk. Instead, they suggest, risk assessments actively construct our understanding of what is the matter with young people (Armstrong 2004; Bottoms 2005; Goldson 2001; Goldson and Muncie 2006; Jamieson 2006; Kelly 2001; Polakow 1993; Wilcox 2003). In particular, several scholars argue, risk-factor research has been extremely influential in reorienting thinking about youth toward antecedents of trouble that are believed to be the responsibility of the child and his or her family, and away from problems rooted in the structural characteristics of the society itself (Fine 1995; Kelly 2001; Parton 1999; Swadener and Lubeck 1995). Swadener and Lubeck (1995) note that the pervasive discourse of risk provides a language of medical pathology to label low-income children, drawing attention toward the personal and behavioral characteristics of these young people, and away from debates about social welfare and educational policies that contribute to child poverty and educational inequality. In the context of diminishing social welfare protections and growing employment insecurity, scholars like Kelly (2001) ask whether the discourses of "youth at risk" serve to focus attention on individual deficits and pathologies in the increasingly uncertain settings of an ever more precarious "risk society" (Beck 1992; Gidden 1994). From this perspective, a preoccupation with risk assessments and interventions that focus on individual behavior and attitudes can be conceived as part of a broader neoliberal project that makes individuals and families responsible for managing their own predicaments even as the society manufactures more risk and uncertainty with which they must contend (Kelly 2001; Rose 1996).

What follows is a brief story that prompts me to take such critiques seriously. I tell this story to bring about a thoughtful consideration of how discourses of risk—and the assessment tools and intervention plans with which these are associated—may reshape our thoughts and actions with regard to young people. Furthermore, I suggest that we might seek ways to understand how schools and social work settings saturated with notions of "risk" might shape, confine, or structure the self-understandings of young people themselves.

The story emerged from an ethnographic study of community-based reform that I carried out in Stockton, Michigan, between 1996 and 1998 (Nybell 2002). In many ways, it seems an act of hubris to raise questions about a powerful scientific discourse based on a simple story of experience. On the other hand, the need for social work students, practitioners, and teachers to think critically includes forgoing the comfortable feeling of certainty, questioning what others take for granted, and being willing to seriously appraise popular ideas (Gambrill 2000). I offer the story as a stimulus to such critical thought. Following the story, I offer a coda about its relevance a decade later.

COMMUNITY-BASED REFORM COMES TO STOCKTON

On the third Friday of every month, 20 or more people gathered around a large conference table at the Community Mental Health Center of Stockton, Michigan,[3] to convene the county's Multi-Purpose Collaborative Body (MPCB). The Stockton MPCB drew together the local public agency directors, the probate judge, the directors of private local agencies, three "consumers" who were longtime agency volunteers and foster parents, and representatives of "citizen groups," including the United Auto Workers.

Stockton, Michigan, where these leaders gathered, is a community of about 20,000 residents that bears nostalgic hallmarks of small-town America. Since its original heyday as an early-nineteenth-century port, Stockton has retained a measure of historical charm, while enduring the rise and decline of the lumber industry, paper mills, steel making, energy production, and auto-related manufacturing. Through the 1980s, Stockton had a history as a center of manufacturing with a high percentage of its work force organized in labor unions. In recent decades, however, nonunion service jobs, with wages of about 50% of the manufacturing sector, expanded while jobs in manufacturing declined. Children in Stockton, like children in other small towns and working-class suburbs across Michigan, faced uncertain and perhaps increasingly disparate futures in the lagging state economy (Michigan League for Human Services 2004, 2005). And as children in Stockton grew up, some portion of them came to the attention of the community's mental health, juvenile justice, or child welfare agencies.

In Stockton in the mid-1990s, the MPCB represented a new forum in which directors of these agencies came together with other community leaders to devise strategies to better assist troubled and troubling young people. The creation of the MPCB in Stockton was a local manifestation of a stream of community-oriented social reform in the United States in the 1990s. Citing the proverb "It takes a village to raise a child," advocates envisioned reintegrating care of troubled or troubling children within networks of local concern (Clinton 1996; Comer et al. 1996; Hagedorn 1995; Knitzer 1996; McKnight 1995; Schorr 1993). In a flurry of activity, the U.S. government, private foundations, and state bureaucracies funded model programs to demonstrate how communities might assume new responsibilities for children. Each of these grantors promoted model programs that shared an emphasis on local collaboration and proposed to demonstrate ways in which communities might assume more responsibility for troubled children (Cole 1996; King and Meyers 1996; Schorr 1997; Stroul 1996).

By the mid-1990s, collaborative structures on behalf of children seemed to be springing up everywhere. For example, in Michigan in 1995, the state department directors identified nineteen different initiatives that required interdepartmental state steering committees and local collaborative coalitions, committees, or councils. The directors wrote that the proliferation of "these innovative activities, all of which have merit, [is] causing confusion in local communities as to what collaborative initiative will lead to true reform" (State of Michigan 1995:2).

Ironically, then, as efforts at coordinating community-based services proliferated in Michigan, the resulting confusion threatened to fragment them further. A 1995 letter from the governor to public agencies indicated that communities wishing to participate in state-sponsored interagency initiatives in the future would be required to have a "multipurpose collaborative body (MPCB) intended to serve as a decision-making body to coordinate human services" (State of Michigan 1995). It was envisioned that by establishing collaboratives, communities would develop more efficient and flexible local services and goad further statewide reform.

Stockton's MPCB was established to meet these state requirements and structured in accord with state guidelines. Local agency directors and prominent citizens met monthly to explore the possibilities of this new form. The MPCB in Stockton oversaw three state-funded interagency initiatives: a program offering wraparound services to children who were understood as "high-risk" youth with complex needs; "Early On," which identified and offered services to "high-risk" babies and their mothers; and "Strong Families / Safe Children," which offered very modest budgets to communities to fund projects to reduce the risk of child abuse. It is noteworthy that each of these initiatives shared a vocabulary of risk. In the context of collaborative efforts uniting social workers, educators, doctors, judges, and other community members—each with their own specialized vocabularies and particular arenas of concern for children—the discourse of risk offered a language that flowed across these professional boundaries.

The director of the county's mental health agency, Samuel Burman, chaired Stockton's MPCB. An imposing man well versed in *Robert's Rules of Order*, he conducted the meetings in a cordial, formal tone. The agenda of each MPCB meeting was devoted to monitoring the status of interagency initiatives, planning responses to new state-funded opportunities, and offering a forum for members to make reports or announcements about new social service developments in the community. In the meetings, members shared the startling and accelerating changes in the policies and programs aimed at serving children in Michigan. Policy makers involved with "ending welfare" rolled back public assistance. At the same time, the state's involvement in the lives of delinquent youth intensified, focusing with increasing intensity on providing punishment rather than guidance or rehabilitation. In an increasing eagerness to treat troubling youth as adults, proponents of "get tough" and "zero-tolerance" policies essentially evicted offenders from the conceptual category of "children," treating them as fully responsible for their actions (Jenks 1996). "Second chances" and "special needs" were increasingly reserved for an expanding group of children considered disabled or mentally ill.

In this context of dramatic change, members of the Stockton MPCB accepted interagency projects as worthwhile endeavors. It was clear that older channels of state funding for programs aimed at children and youth were drying up. Local actors hoped that streams of funding for new, locally driven efforts might eventually rise in their stead. They approached the new project in a practical spirit that was neither resistant nor eagerly reformist. Still, in private conversations, some members expressed suspicions about the degree to which the state's avowed interest in devolution of authority and responsibility to the local level was authentic.

In its initial months of operation, Stockton's MPCB established several priorities of local concern, including youth employment, transportation, and housing. Many members of the MPCB had participated in a comprehensive community needs assessment process sponsored by the United Way just two years earlier, and the MPCB priorities were in line with the results of that study. The United Way assessment process was based on census data and research reports generated from surveys of residents and from interviews and focus groups with key informants. The assessment results indicated that Stockton respondents took pride in their schools, police and fire departments, and the county mental health agency. Their rankings of the problems of crime, mental and emotional illness, and illiteracy were low. The report stated: "The perception was that these needs are being met at more than an adequate level and that makes the quality of life in the county secure." In contrast, housing, health, unemployment, shortages of recreation and child care facilities, and transportation ranked as serious concerns. The most severe problems—housing, access to health care, and family finances—were linked by the authors of the report to the loss of manufacturing jobs, growth in lower-paying service-sector employment, and cuts in government programs in Stockton County.

As the MPCB organized itself in Stockton, it created subcommittees on youth employment, transportation, housing, child care, and public awareness—areas that surfaced as important concerns in the United Way study. The MPCB was saluted on the Stockton evening news for its summer youth employment program, which hired youth from Stockton's east-side neighborhoods to improve city parks. This effort was financed by funds that the MPCB scraped together from unexpended lines of other grants, and members of the body were obviously proud of the effort, which they hoped would be the first of a series of efforts to make a tangible difference in the lives of Stockton youth.

REALIZING RISK THROUGH "COMMUNITIES THAT CARE"

When the well-respected local juvenile court justice "Judge Jerry" returned from a meeting in Lansing with news that Stockton had a chance to compete for a delinquency prevention grant, the Stockton MPCB formed a task force to work on a proposal. Grant funding came from the U.S. Office of Juvenile Justice and Delinquency Prevention (OJJDP). As Judge Jerry described it, the grant-making process required that a committee of "key leaders" in Stockton assemble data on community needs. The roster of key leaders who stepped forward included the city manager, the superintendent of schools, the detective assigned to community affairs, the director of Stockton's United Way, and Blair Thompson, a social worker who staffed the MPCB on a part-time basis.

The OJJDP relied upon a framework for delinquency prevention called "Communities that Care."[4] Communities that Care (CTC) has billed itself as "a community operating system that provides research-based tools to help communities promote the positive development of children and youth and prevent adolescent substance abuse, delinquency, teen pregnancy, school dropout and violence." CTC is described as a comprehensive, community-wide, risk-focused prevention strategy based upon the "latest research about the factors that promote the healthy development of children and youth and the factors that increase the likelihood of problem behaviors" (Hawkins and Catalano 2005). With the support of the OJJDP, CTC is in use in a number of states and, with funding from international foundations, is now an extremely influential model of prevention work with youth, both nationally and—through its projects in Britain, Australia, and the Netherlands—internationally (Crow, France, and Hacking 2006; Toumbourou 1999).

"Community mobilization" in CTC required adherence to specified steps and processes by which local actors identified as "community leaders" were engaged in learning about and then applying notions of "risk factors" and "protective factors" to the development of a plan to promote positive youth development in local settings. Key leaders from interested communities were invited to participate in a training session explaining the CTC approach and its implications for evidence-based programs based on "prevention science." These key leaders then worked together to develop a Community Prevention Board, which was charged with bringing together a larger group of formal and informal leaders and service workers. Once established, the Community Prevention Board would generate a plan aimed at reducing the community's elevated risk factors and propping up depressed protective ones. Once the CTC approved the local plan, it would give technical assistance and training to the local community board in carrying it out.

In Stockton, the city manager, school superintendent, police detective, director of the United Way, and social worker Blair Thompson convened to gather data and assess local needs. They believed that their task was to assemble data that they considered relevant to promoting positive youth development in Stockton and to reflect on this information in preparation for "key leader training." In their early meetings, the data amassed by the membership reflected their diverse backgrounds and interests. The city manager assembled census data, from which he made observations about relatively low to average education levels, unusually high percentages of workers who were "detached from the labor force," and the impact of poverty and housing problems in the census tracts on Stockton's east side. The superintendent reviewed dropout rates and test scores as well as results of a survey conducted in recent years by the Merrill Palmer Institute. The United Way director returned to the survey of Stockton residents that focused concern on lack of affordable housing, inadequate access to health care, unemployment, and shortages of child care and recreational opportunities. The police detective offered data on crime rates. Blair asked questions about environmental risks to youth that stemmed from brownfields, abandoned factories, and deteriorated housing that she observed on her frequent visits to the city's east side. She reported that the director of the community center there, the Joe E. Johnson Center, perceived an urgent need to expand child care and youth programming in other low-income tracts within the city. And she proposed that the task force interview parents of children labeled "disabled," "delinquent," or "disturbed."

Loaded with these varied fragments of information, representatives of Stockton's team of key leaders attended preliminary CTC training sessions. They returned with the news that successful competition for the delinquency grant funds hinged not on the data they had gathered, but on participation in the CTC Youth Survey, an eleven-page survey to be administered to all students in Stockton's sixth, tenth, and twelfth grades (U.S. Substance Abuse and Mental Health Services Administration, n.d.).

ACCOUNTING FOR RISK

The CTC Youth Survey asks all students at the targeted grade levels to respond to a ten-page questionnaire containing 191 items. In the survey, students are asked to report very extensively—on 72 separate items—on their own "experience with tobacco, alcohol and other drugs" (including marijuana, crack, cocaine, steroids, heroin, LSD, hashish, psychedelic drugs, barbiturates, and inhalants); their attitudes toward drugs and alcohol; and the behaviors, beliefs, and values of their family, neighbors, and peers in relationship to these substances. Examples of inquiries about the behaviors of others include questions such as "About how many adults have you known personally in the past year who have used marijuana, crack, cocaine, and other drugs?" "Thinking about your four best friends (the friends you feel closest to), in the past year (12 months), how many of your best friends have: smoked cigarettes? tried beer, wine or hard liquor (for example, vodka, whiskey, or gin) when their parents didn't know about it? used marijuana? used LSD, cocaine, amphetamines, or other illegal drugs?" Examples of questions about the beliefs of others include questions like, "How wrong would most adults in your neighborhood think it was for kids your age to use marijuana? to drink alcohol? to smoke cigarettes?" "How wrong would your parents feel it would be for you to drink beer, wine, or hard liquor (for example, vodka, whisky, or gin) regularly? smoke cigarettes? smoke marijuana?" (U.S. Substance Abuse and Mental Health Services Administration, n.d.).

In addition to the central focus on substance abuse, the survey incorporates many questions about the respondents' delinquent behaviors, such as "How many times in the past year (12 months) have you: been suspended from school? carried a handgun? sold illegal drugs? stolen or tried to steal a motor vehicle such as a car of motorcycle? been arrested? attacked someone with the idea of seriously hurting them? been drunk or high at school? taken a handgun to school?" Other questions inquire about how old respondents were when they first stole anything worth more than $5, drew graffiti, or attacked someone with the idea of seriously hurting them. The survey also asks young people to report if friends or family members engage in these behaviors, and inquire about how much disapproval one's parents express for these behaviors.

Supplementing the questions on substance use, delinquent behavior, and antisocial attitudes are items that seek to identify protective factors, including attachment to family ("I can go to my mom or dad for help"); religiosity ("How often do you attend religious activities?"); opportunities for positive involvement ("I know where to go to get help with my homework"); and rewards for conventional involvement ("My parents notice when I am doing a good job and let me know about it").

The survey poses few questions about the economic realities that young people face. The single question aimed at soliciting respondents' views of material conditions in their communities asks: "How much do each of the following statements describe your neighborhood: crime and / or drug selling? fights? lots of empty or abandoned buildings? lots of graffiti?" Even this question, designed to assess "neighborhood disorganization," focuses more on neighborhood behaviors—fighting, drug selling, and producing or viewing graffiti—than it does on economics.

One can imagine a survey aimed to capture the material realities of young people's lives that would require other sorts of questions, for example: "My house or apartment always has heat, water, and light"; "The owner of my house or apartment makes repairs when they are needed"; "I can find employment in my community if I look for it"; "I always have transportation to work and school"; "There are parks, playgrounds, or community centers in my community where I enjoy spending time." Such a survey might seek to understand the role that young people play in meeting family needs, for example: "My responsibilities to care for members of my family sometimes cause me to miss school"; or "The children in my family sometimes have someone to turn to in an emergency when adults at work." Young people might be asked to comment on the material conditions confronted by others as well. For example, imagine a question like, "Thinking of your four best friends, in the past year (12 months), how often have your friends: been evicted? experienced homelessness? lacked food when they were hungry? found themselves unable to get needed medical or dental care? lacked transportation to school or work when they needed it?" One could imagine a survey that asked young people to report more extensively on their views of the adequacy of the schools, for example: "I believe my school has the resources necessary to prepare me for college"; or "My school provides opportunity to all youth, regardless of race, religion, and culture or language difference."

Instead, CTC survey questions conceive risk primarily as behaviors and attitudes of children and those around them. In the analysis of these data, CTC researchers compare the "elevated risk factors" and "depressed protective factors" in Stockton to other settings, in a move that assumes a normative level of risk and prompts local actors to focus on those areas where risk exceeds standardized ranges. Most significantly, however, this framework of analysis points almost inevitably to educational, therapeutic, or disciplinary solutions, aimed at changing children or their parents.

The CTC risk assessment asked questions about behaviors and attitudes that are undoubtedly important ones. At the same time, the survey screened out concerns of community leaders about whether children and youth in Stockton had access to housing, health care, or prospects of employment by which to earn a living wage in the context of a changing economy. It filtered out suggestions of parents and community center staff about the need to increase young people's access to opportunities for civic engagement, political involvement, or creative expression. It set aside apprehensions about the extent to which some children and youth must struggle against prejudice, harassment, or unjust treatment or suffer the effects of exposure to environmental contamination.

The possibility of addressing or at least approaching some of these concerns existed in initial discussions of the key leaders in Stockton who tried to grapple with this grant opportunity. It is impossible to know what might have emerged from a local effort that was not narrowly disciplined by the CTC framework of risk and protection. Clearly many of the problems that surfaced in early discussions extended well beyond the scope of a local-level demonstration effort.

However, one can still wonder what might have happened if engagement with risk assessment had not changed the subject. At one point, as the task force reviewed the draft survey, I observed to the members that the instrument would not address many of the areas of concern that had emerged in their initial discussions, like youth employment, transportation, and housing. "True," the superintendent of Stockton schools replied, "but those guys are the experts; they must know what they are doing."

The task force used the planning funds they received to conduct the survey and receive the analysis. The data that were returned to Stockton centered on comparing rates of substance use and antisocial behavior in Stockton with data from communities in six other states. Recommendations for drug and alcohol education programs emerged. In part, this outcome seemed inevitable; when risks are conceived in terms of personal behavior, it is not surprising that the recommended interventions are directed at education in life skills or parenting support programs. The local effort lost momentum, and Stockton dropped out of the competition for delinquency prevention grant funds. Still, by means of the grant application process, CTC had disseminated its perspective to community leaders, and by means of the participation in the survey, to 1,125 children in Stockton.

CHILDREN, COMMUNITY, AND RISK

The unsuccessful efforts of the MPCB in Stockton to compete for new funding demonstrated how even this limited and ultimately failed engagement with Communities that Care directed the perceptions of local leaders about the problems and prospects for assisting local youth. Through processes of technical assistance, training, and grant management for a variety of risk-focused demonstration projects, the energies of key leaders in communities like Stockton are channeled toward monitoring and preventing particular conceptions of community risk, or toward efforts aimed at containing the behavior and attitudes of a community's highest-risk children. Despite the considerable skepticism of local actors about the motives of the state in system reform, their involvement in the collaborative directed local actors toward risk prevention and management, and disciplined local perceptions of what constituted risk. While the MPCBs were cumbersome vehicles for the delivery of service, they were remarkably efficient means to disseminate new mind-sets to influential local actors. So, while the proliferating array of funded, collaborative, community-based efforts delivers only a modest amount of direct service to a limited number of children, I suggest that we might consider the possibility that these demonstration efforts play a much larger and more influential role in reconstructing the frame of reference through which children's predicaments are viewed.

CODA

In 2007 there is no sign that the impact of risk and protective factor frameworks on social work practice and policy with children is diminishing. The copyrights to the CTC survey and planning system were acquired by the U.S. Department of Health and Human Services, so that system now has a "home" in the Substance Abuse and Mental Health Services Administration. The risk and safety assessment questionnaire is now available to be downloaded and distributed free of charge from the agency's website. Though the CTC model has been disseminated both nationally and globally since the early 1990s, a full-scale evaluation of 24 projects was launched by the pioneers of the model, with results expected in 2008 (Hawkins Catalano 2007).

A serious assessment of this model obviously requires a great deal more than a simple story from Stockton. But the questions raised by the Stockton story linger. A 2005 study of the impact of Communities that Care in Pennsylvania has appeared as the "first broad-scale evaluation of student outcomes in communities using the CTC Program" (Feinberg et al. 2005:2). This study reports that CTC impacted risk factors in participating communities; the authors also explicitly note that "CTC programs are generally designed to impact youth and families directly" rather than focusing resources on community change (5). For that reason, they exclude community risk factors from their analysis.

Meanwhile, a careful, five-year evaluation of three CTC demonstration projects in the Britain "does not add up to a resounding success of the CTC programme" (Crow et al. 2004:69). At the end of five years, the evaluators identified no evidence of impact in two of the three demonstration sites and only "promising but inconclusive evidence in a third" (70). Somewhat to my amazement, the evaluators provide stories of implementation problems that echo the events I observed in Stockton. They note, for example, a failed effort to rely on locally gathered data, which was abandoned in favor of the standardized survey; funding that allowed the assessment and planning to move forward but ran out when it came time to implement an action plan; a conflict between the "science" of the survey and the interests of local communities in addressing tangible needs; and a growth in cynicism and negativity in sites where hours of planning and work did not achieve any goals (Crow et al. 2004; Crow, France, and Hacking 2006).

Perhaps the broad U.S. study currently under way will prove out quite differently. Nevertheless, what I believe the story from Stockton suggests is that the impact of models like CTC must be more broadly reconsidered. Risk-based demonstration programs like CTC not only affect the services and resources available in local communities, they also shape the ways problems of young people are conceived and addressed within local communities. As the evaluators of the British projects point out, one of the underlying tensions in the project emerges from the interplay of the "science" provided by the risk survey and the local knowledge of professionals and lay people in the community (Crow et al. 2004:81). These authors recommend increasing the level of training, monitoring, and orientation of local people, to insure that they are fully inducted into the premises of the model as designed (69). However, I would argue from another angle that what is required is careful attention and documentation of the particular sorts of local concerns that fall outside of the risk assessment models.

Finally, I propose that a study might be made of how children themselves view these assessments, and in what ways these surveys do (or do not) affect the meanings they assign their own experiences. One concern is, of course, that young people do not take them seriously and supply "phony" data. Surveys like the one devised by CTC are designed to confirm that children provide valid responses. However, one can imagine a variety of possible ways children might react to the instrument—from indifference to silliness to sober reflection. I propose that we might respond by working out ways to discover how children and youth perceive the process and outcome of risk assessment surveys. We might also explore how young people themselves might construe "risk" and "resilience" in their own lives, and perceive pathways in and out of trouble.

Those who are invoking the language of children "at risk" are hoping for the humanitarian consequence that the needs of vulnerable young people will receive more attention. However, we must recognize that all frameworks have flaws; indeed, any model for understanding children's situations will be only a "shaved and quite partial image" (Fine 1995:77). However, we have to be concerned if the prominent and powerful image as "children at risk" is one that "betrays more than it reveals" (86). As Michelle Fine argues, "Diverted away from an economy that is inhospitable to low-income adolescents and adults, particularly U.S. born African Americans and Latinos, and away from the collapsing manufacturing sectors of the country, housing stock and impoverished urban schools, our attention floats to the individual, to his or her family, and to those small-scale interventions that would 'fix' the child as though her or his life were fully separable from ours" (1995:89).

QUESTIONS FOR DISCUSSION

1. What is the primary critique the author has with describing youth as "at risk"? Do you see this label as helpful or harmful? What might be an alternative description of this population?

2. In telling the story of the Multi-Purpose Collaborative Body in Stockton, the author provides a broader context of the political climate at the time. Do you believe this is important in understanding the MPCB? How did the policy climate affect the formation and tasks of this interagency initiative?

3. What was the common factor among the first three programs of the Stockton MPCB? Why do you think this language was used?

4. What kinds of questions did the CTC survey not include? How did this shape the aim of the interventions? What can you infer about the types of questions one asks in shaping what programs are implemented?

5. After the CTC survey, the author pointed out to the task force that it did not seem to address the original areas of concern. What was the response provided? Have you ever been in a professional situation in which a figure of authority had a different perspective from yours? How was it resolved, and what were the outcomes?

NOTES

1. The Council on *Social Work Education* (CSWE) standards for accreditation of social work education programs specifies that all programs provide eight areas of foundation content. One, on "populations-at-risk and social and economic justice," requires that social work education programs "integrate content on populations-at-risk, examining the factors that contribute to and constitute being at risk. Programs educate students to identify how group membership influences access to resources, and present content on the dynamics of such risk factors and responsive and productive strategies to redress them" (CSWE 2001: 9).

2. A search of *Social Work Abstracts* reveals that the term "risk" appeared in 2,700 abstracts between 1987 and 2007. As a point of comparison with other key terms in the profession, the word "justice" appeared in 1,635 abstracts; the word "empowerment," in 613.

3. All names of people and places in this story are pseudonyms.

4. The Communities that Care Youth Survey distributed in Stockton was produced by Developmental Research and Programs in Seattle, Washington (Developmental Research and Programs 1997). The survey was based on work by J. David Hawkins and

Richard F. Catalano, faculty members in the University of Washington School of Social Work. By 2001 the materials were distributed on a fee basis from Channing L. Bete. In August 2005 the U.S. Department of Health and Human Service's Substance Abuse and Mental Health Service Agencies, acquired copyright to the survey and related materials. The survey and guidebooks to the CTC planning process are now available at http://preventionplatform.samhsa.gov.

REFERENCES

Armstrong, D. (2004). A risky business? Research, policy, governmentality, and youth offending. *Youth Justice 4* (2): 100–116.

Beck, U. (1992). *The risk society.* London: Sage.

Bottoms, A. (2005). Methodology matters. *Safer Society 25:* 10–12.

Clinton, H. R. (1996). *It takes a village and other lessons children teach us.* New York: Simon and Schuster.

Coie, J. D., N. F. Watt, S. G. West, J. D. Hawkins, J. R. Asarnow, H. J. Markman, S. L. Ramey, M. B. Shure, and B. Long. (1993). The science of prevention: A conceptual framework and some directions for a national research program. *American Psychologist 48:* 1013–22.

Cole, R. M. (1996). The Robert Wood Johnson Foundation's mental health services program for youth. In B.A. Stroul, ed., *Children's mental health: Creating systems of care in a changing society,* 235–48. Baltimore: Paul H. Brookes.

Comer, J. P., N. M. Haynes, E. T. Joyner, and M. Ben-Avie. (Eds.) *Rallying the whole village: The Comer process for reforming education.* New York: Teacher's College Press.

Council on Social Work Education (2001). *Educational policy and accreditation standards.* New York: CSWE. Accessed September 23, 2007, at http://www.cswe.org/NR/rdonlyres/111833A0-C4F5–475C-8FEB-EA740FF4D9F1/0/EPAS.pdf.

Crow, I., A. France, and S. Hacking. (2006). Evaluation of three Communities that Care projects in the UK. *Security Journal 19:* 45–57.

Crow, I., A. France, S. Hacking, and M. Hart. (2004). *Does Communities that Care work? An evaluation of a community-based risk prevention programme in three neighbourhoods.* York: Joseph Rountree Foundation.

Developmental Research and Programs (1997). *Communities that Care® Youth Survey.* Seattle: Developmental Research and Programs.

Feinberg, M., M. Greenberg, J. Olson, and W. Osgood (2005). *CTC impact in Pennsylvania: Findings from the 2001 and 2003 Pennsylvania youth survey.* University Park: College of Health and Human Development, Pennsylvania State University.

Fine, M. (1995). The politics of who's "at risk." In B.B. Swadener and S. Lubeck, eds., *Children and families at promise: Deconstructing the discourse of risk.* Albany: State University of New York Press.

Fraser, M.W. (Ed.) (2004). *Risk and resilience in childhood: An ecological perspective.* 2nd edition. Washington, D.C.: NASW Press.

Fraser, M.W., and M. Galinsky. (2004). Risk and resilience in childhood: Toward an evidence-based model of practice. In M.W. Fraser, ed., *Risk and resilience in child-hood: An ecological perspective.* 2nd edition. Washington, D.C.: NASW Press.

Gambrill, E. (2000). The role of critical thinking in evidence-based social work. In P. Meares and C. Garvin, eds., *The handbook of social work direct practice.* Thousand Oaks, Calif.: Sage.

Gidden, A. (1994). *Beyond left and right.* Cambridge: Polity Press.

Goldson, B. (2001). A rational youth justice: Some critical reflections on the research, policy and practice relation. *Probation Journal 48* (2): 76–85.

Goldson, B., and J. Muncie. (2006). Rethinking youth justice: Comparative analysis, international human rights and research evidence. *Youth Justice 6* (2): 91–106.

Greenberg, M. E., M. T. Greenberg, and D. W. Osgood. (2004). Readiness, functioning and perceived effectiveness in community prevention collations: A study of Communities that Care. *American Journal of Community Psychology 33* (3/4): 163–76.

Hagedorn, J.M. (1995). *Forsaking our children: Bureaucracy and reform in the child welfare system.* Chicago: Lake View Press.

Hawkins, J. D., and R. F. Catalano. (2005). *Investing in your communities: An introduction to the Communities that Care system.* Accessed August 21, 2007, at http://www.preventionplatform.samhsa.gov.

———. (2007). *Science-based prevention: Testing Communities that Care (research project description).* Accessed August 30, 2007, at http://depts.washington.edu/sswweb/resweb/project.php?id = 25.

Jamieson, J. (2006). New Labor, youth justice and the question of "respect." *Youth Justice 5* (3): 180–93.

Jenks, C. (1996). *Childhood.* London: Routledge.

Kelly, P. (2001). Youth at risk: Process of individualization and responsibilisation in the risk society. *Discourse: Studies in the cultural politics of education 22,* 23–33.

King, B., and J. Meyers. (1996). The Annie E. Casey Foundation's mental health initiative for urban children. In B. A. Stroul, ed., *Children's mental health: Creating systems of care in a changing society,* 249–64. Baltimore: Paul H. Brookes.

Knitzer, J. (1996). Children's mental health: Changing paradigms and policies. In E. Zigler, S. Kagan, and N. Hall, eds., *Children, families and government: Preparing for the twenty-first century,* 207–32. New York: Cambridge University Press.

McKnight, J. (1995). *The careless society: Community and its counterfeits.* New York: Basic Books.

Michigan League for of Human Services. (2004). *Working hard but still poor: An agenda for meeting the needs of Michigan's low-income working families* (August). Accessed April 2, 2006, at http://www.milhs.org/Media/Edocs/MLHS101booklet.pdf.

———. (2005). *Michigan's growing low-wage labor force* (June). Accessed April 2, 2006, at http://www.milhs.org/Media/EDocs/HardWorkNotEnough.pdf.

Nybell, L. M. (2002). Remaking children's mental health: On children, community and care in reform. Ph.D. dissertation, University of Michigan.

Parton, N. (1999). Reconfiguring child welfare practices: Risk, advanced liberalism and the government of freedom. In A. Chambon, A. Irving, and L. Epstein, eds., *Reading Foucault for social work*, 101–30. New York: Columbia University Press.

Polakow, V. (1993). *Lives on the edge: Single mothers and their children in the other America.* Chicago: University of Chicago Press.

Rose, N. (1996). Governing 'advanced' liberal democracies. In A. Barry, T. Osborne, and N. Rose, eds., *Foucault and political reason: Liberalism, neo-liberalism and rationalities of government.* Chicago: University of Chicago Press.

Schorr, L. B. (1993). What works? Applying what we already know about successful social policy. *American Prospect 13:* 93–104.

———. (1997). *Common purpose: Strengthening families and neighborhoods to rebuild America.* New York: Doubleday.

Sharland, E. (2006). Young people, risk taking and risk making: Some thoughts for social work. *British Journal of Social Work 36* (2): 247–63.

State of Michigan (1995). *Systems reform for children and their families.* Lansing: Office of the Governor.

Stroul, B. A. (Ed.) (1996). *Children's mental health: Creating systems of care in a changing society.* Baltimore: Paul H. Brookes.

Swadener, B. B., and S. Lubeck, S. (1995). *Children at promise: Deconstructing the discourse of risk.* Albany: State University of New York Press.

Toumbourou, J. W. (1999). Implementing Communities that Care in Australia: A community mobilisation approach to crime prevention. *Australian Institute of Criminology Trends and Issues in Crime and Criminal Justice 122.* Accessed November 19, 2001, at http://www.aic.gov.au.

U.S. Substance Abuse and Mental Health Administration (n.d.). Communities that Care youth survey. Accessed August 21, 2007, at http://www.preventionplatform.samhsa.gov.

Wilcox, A. (2003). Evidence-based youth justice? Some valuable lessons from the Youth Justice Board, *Youth Justice 3* (1): 19–33.

"At Risk" for Becoming Neoliberal Subjects |

THIRTEEN

Rethinking the "Normal"
Middle-Class Family

Rachel Heiman

During the late 1990s I conducted ethnographic fieldwork on class anxieties and suburban life in Marlboro, New Jersey, a town on the fault line of the economic chasm growing within the middle class. This case study draws on a portion of my research carried out while I was working as an "ethnographic babysitter" for a family. The Sillens, as I call them for anonymity, lived in a subdivision of moderate-sized, colonial-style homes, the type of houses that used to be the norm in the town. But starting in the 1980s, and more so during the economic boom of the late 1990s, huge homes—which some disdainfully refer to as "Mc-Mansions"—were being built adjacent to older subdivisions like the one where the Sillens lived. These huge houses dwarfed their neighbors and produced jarring juxtapositions, providing a visual reminder of the split in the middle class. Like gentrification in urban areas, changes in the grandeur of suburban housing reflect a transformation of the class makeup of a town and reveal shifts in the larger class structure and the structuring of people's social locations. For many people in the town, this changing landscape—occurring in many suburban communities across the United States—provoked class anxieties and roused uncertainties about the fiscal boundaries of inclusion and exclusion in the imagined future of the town and of the middle class itself.

Equally distressing during those years was the volatility of professional-managerial work. When I was being hired for the job, Bonnie, the mother of the family, explained to me that they needed someone to help out because she was going back to work. She had been laid off from her job as a researcher at a university medical center when the grant that she was working under was not renewed. She spent time doing other kinds of work, like residential real estate and part-time tutoring. But now, she was going back to work as a "professional"—as she defined her job status—at a pharmaceutical company. When explaining to me what kind of help she was looking for, she said that she "hated having those depressed women who would go onto the porch and cry that they missed their family in Ghana." So, she wanted to do things a bit differently this time. She was looking for someone who was an "all-around responsible person," who also could help the children with their homework. She assured me that she had "great kids," that she and her husband were "very educated" (he had a Ph.D. degree and she had a Master's degree), and that this would be a good job, "not like working for a blue-collar family."

Bonnie's disparaging, racialized remarks about previous babysitters did not surprise me. Marlboro is a town in which many white adults freely shared this type of racial commentary. Her desire, as well, to hire someone white, educated, and from a middle-class background corresponded with discussions at that time about families who were "choosing similarity" (Wrigley 1995) to shore up their children's surroundings in a time of increased competition. What did feel out of the blue was her comment about not being a blue-collar family. The more that I thought about it, however, her need to assert their class positioning (and their educational credentials) made complete sense when juxtaposed with her narrative about moving in and out of "professional" jobs. In a volatile economy with a neoliberal state offering minimal support for middle-class families, and in a town with architectural reminders that they were teetering on the edge of the middle-class chasm, there was a lot at stake in appearing "as if."

My discussion here draws on what I witnessed and participated in during my time with the Sillens, particularly with Bonnie and her three children. The ethnographic moments brought to life took place in their home, at the mall, and during car rides to and from after school activities. Yet the desires, sentiments, and practices explored here are understood as being inextricable from enduring anxieties about the ability to attain and maintain a piece of the shrinking middle-class pie. Whether these everyday experiences involve yearnings for particular consumer products, efforts to keep the new carpet clean, frustrations about being too busy, excitement about learning the stock market, or racialized reactions to babysitters and school spaces, they are analyzed for how they are both reflections of the political economic moment and conditions for producing neoliberal subjects. It may be surprising to some readers to see an essay in a social work text about a family that is not involved in any way with social workers or social work institutions and that would not—in our current state of thinking—necessitate social work intervention. They are a middle-class family that is "normal" in the clinical sense of the term, and they are relatively privileged in their class and race positioning. At the same time, however, they are struggling to reorient themselves to the changing material conditions undergirding middle-class life, and the ways that they are doing so are producing habits that entrench neoliberal logics: through hyper-consumption and overspending that benefits corporate capital; spatial strategies that further segregation along race, class, and age lines; and acts of self-sufficiency that replace a politics of demand on the state. Rather than challenging the structural conditions that create financial pressure and related stressors in their lives, they are digging themselves in deeper and limiting the possibility that a comprehensive social welfare state—which would benefit all classes, races, and ages—could be imagined.

Social work practice is meant to help people whose lives are limited by structural conditions. It is, at the same time, an effort to change those conditions through policy work. If the ultimate goal of social work is to no longer need social work, then perhaps we need to also focus our attention on families like the Sillens. While they do not behave in ways that resonate with traditional "at risk" categories, which typically refer to children, youth, and families deemed a "threat" to the normative social order (Stephens 1995; Finn and Nybell 2001), their habits are placing "at risk" the possibility that new structural conditions can emerge. In a time when middle-class positionings are increasingly "at risk" and means of appeasing class insecurities are regulating the political economy in favor of neoliberal strategies, perhaps it is time to invert our "at risk" categories and view members of "normal" middle-class families as a "threat" to a healthy social order.

"STUPID THINGS"

One afternoon when I arrived at the Sillens's home, these issues were squarely on my mind. I had parked on the street in front of their house and was walking up their driveway, on which there was a regulation-sized basketball hoop for 15-year-old Julia and 11-year-old Doug, and a plastic, miniature version for 5-year-old Sam. Sam's little hoop was lying toppled over on the grass, as it always was. All it took was a little gust of wind to knock it on its side. It always struck me as a metaphor for the instability of their class positioning. As I walked past, I lifted up Sam's pint-sized hoop and let myself into the house by plugging in the code on the security pad that opened one of their garage doors. I walked through the garage and entered the laundry room, where I took my shoes off. The Sillens had just laid down new bone-colored wall-to-wall carpeting in their den, and no one was allowed to wear shoes while walking on it. In my socks, I walked over the new carpeting and made my way to the tiled kitchen. My first task was to prepare lunches for the next school day.

While making Sam's favorite sandwich—cheese, butter, and peanut butter on potato bread—I was thinking about a conversation that I had had a couple of months previously with Bonnie, before the new carpet had been laid down. She was talking about how financially strapped they felt. Even though she and her husband, Kevin, were earning over $150,000 per year (in addition to stock options that Kevin received through his job at a large communications technology company), she said that it never felt like they had enough. With the kids getting older, the things that they need and want—clothes, video games, soccer cleats, karate lessons, SAT tutors, CDs—took up so much of their money. Plus, she added, they also end up buying what she referred to as "stupid things."

As "stupid" came out of her mouth, Bonnie pointed to carpet samples lying on the couch as an example. Bonnie was in the process of looking at samples because she had noticed that the old carpet was looking a little raggedy. I glanced at the carpet to see if it looked as rundown as she thought. It did not strike me as that bad, so I told her that I thought the carpet looked just fine. As I spoke, Bonnie closed her eyes, turned her face away, and shook her head from side-to-side, indicating that what I was saying was something she did not want to hear. She was already set on laying down new carpet, she explained, despite knowing that it was "stupid." When the new rug came in, she stressed, no one would be able to wear shoes on it or eat snacks in the den.

We can view Bonnie's aesthetics of interior design as a means of consuming class security, that is, providing a temporary appeasement of class anxieties through acquiring a consumer item that is common in one's milieu and mirrors back a feeling of equivalence. It is also an instance of the type of nagging longing for consumer items that is indicative of the contemporary culture of hyper consumption, which puts increasing strain on families' purse strings, and into which children are being habituated in increasingly cunning and often aggressive ways. Take, for example, one afternoon I spent walking around the mall with Sam after I picked him up from preschool. Bonnie had bought some clothing that did not fit her correctly, and she needed me to return it. Since I was going to have Sam with me, she gave me a few dollars so that he could pick out something for himself. As she handed me the money, she told me that she always felt like she "*had to* buy something for Sam" when she was at the mall with him. She wasn't sure why; she just felt like she did.

When we got to the mall, Sam led the way as he told me about all of the stores that he likes: Kay Bee Toys, Noodle Kadoodle, the Warner Brothers Store, and the Disney Store. He knew exactly where each of those stores was located. In fact, he made it a point to note that there are *two* Kay Bee Toys stores, one on each level of the mall. Very handy, I thought. No matter on which level of the mall you're walking, your child can drag you into a toy store to beg you to buy something. Our first stop, though, was at a video game store. Sam's birthday was still a month away, but he already knew what he was getting: Yoshi Story, a Nintendo 64 game. As we walked through the front doors of the store and entered the pop-music-filled space, Sam's eyes grew wide with excitement. He glanced around the room at the rows and rows of video games, dragging me toward the Nintendo area. As we walked past the other brands of games, I asked Sam about the differences between them. He rattled off an explanation of the distinctions, during which I made sure to listen very attentively. His comportment suggested that he was a bit put out by having to explain something that was so obvious. While Sam was sharing all of this information with me, I found myself struck by how incredibly adept he was not only at recognizing a good portion of the video game collection in the store, but also at articulating a broad taxonomic knowledge of their relationship to one another. It is, of course, quite common for kids his age to become enthralled with the order of things in their midst, so it is easy for us to dismiss these kinds of obsessions as being part and parcel of a developmental stage. But as the next couple of stops on our stroll reveal, Sam also was learning particular habits of consumption and expectation.

After we left the video game store, Sam tugged my hand and dragged me into the Warner Brothers Store. We were immediately surrounded by the sights and sounds of Bugs Bunny and friends. I followed Sam as he browsed the vast array of offerings in the store's sections, each of which contained items from the most popular Warner Brothers shows and films. When we got to "The Flintstones" section, Sam got very animated. He loves watching "The Flintstones," and since he knew that he was allowed to get something for himself, he picked out a little stuffed Dino. Together we walked over to the register, where I paid for Dino with the money that Bonnie had given me just for this purpose.

With his new purchase in hand, Sam knew exactly where he wanted to go next: the Disney Store. It, too, was arranged in sections according to the most famous and most recent Disney movies and characters. When we got there, we wandered from section to section, spending most of the time in the *Toy Story* section. Sam was enthralled with a Buzz Lightyear toy that flashed bright lights when different buttons were pushed. After we played with it for a while, I noticed that it was time for us to head home. While making our way out of the store, Sam and I spotted a section of toys that neither of us recognized. We stopped and stood there for a moment, pondering who and what these characters might be. Soon into our conversation, one of the salespeople walked over to us. She looked directly down at Sam, smiling as she explained to him that these were characters from *Mulan*, the Disney film coming out that summer.

On our way to the car, Sam talked incessantly about how excited he was to see *Mulan*. He skipped as he talked, his words blending together in excited anticipation. I often saw this same embodiment of enthusiasm when he spoke about the fact that he was getting Yoshi Story for his birthday. Bonnie and Kevin bought the children games only for special events. In order to play the games that they did not have, they would rent games from a local game store. Video game rentals, like film rentals that include promotional trailers before the start of the film, show scenes from other games. Since Yoshi Story was the hottest new game at the time, the Yoshi Story trailer came on almost every time a game was rented. When it popped up on the TV, Sam would jump in exhilaration, reminding me that he was getting Yoshi Story for his birthday.

On our drive home from the mall that afternoon, Sam continued to talk about all the things that he was excited to get and to play with. As historian Lisa Jacobson (2004) explains, it was during the early part of the twentieth century when children like Sam were first "enlisted" and "cultivated" as consumers. Children learned—for the first time—that they could "cross the boundaries of dependency" and make up for what they lacked in the "power of the purse" through their "power to nag and persuade." Companies charting this new terrain did so with great reservation and hesitation; they feared upsetting parents, particularly mothers, by overstepping their authority to make consumer decisions in the home. Now, as Jacobson discusses, the power dynamic has moved so far in the other direction that parents often feel impotent in the face of excessive marketing and advertising directed at their children. Bonnie was not sure why she felt like she "*had to*" buy something for Sam every time they were at the mall. As Jacobson's work reveals, there has long been a concerted effort to cultivate just this sentiment, a dynamic made more extreme in the late 1990s with the magnification of advertising towards children, the intensification of hyper-consumption, and the expansion of consumer credit. When the costs of things that children want are added to the expenses for the "stupid things" that parents crave, the financial stress is compounded, as corporate capital's earnings swell. Children not only become habituated to this type of consumer expectation, but, as the next set of ethnographic moments reveals, they also learn subtle forms of sacrifice for consumer items, with implications beyond the fiscal.

"I JUST HAVE TO GET USED TO IT"

I was supposed to make sure that the children didn't dirty the rug. Sometimes, they ignored the rules. Every once in a while I'd spot an empty plate with crumbs on it, resting rebelliously on the fireplace ledge next to the television in the den. Other times, I'd catch the children making a quick dash over the rug with their shoes on, following a failed attempt to leap all the way over it. More often than not, however, they actually policed themselves and those around them. I always watched in amazement when Sam would hold up his little hand, all five fingers firmly poised in the "stop" sign, which he would then place in the face of one of his friends who was about to walk onto the rug. He always reminded them to take their shoes off, pointing to a good spot in the laundry room to leave them.

When the new rug was first installed, Sam told his friends about the new rule all by himself. He demonstrated for me during an interview exactly how he told them. His body went rigid and his tone mimicked that of parental author-ity as he declared, "Don't step with your shoes on the carpet!" Sam explained to me that most of his friends have been good about remembering on their own, except for his friend Joey. One time, Sam explained, "[Joey] came. He had his shoes on. He went halfway to the first square. *Then* he went down and took his shoes off." One afternoon, when Sam did not feel like taking his shoes off, I watched in amusement as he crawled on his knees all the way across the rug, carefully making sure that the tips of his shoes stayed well above the carpet the entire time. Similarly, when Doug and Julia were in the garage getting into the car and realized that they had forgotten something in the house, they would often go to another door instead of using the nearby back door, to avoid the rug altogether. They would run around the house and enter through the front door, which opens onto a tiled foyer. This maneuvering to avoid the rug would get particularly tricky if they had left something upstairs. The new carpet also cov-ered the stairs and the platform leading to the bedrooms on the second floor. There was no way to leap over a two-story obstacle.

On separate occasions, I asked each of the kids if they were bothered by the fact that they could not wear shoes on the new rug. When I posed the ques-tion to Sam, at first he uttered, "I mind." But then he immediately switched his answer to "I don't mind," adding, "It doesn't bother me. I just have to get used to it. Now I just don't care." Sam may have been worried about saying the right thing, unlike Doug, who instantly declared the whole thing "a pain." But, he added with a boastful swagger, "I never took my shoes off." Julia, on the other hand, was comfortable admitting that she did *try* to follow the rules, despite the fact that "it's annoying." As she pointed out, "Let's say I'm down here with my shoes on already to be picked up, and then I realize that I forgot something like in my room. . . . That's annoying like when you're already dressed and ready to go, and then you realize you have to . . . just to go upstairs you have to take all your shoes off and everything. Sometimes I don't even care, I just like run upstairs." This was particularly tough for Julia when she had friends over. One time when her parents were away, a few of her friends came by, and each of them ended up bringing other friends. Julia did not want to ask them all to take their shoes off. "I felt bad saying, 'Take your shoes off,'" she explained. So most of the night she kept thinking to herself, "Oh shit, the carpet."

Julia and Doug both told me that a lot of their friends' houses are "no shoe zones," and as Doug explained, "Some kids I know, I can't even go into their [bed]room." When I asked him why, he bellowed as if he was one of his friends' moms: "Because I'll mess it up! It's too dirty! You're gonna make it too dirty!" When I asked him where he and his friends hang out, he matter-of-factly stated, "Basement. Go outside. Living room." When I asked Doug what he thought about this way of living, he said that it doesn't bother him that much. Plus, he added, "It's cool to have a nice house, especially for when people come over." Julia, too, admitted that despite all that is annoying about their new rug, she likes living in a "neat house."

When I was visiting the Sillens a year after I had completed my field-work, the Nintendo—which the boys played in the den on the new rug every afternoon—had been moved down to the basement, taking them down with it. Their time on the rug (and thus the literal and symbolic "dirt" that they brought with them) was reduced. They were supposed to "get used to" keeping the car-pet clean, but in light of their irreverence—of which their parents were well aware—it clearly was not working so well. The cleanliness of the rug and all that it reflected back was important enough to have their presence removed. The children were participating in and sacrificing for the display of anxious class yearnings and tenuous class attainments, often at the expense of feeling wel-come on, in, and near spaces in their own home. Despite their ambivalence, there was at the same time hesitant resolve. They were learning that a part of being able to have and maintain particular consumer objects (and presumably their privilege as a whole) is accepting and becoming habituated to their own marginalized space and place. They "just [had] to get used to it."

"IT SUCKS BEING SO BUSY"

Keeping the rug clean surely did require a lot of effort on the kids' parts. But so, too, did all of the other activities in which they were involved, leading them to seem somewhat exhausted by their busy schedules. One day, I asked Sam if he was excited about turning 6. His birthday was a month away, in July. I expected him to enthusiastically talk about getting Yoshi Story. Instead, with a powerful sense of anticipated relief in his voice, he explained to me what he was really excited for: "That I won't have any school. I can rest sometimes." Julia, too, envisioned their daily life as jam-packed, with weekends as no exception. I once asked her what it was like on a "normal" weekend since I was only with them during the week. She complained to me, "Uch, it's chaos. There's just like so much to do. . . . Everybody's running." This type of scheduling pressure began to receive public attention during the late 1990s, raising questions about the effects on kids of this approach to providing them with a competitive edge.

Doug definitely had the busiest schedule of the three children. One afternoon, he was scrambling to finish up his homework while eating dinner. With a few bites still in his mouth, he raced around the house putting together everything he needed for his soccer practice. We had to get him to practice on time or else his coach would make him run extra laps. Mind you, his grueling soccer practice was just the beginning of his evening. When it was over, I was to pick him up and take him directly to guitar lessons. Just before we ran out the door, Doug complained to me about his schedule. He kept going on and on about how he had no time; how he never had any time; how "it sucks being so busy." Doug's situation was somewhat extreme because of his traveling soccer team. But many children and youth in town faced similar pressures, prompting parents to wonder, "When do they get to be kids?"

The predicament of the busyness in Doug's life took on a whole new perspective in a conversation I had with him a couple of months later. On our way to the track where his soccer team was doing stamina training, I asked him the usual "How was school today?" question. In an overwhelmed and frustrated voice, he told me that he didn't understand why we have elementary schools. He explained to me that he gets that everyone has to learn to read and write, but he still didn't see the point of it all. I threw out a reminder of all the important things that are learned, during which he blurted out, "It's so annoying that we have to go to school and be so busy when we're young. Then, we have to spend the rest of our life working all the time." This sentiment was echoed several months later when I asked him what he thought it meant to become a "teenager" or an "adolescent." I asked him if he felt that he was entering a different "stage" of life. He responded, "I think I'm just entering more and more work. . . . I have to do the stupid exercises my coach gave me. Now I'm going to go to middle school. It's twice the work. . . . More and more work as you get older."

I wasn't surprised to hear these words come out of Doug's mouth. He had a pretty frantic schedule, as did many of the parents in his midst. What did amaze me was what came out of his mouth next that day in the car. He informed me that he wished we had "a society like communism because they don't have to work so much." He then hesitantly added, "They do have to wait in long lines like in Russia, but it seems so much better there." I was struck by this potential seed of radicalism until a few months later, when Doug walked in from school, dropped his backpack, and asked me if I had any stock tips for him. Somewhat bewildered hearing this question come out of his mouth, I said that I didn't know that much about the stock market, but why was he asking? He said that his dad had opened an e*trade account for him with some money so that he could start learning how to invest. Seeing this as a moment for a subtle intervention, I told him about socially responsible funds. He said that he hadn't realized that you could choose stocks that way, but his main goal, he explained, was to make enough money to buy a car for himself when he turned 17.

Doug's critique of his frenzied life and initial desire for a supportive state, combined with his embrace of the stock market's ability to generate capital and enable self-sufficiency, expose contradictions inherent in current neoliberal shifts. We cannot yet know how Doug will end up living his life, but the odds seem to be working against the possibility that the buds of his critical gaze will bloom. When I asked him 9 months later about his Russia comment, he did not remember saying it. In fact, he seemed shocked that he would have said anything like that, remarking, "I would never say that." He then added, "I would rather be busy than always be at home all [afternoon]. . . . It's boring. In a sense, I do like to be busy sometimes. . . . At least I have something to motivate me."

"IT JUST SEEMED SO, LIKE, DIRTY"

Julia was motivated by her desire to become a doctor, and her schedule was made a bit busier because of a volunteer job at the local hospital. She was trying to put in enough hours to qualify for a college recommendation from the supervisor of the program. Julia and I spent most of our time together while sitting in traffic on our way to the hospital each week, during which she often complained to me that her mom was too invested in what she was doing. "I honestly do want to become a doctor," she told me one afternoon, "but I . . . don't want it to come from her. I think it should come from me. . . . Even if she didn't pressure me, I still think I would have wanted to become a doctor. But like, I don't know."

In light of the palpable pressure on Julia fueled by personal ambition and parental desires, I was surprised to learn that Julia was not attending the Medical Sciences Learning Center at one of the local high schools. Marlboro is one of eight towns that are a part of a regional high school district. All students have the option to apply to prestigious Learning Centers located in the different high schools. Julia was instead attending an International Studies Learning Center. I was curious if it had something to do with the fact that the Medical Sciences program is housed in the school with the highest percentage of students of color and students whose parents hold working-class jobs.

During one of our car rides, I asked Julia why she was not enrolled in the Medical Sciences program. She said that she didn't want to go to the school in which it was located. She had gone to visit when she was in the eighth grade and was "turned off," she explained, because it was such a small, old, and rundown school. Plus, she added, the kids there didn't seem "nice," and there were a lot of kids who were from a "bad crowd." When I asked her more about this during a formal interview, her answer was similarly elusive:

> I don't know, like, it's a smaller school. And like I didn't feel like there people that I could relate to, like, I don't know. . . . I guess like I wanted to be around a few people that like, I don't know. . . . Just . . . I didn't want to go there. It didn't seem like a good school, like . . . I went there for a day to see it. . . . I mean I heard that it wasn't in a good area, but I saw it. I don't know. It wasn't that people were mean, but it just seemed so, like, dirty and like. I don't know.

Julia's hesitant pauses and excessive use of "like" and "I don't know" suggested that she was uncomfortable being explicit about her reasons for not wanting to go to that school. Her use of "dirty" and claims about not seeing people that she "could relate to" implied racialized anxieties in regard to the school space.

Also thrown into relief during this conversation with Julia were the further racial implications of my positioning in the domestic service sector. Not only was I hired because I wasn't one of those "depressed women who would go onto the porch and cry that they missed their family in Ghana"; my services were needed, in part, because Julia was going to a school much farther from her house to avoid being among kids from a "bad crowd." I was driving her to volunteer work each week, presumably because she and / or her mother figured that it would help compensate for the fact that she was not in the Medical Sciences program. Julia was made busier because of this added extracurricular activity that, incidentally, was a sacrifice in other ways: she hated every minute that she worked at the hospital. According to Julia, her supervisor was "a real bitch." When racial fears intersect with class aspirations and efforts to shore up educational credentials, busyness and sacrifice take on a whole new appearance, and a key effect of neoliberalization on space—increased segregation of youth and adults along race and class lines—gets exacerbated.

CONCLUDING REMARKS

Like Ben's pint-sized basketball hoop that I picked up every afternoon when I arrived at the Sillens's house, their class security was equally susceptible to unpredictable gusts of wind. With such extreme attention paid to "local" ways of appeasing class anxieties, discussions rarely took place about the structural realities that have placed the financial burden of middle-class life largely on the backs of individual families. As these ethnographic moments have revealed, neoliberal subjectivities are being developed among the middle class through everyday practices and intimates experiences, which get naturalized, regulated, and taken for granted, despite moments of ambivalence, questioning, and doubt. If we continue down this road, we are further entrenching our society in a dialectic that seeks to appease class insecurities in ways that actually make people more insecure and that exacerbate class, race, and age inequalities. We cannot yet know how the members of this family will seek out a sense of class security in the years to come, but as conditions for the middle classes continue to worsen, is it possible to imagine a day when families like the Sillens will enter into cross-class coalitions that call for a committed social welfare state, like in the years leading up to the New Deal? Could we be on the brink of collective efforts to rethink neoliberalism, as is the case in Latin America? Perhaps if we rethink our "at-risk" categories, we can develop social work interventions with families like the Sillens in order to speed up the process of demanding a healthy social order for all.

QUESTIONS FOR DISCUSSION

1. How do changing political, economic, and social conditions alter middle-class family life? What anxieties are shaping the experiences of childhood in this family? Are these anxieties apparent in your own life and work?

2. One of the often unexamined "certainties" of social work is that middle-class life in the United States is "normal" for children and their parents. In what ways does the author challenge this assumption?

3. Another "certainty" that social workers sometimes encounter is that the politics of race are absent in largely homogeneous white communities. In what ways does Heiman introduce notions of race into this account of white, middle-class family life? In what ways does her discussion of race speak to how racial inequalities are reified in everyday life?

4. What does it mean to become a "neoliberal subject?" What sorts of "disciplinary practices" shape the everyday lives and class positioning of middle-class children in the United States? Of working-class and poor children? What are ways in which children and youth resist these practices?

5. Some scholars are calling for social work practice that resists neoliberalism (Ferguson and Lavalette 2006). What does this mean to you? What might be some of the possibilities and consequences of a social work of resistance?

REFERENCES

Ferguson, I., and M. Lavalette. (2006). Globalization and global justice: Toward a social work of resistance. *International Social Work 49* (3): 309–18.

Finn, J., and L. Nybell. (2001). Introduction: Capitalizing on concern: The making of troubled children and troubling youth in late capitalism. *Childhood 8:* 139–45.

Jacobson, L. (2004). *Raising consumers: Children and the American mass market in the early twentieth century.* New York: Columbia University Press.

Stephens, S. (1995) Introduction: Children and the politics of culture in "late capitalism." In S. Stephens, ed., *Children and the politics of culture,* 3–48. Princeton: Princeton University Press.

Wrigley, J. (1995) *Other people's children.* New York: Basic Books.

Reinventing Social Work with
Children and Youth

PART III

FOURTEEN

Child's-Eye View

Janet L. Finn

No one teaches children sociology or psychology;

yet, children are constantly noticing who

gets along with whom, and why. . . .

A nation's politics becomes a child's everyday psychology.

—Robert Coles, *The Political Life of Children*

In this chapter I bring the Just Practice perspective—a critical approach to social justice–oriented social work that my colleague Maxine Jacobson and I have
been developing over the past several years—to bear on thinking about practice
with children and youth (Finn and Jacobson 2003, 2008). Throughout this text,
contributors have argued that contemporary social work suffers from a serious
lack of attention to meanings of childhood and worldviews of children. Further, we have argued that dominant conceptions of childhood, youth, and social
work are inadequate for meeting the profound demands of contemporary practice. Every day social workers confront complex challenges regarding children
and youth. They face the erosion of state-based resources; increased strains on
education, child welfare, mental health, and juvenile justice systems; and competing claims regarding young people's needs and rights. These everyday pressures leave little time for critical reflection on fundamental questions regarding
notions of childhood, the social work policies and practices that affect children's
lives, or the ethical and political obligations social workers have to the self-
determination as well as the safety of children and youth. We seldom have time
to ponder such critical issues as how these constructions variably shape and
constrain the status of children as people; how and where children's worldviews,

the meanings they give to their experiences, and their possibilities for human agency are seen and heard; and how we can become more aware of children as social actors and bearers of rights.

I present the Just Practice perspective as a theoretical, moral, and practical guide to enhance "complexity thinking" and social justice action for and with children (Finn and Jacobson 2008). According to Adams, Dominelli, and Payne (2005:11) "complexity thinking," is the practice of critical thinking that involves the following processes: (1) *being reflexive:* stepping back to observe the situation and reflect on taken-for-granted assumptions; (2) *contextualizing:* giving thought to the wider context of social relations and policy in which practice takes place; (3) *problematizing:* debating, discussing, and deliberating policy and practice; (4) *being self-critical:* recognizing that our actions are never entirely separate from the problems we identify; and (5) *engaging with transformation:* identifying barriers and divisions in social relations that lead to oppression, and helping people move beyond self-blame and consider possibilities for change. The Just Practice perspective offers a way to reframe our thinking and action so that we can better grasp the social construction of childhood and its implications and better learn from the voices, views, and wisdom of children themselves. Using the key themes of Just Practice—meaning, power, history, context, and possibility—I outline an approach that enables social workers to better appreciate a child's-eye view, support children's voices, and craft spaces for their participation in the issues that affect their lives. Drawing from a growing body of literature on children's participation and rights in the United States and internationally, I illustrate possibilities for social justice–oriented practice informed by a child's-eye view.

JUST PRACTICE: A RATIONALE AND OVERVIEW

In recent years, historians, sociologists, anthropologists, legal scholars, and social workers have been critically examining the ways in which we think about children and youth and the implications for policy and practice (Fass and Mason 2000; Hutchison and Charlesworth 2000; James and James 2004; Lansdown 2000; Morss 2003; Sealander 2004). As addressed in detail in the introduction to this volume, they have explored childhood as a social construction, questioned universalist views of childhood; and probed the ways in which popular and professional images of childhood and the problems of children encode and reflect adultist assumptions and concerns. For example, Thorne (1987) has argued that children become viewed as "other" in adult-centered constructions of childhood where children are measured, judged, and classified by adults. Hutchison and Charlesworth (2000) have raised fundamental questions regarding childhood as a social construction and the implications for child welfare policy and practice. They ask why it is that children are seen as a class of people in need of special protection, and they probe assumptions about the distinction between adults and children that underlies our beliefs about protective policies. They ask: How do notions of children as human "becomings" rather than human beings affect policies and practices? How do beliefs about competence, vulnerability, dependency, and rights play into constructions of childhood? They call on social workers to consider childhood in historical, cultural, and political contexts; to examine the interplay of social policies and constructions of childhood; to critically address the impact of social and economic shifts on the meaning and experience of childhood; and to explore the tensions, ambiguities, and contradictions in meanings of childhood. Theis (2001) contends that "We are in the middle of an ongoing paradigm shift in relation to children and childhood. Such a fundamental transformation requires changes at many levels (theory, practice, language, attitudes, laws) and the transition period from one paradigm to the next is likely to take at least one generation" (90).

These inquiries into the meaning of childhood, social experiences of children, and implications for practice resonate with a broader debate about the nature and future of social work in the twenty-first century. Critical social work theorists point to the impact of market forces, neoliberal ideologies, and economic globalization on the profession and call for a transformative approach to practice in which both social conditions and participants, including the social worker, are changed in the pursuit of a just world. Those arguing for a critical, political, transformative practice of social work place social justice and human rights center stage. They call attention to questions of difference, power, and oppression and envision social work as a liberatory practice that promotes the dignity, rights, and participation of all, especially those groups who have experienced greater vulnerability as a result of unjust social conditions (see for example, Adams, Dominelli, and Payne 2005; Allan 2003; Ferguson, Lavalette, and Whitmore 2005; Fook 2000; Ife 2000).

My colleague and I developed the Just Practice perspective as a response to these political, theoretical, practical, and moral concerns regarding the future of social work (Finn and Jacobson 2003). The framework emerged from our own practice, reflection, and long-term dialogue regarding the meaning of social justice work and the challenges of linking thought and action. We sought to bring together a set of interrelated themes and questions that would challenge social workers to examine the forces that shape and constrain human experience, attend to the immediate conditions of people's lives, recognize the partiality of their knowledge and worldview, and, in spite of it all, spark a sense of hope in the possibility of change. The Just Practice perspective revolves around five key concepts and their interconnections: *meaning, context, power, history,* and *possibility*. It brings together these interrelated concepts as a guide to the development and implementation of social justice–oriented practice. A social justice approach to social work with children is especially fitting, given children's own "acute sense of justice" (O'Kane 2004:698). As Claire O'Kane (2004) states, children from diverse national and cultural backgrounds share a sense of justice and fairness when faced with inequalities great or small.

The Just Practice perspective asks us to consider the following questions: How do people give *meaning* to the experiences and conditions that shape their lives? How do we understand and appreciate the *contextual* nature of human experience and interaction? What forms and relations of *power* shape and constrain social relations and experience? Who has the power to have their interpretations of reality valued as "true"? How might *history* and a historical perspective provide us with a deeper understanding of context, help us grasp the ways in which struggles over meaning and power play out, and enable us to appreciate the human consequences of those struggles? How do we claim a sense of the *possible* as an impetus for justice-oriented action? By holding these key themes in relationship to one another, how might we be better prepared to explore and grasp the complexities of the situations we face and our at best partial understandings? How might this framework guide inquiry and action regarding the questions of children and childhood we raise here (Finn and Jacobson 2008:50, 199)? In the following section I address four of the key themes of Just Practice and show how they can be used to help social workers better see and appreciate a child's-eye view. This sets the stage for exploring the possibilities of practice with children.

MEANING, CONTEXT, POWER, HISTORY— THROUGH THE LENSES OF CHILDHOOD

Meaning speaks to how we make sense of the world and our experiences in it. All human beings are meaning makers. We interpret our experiences from our grounded positions in the world and through the personal lenses of culture, race, place, gender, class, citizenship, and age. The discussion of childhood as a social construction goes to the heart of this question of meaning. As addressed above, when we consider the concept of childhood as historically and culturally specific, we come to appreciate differing meanings at different times and places. We have seen children variably constructed by adults as divine gifts, chattel, sources of labor, and icons of innocence (Zelizer 1985). We have thick and contradictory descriptions of children and childhood from the points of view of adults. However, our understandings of children as meaning makers and the ways in which children interpret their worlds and experiences therein is much thinner. The theme of meaning calls on us to ask new questions, such as: How do we construct children and their problems? Who shapes knowledge of children and childhood? What meanings do children give to their experience, and how might those meanings differ from those of adults? How have lives of poor children and children of color diverged from idealized Western concepts of the child and childhood? Where have we failed to recognize children themselves as meaning makers, as fully cultural beings acting in the world as well as being acted upon?

Let's consider a few examples. In my earlier essay, "Making Trouble" (chapter 1), I show the intersectionality of class, race, gender, and citizenship with the meanings of childhood. I describe how children of the poor and working classes have been labeled dangerous and deviant, potential risks to middle-class society and their "innocent" children. From the children of nineteenth-century immigrants negotiating the precarious nature of tenement house life to the children of twenty-first century welfare recipients, children of the poor have faced judgment and scrutiny, the meaning of their existence somehow devalued by virtue of their class status. Both popular and professional discourse has tended to blame the children of the poor for their poverty. Much less is known about the ways in which children living the everyday realities of poverty interpret their own experiences. A few recent studies have sought to illuminate children's experiences of poverty, rather than rely on adult interpretations of children's experience.

In terms of poverty in the United States, statistics tell part of the story. Some 12–13 million children live in poverty in the United States; 5 million children live in households with incomes of less than half the federal poverty level. Poverty rates are highest for young children, with 20% of children under age 6 living in poverty (National Center for Children in Poverty 2005). If we look at a global picture, we see millions of children suffering daily from hunger and malnutrition, and millions working from tender ages to contribute to personal and family survival, at times coming together to make claims for their rights as children (Wordsworth, McPeak, and Feeny 2005). How do children give meaning to their experiences of poverty? Summarizing responses from a qualitative study of children and poverty in North America, one adult researcher reported: "Kids told us that being poor is pretending you forgot your lunch, not getting a pet because it costs too much, feeling ashamed when Dad can't get a job, hearing Mom and Dad fight over money, being afraid to tell Mom that you need gym shoes" (Wordsworth, McPeak, and Feeny, 2005).

Researchers engaged in a cross-national study of children's experiences of poverty found themes that resonated across borders. According to a teenage girl from Belarus, "Children want to be the same as all the others and they can't be because they don't have the same clothes. Some people think they are better than others because they are richer. They think things like, 'You look bad. Where did you find those clothes from? You look like a person from the street.' Just looking you up and down is enough to make you feel bad" (Wordsworth, McPeak, and Feeny 2005:15).

Her experiences resonated with those of a teen girl from Kenya: "I feel bad. I feel like the odd one out. You feel like you shouldn't talk wherever you are, like you shouldn't be expressing ideas. You feel lonely, you feel ashamed" (Wordsworth, McPeak, and Feeny 2005:16).

Their words echoed the sentiments of low-income children in the United Kingdom who shared their fears and struggles attached to the experience of stigma and difference associated with being poor. Some children found their poverty to be a barrier to making and sustaining friendships: "'If you don't have any friends you won't be able to go out and play without being bullied' (Jim, age 10)" (Ridge 2003:7). Children are, as Tess Ridge argues, "keenly aware of the impact of poverty on their lives and on the lives of their parents" (2003:9). Some worry about their parents; some seek work; others keep their worries to themselves and try to minimize the stress on the family. Some have come together to critically question the conditions of their lives and make collective rights claims, as illustrated in the words of Beeru, a 14-year-old rag picker and member of the child workers' union in Delhi: "There should be no poverty, but it has been created by the rich. Furthermore, the rich feel that they are superior to us just because they have money. As street children, they consider us to be even more inferior and downtrodden" (cited in O'Kane 2002:697). As Ridge describes, "Our understanding and perceptions of poor children are often ill informed and stereotyped. Whereas children's lives are very diverse and poor children are not a homogeneous group, their experiences of poverty are mediated by many other factors including gender, ethnicity and age. Children in different circumstances have their own experiences and concerns to relate and their own perceptions of how poverty affects their lives" (2003:8).

Ridge's conclusions coincide with Wordsworth, McPeak, and Feeny (2005), who summarize the results of listening to children in poverty as follows: (1) children understand poverty as a deep physical, emotional, and social experience; (2) children are far more sensitive to and affected by poverty that is generally appreciated by adults; (3) children experience poverty not as a static state but as continuously changing conditions; (4) children are not passive recipients of experience but active contributors to their own well-being.

Context can be thought of as the background and set of circumstances and conditions that surround and influence particular events and experiences. Social work's legacy, and what distinguishes it from other helping professions, is its fundamental assertion that people and their actions must be understood in context, both in terms of immediate circumstance and of the larger structural forces that impinge on and shape circumstances. Social workers' involvement in the lives of children is mediated by the organizational context in which we come to know the child, whether that be through a school, court, mental health center, neighborhood center, or child protective services referral. The organizational context shapes how we see the child, her presenting concern, and our professional role and purpose. Our own contextual lenses can limit our ability to see the situation from a child's-eye view. What are the economic, political, and cultural contexts of children's lives? How do these shape how children feel about themselves and their world? How do children see, experience, and interpret their immediate circumstances?

Let's consider two examples. In *There Are No Children Here*, Alex Kotlowitz's 1991 account of children coming of age amidst poverty, racism, and violence in a Chicago housing project, the author tells the story of LaFayette Rivers, age 10, and his 7-year-old brother Pharaoh as the boys take him into the context of their lives. At one point Lafayette tells Kotlowitz, "If I grow up, I want to be a bus driver." At age 10, Lafayette was acutely aware of the context of his life and his own uncertain future. Lafayette educates Kotlowitz both about the realities of his everyday life and about his determination to create a different future for himself despite the odds: "'You grow up 'round it. . . There are a lot of people in the projects who say they're not gonna do drugs, that they're not gonna drop out, that they won't be on the streets. But they're doing it now. Never say never.' He paused. 'But I say never. My brothers ain't set no good example for me, but I'll set a good example for them'" (29).

Zelizer (2005) offers examples of children's agency in the contemporary context of immigration. Drawing on recent research on the children of immigrant families (Orellana, Dorner, and Palido 2003; Valenzuela 1999) in the United States, Zelizer describes ways in which children serve as linguistic mediators, tutors, and advocates for their parents. Children serve as interpreters not only of language but also of the workings of U.S. institutions, such as schools, banks, courts, social service organizations, workplaces, churches, and hospitals. Children, especially daughters, are often counted on both to understand and to negotiate these complex social contexts on their parents' behalf. Children's practice as translators across these domains may be a source of both skill development and stress as they bear the responsibility for the well-being of their parents and siblings. Moreover, as children assume the responsibility for context interpretation, they also contribute to a shift in parent-child power relations.

Power can be conceptualized in many ways. Some have viewed power from a standpoint of exclusion, domination, and oppression. Others have pointed to the power of language, the power of emotion, and the power of collective memory as sources for resistance and motive forces for action on the part of people in less powerful positions (Freire 1990; Gramsci 1987, Kelly and Sewell 1988). Bourdieu (1977) describes symbolic power as the power to interpret another's reality. In both social work practice and broader social relations, adults wield enormous power over the lives of children. While the power over children is often exercised as a form of protectionism and believed by adults to have the safety and best interests of the child in mind, top-down power often renders children silenced and invisible. In myriad ways, every day adults assert symbolic power over children, interpreting their realities without asking them first.

Janet Townsend and her colleagues (1999) identified four forms of power: (1) power over, (2) power from within, (3) power with, and (4) power to do. Given children's relative powerlessness in society, it is critical that we ask who has the power to impose meanings of reality onto them. How do powerful disciplines such as social work create and reproduce notions of what it means to be a child? How has professional power vis-à-vis children been wielded? Where are the opportunities for power sharing with children? How willing are adults to give up power and entrust it to children?

Children moving through school, justice, and child welfare systems frequently confront people and relations that exercise power over their lives. Adult professionals have the power to name the problem, label the child, and document the "case." Children are expected to conform to institutional rules and practices created by adults for the children's own good. Decisions about out-of-home placement are made by interdisciplinary teams acting in the "best interests" of the child, but often in the absence of the child himself. Court-appointed child advocates are charged with representing the interests of children in contested legal matters, and yet that representation is often filtered through an adultist world view. As social workers we often fail to recognize the paternalism behind our protective stances and actions toward children. Bound to both explicit and implicit models of "power over," we miss opportunities to share power with children. Let us think for a moment about how power might be reconceptualized. How might we build relationships of colearning with children, help children tap into their own internal resources, and engage children actively as participants in the decisions that affect their lives? We start by taking young people's voices and views seriously. Consider, for example, the California Youth Connection (CYC) (see also chapter 20 in this volume). CYC promotes participation of foster youth in the decision making that affects their lives through grassroots organizing, policy development, and legislative advocacy. It is "guided, focused and driven by current and former foster youth with the assistance of other committed community members" (CYC website, 2007). CYC was launched in 1987 and now has chapters throughout the state. It is part of a growing cross-national network of youth activists claiming power and voice.

A recent article authored by six children and published in *Paediatric Nursing* provides another illustration of the power of children's voices, views, and actions (Moules 2004). The authors report on their participatory research study of children's experiences of quality of hospital care and on their recommendations to medical personnel. The authors interviewed 129 children between the ages of 9 and 14 who had been hospitalized. With regard to their expectations of quality of hospital care, the children identified the following factors as key to quality care: (1) good technical skills of care providers; (2) friendliness of staff; (3) being treated with respect; 4) having some degree of choice about care; and (5) being informed about what is happening to them. Fundamentally, they wanted to be asked about their experiences and included in these intimate decisions about their health and lives. We will look at further examples of empowering practice by and with children in the discussion of possibility.

History is much more than a chronological record of events. It is a human creation, shaped by the perspective and experiences of the historian. As Paulo Freire (1990) argues, ordinary people are continually making history and being shaped by history. A historical perspective is vital to our work as social workers. History serves as a warning device. It compels us to scrutinize the present. It helps us create linkages and connect themes across time. It helps us understand the workings of power. History can inspire us to act (Finn and Jacobson 2008). A historical perspective can help us see shifts in constructions of children and childhood, and the concomitant changes in practice and policies. Attention to history reminds us that children are makers and keepers of their own histories, as interpreters of experience, memory keepers, and story tellers. For example, as discussed in previous chapters, our history of child placement from orphanages to "orphan trains" and from the forced removal of American Indian children first to boarding schools and later to placement non-Native families speaks volumes about the ways in which "other people's children" were viewed and (de)valued. These histories should certainly serve as warning devices, challenging us to scrutinize practices of the present done in the "best interests of the child." Moreover, children came to these experiences with their own histories, and they variably acquiesced to and resisted the forces buffeting their lives. For instance, some who have documented the history of Indian boarding schools trace the beginnings of a pan-Indian identity and movement to the resistance of Native children who refused to have their histories erased and who invented ways to preserve language, memory, and cultural knowledge against the odds (McBeth 1983). As the orphan train history came to be known, so, too, did stories of children's resistance, of attempts to claim and tell their own stories, such as Elliot Bobo's: "A farmer came up to me and felt my muscles. And he says, 'Oh, you'd make a good hand on the farm.' And I say, 'You smell bad. You haven't had a bath, probably in a year.' And he took me by the arm and was gonna lead me off the stage and I bit him. And that didn't work so I kicked him. Everybody in the audience thought I was incorrigible. They didn't want me because I was out of control. I was crying in the chair by myself" (Graham and Gray 1997).

More recently young people who have lived the experience of transracial and transnational adoption have come together to tell their stories and to challenge the dominant discourse of adoption that is largely devoid of a larger history of colonialism, imperialism, militarism, and missionizing from which the post–World War II adoption enterprise emerged. *Outsiders Within* (Trenka, Oparah, and Shin 2006) is a compilation of powerful and at times painful accounts of those experiences. Jane Jeong Trenka, one of the editors of *Outsiders Within*, shares her own adoption story in her poignant memoir, *The Language of Blood*. Jane and her older sister Carol were born in Korea and adopted by a white rural midwestern Lutheran couple when Jane was 6 months old and Carol 4 years old. Despite their tender years, both girls carried histories and memories of their Korean life with them. Trenka writes:

> Because I was a baby, I was appropriately cuddly and showed affection to all the right people at all the right times. . . . Carol also assimilated well, just as Mom and Dad were promised she would. Her behavior was polite, clean, and not wasteful: she would dive beneath the table to retrieve a single grain of rice if one fell to the floor. . . . According to Mom, Carol spoke one Korean word repeatedly and for no visible reason. Mom matched it up on the vocabulary list provided by Lutheran Social Service: *apum*, pain. Other than that, Carol didn't even try to speak until the day complete English sentences came out of her just like anyone else. (27)

In sum, a Just Practice approach to working with children challenges us to examine the social construction of childhood and the ways we give *meaning* to the social experience of children. It guides us to look at the *context* of children's problems and question the relations of *power,* domination, and inequality that shape the way knowledge of children and their concerns is produced and whose view counts. It forces us to recognize the importance of *history* and a historical perspective in understanding particular and shifting constructions of childhood and their relationship to child-serving institutions and professionals. Finally, a Just Practice approach opens up the *possibility* for new ways of looking at and thinking about programs, policies, and practices, and for envisioning the children with whom we work and ourselves as active participants in social transformation toward a just world. Let's turn now to possibility.

POSSIBILITY

Possibility enables us to look at what has been done, what can be done, and what can exist. It engages us in reflection and helps us formulate a vision of something different. It is a way to get unstuck from fatalistic thinking where "that which has been will always be." Possibility challenges us to think differently about policies, practices, and children themselves. It draws attention to children's *agency,* or the capacity to act in the world as intentional, meaning-making beings, whose actions are shaped and constrained, but never fully determined by life circumstances. We open ourselves to exploring the possibilities of children as social actors when we refrain from exercising power over children and look to ways of promoting power with them. To do so requires us to follow in the words of Robert Coles and recognize the cultural, political, moral, and intellectual lives of children; to appreciate children as meaning makers; and to respect children as social actors always and everywhere involved in the constructions of their worlds. To shift the balance of power, we need to acknowledge children as bearers of rights and support their right to participation in the issues that affect their lives. We need to resist the pressure to patronize children and to push against the dominant grain wherein adults presumably "know what's best."

Child advocates throughout the world have turned to the United Nations Convention on the Rights of the Child as one resource for acknowledging and promoting children's rights claims. While not without its challenges, the Convention on the Rights of the Child recognizes the importance of children's right to participate in the decisions that affect their lives. It was adopted by the

UN General Assembly in 1989 and entered into force in 1990. This is an extensive document with 54 articles focused on recognizing children as persons with rights including: the right to name, family, and citizenship; the right to education, a safe environment, access to health care, and an adequate standard of living; and the right to be free of violence and exploitation (United Nations 1989). The document attempts to extend fundamental human rights to children while recognizing that childhood is entitled to special care and assistance. The United States is one of two countries, along with Somalia, that is still not a signatory to the convention. Nonetheless, it is emerging as a tool that gives children power, and as a movement it has been redefining childhood internationally. It has fueled the debate on children's rights and forged changes in laws such as promoting the prosecution of individuals involved in child sex trade. Social workers in the United States can expand their own possibilities for promoting children's rights by becoming informed about the convention and the ways in which it is being used for empowering child-centered practice throughout the world (see, for example, Hart 1992; Lansdown 2000; Schwab 1997).

The Child Friendly Cities Initiative offers a powerful example of the possibilities for grounding the principles of children's rights in concrete action on a global scale. The initiative was launched in 1996 to take action on a resolution passed by the second United Nations Conference on Human Settlements calling for cities to be livable places for all and places that promote the well-being of children. The Initiative, spearheaded by UNICEF, seeks ways to put the UN Convention on the Rights of the Child to practice at the local level throughout the globe. Fundamentally, the initiative promotes children's participation in the issues that affect their lives. A Child Friendly City is a local system of good governance committed to fulfilling child rights for all its young citizens. A child-friendly city

> involves children and youth in initiatives concerning their lives; fosters participative planning, implementation and good governance processes; encourages child participation in family, community, and social life; extends basic services such as health care, education, shelter, safe water, and proper sanitation to all; protects children from exploitation, violence, trafficking and abuse; maintains safe streets and places for socialization and play; provides green spaces and playgrounds; controls pollution and traffic; supports cultural and social events; and ensures that all children live as equal citizens with access to every service, without discrimination related to age, gender, income, race, ethnicity, cultural origin, religion, and/or disability. (CFC 2006:1)

Promoters contend that a child-friendly city is friendly to all. The UNICEF Secretariat for Child Friendly Cities has developed a framework for defining and developing a child-friendly city, based on nine building blocks:

1. Children's participation
2. A child friendly legal framework
3. A citywide Children's Rights Strategy
4. A Children's Rights Unity or coordinating mechanism
5. Child impact assessment and evaluation
6. A children's budget
7. A regular "State of the City's Children" report
8. Making children's rights known
9. Independent advocacy for children

CFC provides a framework for ground-up, child-centered planning and policy-making that moves beyond tokenism to support active participation of children in the issues that affect their lives. Hundreds of projects have been launched worldwide. The CFC website (www.childfriendlycities.org) gives examples of child-friendly cities around the world, as well as a framework for action.

Children and youth have also taken grassroots approaches to putting the Convention on the Rights of the Child to practice by developing their own self-advocacy organizations. For example, Article 12 is a youth-driven organization established in 1996 in the United Kingdom to promote youth participation and human rights. The group named themselves After Article 12 of the Convention, which states that states "shall assure to the child who is capable of forming his or her own views the right to express those views freely in all matters affecting the child, the views of the child being given due weight in accordance with the age and maturity of the child" (United Nations 1989). The group is made up of young adolescents who speak out on children's rights and carry the message to other children (Schwab 1997). In recent years they have trained young peer educators to conduct research in their communities and organized international children's rights conferences.

To promote the full, meaningful participation of children in the concerns that affect their lives, Roger Hart (1992) has proposed that we think of participation in terms of levels or as rungs on a ladder (table 14.1). Hart argues that too often adult-driven calls for youth participation are at best acts of "tokenism," whereby a young person is hand picked to serve on a committee or board, but adults control the agenda, processes, and outcome. It is much more chal-

Table 14.1 Roger Hart's Ladder of Young People's Participation

Rung 8: Young people and adults share decision making
Rung 7: Young people lead and initiate action
Rung 6: Adult-initiated, shared decisions with young people
Rung 5: Young people consulted and informed
Rung 4: Young people assigned and informed
Rung 3: Young people tokenized*
Rung 2: Young people are decoration*
Rung 1: Young people are manipulated*

Adapted from R. A. Hart, "Children's participation," UNICEF ICDC/IRC, 1992.
* Hart explains that the last three rungs are nonparticipation.

lenging for adults to truly share power and decision-making or to create spaces and opportunities for children to initiate and lead action as researchers, policy makers, and agents of change (Hart 1992; Schwab 1997). Hart also describes the generative possibilities that emerge when young people's participation is supported with adults as allies. He offers an example from his experience in Brazil where adult facilitators engaged with children living on the streets; they listened to children's stories, learned about their abilities to live independently, and created opportunities for children to learn skills of cooperation. Using popular education strategies, adults and children took part in small group conversations about the conditions of young people's lives. The children learned and discussed the concept of children's rights and identified the systematic ways in which the rights of children living on the streets were violated by agents of the state. The children organized collective action to create policy change, bringing their concerns to the nation's capital and influencing the writing of a new constitution (Hart in Schwab 1997).

Accounts of children's engagement as community-based researchers also abound. The story of ACTIONAID Nepal (AAN) is a case in point (Hill 1998). AAN's mission is the eradication of absolute poverty through empowerment of women, men, and children. AAN has carried out participatory research enabling children to share their experiences and opinions. Their work showed that children need to be integral in the process, their voices and views heard, and their rights and needs considered in order to assure that interventions truly address and improve their quality of life. The researchers began by bringing groups of children ages 11–15 together to analyze their social reality and to serve as ongoing consultants to AAN's planning process. The techniques used included focus-group discussions about changes, diaries to record children's daily activities, and social maps to show how children went to school. Children's thematic drawings presented graphic images of their life circumstances and provided a base for evaluating changes in those circumstances. Rapport between children and facilitators was key to meaningful participation.

The researchers write:

> By forming groups the right of children to have a space to discuss their issues has been formally acknowledged. Adults in the community and AAN are beginning to listen to these groups, and participation in these groups has allowed children to develop skills, knowledge, experience and confidence. . . . A key problem identified by the groups was children being sent for wage labor, which prevented them from attending school. Their groups have raised awareness, for example through street drama, about girls' rights to education. They have directly persuaded male household heads to send girls and women to school. (92–93)

Participants in one of the children's groups write:

> In the past we were innocent and no one would listen to us, and the adults sometimes used to scold and dominate us. Now the situation has changed. We are able to read, write, and speak. . . . We are able to solve our problems ourselves. (93–94)

Examples of children as researchers for social change can also be found closer to home. *Photovoice* is a strategy for promoting children's participation in knowledge development and policy making. Community researchers have invited participants in collective change processes to illustrate the impacts of their participation through "before" and "after" photographs. How did they see themselves and their life situations before becoming involved, and how did those images change through the process of participation? Participants are invited to tell their stories of participation and describe the meanings of their before-and-after images. This approach, which is referred to as *photovoice* in the literature, has been used with increasing regularity as a participatory evaluation method with a strong action component (Wang and Burris 1997). For example, Latino adolescents living in a rural town in North Carolina with documented high dropout rates routinely described the quality of their lives as poor: they felt they were being funneled into low-wage, dead-end jobs in industrial poultry processing plants (Streng 2004). Armed with cameras, the students engaged in a photovoice project where they visually captured what they perceived as the barriers to inclusion and career fulfillment. Their photo display drew the attention of school administrators and provided an opportunity to voice their concerns and to address inequities in school policy.

Another visual method for conducting participatory evaluation is presented by Gallagher (2004) in a description of the Our Town project that involved low-income urban children in designing and building an intervention in their neighborhood. Children, assisted by architects, community planners, and neighborhood residents, first assessed the neighborhood and represented their findings in drawings. Based on what they perceived as the deficiencies and strengths of their neighborhood, the children then designed an ideal living environment. From their ideal images and identified needs, they built a park, which brought neighbors together and served as a site for community events. The project not only helped create a needed neighborhood space informed by the perspectives of children, it challenged assumptions about children's participation in community planning and evaluation efforts. According to O'Kane (2002:702), "Children and youth need to learn how to become citizens through the every day experience of their family, the communities in which they live, their school, and their nation." These grounded examples illustrate the possibilities for promoting the participatory citizenship of children and youth with adults as allies.

IMPLICATIONS FOR SOCIAL WORK

The future of social work practice with children is rich with possibilities. As O'Kane states, "Through concrete and creative actions children and youth have made their parents, local communities, media, judiciary, local and national government officials and institutions take notice of their views and become responsive to injustices in very powerful and transformative ways" (2002:703).

Social workers now face the tough questions: Are we ready for the challenge? Are we ready to share power with children and youth? What it will take to practice "with" instead of "on" children and youth? How would seeing children as capable and competent actors challenge us on personal, professional, and institutional levels and provide us and children with new possibilities for practice? We have so much to gain by being willing to develop respectful, genuine, attentive relationships with children and honoring their views and voices. We have the skills and knowledge to be advocates for children's rights and allies in the creation of spaces for children to come together to share their stories, reflect on their rights, name their concerns, and take action. We now must muster the political will and moral courage to practice against the grain of protection and paternalism. We must engage with the humility of new learners to discover the possibilities of practice emerging within and beyond our borders. Hopefully, the Just Practice perspective offers a guide to thought and action in this exciting and uncertain terrain.

QUESTIONS FOR DISCUSSION

1. How might a child's-eye view of your current social work practice / practicum setting differ from an adult's view? What challenges might a child's-eye view pose?

2. How might you apply the processes of "complexity thinking" in your practice with children and youth. Provide an example.

3. How might thought and action guided by a commitment to child rights challenge social work practice in the United States? What challenges and possibilities can you envision?

4. Use the five key themes of Just Practice to think through a practice situation in which you are engaged. What questions does it raise for you? What possibilities can you see?

5. Identify an issue or concern facing children and adults in your community. Are the voices and views of children being heard? What strategies might you employ to encourage children's participation in addressing this issue? Where might you encounter resistance to children's participation? Where might you encounter support?

REFERENCES

Adams, R., L. Dominelli, and M. Payne. (Eds.) (2005). *Social work futures: Crossing boundaries and transforming practice.* New York: Palgrave / Macmillan.

Allan, J. (2003). Theorizing critical social work. In J. Allan, B. Pease, and L. Briskman, eds., *Critical social work: An introduction to theories and practices,* 32–51. Crows Nest, Australia: Allen and Unwin.

Bourdieu, P. (1977). *Outline of a theory of practice,* trans. R. Nice. Cambridge: Cambridge University Press.

California Youth Connection. (2007). Foster Youth Building a Foundation for the Future. Mission statement. Accessed June 4, 2007, at http://www.calyouthconn.org.

Child Friendly Cities (2006). Homepage, Project of UNICEF. Accessed March 15, 2006, at http://www.childfriendlycities.org.

Coles, R. (1986). *The political life of children.* Boston: Atlantic Monthly Press.

Fass, P.. and M. Mason. (2000). *Childhood in America.* New York: New York University Press.

Ferguson, I., M. Lavalette, and E. Whitmore (2005). *Globalisation, global justice and social work.* New York: Routledge.

Finn, J., and M. Jacobson. (2003). Just practice: Steps toward a new social work paradigm. *Journal of Social Work Education 39* (1): 57–78.

———. (2008). *Just practice: A just-oriented approach to social work.* 2nd edition. Peosta, Iowa: Eddie Bowers Publishing.

Fook, J. (2000). Critical perspectives on social work practice. In E. O'Connor, P. Smyth, and J. Warburton, eds., *Contemporary perspectives on social work and the human services: Challenges and change.* Sydney: Pearson Education Australia.

Freire, P. (1990). A critical understanding of social work. *Journal of Progressive Human Services 1* (1): 3–9.

Gallagher, C. (2004). "Our town": Children as advocates for change in the city. *Childhood 11* (2): 251–62.

Graham, J., and E. Gray (1997). *American experience: The orphan trains.* PBS. Website produced by Joseph Tovares for the American Experience and WGBH Interactive. Accessed March 9, 2007, at http://www.pbs.org/wgbh/amex/orphan/credits .html.

Gramsci, A. (1987). *The modern prince and other stories.* New York: International Publishers. (Originally published 1957).

Hart, R.A. (1992). *Children's participation: From tokenism to citizenship.* Innocenti Essay No. 4, Florence: UNICEF International Child Development Centre.

Healy, K. (2005). Under reconstruction: Renewing critical social work practices. In S. Hick, J. Fook, and R. Pozzuto, eds., *Social work: A critical turn,* 219–29. Toronto: Thompson Educational Publishing.

Hill, J. (1998). Toward louder voices: ActionAid Nepal's experience of working with children. In V. Johnson, E. Ivan-Smith, G. Gordon, P. Pridmore, and P. Scott, eds., *Stepping forward: Children and young people's participation in the development process,* 92–95. London: Intermediate Technology Publications.

Hutchison, E., and L. Charlesworth. (2000). Securing the welfare of children: Policies past, present, and future. *Families in Society 81* (6): 576–85.

Ife, J. (2000). Localized needs and a globalized economy: Bridging the gap with social work practice. *Canadian Social Work* (Social Work and Globalization: Special Issue) 2 (1): 50–64.

James, A., and L. James. (2004). *Constructing childhood: Theory, policy, and social practice.* New York: Palgrave/Macmillan.

Kelly, A., and S. Sewell. (1988). *With head, heart, and hand: Dimensions of community building.* 4th edition. Brisbane: Boolarong Press.

Kotlowitz, A. (1991). *There are no children here.* New York: Anchor Books.

Lansdown, G. (2000). *Promoting children's participation in democratic decision-making.* Florence: United Nations Children's Fund.

McBeth, S. (1983). *Ethnic identity and the boarding school experience of West Central Oklahoma American Indians.* New York: University Press of America.

Meuccia, S., and M. Schwab. (1997). Children and the environment: Young people's participation in social change. *Social Justice 24* (3): 1–10.

Morss, J. (2003). The several constructions of James, Jenks and Prout: A contribution to the sociological theorization of childhood. *International Journal of Children's Rights 10* (1): 39–54.

Moules, T. (Ed.) (2004). Whose quality is it? *Paediatric Nursing 16* (6): 30–31.

National Center for Children in Poverty (2005). Who are America's poor children? Poverty Fact Sheet #2. New York: National Center for Children in Poverty.

O'Kane, C. (2004). Marginalized children as social actors for social justice in South Asia. *British Journal of Social Work 32:* 697–710.

Orellana, M., L. Dorner, and L. Palido. (2003). Accessing assets: Immigrant youths' work as family translators or "para-phrasers." *Social Problems 50* (4): 505–24.

Ridge, T. (2003). Listening to children: Developing a child-centred approach to childhood poverty in the UK. *Family Matters, 65:* 4–10.

Schwab, M. (1997) Children's rights and the building of democracy: A dialogue on the international movement for children's participation. *Social Justice 24* (3): 177–92.

Sealander, J. (2004). The history of childhood policy. *Journal of Policy History 16* (2): 176–87.

Streng, J., S. Rhodes, G. Ayala, E. Eng, R. Arceo, and S. Phipps. (2004). *Realidad Latina:* Latino adolescents, their school, and a university use photovoice to examine and address the influences of immigration. *Journal of Interprofessional Care 18* (4): 403–15.

Stephens, S. (Ed.) (1995) *Children and the politics of culture.* Princeton: Princeton University Press.

Theis, J. (2001). *Tools for child rights programming: A training manual.* Save the Children. Ms.

Thorne, B. (1987). Re-visioning women and social change: Where are the children? *Gender and Society 1* (1): 85–109.

Townsend, J., E. Zapata, J. Rowlands, P. Alberti, and M. Mercado. (1999). *Women and power: Fighting patriarchies and poverty.* London: Zed Books.

Trenka, J. (2003). *The language of blood.* St. Paul: Borealis Books, Minnesota Historical Society.

Trenka, J., J. Oparah, and S. Shin. (2006). *Outsiders within: Writing on transracial adoption.* Cambridge, Mass.: South End Press.

United Nations (1989). UN General Assembly. *Convention on the Rights of the Child*. (UN Document A/Res/44/23). New York: United Nations.

Valenzuela, A., Jr. (1999). Gender roles and settlement activities among children and their immigrant families. *American Behavioral Scientist 42:* 720–42.

Wang, C., and M. Burris. (1997). Photovoice: Concept, methodology, and use for participatory needs assessment. *Health Education and Behavior 24* (3): 369–87.

Witter, S., and J. Bukohe. (2004). Children's perceptions of poverty, participation, and local governance in Uganda. *Development in Practice 14* (5): 645–59.

Wordsworth, D., M. McPeak, and T. Feeny. (2005). Children and poverty working paper #1: Understanding children's experience of poverty. Richmond, Va.: Christian Children's Fund.

Zelizer, V. (1985). *Pricing the priceless child: The changing social value of children*. New York: Basic Books.

———. (2005). The priceless child revisited. In J. Qvortrup, ed., *Studies in modern childhood*, 190–99. New York: Palgrave/Macmillan.

On Project SpeakOUT   **FIFTEEN**

Derrick Jackson

Once, while I was describing Project SpeakOUT (PSO) to a group of educators, an English teacher responded cynically, "You really get kids in Ypsi to write poetry?" Exasperated, I replied, "And they can read too!" Noting my obvious disappointment with his remarks, the teacher pressed on awkwardly. In the course of our discussion, the teacher confessed that he had a terribly difficult time getting his students to pay attention, let alone recite or compose poetry. He went on to tell of a poetry assignment he devised that brought only silence to his classroom. Hence, his conclusion, "Kids in Ypsilanti aren't into poetry."

I couldn't help but wonder if the teacher's classroom was actually silent, or if he had tuned out what his young students were saying instead. Had he created this reaction by his preconceived notions of what poetry is supposed to be? Was it that he had already made up his mind that poetry was foreign to these "Ypsi kids"? For all of his will to do good, was it his desire to be the expert, the adult, the educator that brought silence? Or could it simply be that he was not listening?

I thank the youth of PSO: Brittany, Natalia, Keena, Krystal, Troy, Gabe, J-Fab, Paris, Sulaimon, BMC, Rod and all the young people that continue to speak out for themselves.

Project SpeakOUT is an outgrowth of the Ozone House Drop-in Center in Ypsilanti, Michigan. I served as Outreach Director of the Drop-In Center from 2000 to 2005. My discussion with the English teacher took place in the context of racial and economic divisions between the working-class rustbelt community of Ypsilanti and its neighboring university town of Ann Arbor. These divides are clearly defined, are well known, and have a significant impact on the young people, teachers, and other direct service workers. Michigan, I should note, is a highly racially segregated state, and the divisions within the Ypsilanti and Ann Arbor areas are symptomatic of that larger social ill.[1]

From my viewpoint, youth today are speaking louder and more clearly than ever, within and across these divides. The problem is that we—social workers, teachers, parents, and almost every other person a youth comes in contact with—are simply not listening. We hear the slang-ridden dialogue and dismiss it as broken English, or hear the curse-filled music and distort it as hate-filled gibberish. Even when we hear young people speak about their problems, we too often fail to actually listen to their analysis of the reasons behind them.

CAN YOU HEAR ME NOW?

Never was the inadequacy of my own listening ability more evident than when one of my favorite young people asked for a ride home from the Drop-In one night. As we approached her neighborhood, several patrol cars made their exit. It was common in this area to see the local police making their rounds, and the presence of the patrol cars did not seem significant to either of us. Two blocks later, we pulled up to her home to find a cousin pounding on my passenger side window, front door boarded up, maintenance man packing up. Her home had been raided for drugs and all the adults arrested.

After convincing the maintenance man to let us into her home, the young woman frantically searched through the clothes on the kitchen floor, navigated past the mattress in the living room, found her way around the closet door that lay in the hall, and eventually made it to the space she called her room. She was searching for something more meaningful than the clothes hanging from the ceiling fan, more significant than the photos that covered the couch. I encouraged her to grab the things I thought to be important . . . a change of clothes, a toothbrush, supplies for school. Ignoring my suggestions, she continued to search desperately.

"We don't have much time. What are you looking for?" She looked up at me, picked up a picture of herself as a child with a young woman who resembled her, and continued to search. The look she gave me prompted memories of a poem she had recited several weeks earlier and, for that matter, every other poem she had written. Like the finale to a great mystery, it all began to make sense. I joined her search, and about fifteen minutes later we found what she sought, in the bathroom beneath the toilet. We headed to the shelter with three items: her journals, the picture she held, and her mother's urn. That's all she had and, at the time, it was all that was needed. At that point, I realized the power of the words that she had shared so many times before. She had recounted her entire story week by week, noting every pain that she had ever encountered, every coping mechanism that she had ever learned. She had given me the answers that I had been looking for, and in three poetic minutes she provided what would have taken typical one-on-one work several months to accomplish. In her poems, she said it all.

A couple of regulars at the Drop-In, including this young woman, had been sitting together each week in what they called a "cipher." They shared the writing that they had worked on since the previous meeting. On occasion, I'd be drawn in by the rhythmic cadence or the hard-hitting emotion of the words they strung together. For the most part, though, I just thought of it as a group of kids getting together and sharing ideas.

So, what was it that kept me from hearing more than rhythmic lines strung together? What prevented me from listening to what she was saying so clearly? Anxious to find out, I asked for a copy of one of her poems. While I read, it quickly became clear what she had been saying during the "cipher." I'd missed it.

THE CIPHER

> She's dying, slowly dying inside, dying to forget, dying not to remember.
> Her childhood flies by her eyes at night . . . and she sighs.
> As flashbacks of her mom float freely on her mind.
> She's mentally tired; emotionally worn out feeling chained in by hate . . .
> Like a bird with no wings that can't fly.
> To fly away from sorrow she's dying.
> Like a tree with no roots she's broken.
> I can feel It, I'm crying for her . . .

Was it my preconceived notions of this "Ypsi kid" that made me doubt her ability to know what was going on in her own life? Had I already made up my mind about the issues she was dealing with and how to help?

I sit holding a pen describing my pain.

I no longer have a heart to break its broken already.

Killed by life and tears that are left unshed turned to poison in the dust . . .

Was it my own professional arrogance that led me to believe that sitting in a one-on-one session and asking questions was the only way for me to get the answers I was searching for? For all of my will to do good, was it my desire to be the expert, the adult, the educator that led me to hear silence when she was telling me everything I needed to know?

And inside her blood no longer runs warm but cold,

She's a lie inside and out and no one knows this but her,

She hides behind her smiles and bats her eyes and says I'm fine.

Fine even though she's crying tears of rebirth wishing to begin again and be normal.

Fine even though her soul aches to be set free breaking dreams of cold memories

into shattered glass . . .

Showing her reflection, not her own but someone she pretends to be.

She's depressed and knows it, tired of being alone, holding on and being strong

But she smiles when asked and says I'm fine.

Sitting there, dissecting each line, I wondered how often I had been fooled by smiles that said, "I'm fine." After pondering those questions for days, I began to understand that I had missed more than just the lines of her poems. It hit me that a few young people had formed their own support group right before my eyes. No adult supervision, no curriculum, no long-drawn-out service plan, and no group facilitator needed. These young people had created something that I struggled to construct—a group that was well attended and extremely successful. Sure, I'd had successful programs in the past. But despite all my years of social work education, I had accomplished nothing that compared to what they had so naturally created and so easily sustained. This realization forced me to step outside of my comfort zone and evaluate my previous professional beliefs. In retrospect, I can acknowledge that the Drop-In Center was doing something right by providing a safe space that encouraged creativity and individual growth. Beyond that, it was the teens themselves who created, facilitated, and helped nurture this small group into what would become Project SpeakOUT.

I realized that the perception I held of myself as "expert" had prevented me from providing the best possible service to the people I wanted to help most. I was actually standing in the way of their full potential. By creating programs from my perspective, I wasn't allowing the young people at the center to fully participate in their own development. Yes, I would ask participants to brainstorm as a group and generate some ideas, but after that the "expert" would kick in. Planning the group, getting the space, buying materials, setting up the service plan, and making goals were all things that were done by the "expert." The young people participated in what I had developed. Ultimately, I was holding them back.

In contrast, the "cipher" generated instant buy-in and immediate success because it was theirs. These young people knew exactly what would keep them interested, and they knew how to get others to take part. They set ground rules without meetings dedicated to brainstorming; they made a game plan each week without hour-long planning sessions; they challenged, encouraged, empathized, developed, and enacted every other social work term in the book without ever calling themselves social workers. The "cipher" was based upon the participants having real power within the group and understanding that they are the experts about themselves.

After weeks of informal meetings, the "cipher" was added to the weekly Drop-In Center schedule. Of course, it had to have a catchy name and logo to go on all the fliers the kids wanted to post around town. Someone suggested Lyricist Lounge; another sat sketching a teen holding a microphone that would later become the logo; several others got together to design the flier that was posted in every nook and cranny of Ypsilanti. In short, they did more than come up with an idea and hand it over to the "expert"; they actually developed the entire program and developed as individuals along the way. My definition of a successful youth development program was forever altered, and the impact would transform the center.

THE DROP-IN

Established in 1994, the Drop-In Center is the Ypsilanti satellite office for Ozone House Youth and Family Services. Ozone is a safe haven for runaway and homeless teens and has been around since the early 1970s. It consists of a 24-hour hotline, an emergency shelter, a long-term independent living facility, numerous off-site residential apartments, counseling services, street outreach, and the Drop-In Center. In short, it's a safe place for anyone between the ages of 10 and 20. Ozone House was designed as a holistic approach to serving the teen homeless population. The Drop-In Center was an entry point for many of the services.

The Drop-In Center was established to build bridges with young people of Ypsilanti. In spite of Ozone House's many years of successful programming and numerous awards for its accomplishments, it had become evident that the economic and racial divide between Ypsilanti and neighboring Ann Arbor was interfering with our ability to effectively reach the young people we so desperately fought to serve. Our main site was located west of the "US-23 divide" in Ann Arbor, and a large population of our young people lived on the "other" side of the US-23 border. We began to understand that perceptions of Ozone House and popular notions of who it was that we served and hired had become tainted by racial undertones.

There were times when a professional social worker would hesitate prior to sending a young person of color to our shelter in Ann Arbor, fearing that the young person might encounter race and class prejudice. On the other hand, the 15-year-old peer outreach workers in Ypsilanti who traveled from neighborhood to neighborhood would roll their eyes and dread the times we crossed the border into the city of Ann Arbor. The relationship among Ann Arbor, Ypsilanti, and the smaller, more rural surrounding towns and villages was complicated, too. We even set up a program where students from a predominantly white high school in neighboring Saline would spend several weeks working with us in downtown Ypsilanti. At the conclusion of the semester, those students made presentations to their classmates back at the high school and the question, "What did you think when you first went to Ypsi?" inevitably arose. It was usually followed by the all too familiar, "I was terrified at first." Although much of this was perception, there was no denying that the divisions that separated our community were deep and very real.

In an effort to bridge these gaps and simultaneously change the perception of Ozone House, a decision was made to place a satellite office in the downtown business district of Ypsilanti. Ypsi itself is hardly a homogenous community, and numerous boundary lines divide it—South Side, West Willow, and Prospect are all clearly defined divisions. As a result, it was important to have the Drop-In Center centralized within the city, in a "neutral area," so that young people could participate and feel welcome. More important, I suppose, was the idea that no matter what area of the community you were from or what boundaries you encountered, you would cross them if something on the other side of that invisible wall was worth it. Maybe it was the draw of the stage and the chance to get on the microphone and perform. Maybe it was the supportive atmosphere or the opportunity to express yourself and have someone listen. Whatever the reason, it was clear that kids from all over the community were coming together to read, write, and listen to poetry at the Drop-In.

One young person described the center as his "second home." To him, the Drop-In was a place where he didn't want his younger brother tagging along, invading his private space. Yet, at the same time, it was a place where he felt obligated to bring that same younger sibling because it was "one of the few fun safe teen spots" in the community. The Drop-In was arranged in a way to have a relaxed, rec room feel. Upon entering the building, you stepped into a large gathering area with couches, a big screen television, and a couple of recliners. Further down the hall was a little hang-out area for reading and a quiet space to just get away. Several computers made up "the lab," a space used for mostly surfing the Net, but, as one teen put it, "It sounded so intellectual to say the lab, like I was learning or something." The irony in that statement, about learning when you don't know that you are learning, always caught me, but that's just what the center was based upon. Fun, innovative programming is what brought people in, but it was what I called "backdooring" that really set it apart.

For example, every Wednesday was movie night. After the movie, we would sneak in an educational component through some activity that related the premise of the movie to real-life experiences. Try taking the meaning of life from Happy Gilmore, but that was "backdooring," and that was what we were good at. Bring in a video game and just see how many young men show up for the "Men's Movement," our Friday night male support group. The young men would come in to play games for an hour or two, then four hours later we would be wrapping up our conversation on relationships, sex, parents, school, or any number of other topics, finally forcing the participants out the door so that we could lock up for the night. Out of the Men's Movement grew "Time to Shine," an hour given to one person to present himself to the group. Each young person could do whatever he wanted to teach us about himself in one hour. Teaching and learning about yourself was "backdooring" at its best.

LYRICIST LOUNGE

Every night of the week the schedule was full and the rooms were continuously occupied by young people, but Lyricist Lounge was unique. It took what we were good at, "backdooring," and combined it with true youth development to form the beginnings of a one-of-a-kind program.

Lyricist Lounge jumped from 5 or 6 people in the "cipher" to 10 or 20 and then upwards of 50 visitors each week. It quickly went from sitting in a circle taking turns to having sign-up sheets so that everyone had time to "spit," a term seared into my mind thanks to weeks of Lounge performances. We went from sitting around reading with the lights on, to performing under dim stage lights—more like Christmas lights left up all year round—to set the ambiance.

We went from listening to one person's radio to the demand for a stereo to occasional nights with a live DJ or band. The Lyricists even developed their own language and cultural norms; for example, "snapping it up" instead of clapping. Clapping caused too much of a ruckus. You can't clap in the midst of a performance or you miss that all-important next line. So one day someone began to snap in the middle of a performance, and the notion of "snapping it up"—showing how much you enjoyed the piece without interrupting it—began.

MAGIC GLASSES

All the performers understood how uncomfortable it was to be new to the Lounge, and how important it was for each new person to get past this uncomfortable stage. In recognition, they gave all first-timers a grand introduction complete with drum roll. The look on a newcomer's face as everyone in the room stomped out a drum roll on the wooden floor was wonderful. If the drum roll didn't work to relax a newcomer, the young hosts insisted that the entire audience turn and face a wall so that the first-time performer felt alone in the room. For would-be performers who were still experiencing nerves, there were the "magic glasses." This tradition started after one young performer was asked why he always wore sunglasses during his readings. He described the way that hiding behind his glasses made it easier to stand on stage, and soon it became common for every nervous performer to be offered the "magic glasses." Over time, one after another, participants moved from experiencing total fright to gaining comfort performing with the rhythm of the booming floors that so irritated our neighboring businesses.

It was truly amazing to sit back and watch the development of these customs. Young people were taking suggestions or weaknesses of performers at the Lounge and folding them into the culture of the group. Without knowing it, they were "backdooring" a therapy session, meeting the clients "where they were" and turning weaknesses into strengths. Even a few individuals who found it challenging to read and write felt supported enough to stand on stage and struggle through a piece that they had prepared. Sometimes social workers and other service providers visited the Drop-In and perceived nothing more than a "group of kids hanging out." Once a week however, one of the young participants brought therapy to the front door and made the benefits of this process evident to anyone who was looking. A young poet would step up to the microphone, make the all-too-common disclaimer, "I've never said this to anyone before," and then the room would fall silent, serious, intent. The speaker would spew words full of anger, hate, sadness, disappointment—messages full of those red flags that we all look for but sometimes don't see, or distort or dismiss. Some members of the helping professions resisted the transition from a quiet one-on-one therapy session to the loud, in-your-face therapy performances of Lyricist Lounge. Was it the struggle to stay within our comfort zone that caused some of us to miss that all-too-important next line?

POETRY IN THE PARK

During the summers, the cramped center was bursting at the seams. Following one of our jam-packed, sweat-filled Lyricist Lounge performances, a young participant suggested that we move outdoors to the park behind our building. Although we didn't go that night, the seed was planted. In the weeks that followed, we feverishly planned for our first community-wide outdoor performance. These performances became an annual event known as Poetry in the Park.

We had planned for one event during the summer that would build upon the laid-back beginnings of Lyricist Lounge, which, although growing in popularity, still remained an intimate, safe space for the beginning poet. Poetry in the Park, however, stepped it up a notch. The outdoor performance produced a larger audience full of strangers, without the comfort and familiarity of the Drop-In. This performance opportunity helped some to see how much they had grown and pushed others toward further development. It also showcased the great work of the young people, which to this point had been appreciated only by staff and participants at the Drop-In. Members of Project SpeakOUT applied for the permits, set the stage up in the busiest area of the park, provided food, hired a DJ, and placed fliers in every nook and cranny of Ypsi. Young people took an idea for an outdoor performance and developed it into the second component of Project SpeakOUT.

GUERILLA POETRY

With time and experience, several participants had developed the ability to perform their work almost anywhere. At that point, "guerilla poetry" evolved. While waiting for the bus one afternoon, Natalia began rehearsing one of her new pieces, and soon a small crowd gathered. She explained what she was doing, and at our next Lyricist Lounge some of those same young people made their first visit. That's how we discovered how powerful a tool "guerilla poetry" was. After that, we would head to the bus stop, library steps, arcade, or any other space where young people might be and launch an impromptu performance. Guerilla poetry was a unique way to advertise, recruit potential participants, push participants to another level; most importantly, it was created by the young people themselves.

The goal of Project SpeakOUT was to provide a space for both the beginning and the experienced poet to become involved and to flourish. It is important to point out that not everyone who participated in Project SpeakOUT came into the program as a poet or writer. In fact, most of the teens who visited came because it was a "cool spot" and they wanted to be entertained. Others came because a friend was performing, or because they were receiving services at Ozone House. Some would visit and jump right in, while others took months to feel at ease. For example, I had known J-fab for several months before I even knew he was interested in writing. One day, without warning, he stepped up to the microphone and wowed us all with his talent. Both Keena and Krystal started out as rappers. Their hard-hitting, in-your-face rhymes poetically shed light on the plight of neighborhood life, but they never did think of themselves as poets. In fact, they fought against the title. Both later developed into well-rounded performers, one pursuing a career in social work while the other focused on her music. Other participants, like Natalia, were writers who refused to perform in front of an audience. Now, seeing her alone on stage . . . microphone in hand . . . "I bear my soul for the sole purpose of education" . . . the crowd roars with approval . . . she smiles with confidence . . . exits stage right.

By this point, there were three levels to Project SpeakOUT, and soon a fourth was added. Lyricist Lounge provided a safe space for the beginner and allowed the experienced poet to practice, host, and encourage those that were new to the program; Poetry in the Park gave those who practiced the venue to showcase what they so diligently had been perfecting; guerilla poetry provided outreach and recruitment by taking now confident and polished participants to perform in school presentations, social gatherings, university events, and local community shows. We had a complete cycle: someone could see a performance, become interested, visit the safe confines of the Drop-In, perform for the first time at Lyricist Lounge, hone their skills from week to week, and move on to perform in front of an even larger audience through Poetry in the Park. Finally, participants organized and participated in the same sorts of community shows that had first introduced them to the program.

THE SLAM

As we traveled around the community performing and recruiting, someone suggested we attend a local area poetry slam. A slam is a competition between poets. You take a piece that you have written, stand on stage, perform, and then receive a score based upon a number of criteria—how well written the piece was, how well it was relayed to the audience, how much the audience enjoyed it. To that point, we had never seen anything like a slam. Once the kids saw one, they wanted nothing more than to see another. The day following that first slam was spent reenacting the highlights and talking about this piece or that piece. Instantly, I knew that we would soon see Project SpeakOUT members gracing the slam stage.

Participating in a slam was an important transition for the program. I was reminded of a time when Project SpeakOUT performed for and answered questions from students in the Social Work program at Eastern Michigan University. One student asked, "Why is it easier to be so vulnerable in your poetry but not in a one-on-one session?" The response, "Because you can't say anything when I'm on stage. You just have to listen." I knew that when young people were allowing judges to assess their work, they were giving the judges a "say." That dynamic added a tremendous amount of pressure for even our most experienced poets. The issue was that slamming was a competition. How could someone judge the work that these young people put forward? Placing points on the narrative of people's lives just didn't seem to fit. Deep down I was concerned with how a competitive environment might change the culture of the program, but the young people so wanted to be a part of the slam movement. Ultimately it was their program, so who was I to stop the inevitable? By this point, I knew that my job was helping the young people at the Drop-In figure out what they wanted and assisting them in seeing it through.

Months after we saw that first slam, we were invited to perform during the National Youth Slam competition, Brave New Voices. This Olympic-style event brought youth slam teams from around the country to Ann Arbor for one weekend. That first year we struggled and never made it past the first round, but the lessons learned during that first National Slam would once again change our center and Project SpeakOUT.

These young people were developing step-by-step; from asking their audience to turn and face the wall to performing in front of judges who were scoring their work, the transition was both obvious and astonishing. Quiet newcomers who at one time required the "magic glasses" were now confident performers willing to place their work before a raucous audience and five judges whose sole purpose was to pick a winner. The "I've never said this before" kids were standing on stage—hearts open, personal stories on display—allowing total strangers to assign points to the hardships of their lives.

When a newcomer joined Project SpeakOUT, we often heard that person perform the same poem numerous times. If we ever canceled a Lyricist Lounge, you could rest assured that several poets would be waiting at the door to recite the same piece they had presented several weeks in a row. I came to see that it was the therapeutic nature of poetry at work. The issues contained within the poems that they repeated were still pressing and raw. Performing the poem was a way of discussing these pressing issues and relieving the stress of holding it all in.

By the time poets were ready for the slam, however, they had moved beyond the issues that confined them to that same poem. Experienced poets had written, performed, critiqued, and discussed the issues within the poem so many times and with so many people that they were no longer confined by the same concerns. Some who reached this point simply refused to read a poem once they moved beyond it. Others actually destroyed the books that they had written in once they moved past the accounts recorded there.

Poets who repeated a poem reached a point where they had presented the problem, dealt with it, and moved beyond it. Now, there were other issues to analyze. No longer were the writers confined to the frequent topics of the neighborhood or family issues. Their horizons expanded, their vocabularies exploded, and their sense of themselves matured. Accomplished poets, they now discussed complex relationships, personal growth, politics, and history. Even the common "where I'm from" poems had a depth that was not there months earlier. The slam had opened their eyes to the fact that there were young people from all over the country dealing with the same issues they faced back home in Ypsilanti. Their struggles and hardships were validated, and they were determined to bring that validation back to the center for others to experience.

BRAVE NEW VOICES

Over the next four years, we continued to grow the program by adding our own slam competitions. We held a qualifying slam that allowed teens from our area to compete against one another with the top seven poets making up the Ypsilanti Area Poetry Slam team. After several months of Lyricist Lounge, tons of guerilla poetry readings, and a summer of Poetry in the Park, each year culminated in the National Slam. We competed in Chicago, New York, San Francisco, and Los Angeles. Every time the poets returned to Ypsilanti, they brought with them the stories and styles of their peers. They were so determined to share these experiences with others that one year several team members decided not to compete so that the next poets in line would have the chance to travel and experience the National Slam firsthand. These young people were growing beyond the written word and developing as individuals. Their vocabularies expanded, but so did their commitment to community. They were becoming civically involved, and they were concerned with the social ills affecting their peers.

The 2004 National Slam started as they all had: travel, excitement, reunions, guerilla sessions. and then the competition. After our first round, we found ourselves near the top of the points list with our second round approaching. Round 2 was no different, and by the end of that first day the rumor was that we were the team to beat. Still, in my mind, placing points on the narrative of people's lives just didn't seem to fit. We played along, but it didn't fit. Just as our program was unique to our community, Ypsilanti was unique to the National Slam. Not only was our style of performance slightly different, but, unlike many teams, ours didn't really have a coach. I was there to assist, but it was rare that I would coach them on how to write or advise them to change something in their performances. If anything, they taught me the value of the spoken word, and, besides, to this point they had done just fine with limited input from any adults or experts.

Still, it was a competition. Every year, between the first two rounds and the finals, a coaches' meeting was held, and every year I encouraged our entire team to attend. Every year, the focus was expected to be on the poets, but somehow. without fail, each year the coaches became embroiled in an argument about the points. It was funny how the young people embraced self-expression and creativity as the true essence of the slam, but once the adults were left alone, they threw those values out the window. This year, once again, the coaches began arguing about how this team made it in to the finals in error or how that judge was biased. Even in the midst of this national movement centered on the spoken word, the adults were not listening.

Sitting toward the back of the room, watching as the ugly nature of competition emerged, our kids witnessed the betrayal of the movement's ideals. "Can you believe it?" was followed by "What can we do?" Our team members told everyone who would listen what had happened, but to most it did not seem to be that big of a deal. Unlike the young people on other teams, these "Ypsi kids" had built our program from scratch, and the hypocrisy they had just observed was too much for them to bear. Instantly, various poets proposed quitting, forfeiting, or making some sort of a statement. Half the team wanted to leave, and the other half focused on being so close to our first national title that they couldn't care less about hypocrisy. The entire night was spent discussing what could be done, going back and forth from throwing the finals to winning it all and then making some important speech at the end.

Every time we thought we had reached a decision, someone would ask another question, and then the entire debate would begin again. Someone stormed out, tears were shed, "I quit" was yelled at least ten times. I wondered if they would give up what they had worked so hard to build for the sake of winning. Yet, I remained certain that as a group they would make the decision that was right for them. I had learned a long time ago that they knew what was best for them. As much as they wanted an answer from me, I refused to give one. I watched, confident because the wheels were turning. They struggled, but they were working it out among themselves. They had seen a problem, decided to address it, experienced conflict, debated the issues, and ultimately reached a group decision. Tears eventually dried, and everyone was on board.

The finals consisted of the eight top-scoring teams receiving three slots in which to have their finest poets perform their best stuff. Gabe had received perfect scores the day before, and he led off for us. He didn't disappoint—another perfect score, and we were leading. Natalia and Keena performed a collaboration poem to perfection, and although the scores didn't reflect it, they scored high enough to keep us in first place as we headed to the third and final round.

To start this round, Gabe began from the crowd, walking slowly to the stage, embracing the applause as he repeated "boom-bip-bap, see how we hit you with the boom-bip-bap." Keena and Natalia followed, both in repetitive unison, "Y-P-S-I-L-A-N-T-I." Brittany sang out from the crowd, "It's not all about the competition." We had reached our participant limit and the crowd anticipated the poem's official start. They continued the chant; serious, intent. Krystal headed to the stage for an impromptu freestyle blasting the high regard for points that they had witnessed in the coach's meeting. Troy merged in with Krystal's verse and then transitioned to add his own, as his five teammates continued the chant. The Ypsi team had already exceeded the allowable number of performers on stage, and Troy's verse pushed them well beyond the time limit, too. They had done it—disqualified themselves. They sent a message. I marveled at their courage and willingness to embrace the moment—and to give up the gratification of winning.

As I sat transfixed on what they had accomplished, I saw a flash from the corner of my eye. It was members of the team from Leeds, England, jumping on stage one by one to join in with the chant. "L-E-E-D-S" blending with the "Y-P-S-I-L-A-N-T-I." The San Francisco team piled on stage, "It's not all about the competition." One by one, each and every participant in the slam made their way to the stage, leaving the sold-out arena in awe. The chant blended together as they all shouted, "It's not all about the competition." In fact, they had ended the competition. Some adult grabbed a microphone and attempted to announce the winners, only to be drowned out by the ongoing chants of kids from around the country and world screaming loud and clear what they felt.

I wondered if the adults in the room had their preconceived notions of these "Ypsi kids" changed; if they were hearing more than just slang-ridden dialogue or rhythmic lines being strung together. One thing was certain: for that moment, there was no mistaking the fact that every adult in the place had to pay attention to these young people speaking out for what they believed in and what they had built.

QUESTIONS FOR DISCUSSION

1. Jackson asserts that all too often adults are "simply not listening" to children and youth. What is your perception of communication between young people and adults in your practice? In what forums or settings do you observe young people speaking or remaining silenced? In what forums or settings do you observe adults listening or failing to hear?

2. Work in Project SpeakOut pushed Jackson outside of his "comfort zone." What might make this sort of social work practice uncomfortable for workers? What professional encounters have you had with young people that felt "out of your comfort zone"? How did you adapt, grow, or retreat?

3. Jackson briefly notes that some professionals were not receptive to Project SpeakOut as a form of social work practice. In your own work, have you challenged or changed the expectations of other social workers? What did you learn from these encounters?

4. How does Project SpeakOut challenge assumptions about children and youth at the Drop-In Center? How does it challenge assumptions about race and gender in the Ypsilanti community?

5. Use the five themes from Just Practice to think through the development of Project SpeakOut. What lessons does Project SpeakOut offer for your own work with young people?

NOTES

1. The standard "index of dissimilarity" used to measure residential segregation between whites and blacks for metropolitan Detroit is 88 — ranking Detroit just behind

Gary, Indiana, on a list of the most segregated major metropolitan regions in the country, and placing it not far from the 100 that would result from complete apartheid on that index. Michigan includes four of the metropolitan areas ranking in the top twenty for white-black racial segregation, including Flint (with a white-black dissimilarity index of 81.2), Benton Harbor (81.2), and Saginaw (79.1), along with Detroit (Social Science Data Analysis Network 2007).

REFERENCE

Social Science Data Analysis Network (2007). *CensusScope: Segregation.* Accessed July 31, 2007, at http://www.censusscope.org/segregation.html.

The Marshall-Brennan
Constitutional Literacy Project

SIXTEEN

A Case Study in Law and Social Justice

Maryam Ahranjani

Over 30 years ago, my parents fled a corrupt regime in their home country of Iran in search of a society based on fairness and a sense of justice. They wanted to live in a place free from nepotism and greed by the ruling oligarchy, where there was a direct, or at least somewhat direct, correlation between hard work and achievement. Whether the United States is such a society is debatable. However, I argue that at the very least, the U.S. Constitution and legal system provide a framework for citizens to turn to in seeking fairness and justice. This framework can evolve into a firm structure only if our citizenry, and specifically youth, activates the principles and ideals of the Constitution in our daily lives.

At least one study has found that when students are *taught* their constitutional rights and when they practice the freedoms protected by the Constitution, they are far more likely to champion the Constitution.[1] Other studies show that greater knowledge of the Constitution leads to greater civic participation—including voting, running for office, and participating in community development.

Some lawmakers have realized the importance of educating children about the U.S. Constitution. In December 2004 U.S. Senator Robert Byrd proposed legislation requiring all educational institutions that receive public funds to recognize the U.S. Constitution on September 17 every year. This legislation was passed by the House of Representatives and the Senate.[2] Educators and administrators around the country reacted with a mixture of applause and skepticism about how best to comply with the general language of the legislation. Those of us who view every day as Constitution Day were elated.

Named for the late Supreme Court justices Thurgood Marshall and William Brennan, Jr., the Marshall-Brennan Constitutional Literacy Project has worked for eight years to mobilize talented law students to serve as mentors to junior high and high school students, learn about the importance of democracy and citizenship, and share their knowledge of the law with high school students. Besides the substantive curricular goals of the project, one of its social goals is to promote the pipeline of students of color to college, law school, and the practice of law.[3]

To a certain extent, the project is subversive in its approach. Unlike traditional curricula covering the Constitution, which tend to be dry and straightforward, the founders of the Marshall-Brennan Project set out to inspire young people to care about the Constitution by showing them how it affects them every day in schools. The curriculum takes Supreme Court cases about public school students and asks students to read and analyze critical issues of constitutional law through their own lens.

The project has enjoyed tremendous success and has been recognized as a model for civic education. After seven years in existence, there are now chapters in six states across the country. Supporters include local politicians, school board members, teachers, administrators, and constitutional rock stars such as Cissy Marshall, widow of Thurgood Marshall, the great civil rights leader and Supreme Court justice, and Mary Beth Tinker, a plaintiff in the landmark 1969 case about the First Amendment right of students to wear black armbands to school in silent mourning of the loss of life in the Vietnam War.

This chapter explains how the Marshall-Brennan Project started, how it works, and how it has expanded. In conclusion, some ideas will be presented in terms of lessons that can be applied to other civic learning projects aimed at engaging youth in the process of citizenship.

HOW THE PROJECT STARTED

The seeds were planted when Professor Jamin Raskin was approached by a group of high school students in Montgomery County, Maryland, who felt their freedom of speech was being violated.[4] The students were part of a communications academy at their school and helped run a talk show on a local cable television station affiliated with the school. They had put together a program called "Shades of Gray," during which they interviewed experts on difficult topics of the day. One particular show included a debate on gay marriage, and the students had lined up two speakers in favor of gay marriage and two against. The program was taped and approved by the teacher who oversaw it.

However, the show was pulled before it aired. School officials deemed the show "inappropriate" for the station. When the students contacted him, Professor Raskin wanted to go straight to court, but the wise students asked for help in first exhausting all remedies at the school district level before pursuing litigation. In the end, the students appealed to the school board and won a reversal of the superintendent's censorship of the program. The program aired six times instead of the one or two times it would have aired had the superintendent allowed it in the first place.

This experience led Professor Raskin to the realization that high school students, especially urban students, are not taught about the Constitution and how it affects their daily lives. When he compared the resources he had (access to overly enthusiastic law students) to this need for constitutional literacy, the idea for the project was born.

The project started in the fall of 1999 with 20 idealistic law students who volunteered to teach in 8 public schools in the District of Columbia and Montgomery County. There was no formal academic component and no formal curriculum in that year; students met with Professor Raskin on an informal basis every week to share ideas and process their experiences. Today, the project recruits 60 law students from American University's Washington College of Law and Howard University's School of Law to teach in fifteen public and public charter schools in the District of Columbia, and the academic component includes a mandatory orientation to theory and pedagogy, as well as a yearlong mandatory weekly seminar.

HOW THE PROJECT WORKS

The model is a simple one: harnessing the surplus energy of relatively privileged law students into teaching disenfranchised public high school students about the Constitution through cases that directly affect them, and motivating young people to become civic actors. As one recent moot court competitor, a tenth grader named Ade Ademisoye from Washington, D.C., said, "[T]his program . . . inspired me to improve my civic involvement and helped me understand the government. Now I can't wait to vote."

Each January, we invite some 800 first- and second-year law students to information sessions about teaching in the public schools. The application process to become a Marshall-Brennan Fellow is rigorous. It includes attendance at one of the information sessions; guest teaching an existing course; submission of a lengthy application, which includes a letter indicating interest in serving as a Marshall-Brennan Fellow, a resumé, a self-evaluation of the guest teaching visit, an evaluation from the Fellows whose class was visited; and an interview with the project's associate director. The Fellows are ultimately selected by a committee of faculty who know all of the applicants and are able to contribute their personal insights in addition to the other elements of the application process.

Considering the other responsibilities most law students have, the time commitment is a significant one. Many senior lawyers and law professors are shocked that so many students choose to make such a significant commitment of time and energy. However, many law students have found that the commitment is more than worthwhile. Julie Yeagle, a law student teaching at a public charter high school in the District of Columbia wrote in one of her final papers for the academic seminar accompanying the Fellows' fieldwork, "I've never regretted my decision to teach in the Marshall-Brennan program. Just the opposite: I come home each day raving about how much I enjoy it."

Other students find that teaching helps them contextualize what they are learning in their law school classrooms. Zahida Virani, who teaches at one of the lower-performing D.C. public schools, explains, "To anyone who asks about my law school experience, I explain that the best law school feeling, by far, is walking into a classroom filled with teenagers and being able to teach them about their rights. I always look forward to teaching, even when I am tired and stressed about my classes."

Professor Raskin created *We the Students: Supreme Court Cases About Students* as the first text for the project. The Fellows now also teach from *Youth Justice in America*, an additional text that I coauthored with Jamie Raskin and Andrew Ferguson, a public defender in the District of Columbia, which we developed specifically for young people involved in or familiar with law enforcement. The District of Columbia Public Schools (DCPS) recognizes both courses, Constitutional Law and Youth Justice, as elective courses. Credits earned from these courses are applied to the Carnegie units required for graduation.

Both curricula were specifically designed to speak to students in their own language. *We the Students* is a compilation of all the Supreme Court cases about the rights of students in public schools. The casebook covers freedom of speech, freedom of student press, students' freedom to practice religion, freedom from government establishing religion, freedom from unreasonable searches and seizures in schools, racial segregation and desegregation, and the rights of students with disabilities.

The first edition of *We the Students* was printed in 2000. We quickly realized that the students we teach are most interested in issues relating to crime and punishment since these issues permeate their daily lives. So we began to collect cases, stories, and pictures, and in 2005 *Youth Justice* was printed. An immediate success, *Youth Justice* includes cases and hypotheticals around the history of the juvenile justice system, different theories of crime and punishment, the proper role of police in a society that values personal liberty as well as safety, juveniles' right to counsel, the abolishment of the death penalty for juvenile offenders, felon disenfranchisement, and other topics of interest. *Youth Justice* is a relevant tool to reach youth in detention. During the 2006–07 academic year, I led a spin-off group of Fellows and others to teach at the Youth Services Center, the District of Columbia's detention facility for youth awaiting adjudication of criminal charges against them. The youth have made comments like, "Can I take this book to court with me so the judge knows I have rights?" and "I want to learn. Please teach me."

Julie Yeagle explains the impact of the Youth Justice curriculum on her students at a residential charter school in the District of Columbia: "I'm so pleased that my students have the opportunity to learn their rights under the Constitution and to learn how to become effective democratic citizens. I think that both lessons are indispensable to a student's social and intellectual growth." Matthew Wright, another Fellow who taught Youth Justice at a public high school in D.C. feels that his students actually changed their personalities and became more assertive and confident after learning about their rights. According to Matt, the curriculum "in a very real way empowered [my students] and instilled a sense of pride and awareness of their rights in this society."

The project heavily focuses on practical, experiential opportunities. These include visiting the U.S. Supreme Court to take tours and hear oral arguments; participating in debates; interacting with guest speakers such as attorneys, police officers, and law professors; participating in financial literacy workshops; meeting judges and watching trials in state and federal courts; and competing in various moot court competitions (in-class, citywide, and national).

Moot court, or appellate argument, is a critical component of the experience for both the high school and law students. The project produces new local and national problems each year, and every Fellow teaches the substance of the problem, as well the art of oral advocacy. Past moot court topics have included, among others, free speech rights of students on the Internet, the equal protection rights of same-sex couples in schools, and students' Fourth Amendment rights in the parking lot of the school. The project hosts a fall citywide competition at the federal courthouse, and the finals are judged by a panel of U.S. District Court judges. The spring local and national competitions are held at the Washington College of Law and rounds are judged by Washington attorneys, law professors, and judges.

Because the students spend an entire day with their teachers during the competitions, the Fellows find that they are able to bond with their students and with their students' family members and friends throughout the moot court process in meaningful ways. In fact, some students, like eleventh grader David Mikel, decide to become attorneys because of the moot court experience. David said, "I think I know more about my rights than ever before, and now I think I want to study law."

Through moot court and regular presence in the schools, Fellows clearly develop meaningful relationships with their students. Julie Yeagle opined,

> I know how critical it is to provide enthusiastic support for high school students because for many of them, this is the last chance to live a somewhat structured life, to receive positive reinforcement, and to grapple with complex intellectual issues. Sometimes the students are apathetic and irreverent, but more often than not, they're engaged and excited by the fact that they now know a thing or two about the system of law. The other day, for example, a student said, "That would be so tight if I was in court" and was like, "You need to suppress my statements because the interrogating officer didn't read me the Miranda warnings!" How can such a statement not force a wide, toothy grin?

CREATING A NETWORK: NATIONAL EXPANSION

We quickly realized that this model of spreading constitutional literacy through law students worked, and it could work all over the country. Once we felt certain our infrastructure and track record of success were strong enough, we felt prepared to respond to requests for more information and to help set up chapters around the country.

I recently had the opportunity to travel to Jackson, Mississippi, to help start up a Marshall-Brennan chapter through the Mississippi College School of Law, one of two law schools in the state. Sitting around a table of public school students and teachers, the director of the ACLU of Mississippi, two privileged private school students, a veteran Mississippi organizer, and three young attorneys who represent youth, it struck me that this project touches so many people. Little did we know that our message of constitutional literacy would strike a chord with so many. Sheila Bedi, a civil rights lawyer, codirector of the Mississippi Youth Justice Project, and a Marshall-Brennan alumna, explains how she and other volunteer lawyers kept juvenile offenders who were deprived of education after the disaster distracted with the *Youth Justice* curriculum: "We used the book . . . during Hurricane Katrina, when they would have otherwise been locked in their cells for 24 hours a day, and they found it fascinating and asked that it become part of their regular curriculum."

With chapters at Sandra Day O'Connor Law School of Arizona State University, Northeastern University Law School, Rutgers University Law School, University of Oregon Law School, and the University of Pennsylvania Law School, as well as the Washington, D.C., partner Howard University Law School, the project has experienced tremendous growth in seven short years. Each chapter has a different flavor in terms of how it is run. Some chapters are very large (in the District of Columbia, we have 60 students each year, whereas the Rutgers program carefully selects 8–10 Marshall-Brennan Fellows each year).

The common thread is a commitment to empowering underserved public high school students to learn about the Constitution from energetic, motivated law students. Because the mostly urban schools in which the law students teach across the country are predominantly low-income schools attended by students of color, we are considered a "pipeline project." As such, we have had an opportunity to create relationships with the American Bar Association's diversity efforts, the Council on Legal Education Opportunity, the Law School Admissions Council, and many other groups dedicated to diversifying the legal profession.

The Marshall-Brennan chapters have evolved in different ways. However, they all have five basic elements in common.[5]

First, the Marshall-Brennan Constitutional Literacy Project requires a partnership with the local school system and/or individual local schools. Because of these close partnerships, law students become full participants in the teaching process: they run their own classrooms, assign grades, attend parent-teacher conferences, and manage all aspects of their classrooms, including dealing with discipline and attendance issues.

Second, the Marshall-Brennan Project requires an academic component and supervision. At American University, the Marshall-Brennan Fellows do not receive academic credit for their teaching, but they earn credit in a mandatory two-semester seminar that we offer as a three-hour class in the fall and a two- or three-hour option in the spring. Generally, the seminar covers both pedagogical issues (how to teach effectively, how to motivate students) as well as substantive law (the cases and material in the textbook).

Third, the Marshall-Brennan Project enriches the high school experience for students in many different ways (i.e., not just creating mentoring or sporadic teaching).

Fourth, to be successful, a Marshall-Brennan Project chapter requires a commitment of staff and resources. Without the support of the law school dean and faculty, it would be difficult to foster the kind of environment necessary for a chapter to be successful.

Finally, affiliation with the Marshall-Brennan Constitutional Literacy Project is a straightforward process that simply involves regular communication with headquarters. To foster communication with headquarters and between chapters, a summit is held in Washington, D.C., each year.

CONCLUSIONS AND OUTCOMES

Mary Beth Tinker, plaintiff in the leading case establishing students' First Amendment rights, often calls young people to action by explaining how, "throughout history, social change has always been initiated by children."[6] While our role as teachers is to remain as objective as possible and to avoid giving direct legal advice to our students in terms of how to protest against unfair school policies, we have always maintained that the law and reality on the streets are often in conflict. Mary Beth, who has worked as a union organizer and a pediatric nurse, is so committed to our cause that she often speaks at our moot court banquets, annual summit, and end-of-year student awards ceremony. In fact, she has become our best ambassador. As she travels around the country in her spare time speaking to youth about her case and about the First Amendment, she promotes our model as one that works—young adults teaching and learning from young people.

In terms of measurable outcomes, students involved in the project complete pre- and posttests designed to assess their basic civic literacy. In the short term, students demonstrate increased knowledge of their constitutional rights and responsibilities and also develop key lawyering and advocacy skills. These include improved reading, writing, and oral advocacy skills, and an ability to read and digest case law. When we talk to the students at the annual awards ceremony in May, attended by hundreds of high school students from around the city, they also report numerous sociocultural benefits. These include mentoring from law students and lawyers; positive reinforcement that leads to improved confidence and greater engagement in an academic setting; development of life skills such as advocating for oneself as a consumer and citizen; increased community involvement, through volunteerism, working at election polls, and other outlets; greater awareness of college and graduate school options; and referral services for legal and other needs for themselves and their families. We encourage the students to stay in school, as data have indicated a correlation between civic involvement (specifically, voting) and high school dropout rates.[7]

One area we wish to better track is the long-term effects for high school students. While we have anecdotal evidence that such effects can be profound, we have not collected formal data, mostly because it is almost impossible to acquire contact information for high school students once they have left their schools.

The benefits for Marshall-Brennan Fellows include improvement of managerial and organizational skills; active participation to effectuate positive change in their adopted community; improved confidence and public speaking skills; networking opportunities with affiliated lawyers, judges, and education officials; higher achievement in law school and greater confidence with the bar exam; and an opportunity to escape the law school "bubble."

We are very proud of our Marshall-Brennan alums. In the last eight years, alums have gone on to work as senior staff in the District of Columbia government, public school teachers, public defenders, nonprofit founders, and staff attorneys for various education-related advocacy groups. They have become law school professors and elected officials in their community. Many of them keep in close touch with us. Many, including me, feel forever changed by the students they taught and the sense of empowerment engendered by teaching the Constitution.

For example, Nisha Thakker, a former Fellow and 2007 graduate of Washington College of Law, was so moved by her experience teaching at a D.C. residential charter school and at the Youth Services Center that she cofounded a national nonprofit called the National Youth Justice Alliance (NYJA) to create and support partnerships between lawyer and law student volunteers and local detention facilities around the country. NYJA's goal is to use the Constitution to empower youth in fighting against recidivism.

Also, Eric Lerum, a former Fellow, 2003 graduate of Washington College of Law, and current chief of staff to the deputy mayor for education in the District of Columbia, explains, "My Marshall-Brennan teaching experience shaped my career path. After my year as a Fellow . . . I saw how much of a need there was for lawyers to work to improve the state of education in DC. . . . This program set me on the path to work in education reform."

QUESTIONS FOR DISCUSSION

1. In what ways do young people learn about their rights? What issues of rights are currently contested by young people in your communities? How have these struggles changed over time?

2. In your experience, in what ways do social workers build on or fail to engage with the idea that young people hold rights?

3. One of our unspoken "certainties" in social work practice may be that there is a widespread lack of concern for disenfranchised high school students. Yet Ahranjani describes harnessing the "surplus energy of relatively privileged students" to teach students about the Constitution. Are there sources of "surplus energy" in your communities that might be harnessed for work with children and youth? Where are they? What issues might engage them in partnership with young people?

4. In what ways do social workers in your communities engage with those who provide legal advocacy or education for young people? What supports exist for such collaborations? What resistances might arise?

5. What implicit or explicit assumptions about young people are built into the Marshall-Brennan Constitutional Literacy Project? What lessons does this project offer you for your own work with young people?

NOTES

1. See "The Future of the First Admendment: What America's High School Students Think About Their Freedoms: Executive Summary and Key Findings," accessed January 16, 2007, at http://firstamendment.jideas.org/.

2. "Consolidated Appropriations Act, 2005," Dec. 8, 2004; 118 Stat. 2809, 3344–45 (Pub. L. 108–447, Sec. 111, Div. J).

3. The American Bar Association produced a report dubbed the "pipeline report" in 2005 documenting the lack of racial and ethnic diversity in the legal profession and in law school. The report is available at http://www.abanet.org/op/pipelineconf/PipelinePostReport.pdf.

4. From an excerpt in J. B. Raskin, *We the students: Supreme Court cases for and about students* (2003): 64–66.

5. Adapted from a basic list of requirements produced by Professor Stephen Wermiel.

6. I have had the opportunity to hear Mary Beth, a great supporter of the Marshall-Brennan Project since its inception, speak many times. She reiterated this sentiment at an ACLU conference on students' rights held in Washington, D.C., in October 2006.

7. National Conference on Citizenship, *Broken engagement: America's civic health index report,* September 18, 2006. Accessed January 16, 2007, at http://www.ncoc.net/conferences/2006civichealth.pdf.

"You May Even Be the President
of the United States One Day"?

Challenging Commercialized Feminism in
Programming for Girls in Juvenile Justice

Sara Goodkind

SEVENTEEN

"You may even be the president of the United States one day." These are words
of encouragement from a staff member at a residential program for adolescent
girls in a midwestern U.S. city. She offered these words to describe how she tells
the girls that they can be whoever or achieve whatever they want, as long as they
work hard and believe in themselves. Similarly, another staff member said of
the girls, "If they dream it, then they can achieve it—they just have to believe."
These quotations illustrate underlying assumptions about the girls and the world
in which they live that are central to the program's intervention efforts. In this
chapter, I suggest that these beliefs represent a gendered version of the American dream that is promoted by such programs and enabled by a commercialized version of feminism resulting from the intersection of neoliberalism and
feminist ideals.[1] Feminism, in its many forms, has always endorsed both individual and societal change, grappling with contradictions between the two and
endeavoring to make them complementary. Commercialized feminism, however, represents a triumph of the focus on the individual. Thus, commercialized
feminism represents a neoliberal "abduction" of a long-standing feminist tradition of at least partial focus on transforming society, which has the potential
to lead to the disempowerment of the girls and women that it claims to assist.

This chapter builds on my previous examination of the application of commercialized feminism in two residential programs for adolescent girls. It is based on ethnographic research designed to explore the effects of a 1992 federal initiative to provide "gender-specific" programming to girls in juvenile justice, with the goal of understanding the beliefs and assumptions about gender, race / ethnicity, class, sexuality, and age held by program designers, staff, and the girls themselves. One program studied was a "traditional" juvenile justice placement, a group home for adjudicated girls run by a faith-based nonprofit organization, which I call "Kidstown." The second was a community-based residential program for young women, which I call "New Choices," considered to be a model program because of its explicit feminist orientation. It works with homeless girls who have been diverted, sentenced to community-based placement, or are generally considered "at risk."

In this work, I found that the commercialized feminist approach risks reproducing hierarchies of gender, race / ethnicity, class, and sexuality by convincing girls to blame themselves for their failure to transcend such hierarchies (Goodkind 2008). In this chapter, I review this argument, applying a critical lens to four key aspects of commercialized feminism suggested most often in discussions with program staff and girls about program goals—independence, self-esteem, choice, and empowerment. I thus conclude that feminist ideals based on freeing women from dependence on and control by men have been transformed in the neoliberal U.S. context into imperatives for emotional and economic independence from virtually all sources of support. These imperatives are not evenly applied to all women but rather are focused on those who are young and poor and disproportionately women of color. I then present suggestions for challenging the application of commercialized feminism in such contexts, focusing on specific policy and practice changes that can enable programs for girls to meet the girls' individual needs while simultaneously working to change the unjust social structures which have contributed to their program involvement. In order to better understand the current context, I begin by providing background information on the juvenile justice system's history of reinforcing gendered expectations of girls.

GENDERED EXPECTATIONS IN THE JUVENILE JUSTICE SYSTEM

Girls' involvement with the justice system has recently been the focus of increased popular and academic attention. Specifically, much has been made in the media and popular press of a supposed increase in violence among girls. In fact, girls' arrests for simple assault did increase over 300% from 1983 to 2003 (Snyder and Sigmund 2006). Yet a recent analysis by Steffensmeier and colleagues (2005) comparing official arrest rates with girls' (and boys') self-reports of violent behavior and victimization surveys demonstrates that girls' behavior has not changed. Thus, they conclude that changing system policies and practices, rather than changes in girls' behavior, are responsible for the increase in girls' arrests for violent offenses. They cite three trends to support their conclusions: (1) increasingly broad definitions of youth violence, as police arrest youth for more minor types of offenses, which girls engage in at rates more similar to those of boys (as opposed to more serious violent acts in which boys are much more likely than girls to engage); (2) greater policing of domestic and relational violence, as police are increasingly called to intervene in cases of violent behavior in "private" situations and between intimates, again arenas in which girls are relatively more likely to engage in violence than in "public" settings; and (3) changing attitudes toward girls—in particular, families and society in general have become less tolerant of adolescent girls (Steffensmeier et al. 2005).

Such increased attention to girls contributed to an initiative in the 1992 reauthorization of the Juvenile Justice and Delinquency Prevention Act (JJDPA) for juvenile justice programs to provide gender-specific services. Such services were defined in the JJDPA as services that address the "unique" needs of the individual recipient's gender and have been interpreted to mean services designed specifically for girls. As a result of this initiative, government agencies such as the Office of Juvenile Justice and Delinquency Prevention have commissioned programmatic manuals to give service providers guidance about what "gender-specific" services should encompass (e.g., Greene, Peters, and Associates, 1998). While helpful in highlighting the differential experiences of and pathways by which girls and boys become involved with the justice system, much of this work has employed essentialized notions of gender, which has served to reify socially constructed differences between girls and boys and neglect racial/ethnic, class-based, and sexual diversity among girls and women (Goodkind 2005). In particular, it is often based on analyses of experiences of white, middle-class girls, despite the fact that girls in the juvenile justice system are overwhelmingly working class and disproportionately African American and Latina. Further, these programmatic guides frequently presume that girls' rising rates of justice system involvement are the result of changes in their behavior and thus focus primarily on individual-level solutions, rather than offering suggestions for addressing the systemic problems that have contributed to this rise (Goodkind 2005).

I became interested in the implementation of this federal initiative as a result of my involvement in evaluating an art therapy program at a residential facility that was instituted as part of its "gender-specific" programming for girls. Specifically, I was troubled by the evaluation findings, which suggested that despite the good intentions of the staff, their gender-specific treatment was serving to reinforce oppressive gender expectations, thus perpetuating the juvenile justice system's history of policing sexuality and maintaining gender conformity (see Goodkind and Miller 2006). For over 100 years, the juvenile court and residential institutions together have policed and controlled the sexuality and gender conformity of girls, most of them low income and many of them girls of color (Abrams 2000; Chesney-Lind 1997).

The juvenile justice system was founded by social workers and child advocates whose goal was to protect young people from the harsh treatment of the criminal court and adult institutions. With the invention of the juvenile court at then end of the nineteenth century, a special category of offenses that apply only to youth was created. Known as "status offenses," such offenses are not criminal acts when committed by adults; instead, they are actionable behaviors only if undertaken by minors. Today they include truancy from school, incorrigibility, running away from home, and underage drinking; in the past "immorality" and sexual offenses were also included. At the inception of the juvenile court, most girls were charged with "immorality" or "waywardness" (Chesney-Lind 1997). Immorality meant sexual intercourse, evidence of which was often provided through mandatory gynecological exams (Abrams and Curran 2000). "Waywardness" (now termed incorrigibility or ungovernability) meant being beyond parental control; such charges have been frequently filed by parents, particularly those concerned about their inability to control the sexual behavior of their daughters. Throughout the first half of the twentieth century, girls were twice as likely as boys to be sentenced to out-of-home placements by the juvenile court (Chesney-Lind 1997), and status offenses accounted for the vast majority of commitments of young women to state institutions (Odem and Schlossman 1991).

With the development of the juvenile court came the creation of increasing numbers of residential institutions for youth, whereas previously most were incarcerated with adults (Stein 1995). There was a particularly large growth in reformatories for girls between 1910 and 1920 (Abrams and Curran 2000). Such institutions were focused on education, treatment, and helping the youth "fit in" to society. Much of this was done through work—girls and boys were given tasks and instruction associated with female and male roles, respectively, and their "likely vocations" (Stein 1995). Girls were prepared for motherhood and domesticity and were instructed in cooking, sewing, and cleaning (Abrams and Curran 2000). In this way, girls were "resocialized" to adhere to traditional gender expectations and were institutionalized until they reached "marriageable" age (Abrams 2000). Yet, despite the significant role of the juvenile justice system in constructing and perpetuating gendered, raced, and classed expectations of the girls involved with it, most scholarly work on juvenile justice has focused on boys.

THE NEOLIBERAL ABDUCTION OF FEMINISM

The concept of commercialized feminism (Kelly, Burton, and Regan 1996) is fundamental to understanding the goals and effects of the programs I studied.[2] Commercialized feminism has resulted from the intersection of neoliberal ideas about the individual with feminist ideals. Kelly and colleagues (1996) highlight the rise in therapy, self-improvement, and self-help marketed toward women, all of which draw on feminism for their theory, methods, and goals, as indicative of the ascendance of this concept. The aim of such therapeutic efforts, however, is not to help women as a group, but rather to encourage individual women to transform themselves. Thus, Kelly and colleagues (1996) explain how what began as a problem with men and patriarchal power has been transformed into a problem with women, who, it is suggested by the self-help industry, are not confident and independent enough to utilize the power now available to them to achieve what they want and need. Commercialized feminism instructs each woman that it is she who needs changing and that she is responsible for enacting this change.

Scholarship on "therapeutic governance" and the neoliberal state furthers this analysis by revealing that the individual change promoted by commercialized feminism is intended not only to create personal fulfillment but also to produce citizens who will regulate and govern themselves. Under neoliberalism, "citizens shape their lives through the choices they make. . . . Government works by 'acting at a distance' upon these choices, forging a symmetry between the attempts of individuals to make life worthwhile for themselves, and the political values of consumption, profitability, efficiency, and social order" (Rose 1990:10). So, what is sold to women to raise their self-esteem will also turn them into the kind of citizens needed for the successful operation of the neoliberal state. While illuminating in this regard, most literature on the therapeutic state does not directly address feminism (e.g., Furedi 2004; Nolan 1998; Rose 1990).

Examples of neoliberalism's effects on feminism are not difficult to identify, however. Representative of such effects is Gloria Steinem's *Revolution from Within: A Book of Self-Esteem* (1992), heralded on its back cover as "the ultimate self-help book." This version of self-help, according to Steinem, inverts the feminist adage "the personal is political" to "the political is personal." Steinem argues that women's lack of self-esteem has contributed to a stalling of the feminist movement. Cruikshank, in a critique of Steinem and the societal obsession with self-esteem, explains why this framing is problematic, as "thousands of people now define their lack of power and control in the world as attributable to their lack of self-esteem" (1996:247). Cruikshank further notes how even many critiques of the self-esteem movement miss the extent to which "the self is . . . not personal but the product of power relations" (248). In other words, the self is created through social interaction. Thus, an examination of residential programs for girls must consider the types of selves that they seek to create.

Similarly to Kelly and colleagues, Hochschild analyzes the growing popularity of advice books for women, which she believes is indicative of an "abduction" of feminism. She suggests that through such books, "feminism may be 'escaping from the cage' of a social movement to buttress a commercial spirit of intimate life that was originally separate from and indeed alien to it" (2003:13). This "abduction" of feminism is based on ideals of an independent, low-needs self; Hochschild explains, "The ideal self doesn't need much, and what it does need it can get for itself" (24). Weiner (2007) demonstrates that under neoliberalism a "good citizen" is conflated with an "ideal worker," both of whom, Hochschild's work implies, have the same characteristics as an "ideal self"—independent and personally responsible for one's own well-being and happiness. For this reason, self-help approaches can be appealing to those working in social service and penal settings, as they absolve staff of much of their responsibility by placing it on the clients or inmates and present opportunities to create "ideal selves" among those who have been labeled as less than ideal.

FROM DELINQUENT DAUGHTERS TO INDEPENDENT MOTHERS: COMMERCIALIZED FEMINISM IN PRACTICE

This section briefly reviews arguments I have made elsewhere about the application of commercialized feminism in the two programs I examined and the types of "ideal selves" they seek to develop (see Goodkind 2007a, 2007b, and in press for evidence for and elaboration of these arguments). These programs, like past juvenile justice and residential treatment programs for girls, are shaped by, and in turn help to shape, prevailing societal and cultural ideas about gender, race/ethnicity, class, sexuality, and age. Similar to past programs, they attempt to prepare the girls to be "good" mothers and push them to conform to social norms around female sexuality, which define girls' agentic sexuality as inherently "bad" and dangerous. Thus, the programs both illustrate and reinforce societal and cultural beliefs about and ideals for motherhood and sexuality. However, some of these ideals seem to have changed. While girls are still expected to learn to adhere to middle-class norms of behavior, the programs are no longer preparing them for domesticity and dependence on men. Instead, these girls are supposed to become "independent" mothers who both can and should solely and completely provide for their children's emotional and material needs (Goodkind 2007a). I contend that this altered vision of a "successful woman" has been enabled by commercialized feminism. Thus, feminist ideals based on freeing women from dependence on and control by men have been transformed in the neoliberal U.S. context into imperatives for emotional and economic independence from virtually all sources of support. These imperatives are not evenly applied to all girls and women, however; instead, they are focused on those who are young and poor and disproportionately girls and women of color.

Motherhood is an important lens for understanding intersections of gender with race / ethnicity, class, sexuality, and age in the lives of the girls in these programs. It is one of the primary means through which staff and the girls themselves understand these intersections, and it provides a basis for elaborating on their perceptions of their "problems" and needs. Girls in the juvenile justice system have long been viewed, and, I found, continue to be viewed, as "delinquent daughters" (Goodkind 2007a; Odem 1995). This is not so surprising, considering that the juvenile justice system is based on the idea of *parens patriae*, or state as parent. If the court itself serves as the paternalistic father, though, the institutions to which girls are sent serve a maternalistic function. Many staff describe their work as that of a mother and speak of the young women as their daughters (Goodkind 2007b). Further, a number of staff feel that the girls' problems are due in large part to inadequate mothering, and thus that many are searching for what one called "mother love." They recognize too that girls often treat them like their mothers. Likewise, girls refer to staff, particularly those that they like, as motherlike in many ways; as one said, "I consider most of the staff is like my mother or aunt. . . . To me, they are like moms or second moms."

While some staff and girls seem to enjoy this mother / daughter dynamic, many also recognize that it is fraught with tension. Staff, in particular, are caught between the standards of professionalism and the definition of "good" mothering (Goodkind 2007b). On the one hand, it is their job, and therefore they must act "professional" and maintain appropriate boundaries. On the other hand, the job they have is, in many ways, that of mothering the girls, and a "good" mother is not professional, detached, and operating according to a manual, but rather warm, caring, and directed by love and instinct. Their job, in many ways, is the ultimate example of what Hochschild (1983) calls "emotional labor." As one staff member explained, the girls "need to feel and know that they are loved and cared for. That is the reason why we are here. That's the reason why we have a job." Many girls feel, similarly to staff, that their problems stem from abandonment by or conflicts with their own mothers. Thus, the fact that someone has to be paid to "mother" them often serves to reinforce notions of themselves as unimportant and worthless.

Based on the widespread assumption among staff that the girls will be mothers themselves one day (if they are not already), a main goal of staff and programs is to prevent these "delinquent daughters" from becoming what Douglas and Michaels (2004) call "delinquent mothers." Many staff and girls view motherhood as a potential source of valuation, noting the motivation it can provide to get or keep one's life on track and the value placed on women as mothers. However, it is also an important arena for the internalization and reproduction of their devaluation. Specifically, the girls' abandonment by their own mothers—the one person you should be able to count on, their sense that someone must now be paid to mother them, and their recognition that becoming mothers themselves may be one of the only ways they can gain value all contribute to feelings of worthlessness. I argue that idealized notions of motherhood, which include the centrality of motherhood in women's lives as well as the expectation that mothers can perfectly and solitarily meet all of their children's needs, shape these understandings and processes (Chodorow and Contratto 1992; Douglas and Michaels 2004; Hays 1996). Based on these idealized notions of motherhood, the assumption that the girls will be mothers, as well as on stereotypes about African American women as strong and independent and African American men as unreliable, the staff ultimately view their task as that of transforming the girls from "delinquent daughters" to "independent mothers" (Goodkind 2007a).

I have found that commercialized feminism holds particular appeal in these efforts for many reasons (see Goodkind 2008). First, it fits well with the mandate of the juvenile justice system to focus on the *individual* needs of the young people involved with it. Second, it allows programs for girls to appear to comply with the federal initiative to provide gender-specific services within juvenile justice in a "feminist" manner, while remaining consistent with assumptions about gender difference and failing to challenge prevailing social hierarchies of gender, race/ethnicity, class, sexuality, and age. Third, it is congruent with stereotypes of African American girls and women—who are vastly overrepresented in juvenile justice and among girls characterized as "at risk"—as strong and independent. Finally, it presents a resolution to the ubiquitous tension within both social work and juvenile justice between helping and control because it allows the programs to serve both functions simultaneously.

In demonstrating the application of commercialized feminism in these programs, I have focused on four key concepts suggested most often in discussions with staff and girls about the program goals—independence, self-esteem, choice, and empowerment—which were also evident in the stated goals in the programs' written materials and in my observations at the two programs (Goodkind 2008). In the remainder of this section, I briefly introduce these concepts and demonstrate the tensions, contradictions, and challenges they present.

Independence

Independence was the program goal expressed most often, by both staff and girls. From what they said, it was apparent that independence, as defined by the programs, entails the ability to provide for oneself both materially *and* emotionally. Further, while independence was expressed as a goal for all of the girls, it became clear that some staff members' beliefs about independence are racialized. For example, some African American girls discussed how a white girl was receiving preferential treatment from the white director of one of the programs. One girl said, "That doesn't make sense for her not to get in trouble because she is weak and I and other people are strong." The director's behavior thus reflected stereotypical assumptions about African American girls and women as strong and independent (Collins 1992; Davis 1981), assuming the sole white girl to be weaker and in need of help.

This uneven promotion of independence raises questions about whether it is a desirable or achievable goal. While dependence is considered a "normal" period of children's lives, prevailing stereotypes of working-class women of color and women in prison as "welfare queens," "crack hos," and "criminally dependent" suggest that dependence may not simply be a normal period of these particular girls' lives, but rather a potential or actual "problem" (see McCorkel 2004). The self-help and advice books for women critiqued by Kelly and colleagues (1996) and Hochschild (2003) for their commercialization of feminism often feature this concept; in particular, many focus on the problem of "codependency"; further, "dependent personality disorder" is defined as a psychological disorder in the *DSM-IV*. In addition, most middle-class youth are not expected to be independent at such a young age. In fact, they frequently experience this transition much more gradually and are never truly "independent." Propp, Ortega, and NewHeart argue that "being independent or self-sufficient is a myth at best and unhealthy at worst. Research indicates that people who experience life without support are prone to loneliness, depression, and other poor mental health outcomes" (2003:262).

Self-esteem

Staff and girls cited self-esteem as a prerequisite for the achievement of independence. Given the extensive devaluation they have experienced, it is difficult to argue with the benefits of the girls viewing themselves positively. However, I question the implication that high self-esteem is the primary solution to their problems, which suggests that such problems are caused by their low self-esteem, and that to become "successful" they must simply value and love themselves. There is evidence, however, that low self-esteem is not a principal cause of delinquent behavior (or of school failure, teenage pregnancy, welfare "dependency," and substance abuse; Schwalbe 1991). Further, recent research problematizes the link between self-esteem and improved adult outcomes. Mahaffy found that self-esteem during adolescence did not have a significant effect on girls' adult educational status, occupational status, and earnings when controlling for background factors, and concluded that "The focus on self-esteem as a solution to many of society's ills diverts our attention from more insidious influences such as social structural arrangements that not only deflate self-esteem but also make participation in the labor force difficult for both women and men" (2004:324).

Thus, the focus on self-esteem is troubling because, similar to the other individualizing strategies utilized by the programs, it leads the girls to believe that *they* are the cause of their problems, if not the problems themselves. It suggests that they would not be there if they had high self-esteem, and that the solution is to "fix" themselves by improving their self-esteem. That girls and women value themselves and not depend on men to prove their worth has been an important feminist goal. However, such individual valuation is intended to be facilitated by a context of broader social change in which the social value of all women is enhanced. Further, the promotion of self-esteem absolves staff of responsibility for "fixing" the girls; Cruikshank explains, "Self-esteem is a technology of citizenship and self-government for evaluation and acting upon our selves so that the police, the guards and the doctors do not have to" (1996:234).

Choice

Low self-esteem was frequently viewed by staff as the cause of girls' poor choices, which are often seen as the most immediate causes of their program involvement. Choice is an important aspect of the lives of neoliberal individuals. The range of choices available in capitalist societies, enabled by competition, distinguishes them from socialist ones. Choice is also a feminist ideal, specifically represented by the idea that women should be able to choose to involve themselves with men but not be forced by these men or by economic need to do so. However, a focus on choice obscures the contributions of structural and relational factors to the girls' problems. It suggests that the solution is for the girls to make better choices, which implies that their futures, like their pasts, are also unaffected by forces outside themselves. This demonstrates a conflation of freedom and agency—the idea that one's power to act means one's actions are unaffected by relational and structural restrictions (Hannah-Moffat 2004). Thus, emphasizing "the power of positive choices" (an oft-cited motto at New Choices) risks leading the girls to believe that they have only themselves to blame if they face obstacles or fail in some way to achieve their goals.

Empowerment

Empowerment can be thought of as an umbrella under which the specific aims of achieving independence, raising self-esteem, and promoting positive choices are collected. Empowerment originated as a process by which disenfranchised individuals and groups raise their consciousness, develop self-efficacy, and work together for broader change (Freire 1973; Gutierrez 1990); however, it is currently implemented in many social service agencies in a very individualized way (Gutierrez, DeLois, and GlenMayer 1995; Young 1994). Specifically, Gutierrez and colleagues found that "practitioners generally think of empowerment in terms of a psychological process of change" (1995:541). These programs similarly operationalize empowerment by focusing on the individual development of confidence and independence rather than on consciousness-raising around structural oppression and the development of a collective effort to change these conditions. Such an approach may ultimately be disempowering, especially if a limited range of options and opportunities means that making "good" choices is not enough or not possible. Gutierrez (1990) defines the goal of empowerment as the creation of power for individuals and groups. Yet, I found that it was often employed in these programs as a means to shift the responsibility for transforming the girls from the programs and staff onto the girls themselves.

For example, a staff member at New Choices explained how she told the girls that discrimination should not limit them: "'You can be the president of a company, you may even be the president of the United States one day.' . . . I told them, 'You have to know that you are not limited because you are a woman and because you are black. You turn that around and make that work to your advantage. . . . You can be anything you want, but you have to believe it.'" According to this staff member, she told the girls only what she believes and has tried herself. However, she neglects the fact that many have had very different experiences (e.g., parental abandonment, incarceration, homelessness, drug addiction). Thus, she discounts the effects of such obstacles when she states that they now have all the necessary support.

As I have argued elsewhere (Goodkind 2008), empowerment, independence, self-esteem, and choice all appear on the surface to be positive goals. Who would not want the girls to feel a sense of power over their own lives, in their relationships, and in the larger world, to be able to care for themselves without having to rely on people who will harm or take advantage of them, to feel a greater sense of self-worth, and to be informed and skilled enough to make "good" choices? I question, however, whether such goals are achievable through efforts focused solely on changing them. Is it reasonable to think that they will be able to be solely and entirely responsible for the economic and emotional support of themselves and their children when we do not have such expectations of girls who have come from more privileged backgrounds? Is it fair to expect these girls to be able to value themselves when the world around them devalues them so completely? Does it make sense to fault them for their "poor" choices when their options and opportunities are so limited?

I do not mean to criticize these two particular programs; they did not invent commercialized feminism but rather represent just one location where it is employed. It is attractive in such contexts because it allows the programs to focus on the individual needs of the girls as mandated by the juvenile justice system, to seem to be both "feminist" and "gender-specific," to accord with stereotypes of African American women as strong and independent, and to resolve the omnipresent tension between helping and control in social work and juvenile justice interventions by doing both at the same time. Yet, the employment of commercialized feminism legitimates the increased involvement of girls in juvenile justice by highlighting the helping aspect of the programs and deemphasizing that of control because it focuses on self-control rather than staff control of the girls. In addition, by focusing on changing the girls, it does not challenge existing social hierarchies of gender, race / ethnicity, class, sexuality, and age or the oppressive social conditions that play a role in the development of these hierarchies. Rather, it helps to make girls more complacent about their social positions because it tells them they are responsible for where they find themselves, a message made more effective by the "feminist" face it puts on the perpetuation of injustice and inequality (Goodkind 2008).

CHALLENGING COMMERCIALIZED FEMINISM: SUGGESTIONS FOR CHANGE

In the remainder of this chapter, I present policy and practice suggestions for girls' programming as an alternative to the commercialized feminist approach. An overarching theme is that intervention and change must be focused on multiple levels. I advocate involving girls in broader change efforts, as well as in program design, evaluation, and improvement. Programs focused solely on individual change suggest to girls that *they* are the problem, whereas involving girls in broader change efforts helps them make connections between their individual circumstances and the inequities of the world around them and demonstrates to them that they can be part of the solution. By doing this, we can create new definitions of and methods for promoting self-esteem, positive choices, and empowerment. In addition, we should abandon the goal of independence, instead recognizing that everyone is interdependent, and assist girls in working toward this goal by providing guidance in the development of supportive relationships with each other and those around them. These change efforts call on us to challenge the frameworks through which we understand girls' lives, for example those of victims / agents and dependence / independence. We must also challenge the conflation of freedom and agency inherent in commercialized feminism, which implies that because a girl has the capacity to make choices, she has the power to make choices without external constraints. Further, we need to address the sources of such external constraints, find ways to help girls and their families sooner and in less restrictive settings, and promote an integrated approach to practice.

Take action at multiple levels. Programs for girls should address change at the individual, social network, community, and institutional levels (Ms. Foundation for Women 2001). Support at the individual level should be just one component of a broadly targeted intervention effort. We must conceive of the girls' environments much more broadly, looking beyond the family to consider changing girls' broader social networks, communities, and societal institutions. Attention to multiple levels is congruent with the work of social work scholars who have merged the traditional social work focus on person-in-environment with a framework that incorporates power, history, and change, in what has been termed "structural" or "critical" social work. From this perspective, need and structural location are understood as connected, and solutions are focused on both immediate assistance and longer-term institutional and structural change (Figueira-McDonough 1998; Mullaly 1997). As Michelle Fine warns: "Supply-side interventions—changing people but not structures or opportunities— which leave unchallenged an inhospitable and discriminating economy and a thoroughly impoverished child care/social welfare system are inherently doomed to failure. When such programs fail, the social reading is that "these young women can't be helped" (1988:48). In other words, enabling girls to make better choices will be ineffective and impossible if we do not also try to increase the options and opportunities available to them.

Parents of these girls also need support, particularly those with low incomes. Many of the reasons that the mothers of the girls in these two program were "not there" for their daughters were directly related to structural and institutional barriers and constraints, such as a lack of decent, affordable child care, jobs that do not pay a living wage, limited effective and affordable substance abuse treatment programs, inadequate schools, and racial discrimination. There are similar structural and institutional impediments to fathers' involvement in their daughters' lives. Many low-income parents and their children need improved economic, material, and social service assistance. We also need to challenge and change prevailing cultural expectations of mothers and ideals about motherhood, which suggest that mothers are solely and entirely responsible for their children. Similarly, fatherhood should be viewed as entailing more than just economic support (Ruddick 1990). Further, we need to think about children not so much as a personal responsibility but as a societal one. The perpetuation of structural inequality requires ideological rationalization for it, and the resulting cultural ideologies then enable structural oppression and disadvantage to be blamed on those experiencing it.

Another system-level change needed is the creation and enhancement of ways to help girls sooner and in less restrictive and punitive settings. It also entails dealing with the disincentive for the use of alternative and less restrictive programs created by the privatization of juvenile justice services in many areas throughout the country, including the one on which I focused. Thus, it is important to find ways to challenge the perverse incentives for locking up youth (and adults) provided by privatization of the system. Obviously, this cannot and should not be accomplished solely within the juvenile justice system. Rather, there is a need to rely on and integrate with other social service systems, particularly for help in dealing with trauma and other mental health needs. Dohrn (2004) suggests abolishing status offenses and releasing almost all girls from secure confinement. This involves not just institutional change (developing alternative programs), but cultural/ideological change as well. Particularly important are efforts to combat racial and class prejudices and biases; we need to consider how we perceive youth in general as problems and particular categories of youth as especially problematic. Thus, social, cultural, and psychological devaluation are intertwined and require both individual and societal-level intervention.

Involve girls in these broader change efforts. Involvement of girls in the change process is a powerful way to demonstrate to them that they are not the problem—the message they get from programs that focus solely on fixing them. Such efforts can promote critical consciousness among the girls, their families, and professional helpers, raising awareness of the structural roots of the challenges they face. In addition, involvement in broader change efforts can provide a source of value and meaning in girls' lives. Girls can be powerful advocates for themselves. Listening to them talk about their challenges and the injustices they have faced is much more moving than reading a report that "objectively" attempts to document such experiences. In a conference planned by an advisory committee of which I was a member, girls were essential participants on the planning committee. They kept us focused on what was important and relevant to girls and pushed us to promote meaningful change. At the conference itself, there was a girls' "speak out" during which any girl could come to the microphone to share her experiences and opinions with the group. Many participants cited this as the best part of the conference. Clearly, girls can be effective change agents, and many are eager and ready to get involved. It is up to adults to see them as part of the solution rather than merely part of the problem.

Involve girls in program design, implementation, and evaluation. Within programs, such involvement offers an additional means to empower girls in the collective action sense of the word. Three young women from a secure juvenile justice facility who were participating on the advisory committee of which I was a member were inspired by their involvement with the committee to design and conduct a survey of girls in their program. Their report provided useful, important information to the committee, as well as to staff, administration, and girls at their facility. Involving girls in these ways gives them a stake in the program and a sense of ownership that can contribute to more willing participation and greater program benefits. The girls at Kidstown and New Choices demonstrated not only their ability to undertake such endeavors, but also their enthusiasm for them, through their engaged focus group participation.

Peer education provides another way to involve girls actively in program implementation. New Choices has had great success with peer education programs. As staff member there explained, "I think when the girls really have a chance to be part of planning the workshops and they are engaged in them that makes a difference. When there is a product, when they see the fruits of the labor, I think that's also really important." "Empowerment" can be more than a buzzword for programs that require girls to "fix" themselves; instead, it can and should guide efforts that provide meaningful opportunities for involvement in program, community, and societal change.

Promote mutual support and respect among girls and staff. We cannot expect girls to value themselves without trying to demonstrate in programs that they are valued by staff and society more broadly. Programs can acknowledge girls' societal devaluation and engage them in efforts to change it. Further, staff can model respect among each other and toward the girls, thus encouraging a climate of respect and support among the girls. Respect and support can be nurtured through caring relationships. Many girls at both Kidstown and New Choices noted that what had made a difference for them was not the programs as much as the support of specific staff members. A number of staff articulated this belief as well. For example, a staff member at New Choices said: "I think more than honestly actual types of programming, that it's the type of people that are implementing them that makes the biggest difference. If you have someone who is able to really bond with the girls and reach them, they could be counting beans and it wouldn't matter. Do you know what I mean? It's the kind of conversations that come out of those interactions and the way they are treated in those sessions that makes a huge difference, I think."

Thus, it takes much more than simply designing a good program to engage girls. Most important, according to many staff and girls, are the staff running the program.[3] This highlights the necessity of valuing and respecting staff and the care work in which they are engaged. Staff, like the parents for whom they are substituting, need support. This includes creating opportunities for direct service staff members to have input in the design and implementation of the programs and to provide them with recognition of and assistance with the challenges of their jobs. It also includes structural issues such an ensuring that staff earn a livable wage and have a voice in the decision-making processes that affect their jobs. As with girls, involving direct service staff in program design can help to give them more ownership. Similarly, greater treatment responsibility shows that they are respected and viewed as competent and important. Direct service staff can be particularly effective as they are often the ones that best know and understand the girls. This is corroborated by girls' comments, which reveal that girls often feel closest to such staff and find them most helpful.

Think critically about the frameworks through which we understand the girls, their problems, and their possibilities. Too often, ideas about gender and policies and practices affecting women and girls have been informed by dichotomous, us-and-them thinking. Dichotomous thinking about gender perpetuates gender inequity by reinforcing notions of essential gender differences and reproduces other inequalities by ignoring important differences within gender categories (Goodkind 2005). With regard to girls in the juvenile justice system, we need to challenge and deconstruct false dichotomies. We should not think of the girls as victims in need of assistance, unable to help themselves or participate in efforts to change the world around them; nor should we believe that because of their agency they can make choices without external constraints and overcome every obstacle. Viewing girls as either powerful or powerless neglects the importance of the contexts of their lives. Thus, consciousness raising can provide awareness of these constraints at the same time that service recipients and providers can collectively consider possibilities for and work toward dismantling some of these barriers.

Similarly, we must challenge binary constructions of these girls as dependent or independent. Leonard (1997) reframes the dependent/independent dichotomy as a matter of being dependent on the state (what is currently thought of as dependent) or being dependent on the market (what is termed independent). Based on the idea that all are dependent on others for survival, Leonard advocates mutual interdependence as a goal. He argues that this notion is "at the root of a reinvented idea of welfare" and "crucial to a politics of collective resistance and . . . community action" (1997:159). While some amount of self-reliance may be a good thing for girls in programs such as these, then, it is essential to recognize our interdependence and offer girls guidance in the development of supportive relationships with each other and those around them.

My final recommendation is to adopt an interpretivist/constructivist epistemology, which contrasts with the positivist approach that informs much U.S. social work and justice system scholarship and intervention. Such an approach recognizes that identities (race/ethnicity, class, gender, sexuality), labels (victim, delinquent), and problems (delinquency, crime) are all socially constructed. It also acknowledges and embraces social science as normative (Ife 1999) and highlights the fact that knowledge is a tool that can be (and is) used to promote certain positions or achieve certain objectives. When we embrace the normative function of knowledge, we can begin to think about the perspectives and interests of those generating knowledge and to examine their motives and intentions. Thus, as we consider alternatives to commercialized feminism as frameworks for programming for girls in the juvenile justice system, we must challenge the oft-cited justification for attention to girls—that of their rising rates of involvement. Instead, we need to recognize that what has changed is society's response to them and make the case that they deserve attention because of their inherent value as people, not as threats to public safety or as potential (or actual) mothers.

QUESTIONS FOR DISCUSSION

1. Have you ever been told, "You can be anything you want to be"? Who said this? In what context? To what ends? What is your reaction to having (or lacking) this experience?

2. From your standpoint, how does social work engage or fail to engage with feminist concepts in practice with young women? How is this "feminist approach" conceived? How are ideas about "womanhood" in social work practice inflected with notions of race, class, or sexual orientation?

3. Goodkind challenges us to think critically about some of the most widespread and popular "certainties" in work with youth—including the need to place strong emphasis on "building self-esteem." In your experience, how is the concept of "building self-esteem" implemented in practice? What strengths and limitations do you observe in the ways that these concepts are deployed?

4. What does it mean to challenge "dichotomous thinking"? Do you observe such thinking in your own life and work? What strategies could be used to challenge this example of "dichotomous thinking" in practice?

5. In her recommendations for practice, what assumptions does Goodkind make about young women in the juvenile justice system? How does her vision alter your sense of the possibilities for action with young women in the juvenile justice system?

NOTES

1. See Goodkind (2008) for further elaboration of and evidence for this argument.

2. I did not begin my study of the programs with the idea of examining their application of commercialized feminism. Rather, this notion emerged through my analyses of them. However, I begin by introducing this concept for the sake of conceptual and analytic clarity. For a more detailed definition and illustration, see Goodkind (in press).

3. In this vein, Martinson (1974) suggests that the success of a group psychotherapy intervention with incarcerated girls, documented by a study that found that those receiving this treatment were likely to spend less time (than a control group) reincarcerated in the future (Truax, Wargo, and Silber 1966), was due more to the therapists' interaction styles and personal qualities than to the therapy itself.

REFERENCES

Abrams, L. S. (2000). Guardians of virtue: The social reformers and the "girl problem," 1890–1920. *Social Service Review 74:* 436–52.

Abrams, L. S., and L. Curran. (2000). Wayward girls and virtuous women: Social workers and female juvenile delinquency in the Progressive Era. *Affilia 15:* 49–64.

Chesney-Lind, M. (1997). *The female offender: Girls, women, and crime.* Thousand Oaks, Calif.: Sage Publications.

Chodorow, N., and S. Contratto. (1992). The fantasy of the perfect mother. In B. Thorne and M. Yalom, eds., *Rethinking the family: Some feminist questions,* 191–214. Boston: Northeastern University Press.

Collins, P. H. (1992). Black women and motherhood. In B. Thorne and M. Yalom, eds., *Rethinking the family: Some feminist questions,* 215–45. Boston: Northeastern University Press.

Cruikshank, B. 1996. Revolutions within: Self-government and self-esteem. In A. Barry, T. Osbourne, and N. Rose, eds., *Foucault and political reason,* 231–51. Chicago: University of Chicago Press.

Davis, A. (1981). *Women, race and class.* New York: Vintage Books.

Dohrn, B. (2004). All Ellas: Girls locked up. *Feminist Studies 30:* 302–24.

Douglas, S. J., and M. W. Michaels. (2004). *The mommy myth: The idealization of motherhood and how it has undermined women.* New York: Free Press.

Figueira-McDonough, J. (1998). Toward a gender-integrated knowledge in social work. In J. Figueira-McDonough, F. E. Netting, and A. Nichols-Casebolt, eds., *The role of gender in practice knowledge: Claiming half the human experience.* New York: Garland.

Fine, M. (1988). Sexuality, schooling, and adolescent females: The missing discourse of desire. *Harvard Educational Review 58:* 29–53.

Freire, P. (1973). *Education for critical consciousness.* New York: Seabury Press.

Furedi, F. (2004). *Therapy culture: Cultivating vulnerability in an uncertain age.* London: Routledge.

Goodkind, S. (2000). The rehabilitation and control of young women in the U.S. juvenile justice system: An evaluation of an art therapy program. Ms.

———. 2005. Gender-specific services in the juvenile justice system: A critical examination. *Affilia 20:* 52–70.

———. (2007a). From delinquent daughters to independent mothers: A critical analysis of the promotion of independence in programs for African American girls. Ms.

———. (2007b). Program staff as (other)mothers: Navigating the tension between providing care and being "professional." Ms.

———. (2008). "You can be anything you want, but you have to believe it": Commercialized feminism in gender-specific programs for girls. *Signs 34* (1).

Goodkind, S., and D. L. Miller. (2006). A widening of the net of social control? "Gender-specific" treatment for young women in the U.S. juvenile justice system. *Journal of Progressive Human Services 17:* 45–70.

Greene, Peters, and Associates. 1998. *Guiding principles for promising female programming: An inventory of best practices.* Washington, D.C.: Office of Juvenile Justice and Delinquency Prevention.

Gutierrez, L. M. (1990). Working with women of color: An empowerment perspective. *Social Work 35:* 149–53.

Gutierrez, L. M., K. A. DeLois, and L. GlenMaye. (1995). Understanding empowerment practice: Building on practitioner-based knowledge. *Families in Society 76:* 534–42.

Hannah-Moffat, K. (2004). Losing ground: Gendered knowledges, parole risk, and responsibility. *Social Politics 11:* 363–85.

Hays, S. (1996). *The cultural contradictions of motherhood.* New Haven: Yale University Press.

Hochschild, A. R. 1983. *The managed heart: Commercialization of human feeling.* Berkeley: University of California Press.

———. 2003. *The commercialization of intimate life: Notes from home and work.* Berkeley: University of California Press.

Ife, J. 1999. Postmodernism, critical theory and social work. In B. Pease and J. Fook, eds., *Transforming social work practice: Postmodern critical perspectives,* 211–23. London: Routledge.

Kelly, L., S. Burton, and L. Regan. (1996). Beyond victim or survivor: Sexual violence, identity and feminist theory and practice. In L. Adkins and V. Merchant, eds., *Sexualizing the social: Power and the organization of sexuality,* 77–101. London: Macmillan.

Leonard, P. (1997). *Postmodern welfare: Reconstructing an emancipatory project.* London: Sage.

McCorkel, J. A. (2004). Criminally dependent? Gender, punishment, and the rhetoric of welfare reform. *Social Politics 11:* 386–410.

Mahaffy, K. A. (2004). Girls' low self-esteem: How is it related to later socioeconomic achievements? *Gender and Society 18:* 309–27.

Martinson, R. 1974. What works? Questions and answers about prison reform. *Public Interest 35:* 22–54.

Ms. Foundation for Women. (2001). *The new girls' movement: Implications for youth programs.* New York: Ms. Foundation for Women.

Mullaly, B. (1997). *Structural social work: Ideology, theory, and practice.* New York: Oxford University Press.

Nolan, J. L., Jr. (1998). *The therapeutic state: Justifying government at century's end*. New York: New York University Press.

Odem, M. E. (1995). *Delinquent daughters: Protecting and policing adolescent female sexuality in the United States, 1885–1920*. Chapel Hill: University of North Carolina Press.

Odem, M. E., and S. Schlossman. (1991). Guardians of virtue: The juvenile court and female delinquency in early 20th century Los Angeles. *Crime and Delinquency 37:* 186–203.

Propp, J., D. M. Ortega, and F. M. NewHeart. (2003). Independence or interdependence: Rethinking the transition from "Ward of the Court" to adulthood. *Families in Society 84:* 259–66.

Rose, N. (1990). *Governing the soul: The shaping of the private self*. London: Routledge.

Ruddick, S. (1990). Thinking about fathers. In M. Hirsch and E. F. Keller, eds., *Conflicts in feminism*, 222–33. New York: Routledge.

Schwalbe, M. L. (1991). Review of *The Social Importance of Self-Esteem*. *Social Forces 69:* 974–75.

Snyder, H., and M. Sigmund. (2006). *Juvenile offenders and victims: 2006 national report*. Washington, D.C.: U.S. Department of Justice, Office of Justice Programs, OJJDP.

Steffensmeier, D., J. Schwartz, H. Zhong, and J. Ackerman. (2005). An assessment of recent trends in girls' violence using diverse longitudinal sources: Is the gender gap closing? *Criminology 43:* 355–405.

Stein, J. A. (1995). *Residential treatment of adolescents and children: Issues, principles, and techniques*. Chicago: Nelson-Hall.

Steinem, G. (1992). *Revolution from within: A book of self-esteem*. Boston: Little, Brown.

Truax, C. B, D. G. Wargo, and L. D. Silber. (1966). Effects of group psychotherapy with high accurate empathy and nonpossessive warmth upon female institutionalized delinquents. *Journal of Abnormal Psychology 71:* 267–74.

Weiner, E. (2007). *Market dreams: Gender, class and capitalism in the Czech Republic*. Ann Arbor: University of Michigan Press.

Young, I. M. (1994). Punishment, treatment, empowerment: Three approaches to policy for pregnant addicts. *Feminist Studies 20:* 33–57.

Youth Uprising | **EIGHTEEN**

Gritty Youth Leadership Development and
Communal Transformation

Jennifer Tilton

Olis Simmons, executive director of Youth Uprising, talks a lot about "picking up kids." One afternoon she rolled up on a group of young black men at a bus stop in East Oakland. "Don't you know there's a truancy sweep? Are you not in school? Do you need a job?" She finally convinced them to get in her car and drove them to the center. "When we get there, the kids say, 'This is a trick. This is a truancy center. Do you work for the DAs office? Is this a cult?'" She laughed, "No baby it's not." A youth staff member gave them a tour, through the youth-run café, the computer center, the "Moroccan ghetto" living room with its plush couches and overstuffed chairs, the state of the art music and video production facilities, the health and mental health center, the dance studio and outdoor amphitheater where YU has hosted dance battles for 600 kids. Youth sometimes see the facilities and meet Olis, in a suit and Mercedes, and they think, "It's a trap. It's not possible in my world."

The beauty of the Youth Uprising Center is most immediately striking, its inviting glass-lined façade and café patio with wrought-iron chairs and tables. Large block letters in the cement—Knowledge of Self—lead you toward the wide-open glass-front doors. Inside, textured steel, dark gray marble, and polished cement surfaces contrast with brightly colored walls, gold and purple words embedded in the floor read "inspire," "focus," and "skills." Loretha "Lil' Scrappy" Henry, a petite 16-year-old African American young woman with braids and a quick smile, explained that the space conveys respect for young people, "It's giving us the chance to be part of something that is beautiful, that has resources. It feels like we're kind of important. We don't have to beg for it. It's just there for us."

The open spaces of Youth Uprising stand in stark contrast to Castlemont High School next door, surrounded by a tall wrought-iron fence. The fence was built to protect students from the dangerous streets of East Oakland, but in the eyes of many students, it made the school feel like a prison. The Youth Uprising Center offers an alternate vision best articulated by a youth-designed public art poster. Grey and black silhouettes fill the background, while a young black man with short dreads stares thoughtfully at the viewer. "From chillin' at the corner, to building a corner store. We're lifting our community."

Youth Uprising describes their philosophy as "gritty youth leadership development." YU aims to "develop and harness the leadership of young people to create healthy and economically robust communities." They use youth music, language, and culture—which are often framed as the source of neighborhood problems—as the tools for personal and community transformation. This philosophy is embedded in the space and culture of the center because young people led both the initial campaign and the planning process for the youth center.

YOUTH RESEARCH AND ACTION

Youth Together, a multiracial, antiviolence organizing collaborative, began the research and organizing campaign that led to the creation of Youth Uprising. The mid-1990s saw yearly race riots between Black and Latino students at Castlemont, as the Latino population of East Oakland grew rapidly. Youth Together did conflict resolution with students who were involved in the fights, but they also organized students to identify the cycle of violence and to learn shared histories of racial and class oppression. Based on a survey of 1,200 students, parents, and staff, students identified three root causes of violence that they could address: inadequate educational resources, insufficient employment opportunities, and a lack of things to do. Students then developed a detailed proposal and business plan, met with policy makers, canvassed door-to-door, spoke at churches, and collected 900 signatures to build support for their vision a youth center that would address the root causes of violence in the community. Margaretta Lin, former director of Youth Together, emphasized how impressive this kind of youth activism was to local policy makers, "We're used to young people talking about their problems, but not talking about research-based solutions." At a kick-off conference for the One Land One People Collaborative, young people presented their plan to policy makers and asked for signed commitments of support on huge posters placed on the school walls.

The research and activism of these students caught the attention of County Supervisor Mary King, who identified an abandoned county-owned building next to Castlemont as the ideal site for a youth center. The history of this building illustrates the broader historical pattern of disinvestments in East Oakland, a working-class black and Latino neighborhood sometimes described as Oakland's "killing fields." Originally built as a Safeway grocery store, the store closed in the 1970s as a familiar pattern of white flight and economic disinvestments made East Oakland a majority black neighborhood with few thriving businesses, escalating unemployment, and problems with drugs, crime, and violence. The county purchased the building for a neighborhood health center, but county workers were so afraid of the neighborhood that they bricked over the windows and retreated into a maze of offices hidden from the street. The health center closed due to county budget cuts in the 1990s, and this county building sat abandoned, like many others in the neighborhood, until construction began on Youth Uprising in 2002.

As the county took on an increased role in planning the rehabilitation of *their* building, youth participation declined. Even though Youth Together staff continued to participate in planning meetings, the initial county plan was more adult-centered. The plan for a multiservice youth center included performance arts programs, but it prioritized office space for case management, mental health, and educational services. To Olis Simmons, a partnership with the probation department highlighted the absence of young people in the planning process. "What young person is going to say, I want juvenile probation here so I can get a pee test?"

When the county asked Olis Simmons to take over the planning process, she created a new youth planning team and gave them a blank slate. "We have a building and want to build a youth center." She emphasized that people in traditional positions of power need "to know that they don't know" and need "to get out of the way." Rashawna Clay, one of the original youth planning team members, explained that young people know best what will attract, motivate, and retain other people. "We know what we like. We know how the culture is. *We* made it popular."

They recruited kids from the best youth development organizations to represent diverse constituencies across race, class, and sexuality, including youth both in and out of school and on probation. Over the course of two years, 38 young people participated in the youth planning council and were paid a stipend of $500 every six months for their participation. As Olis Simmons explained, "It's a simple reality that if you want poor kids to participate you have to hear that they need money."

The separate youth planning board, instead of placing youth members on an adult board, was vital for establishing an atmosphere where youth believed that their voice really counted. But just as important was investing this youth board with real power to make decisions about architectural design, programming, and staffing. Daniel Mora, "a founder," explained, "Talk is cheap, but they always emphasized that we were going to be the lead. You all tell us the name, the color, the hours, what programs. And it was really happening. What we said was being put out there." Several of the original youth planning team members also emphasized importance of adult engagement and mentoring. The planning process worked best when adults established clear goals, held the group accountable to the rules and agendas that youth themselves had created, and made sure policy makers implemented the plans.

The youth planning team transformed the center in many ways. They established the center's ground rules, expanded the emphasis on music production and media arts, added the dance studio, and developed many of the public art and design components in the building (like the DJ booth attached to the front desk) that establish the distinctive cultural feel of the space.

The youth team also pushed the county to rethink their understanding of transitions to adulthood. The county had planned on serving high school–aged youth, but the youth team "kept telling us that 18 is not a magic number where suddenly you wake up and are an adult." Slowly the plan shifted to include youth and young adults, ages 13–24. In practice, the center has become even more flexible. One youth staff member told me about a 10-year-old boy that members brought to the center. "If he's old enough to be smoking weed, he's old enough to be at the center." Listening to young people has prepared YU to deal with the reality of both accelerated and delayed paths to adulthood.

Finally, youth leadership shaped the way the center conceptualized safety and security. Youth insisted that the center open onto Macarthur Boulevard with a welcoming façade that would draw people in from the street, and they refused suggestions to fence the entrance or retreat from the high-traffic, and often dangerous, thoroughfare. Many youth planners originally opposed having any visible security force at all because, as Daniel Mora explained, "security would bring tension like it always does" in a neighborhood where many young people feel harassed by the police. Finally, at the insistence of adult staff, the youth planners agreed to hire the Fruit of Islam, whose guards were unarmed, did not wear uniforms, and had moral authority in the neighborhood.

Empowering youth in this planning process did not mean that youth took charge of all aspects of planning. Adults retained control over core functions of fund raising and budgeting, and in some cases, like security, adult planners pushed youth to compromise in ways that would address everyone's concerns. Some youth council plans, like late-night and weekend hours, have not yet been fully implemented because of budget and staffing constraints.

Youth Uprising opened in May 2005. Since opening, it has expanded its staff from 8 to 27, and YU has become a separate nonprofit instead of a county program. YU constantly experiments with new programs, adding dance battles, field trips, and a new basketball team at members' requests. The center has almost 2,500 members, and roughly 350 young people come to YU everyday. Some members come every day to take modeling, music and video production, and hip-hop dance classes, while others spend months hanging out in the café before ever even becoming members.

BUILDING THE EMERALD CITY: YOUTH CULTURE AND STREET CREDIBILITY

"I saw it like Oz, like the Emerald City," Preshona Gonzalez, the 23-year-old youth leader of the Rise-Up Team, said, describing her first visit to YU. "Everything I've ever had in me, it's here, the poetry, dancing. You can make movies. It was a mini-Hollywood. Here you create your fame."

Youth Uprising works hard to stay on the cutting edge of local hip-hop culture, cultivating close relationships with artists like E-40, Little John, Too Short, and Mistah F.A.B, and hosting *VIBE Magazine* and music video shoots at the center. Pictures of these hip-hop icons, often with their arms around staff members, are prominently displayed on the YU website and My Space site. Ultimately Olis Simmons would like to make YU "the unquestioned cultural mecca of the Bay. Nobody comes to town and they don't come here."

Olis Simmons herself is not a huge hip-hop fan, "I don't know who these people are. I don't care. But it doesn't matter. I run a youth center. My job is to navigate their world and to attach to it. Rappers have a responsibility to give back. *And* the kids care." Monique, a young adult worker at the Corner Café, described how amazing it is for young people to see their idols supporting them. "They're too juiced to be juiced. Stuff like this comes once in a lifetime. Mistah F.A.B. and Too Short come here like they're members."

Olis Simmons explained the importance of youth culture in their philosophy of gritty youth leadership development, "We go onto the street to get kids. . . . They are not blank slates. They have a language, social norms, a whole set of things that are true and comfortable to them. I have to meet them and show them that those skills are transferable. There's nothing wrong with who they are. What's wrong is the choices they've got. Sure they've got to know how to cross-over culturally, but we make it clear it's not because their culture was wrong."

Youth leadership has enabled YU to incorporate the newest hip-hop trends—like turf dancing and dance battles—that generate real street credibility and excitement among young people who wouldn't normally consider going to traditional youth programs. Monique was skeptical when her friend recommended that she come to the center. She thought that she was too old for a youth center—"My Boys and Girls club days are over." But once she came, she found "it was more real, more mature. It fit the interest of the youth. You want to go party? Come up here." Competing with the streets, Olis Simmons said, means that Youth Uprising has "to be more sexy, more lucrative, fun and attractive to succeed" (Johnson 2005).

Youth Uprising uses their connections with youth culture and hip-hop cultural icons to develop economic opportunities for young people. Youth develop skills in music and video production and then can make money selling beats, teaching classes, or doing tech work at events. Instead of simply preparing low-income youth for low-wage service work, YU emphasizes the importance of encouraging young people to find and follow their passions. As Evette Brandon, YU's development director, explained, "You can make a living doing what you love." Allati, a 16-year-old artist and member of the Rise-Up Team, gets most of her business doing sketches and illustrations through Youth Uprising. For Nahh Dahh, a young adult member and part-time music production teacher, YU helped him refine his skills and connect to people in the music industry. Nahh Dahh's My Space page illustrates the way YU uses hip-hop language and culture to compete with the street and to develop positive outcomes for youth. Celebrating his ability to make money with his art, Nahh Dahh posted a picture of himself holding a pile of money with the caption, "Dis all off music pimp n—i sold 100 n 2 weeks—i aint even post on [the] block."

But their focus on hip-hop culture also brings some of the contradictions of contemporary youth culture into Youth Uprising. A few Oakland activists have repeatedly attacked the center for promoting "hyphy culture," a local form of hip-hop, which they define as inherently pathological. The center has wrestled with how to harness the excitement that big hip-hop events generate, while avoiding the chaos that sometimes follows. After several entirely peaceful dance battles, YU struggled with fights on surrounding streets as 400–600 kids left the dance battles, and they decided to suspend their most popular event. Young people missed the dance battles that made YU "really crank" and brought "youth busting through the doors." "I want that back sooo bad," Lil' Scrappy said.

As staff considers how to bring back the popular battles, YU has begun to think more strategically about how to use its close relationships with local hip-hop artists to do consciousness raising and real violence prevention within hip-hop culture. They recently joined in a partnership with the documentary *Hip-Hop: Beyond Beats and Rhymes* to promote dialogue about violence and misogyny in hip-hop. Ultimately, the challenge, Olis Simmons explained, is to "get the industry to push content that's in the interest of young people."

Finally, despite YU's origins in a multiracial youth organizing effort, YU attracts primarily black youth in a neighborhood that is now half Latino. Although the staff is multiracial, grounding the center in hip-hop culture—which remains marked as "authentically" black despite its appeal across racial lines— may reproduce racial divides in Oakland's youth culture and social networks.

CREATING A CULTURE OF YOUTH LEADERSHIP

"When people walk into center, they are greeted by young people. Get food from café, the staff is young people. Tours—given by young people. With young people seeing other young people taking adult responsibility, it's something different than being greeted by adults," explained Danny Mora, former youth staff member.

In my visits to Youth Uprising, I didn't meet any gang members, high school dropouts, or kids on probation. I met Porshia, who planned to go to Stanford, and talked with Danny, who had recently come back from making a film in Chiapas. I met Allati, who could talk for hours about the importance of shading in her portraits, and saw Chris's quiet excitement as he carried his new suit and talked about his new job as a culture keeper. I began to doubt that these were the "hard to reach kids" that Youth Uprising claimed to attract. When I talked to members about why they came to the center, they often said, "It keeps me off the streets" or "out of trouble." I saw the memorials to lost friends and families worn on their bodies, like the white hoodie covered with pictures of a young boy with the words "Stuntin' in Heaven" and "Brother Love." But it wasn't until I talked in more depth with staff and young people that I heard the harsher stories of some of their lives—the months spent homeless or without lights and heat, the death of parents, the lost friends, the years spent dealing drugs or gang-banging on East Oakland streets.

Youth Uprising is one of the rare youth centers where all young people are welcome to be leaders and staff members. "Our young people are everything. Some are on probation. Some are 4.0 students. They could be all at once," explained Jackie Johnson, one of the original youth planning team members, who became performance arts coordinator before leaving for college.

Olis Simmons met one youth staff person when he jumped up from behind her car and said, "Give me your purse." She told him that he was going to get shot doing that and walked away. He started coming to the center and decided he wanted to work in the café. Olis's first thought was "Lord Jesus," but "he works hard, has great customer service skills, and is academically gifted, though he doesn't want people to know that. So things are often not as they appear."

Youth Uprising makes a fundamental commitment not to define youth by their problems or their histories. Staff members generally avoid using bureaucratic labels and funding classifications, like at-risk, violence-prevention, and anger-management, in their daily practice. In a staff meeting, when one employee used the phrase "Measure Y kids," referring to a violence prevention fund, the development director interrupted to say, "There's no population in the building that should be identified as Measure Y kids. It's an important part of the culture of our organization not to call anyone 'the bad kids.'"

Instead of providing services that respond to the problems young people present, Youth Uprising gives young people opportunities to lead and to give back to their community. Olis Simmons explained that their model is "to hire the kids and train them to help other kids. When you look at the composition of our team, it's much more aligned with the streets. We do what Starbucks or Cisco Systems does for senior vice presidents. We take people that we believe are talented and invest in them."

Many youth staff talked about how much this opportunity to help transform their community meant to them. "I love helping people rise up," said Porshia Butler, a 17-year-old member of the youth leadership team. And Jackie Johnson emphasized the importance of leadership in helping young people transform their own lives, "Especially if you're going through things yourself, helping other people really helps you heal."

In a neighborhood with few legitimate economic opportunities and many families struggling economically, Youth Uprising's focus on creating economic opportunities for youth is particularly important. "They're giving out jobs like crazy," Cyrioco Robinson, a 19-year-old member of YU, told me as we sat outside in the sun one fall day. Thirteen out of 27 full time staff positions are within the membership age group. This includes receptionists, intake workers, janitors, and the youth leadership team. Youth and young adult staff operate the Corner Café in partnership with Global Exchange Partnership. YU also writes stipends for youth into every grant, so many other young people work in part-time positions as dance or music production teachers and program assistants. When one member asked to teach a dance class, the program director sat down with her to develop a contract, a class description, and an outreach plan. As Jackie Johnson said, "That's a real leadership position, not tokenizing youth." Youth Uprising has developed a cascading mentoring model of leadership development and staffing. Youth do not run all aspects of Youth Uprising and are not necessarily consulted with for most administrative or even all programmatic decisions. But youth recognize the existence of an informal career path within the center, from volunteering, to working on stipend, to positions of higher responsibility on the paid staff. Similar to Ben Kirshner's (2006) model of "apprenticeship learning," adults mentor youth staff, while youth staff themselves mentor members. One young adult staff person explained that she wanted "to move up in the company. There are a lot of smart people here, and they don't hold onto all that knowledge."

Youth and young adult staff model a range of paths for youth members, according to Luke Breckimeiser, a youth staff member now in college. Some dropped out of high school, some have a GED or attend junior college, others went straight to a four-year college. "No matter where you are, there's a way up for you. The example is way more effective than preaching." Lil' Scrappy agreed on the importance of seeing youth and young adult staff. Because many staff themselves are young, "they know what we're going through."

Preshona, 23-year-old youth leader of the Rise-Up Team, described her struggles with self-confidence as she took on new leadership roles in the center and dealt with "a lot of drama" in her personal life. She has been inspired both by the older staff and by the young people she works with. "When you work here it's almost a mentorship, they're developing our own self-confidence and skills. When I look around and I see Omana, and I see she been through it, and she's a strong woman. I think that's what I've looked for all my life, strong female role models that have been through it too, but they're a strong queen."

The Rise-Up Team acts as the primary liaison between adult staff and members and is central to creating a culture of youth leadership. Five youth and one young adult are paid to work 20 hours a week at the center. They monitor the open spaces, enforce the ground rules, host bimonthly house meetings, and serve as the primary youth spokespeople with media, community groups, and visitors. A full-time adult staff person does intensive leadership development work with the Rise-Up Team, holding staff meetings twice a week and meeting one-on-one with each team member once a week.

Youth leadership in the planning and operations of YU has helped to establish a culture of youth ownership at the center. Rashawna explained that youth feel the center is theirs. "This is your house. You make sure the center is safe. You don't disrespect the center. Adults can't do nothing with the center. Adults can't even walk through the center without permission." For a lot of youth, she explained, "there is nowhere else you can say this is my space."

One afternoon, I heard Pharoah, an 18-year-old Rise-Up Team member, directly challenge an adult staff member for not consulting with the youth leadership team before shutting down programming for a special event. The adult staff member apologized, and later at the Rise-Up Team meeting, youth leaders decided to set up a meeting with him to improve communication. Preshona reiterated a phrase I heard repeatedly from youth staff whenever there were conflicts with adult staff or teachers, "This is *our* culture."

Lil' Scrappy is also on the Rise-Up Team and dreams of becoming the director of Youth Uprising someday. She's the only female member of one of Oakland's professional turf dancing crews, and one day she dropped in to watch part of a dance class during her break. The adult teacher, from a partner organization, yelled at Lil' Scrappy to leave because too many people had been coming in and out of the room. Lil' Scrappy was angry because she felt the teacher didn't understand the culture of the center. She explained, YU "is a space where youth come in and chill and hang out." She thought the teacher should have put up a sign if she didn't want people coming in to watch, so she talked to two adult staff people about the conflict. All the staff came, and they met with the teacher. Lil' Scrappy explained that Youth Uprising was nothing like school, where "adults say this is the rule" and what a young person has to say doesn't matter. "It made me feel good that all the staff were there to back me up."

Both of these conflicts emphasized young people's sense of ownership at YU, but also the ongoing work that is required to maintain a culture of youth leadership. Adults often come to work with a practice and set of assumptions about how adults interact with young people, so Youth Uprising has to work with adult staff just as consistently as it works with young people to create the space for youth ownership and leadership at the center.

YU recently extended their leadership development approach to security. After 18 months, Youth Uprising ended its contract with the Nation of Islam and decided to transform the idea of security. They hired some older members and neighborhood adults with significant street-credibility to become culture keepers. Olis Simmons explained, "If you're a security person, kids'll clip you. They'll fight. But if you do it in a culture where they love you, even the very grimy kids. It's not about security, it's about culture." In many ways, this plan marks a return to the original vision of the youth council, which didn't want a formal security force. Some of the people they hired have criminal records, while others have never been in trouble. One was the founder of a notorious clique that used to rob people in the neighborhood but grew out of it. Olis said, "Who better to keep the culture? By turning the leaders, you turn the group. It's taking risks with people like that that gives you standing."

Chris, a 23-year-old, soft-spoken young man, was a member who became one of the new hires, proudly carrying his new gray suit over his shoulder. "When they told me what the job was I was shocked. Is y'all serious? I never thought I'd be sittin' up there in a suit. It makes me feel like they look at me different. A couple said that I might have potential." Chris seemed particularly excited about his new role as a mentor. "I wouldn't mind being somebody people could talk to about anything. . . . Not that I have all the answers, but you might be going through the same thing. I needed help before. I'm young, and I'll need help again."

IT'S LIKE FAMILY: RELATIONSHIPS AS THE GROUND FOR PERSONAL TRANSFORMATION

One day as I hung out by the entrance, I saw the lead case manager, Emani Davis, walk into the building in the midst of a cluster of teenager girls. One girl with braids and a backpack idled up beside her, looking shyly down, as she said, "Guess what I got on my report card?" Tall with long wavy brown hair, an infectious smile, and a hint of the streets of New York in her voice, Emani stopped and looked at her, "What'd you get baby?" The young woman grinned, eyes shining, "3.6." Emani put her arm around the girl, "That's great. Bring me that report card so I can put a copy on my wall." She paused and added, "Next time you know what you're going to get?" She smiled and signed 4–0.

Preshona Gonzales described Youth Uprising as a kind of family, "a place that you want to raise you as a person." Youth Uprising's approach to youth leadership development relies heavily on intensive relationships between staff and young people that many members and staff described as like a family. Most staff people carry an informal caseload, but even the formal case management doesn't feel like it to young people. One young woman explained that when she's talking to her case manager, "I don't feel like it's a session." "Hey girl, wha's going on wit' you today?" Another young woman described the kind of family support she received from YU: "Y'all love us when we are good and even when we act up."

Omana Imani, the youth leadership coordinator, described how she worked to build consistent, loving relationships with youth. "We're openly loving to the young people. We slowly build trust. Individual relationships are what enable personal transformation, skills building, and community transformation." Omana emphasized the importance of just hanging out with youth in her office, but also the difference between working with youth and "kicking it with a girlfriend. . . . It's kind of like parenting, sometimes its friendship and sometimes its not. It's always focusing on how to develop them. You need to hone in on what they're passionate about and understand what issues they face. It takes a long time."

Sometimes the family relationship between staff and youth means stretching professional standards. Staff regularly hug young people, tell them they love them, and some youth even call staff members "Mama." Lil' Scrappy explained, "Everyone here is like a parent. Even if they're really busy, they'll still help you." Staff buy school supplies if young people can't afford them, take them to the doctor, and go on shopping trips to buy what they need as they leave for college. Lil' Scrappy added with a sense of awe in her voice, "It's like family. I know Olis and the case managers have literally let someone stay in their house." Reflecting on tension between the professional boundaries social workers are supposed to maintain and the urgent needs of young people, Olis Simmons asked, "What am I supposed to do when a foster care kid says to me she's not going to the diagnostic center, and she's going to do what she has to, to get a place to stay? I know what that means."

Daniel Jones, nicknamed 1 Tyme, is a soft-spoken and thoughtful 20-year-old who has been a YU member and volunteer since shortly after it opened and recently joined the YU staff as a music production and media arts teacher. When he speaks about teaching at YU, his eyes sparkle. "YU has given me a lot of responsibility. I found Youth Uprising, and now Youth Uprising has found me and so many other youth. It's found us and made it possible to dream. It's almost like here you feel like staff people are not staff. They are cousins, aunts, sisters, and brothers. It's a second home. To some young people, like myself, it's a first home." He paused, and said quietly. "I had never really thought of it that way before."

This family commitment generates significant trust among young people, and it also creates a web of mutual obligation. Olis Simmons gives one girl who was thinking about prostitution $10 a day and her aunt $10 a day to help support her. "She will do whatever I need her to, but she'd never come to me and say she's working for $10 a day. It's not that way. I love her, and she loves me back." At a YU staff meeting, Olis emphasized the importance of these close relationships to the mission of the center. "I can get 10 kids to show up and wash windows. If you can't do that, you better figure out how, because it's that kind of relationship that's at the center of this work. If you can't do that, you're not going to be here for long." These relationships and mutual obligation give Youth Uprising significant authority over youth, according to Simmons. "They'll self-monitor their behavior. They'll unload trucks, go to the store for you. They need to give back, to evolve into givers. It gives them meaning and purpose. They know if they need you, you'll be there for them."

"It's never like a movie story, black and white," Preshona explained, as she told me the story of one young woman who had really blossomed at the center. "She's got a lot of violence and anger in her. But now she be texting me, 'Big sis, I did this. I lost control.' She'll be checking in. No fake stuff. She'll let us know when she messes up."

The story of Cyrioco Robinson demonstrates some of the struggles of gritty youth leadership development. I first met Cyrioco when I walked up to a group of young people joking around in the café to ask if I could talk to them about YU. Cyrioco, dressed in baggy jeans, a bright red oversized T-shirt, and a matching baseball cap over his chin-length dreads, looked up with a beaming smile and said, "You are talking to the right man." He led me outside, explaining, "The center is everything to me. I be here around 11 and stay til it closes. When it closes, I walk out with my head down. I can only go back to my house or to the studio to make beats. If I try to go somewhere else, I'll be back on that block." Later he explained what made the center special to him. "Olis is the only person who can tell you the truth about yourself, but you don't be mad."

At 19 years old Cyrioco already had a long history of drug dealing, cycling in and out of jail. But he had the kind of personal charisma that would have made him a leader anywhere—on the streets, in a boardroom, and at Youth Uprising. One sunny day, I watched him herd a group of skeptical young people into a dark screening room to watch a documentary that they had no interest in. He came back out grinning with his success and walked toward where I sat talking with Rise-Up Team members. He looked each of us in the eye as he shook our hands, saying, "You are all my favorite people." Cyrioco was training for his new job as a culture keeper, and it was easy to see why he would excel at the job. But during my visit, Cyrioco violated parole by driving a stolen car. The YU Staff was devastated, but they welcomed him back to the center months later when he was released from jail. YU is committed to creating a space where young people can be leaders even before they have fully transformed their lives.

BEYOND AN OASIS

Monique, one the young adult workers at the Corner Café, described YU as her "safe haven," "I can look forward to this, to waking up everyday. But no matter how good these programs are, I still have to worry that they are going to do a drive-by at my house. I feel safer at work than at home."

In our last interview, Olis Simmons reflected on the problem with being "an oasis in the desert." Youth do "great when in the oasis, but when they go out, will they make it back?" When youth go home, the fundamental problems that created their reality remain: unemployment, failing schools, poor housing, underemployed parents, and pervasive illegal markets that offer at least the illusion of success. The depth of young people's simple material needs was clear when, in a survey conducted by youth staff, youth members asked for socks and toiletries as presents at the YU Christmas party. Olis worried, "I can't create as many living wage jobs as I need to for them."

The ultimate question facing Youth Uprising is how a youth center can become the vehicle for lifting up a community and addressing fundamental problems of economic development. In their first couple of years, they have taken some small but significant steps toward this goal. The youth-run Corner Café operates one of the only sit-down restaurants in the neighborhood. They have hosted community festivals, mayoral debates, and voting registration concerts. Youth Uprising has itself become a major neighborhood employer and helped train young people and connect them to educational and employment opportunities outside of the neighborhood.

Instead of isolating itself from the East Oakland's often-violent streets, Youth Uprising has cultivated deep roots throughout East Oakland. When the center first opened, Olis Simmons met with homeowners and community policing activists to solicit their support, but she also met with the major drug dealers in the neighborhood to tell them she was doing something for the kids and they needed to make sure the center was protected. They have partnered with African American fraternities, but also less traditional stakeholders like neighborhood motorcycle clubs, to put on different events at the center. Youth Uprising builds bridges between these diverse neighborhood stakeholders in order to explore how youth in the neighborhood can be leaders in community transformation.

Youth Uprising has managed to parlay its street credibility and close relationships with young people into a position of some political influence in the city. They actively seek ways for youth to participate in arenas outside the center—both to develop their leadership skills and political engagement, but also to transform local politics around youth. When two Oakland City Council members held a community forum to address the question of whether Oakland "took youth crime seriously enough," many youth activist groups talked about protesting the event. Olis Simmons asked to be on the panel along with two youth council members. The City Council was so excited by the possibility of including youth that they rented a bus for 40 youth from YU. With youth as almost half of the audience, the conversation subtly shifted from one that initially focused on problems of policing and whether the criminal justice system treated youth "less seriously" to one that focused on how the city could better support young people in transforming their lives. Most recently, Youth Uprising has partnered with Senator Don Perata to launch a peace-keeping initiative in response to Oakland's rising murder rate. They are hiring and training men with significant street credibility to reach out to do conflict resolution with young men on Oakland's most violent street corners and to connect young men to case managers, to employment training, and ultimately to the legal labor market.

Youth Uprising's long-term strategy is to become a production house, to build the infrastructure to support youth ideas for entrepreneurship, and to expand paths to living-wage jobs. They recently contracted with a hip-hop entrepreneur to help them explore how better to support, develop, and market young people's ideas into social enterprises. Since hip-hop is a multi-billion-dollar industry, they hope to leverage their relationships with cultural icons and young people's creative ideas toward solving the fundamental problems of economic development in the neighborhood.

QUESTIONS FOR DISCUSSION

1. What does this chapter indicate about the importance of space in work with young people? How does the arrangement of space in schools, agencies, and youth programs impact your practice with young people?

2. How does the organization of space at Youth Uprising challenge existing policies and practices toward youth? How does it challenge our notions of youth?

3. Why did this particular space work? What, in particular, do you feel contributed to the success of Youth Uprising in creating a place where youth would feel accepted and would contribute to maintaining this environment?

4. Are there ideas or understandings that social workers would have to "let go of" to help create and practice within this type of space? In what ways are the

"boundaries" between adults and young people, workers and youth, reconfigured in this space?

5. What lessons does this chapter offer for social work practice with youth? What spaces of possibility does it open up?

REFERENCES

Johnson, C. (2005). Youth haven in East Oakland. *San Francisco Chronicle.* Accessed June 24, 2005, at http://www.sfgate.com.

Kirshner, B. (2006). Apprenticeship learning in youth activism. In P. Noguera, J. Cammarota, and S. Ginwright, eds., *Beyond resistance: Youth activism and community change,* 37–58. New York: Routledge.

Young People as Leaders in Conflict Resolution

Charles D. Garvin

This chapter describes a project to train adolescents to assume leadership positions in their schools and communities to peacefully resolve intergroup conflicts that arise between youth who differ with respect to social characteristics such as race, ethnicity, gender, culture, class, neighborhood of origin, or sexual orientation. Although the primary source of these conflicts can be found in the persistent social injustices that pervade the educational system, job market, housing market, criminal justice system, and political system, they often manifest themselves in interpersonal and intergroup conflicts. Thus, the goal of the project was to enable students to move beyond these differences, recognize the sources of such conflicts, and begin to address them in their everyday lives.

The project, as the name implies, Enabling Adolescents in Culturally Diverse Environments to Peacefully Resolve Ethnic Group Conflicts focused on adolescents because of the special concern of project staff about the existence of social conflicts in high schools and the likelihood that schools seldom bring conflicting groups together to create solutions to such conflicts. We also focus on young people because we believe that they represent an important opportunity to begin to address social injustices and inequalities based on characteristics such as race / ethnicity, class, gender, and sexual orientation. It is no secret that these injustices continue to persist and that society has largely been resistant over the last several decades both to acknowledge the extent of inequality and to address it in a meaningful way. Instead, these injustices and inequalities have been increasingly institutionalized in policies, practices, and institutions.

Young people, however, are coming of age in an increasingly diverse society where technological change has expanded the opportunity to connect with individuals of different backgrounds. Although we are modest and realistic with regard to the direct effects of this specific program, enabling young people to move beyond these differences and the lack of understanding and empathy they engender is an important goal because it can also help us focus attention on the structural and institutional sources of these conflicts.

Thus the purpose of this chapter is to introduce the program that we developed and implemented in two high schools, to discuss the philosophy and principles guiding the program, and to present data regarding some of its direct effects. We conclude with a more general discussion of the importance of leadership and participation of youth in solving the problems that affect their lives.

PARTICIPATION ACTION RESEARCH MODEL

The project was designed and staffed by faculty of the School of Social Work at the University of Michigan who were working in the area of improving intergroup relations. After reviewing the literature and developing case studies of relevant projects, they began work on a program manual for implementation in selected high schools. The approach to the development and implementation of this program was guided by the principles of action research. Action research is a methodology initially introduced by the late Kurt Lewin in papers published in the last period of his life. (Lewin 1946, 1947). Action research, according to Lewin, integrates the systematic study, preferably experimental, of a social problem with efforts at its solution. Since Lewin introduced the construct, it has been utilized in many domains of study and social change, such as education, organizational development, and health promotion projects (see Reason and Bradbury [2001] for a discussion of the theoretical, conceptual, and empirical importance of the action research model). Action research was chosen for the project because of our threefold aims: to change the culture of schools and turn them into intergroup aware organizations, to develop an intervention technology, and to document and evaluate the results of this intervention. Thus, the students themselves were to be full participants in this program.

SCHOOL SELECTION AND PARTICIPANTS

For this particular program, two schools in different cities were selected as sites based on their ethnic diversity and geographic proximity to research staff. In City A, residents have a higher average income than those of the second city, and adults have a higher average level of education. City B has a larger proportion of nonwhite citizens and is the location of several large factories that employ many of its families.

At the beginning of the project, the high school in the more affluent community had a student body of about 2,000 students, with 55% of the students white, 20% black, 10% Arab American, 10% Asian American, and the rest either Latino or Native American. The other high school had a student body that was almost equally divided between white and African American students, although Arab American families were beginning to move into the area and the proportion of African American students was increasing due to so-called white flight.

The intergroup conditions of these schools were related to the broad objectives of the project. The school in City A had a good deal of informal segregation of ethnic groups, although this was not usually talked about in the school or community. Extracurricular activities were undertaken predominantly by one or another ethnic group; students tended to congregate in a "hall" composed of members of the same ethnic group as themselves. The often-encountered pattern of students sitting with others similar to them in the lunchroom existed. The school personnel did acknowledge tensions between Arab American and African American students, which they attributed to African American males seeking social contacts with Arab American females in response to Arab American males seeking such contacts with African American females. This pattern was a particular source of tension as Arab American families sought to protect their daughters from any out-group social contacts. The school in City B also had informal social segregation between black and white students, and this led to tensions at such all-school events as those held on Martin Luther King Jr. Day.

A total of 178 eleventh graders at the two schools participated in the intervention over a three-year period (Year 1, n = 68; year 2, n = 67; year 3, n = 43).

Of this number, 63% were female. As for racial and ethnic background, 48% were African American, 24% Caucasian, 4.8% Latino, 8.4% Asian American, 7% multiracial, 3.6% Arab American, and 3.6% "other." Some 66% were Christian, 15% no religion / atheist, 7% Jewish, 5.9% Moslem, and 6% "other." No students self-identified as gay-lesbian-bisexual; 4 students identified as having a disability. Program meetings were facilitated by trained interns pursuing degrees in social work and teachers at the schools. The project also utilized twelfth graders, who had participated in the intervention the previous year, as peer facilitators who were trained to work collaboratively with the adult facilitators.

PHILOSOPHY OF PROJECT

Social work practice with youth has often focused on reducing the frequency of behaviors such as substance abuse, poor school performance, irresponsible sexual activity, and criminal actions. Thus, youths have been typically seen as the targets of the social work activity rather than as citizens who determine their own goals and the means of attaining them. The driving philosophy of this project, however, was the idea that youth are citizens. We defined citizenship as "the numerous ways in which children are expressing their sense of belonging to and intervening in their environment" (Golombek 2006:14). This is a less restrictive definition of citizenship than those that define it in terms of reaching an age to do such things as voting for elected office holders or joining the armed services, and it provides a means to think more progressively about citizenship through youth participation and leadership.

Further, as discussed above, a research perspective is emerging that advocates for the full participation of young people in all aspects of knowledge development that relates to their lives. As Golombek, citing the work of James and Prout (1990), writes:

> This conceptual framework advocates for a recognition and inclusion of children's opinions, worldviews, and experiences into all relevant processes—from participatory research to community building. Key viewpoints of this conceptualization include an understanding that "children's social relationships and cultures are worthy of study in their own right, independent of the perspective and concerns of adults," that "children are active in the construction and determination of their own social lives, the lives of those around them and of the societies in which they live" and that ethnography is an effective methodology for the study of childhood as it allows to incorporate their own voice in the production of sociological data. (2006:8)

We join Golombek in seeing this perspective as underlying prevention programs such as ours, which assert that young people, given sufficient support and opportunity, can significantly alter their social environments and can continue with this kind of effort throughout their adolescent development and into adulthood. We also propose that this approach to program development and research is an empowering one. First, participants gain skills that they can use in conjunction with others to alter their relevant environments. Second, success in this type of program has a reinforcing quality that will lead to future behaviors to realize similar goals. Finally, youth who achieve change in their environment will be viewed by others, especially adults with whom they interact, as important allies in the struggle for a more just society. Consequently, the program was designed to follow these principles in very specific ways.

First, we saw the student participants as "citizens" of their schools who have a right to contribute to creating a school environment that is conducive to their learning. One important aspect of such a school environment is the way that different social groups in the school interact with each other to create a peaceful learning environment, and whether groups within the school are treated equally in terms of access to both curricular and extracurricular opportunities the school offers. In addition, students were accepted by the project in terms of what they can contribute to the program rather than in terms of "problems" they may evidence, such as poor school performance or inappropriate behavior. We made the assumption that many such problems will be reduced as students see themselves as potent members of the school community. This will apply both to active participants in the program as well as to other students who observed or were influenced by these participants or who benefited by the school environment created by participants. We expect to test this assumption in future phases of the project.

In the spirit of participatory action research, students were seen as research collaborators as well as participants. The students were given the opportunity to contribute their ideas about the success of the project through both qualitative interviews and responses on quantitative instruments. Students also participated as peer facilitators for the succeeding cohort of students. In this capacity they attended planning and debriefing sessions with the adult facilitators on a weekly basis. In addition, the project was seen as a step in *preventing* problems rather than only *treating* problems that exist. The kinds of problems we directly sought to prevent were school violence, bullying, and the consequences for individual students of exposure to intergroup tensions such as failure to learn and absenteeism. It was our aim that students will feel empowered through the use of the skills they gain through the program and their awareness of changes they have created in the school.

THE PROGRAM

The program processes were informed by group development theory. Based on a large body of research, group development theory posits that groups tend to have a pattern in the ways they develop over time and that their development occurs in phases (Garvin 1997; Toseland and Rivas 2005; Tuckman 1963). We drew upon group development theory in this project because we assumed that other programmatic elements that we intended to introduce would be rejected or would be ineffective if they ran counter to the processes that occur in groups over time. For example, a program activity that asked members to provide personal information that required them to trust one another would not be accomplished if introduced before members had developed this kind of relationship in the group.

The first phase, often referred to as formation, involves the initiation of relationships among members, creation of group norms, clarification of group purposes, and initial decisions on group activities. In this process, members resolve ambivalent feelings about affiliating with the group. The second phase is a "middle" or "working" phase that involves enacting activities to achieve group purposes. It also often entails a degree of intragroup conflict as members resolve power and control issues as they carry out their activities. The final phase, referred to as "termination," involves an evaluation of the performance and outcomes of the group, a response to the end of the group, and a possible end to relationships among members.[1] A program plan should present program elements in a sequence that is consistent with and utilizes processes that are likely to occur in groups at different stages of their development.

Our program also used a "stages of change" strategy, which postulates (see Lewin 1946/1948) that a major change in the culture, structure, or other elements of any individual, group, or collection of people in an institution is most likely to occur if a change sequence is followed by an "unfreezing" phase, in which existing attitudes are identified and challenged and the motivation and readiness for change are emphasized. The next stage involves a change process referred to as a "movement" phase, in which participants gradually change their attitudes and reframe their cognitive beliefs, and new conditions are introduced and are learned/incorporated by the entity in question. The final state is a "refreezing" phase, in which the new conditions are institutionalized into the ongoing operation of the individual, group, or institution (Lewin 1947, 1951).

To accomplish change, our intervention utilizes intergroup dialogue among high school students and is complemented by incorporating conflict mediation in the curriculum (Stephan and Stephan, 2001). We also explicitly incorporate an action component into our intervention, a noted limitation of other inter-group dialogue interventions with young people. While the process-content model of intergroup dialogues includes a social action stage, these activities typically include more reflective action that takes place at a cognitive and emotional level. Our intervention proposes that students initiate a schoolwide action activity that puts into practice the skills that they develop through our intervention. Thus, we adopt the approach of Gurin and colleagues (1999) with college students and extend this model to a younger audience that we think would benefit greatly from it.

Based on these ideas, the program was divided into the following four sections.

Section 1. This section sought to accomplish the tasks of group formation as explicated in group development theories. These tasks include clarification of group purposes (to improve intergroup relations in the school), establishment of group norms (e.g., confidentiality, safety in expressing one's views, commitment to the group through regular attendance), openness to expressing one's viewpoint, development of relationships among members and between members and facilitators, and promotion of trust among members. This section also sought to initiate the "unfreezing" process as outlined in social change theory. Specifically, the members were given an opportunity to share aspects of their identities and to learn the same about other members. It was also hoped that the trust-building activities called for in group development theory would have the effect of eventually enabling members to challenge existing conditions within as well as outside of the group with a sense of safety.[2]

Section 2. This section sought to initiate the middle phases of group development in which a group undertakes activities to accomplish its goals. These activities promoted intergroup dialogues as members further discussed aspects of their identities, such as those related to ethnicity, gender, and national origins. We also sought to help members recognize differences that existed related to sexual orientation. In group discussions, however, we found that members were not prepared to reveal their sexual orientations to each other. Group development theory also indicates that intragroup conflicts are likely to arise during this phase related to members' discussions of personal identities, members' initial awareness of power differentials in the group, often related to their roles in the school (e.g., athlete, scholar, economic position), and a recognition of the power inherent in being an adult group facilitator (especially related to the fact that one of the facilitators was a teacher in the school). We dealt with such conflicts at this phase by acknowledging them, supporting group members' disclosures, and reinforcing the group norms regarding respect for difference. We indicated that a full discussion of conflicts in groups and techniques for conflict-reduction was yet to come. The process of "unfreezing" continued through an analysis of the nature of intragroup relations as well as relationships that existed among various social groups within the school and community. For example, students typically were aware of informal social segregation within the school, such as seating patterns in the lunchroom or at extracurricular events. Students often were unaware that many school activities were also segregated or that conflicts existed among groups but were seldom discussed.[3]

Section 3. In developing the program, we expected that conflicts would arise in the group as some members competed for leadership (either with other members, with the facilitators, or with the peer counselors selected from the previous year's participants). We anticipated, however, that many of these conflicts would have been resolved with the help of the facilitators and, consequently, and that this phase would usher in a period of more intensive investment in achieving the goals of the group in the form of identifying issues within the school to resolve and in being open to learning about conflict resolution strategies. Thus, in terms of "stages of change," members are likely to be open to ideas about how their relationships within the school, and the school climate itself may take on new forms, thus creating a new set of conditions. These forms should be manifested in fewer occasions of stereotyping, more relationships with others from different identity groups, and a school climate that is more conducive to these. Activities during this section focused on forms of conflict resolution and the application of these in the group. In addition, students were encouraged to define conflict situations in the school and to consider the nature of a project to address these.[4]

Section 4. This is the termination phase, in which we planned for the members to evaluate the group experience and to plan ways they individually might continue to carry out activities such as those they encountered in this program. In addition, assuming that the relationships they formed in the group were important to them, the members could find ways of ending these in their current forms while continuing to find ways to remain in contact with other members if they wished. One vehicle that we offered for this to occur was for those members who chose to do so to function as peer facilitators for the cohort to be enrolled in the program the following year. In terms of "stages of change" concepts, we sought to help the students begin a process of integration of the learning from this program into their own sense of identity, and to consider what a different school climate may consist of that fosters these things. Students should also begin to hold the view that this kind of change is possible through their own efforts.

While work in earlier stages of the project often made use of specific exercises, we sought in the final sessions to help the students undertake a project in which they applied what they had learned to an actual intergroup problem in their school. The first pilot was limited in this respect as there was insufficient time to fully develop a project. In one school, however, the students were aware of a problem that emerged between racial groups in the school related to the graduation exercise. In this school, the custom was to engage in cheering as each student marched across the stage. The African American students supported this practice while white students thought it lacked decorum. The students in our project sought to mediate this dispute.

The following year, the students in our project in one school sought to create a mural in which each social or ethnic group was represented in some way that portrayed peaceful relations. This mural was completed and displayed in the school. The third year, the students in one school participated in "tolerance" week, an event organized by the school, by visiting classes and, with the permission of the teacher, leading a discussion on this topic. The students in our project who did this believed they gained many ideas on why "tolerance" was a problem in the school, and they were invited to address a meeting of the entire faculty to report their findings.

In the most recent year, one of the most successful in terms of student commitment to the project, students plan very ambitious projects. In one school, the students sponsored a major musical presentation for incoming students that focused on the principles of intergroup dialogues. Coincidentally, the other school also planned to meet with smaller groups of incoming students to discuss intergroup conflicts and principles of conflict resolution.

EVALUATION OF THE PROGRAM

We conducted an evaluation of the program using both quantitative and qualitative methods. The quantitative findings are based on pre/post questionnaires that examine youth development and intergroup relations outcomes using measures of social identities, intergroup contact, critical social awareness, communication with persons of different social identities, bridging differences, and taking action. Although limited by the sample sizes, the quantitative findings provide some important insights. In particular, they show that students reported thinking after their exposure to the program more often about social identities and sexual orientation. Students' also reported increases in their degree of critical social awareness, their commitment to building bridges among groups, and their willingness to take action. Further, they reported being more likely to notify authorities about intergroup conflicts. On the intergroup contact scale, white students reported more contact with people of different identity groups compared to the nonwhite students, while on the critical social awareness measure, young women reported higher scores than young men. Similar gender differences existed across other measures, including the communicating across difference, building bridges, and taking action measures. White students also scored higher on the taking action scale than African American students.

The qualitative data include individual interviews in which students were asked to reflect on the group experiences that did or did not have an impact on them, what that impact was, and how they would like to modify the program. Qualitative data were transcribed and analyzed for emerging themes using content analysis. "Open coding" (Strauss and Corbin 1990) was also used, and this involved systematic review of transcripts to capture important embedded concepts. Overall, the qualitative data reveal that students almost unanimously described their experiences as positive. The following summarizes their more specific responses.

Making new friends and building close relationships. Many of the students expressed that they met students whom they would not have gotten to know if not through the project, such as individuals of different social identity groups, including but not restricted to race. A number of students talked about how the program influenced how they think about others and their recognition of the importance of getting to know others in ways that avoid stereotyping. Students also talked about their discovery of how much more they had in common with others than they previously realized. One student talked about how she can now meet with new friends of different backgrounds to talk about problems in the school and community. An African American male stated: "It was weird to be meeting people I have seen everywhere in the school. I knew them but I did not know much about them. I felt blind and now I feel like the blinders were taken off. The interactions in the group kept me coming back for more [of this experience]."

Building close relationships with new and different people is an important part of unlearning stereotypes, and several students provided evidence for how the program accomplished this goal. For example, one Jewish female stated: "It made me realize that even though you should not judge people, I did this and I am learning not to."

One aspect of the program the students particularly enjoyed was the joint sessions held between the two schools. The students reported that they previously held stereotypes of students at the other school. These stereotypes were related to the fact that one school was located in an affluent college town and the other in a more industrial city where a larger proportion of individuals were people of color. Many students commented that they had learned they had much in common with the other high school's students despite their differences. These sessions also pushed students from the college town to question their negative and false assumptions regarding the physical condition of the other school.

Open and honest dialogue. Students indicated that they appreciated the openness in dialogue of their fellow students. Comfort with discussing difficult and uncomfortable issues was particularly noted. Several participants expressed relief when they learned about some of the views held by other students. As one African American male stated: "In some of the discussions, there were actually people who thought like I did! So I found out that I wasn't really alone on some issues. Before, I thought nobody else could relate to the way I saw things. When I'm with friends, we don't talk about important type issues like we did with the group."

Trust also emerged as a theme in that students reported an increase in their ability to trust one another and work as a team for larger causes. This allowed students to relate personal stories and histories, which in turn allowed others to hear new perspectives. One Latino male stated: "I got to hear their stories and personal experiences and opinions. This was really cool because usually you don't know what peoples' situations are and why they believe the way they do."

Learning about social issues. Students thought that they became more aware of social issues that enabled them to be more open to people of other ethnicities and cultures. For example, one African American female student spoke about how the discussion on gay rights was one she might not have experienced otherwise because of the nature of her religious roots. A number of students said that the program allowed them to discuss topics that people are usually too afraid to bring up. A Latina student stated that this group was "the only time we really talk with each other about serious problems and issues." A white female who is an immigrant from an Eastern European country said: "Just talking about problems with other teen-agers . . . I would never sit down with a group of friends and talk about real-world issues and current events because that's just not something we do. So, this group is a unique chance to talk about real problems with people our own age."

Other students expressed the fact that they had thought about these issues before but not to the degree that they did in this group. Students also talked about how they had not been aware of some of the social issues that exist within their own school. Participants described that they had not realized how segregated students tend to be in their school, particularly in the lunchroom. This realization led one of the groups to engage in a "mix-it-up" lunch day when students were encouraged to eat with different individuals for one day.

Problem-solving and conflict negotiation. Students indicated that they had not only learned about social issues and the conflicts that can arise from them, but also ways to resolve them. They also spoke of their increased desire to solve social conflicts. They indicated that, in the past, they might have addressed these conflicts negatively but are now more convinced that such conflicts can be resolved in a respectful manner. Participants also expressed that they now had a better understanding as to how to respond to people whose views conflict with their own. They now understood that an important part of dialogue is the ability to listen to others. For example, one African American female stated: "I learned you have to listen about where someone is coming from before you just go out and yell." A white female also described a listening exercise as one of her most memorable moments. She stated: "I also liked the one [exercise] about being empathetic and how to be a better listener. That's something I have a hard time with because I like to talk and always try to give advice. I learned a lot from that lesson."

An African American male student stated: "It's definitely influenced the ways I think about relationships and conflict. Before, when I was in conflict with someone, normally I'd stick to my own opinion and not care what anyone else had to say. Now I'm a little more open to what other people say and feel. I'm more likely to try to negotiate than before."

Students also expressed awareness that there will always be moments in life when one will be in conflict with others, and that the information gained from the program can be applied throughout life.

Taking action. Many students indicated they learned from the program that talking about social issues is not enough—one has to take action. Students indicated that they thought they can make a difference around issues of oppression. One student indicated that in the future she will "not be afraid to step up to the plate and take chances." Other students stated that the program motivated them to be more active, not only in their school, but also among family and friends and in their community. When asked about ways in which the program influenced how they think about intergroup relations and conflict, one white female student stated: "I help people out with conflicts and problems they are having. I tell them options and to talk about issues." Another white female student stated that the best part of being a participant was that she "knew that you could positively make a difference by resolving a conflict and learned new ways to handle situations and to prevent small conflicts from escalating into bigger ones."

Personal growth. Several students talked about the personal growth that ensued from their participation. Some stated that they had previously been quieter and may not have addressed problems or expressed how they felt. For example, an African American student with a disability stated: "I hoped to get more self-confidence as a person and [learn] how I can make the school better and to learn about the diversity here."

A number of students talked about how the program will help them in their future endeavors. They said it will help them to know how to get along with others who are different from themselves as they are likely to be working with such people in the future. Others talked about how these skills will be useful when they go to college or when they live in communities that are less tolerant than their current one. One African American female said: "This program started me off into community involvement and I want to get more involved."

Additionally, students spoke about the importance of being leaders in this area. One African American male stated:

Being in this group wasn't about your intelligence; it was about being a leader. There were some people in the group who weren't the smartest students, but they were leaders among their peers in one way or another. This was a chance to be around other leaders in the school and to cut across lines that sometimes divide us when we are only in classes with some kids. We actually don't have opportunities to get together with other leaders in the school.

Leadership was also demonstrated in students' desire to become involved in other school activities and in their desire to continue with the program in the role of student facilitator for the next cohort. This was reflected in the statement of an Asian American male participant:

[I benefited from] thinking of ways to improve the school as the school is not as great as others think. You meet pretty motivated people and more unselfish people and who care about others. It is a good experience to work with others and improve the school. I went to the Youth Senate and now I am [also] a participant there. IGR [this program] itself open up a whole new way of getting involved in other projects and broaden your horizon. IGR is great and was a great experience and I want to be involved as a senior [next year as a peer facilitator].

PROBLEMS AND ISSUES

Several types of problems emerged as we implemented the program. A major one was that the discussions we promoted, according to our judgment and observations, at times created anxiety in the students. We postulate that behaviors such as inappropriate laughter and joking, side conversations, and occasional hostile challenges to the facilitators are manifestations of anxiety. Even occasional expressions of boredom may have been due to such anxiety. Interviews with students suggested that such anxiety was due to fears of disclosing personal information that might elicit negative reactions from other students, fears of being seen as inadequate by other students, or fears of having the shared information repeated outside of the group.

Another problem was that many students "denied" that intergroup conflicts existed in their school. This was especially true of the program conducted in the more affluent of the two communities, despite the fact that there were conflicts, such as those manifested by informal segregation in the school. Certain extracurricular activities were understood to be reserved for members of one ethnic group or another, and some hallways in the school were similarly "owned" by one or another ethnic group. Students found it desirable to believe that "problems" existed in cities such as Detroit, but not in their "privileged" college town. Others in the town, we postulate, share this belief system. As a result of this program, many students indicated that they had begun to think more deeply about their community, and they indicated this was not a comfortable process.

FUTURE PLANS

After we complete the fourth pilot during the winter term of 2007, we plan, if we are successful in obtaining funding, to conduct a full-scale experimental study of this program. This would involve the use of control groups, the employment of better-trained facilitators, and the administration of a larger array of instruments to measure the impact of the program on the identity and social development of the participants. We will also be exploring with the schools means of institutionalizing this program so that it is maintained as a permanent part of the curriculum in each school. This is likely to mean that we will devise ways of the students obtaining course credit for their participation and/or embedding this content in the curriculum of a "regular" course. In any case, we will make our manual as well as all of the feedback and other evaluative material we have collected fully available to interested parties .

This project accomplished several things. First, it demonstrated that adolescents could manifest a strong commitment to improving intergroup relations in their schools. Second, it showed that these students can invest a great deal of energy in creating changes in their schools that will maintain better intergroup interactions. Third, it indicated that intergroup dialogue programs could incorporate elements of conflict resolution and social change that grow out of such dialogues.

This project was also highly related to the theme of this text, namely, that an important transformation of childhood is to learn to value one's personal identity while also valuing the identities of those who differ from one's self. Furthermore, this transformation includes placing a high value on peaceful relations among social groups and investing one's energy in reducing conflicts so that such relations can be maintained. The task of social workers should be to understand the processes discussed in this chapter so that they can facilitate them more adequately. This is a much more constructive and strengths-building perspective for social work than one that is restricted to a focus on pathology. This perspective focuses on supporting individual and social development of citizens of all ages thriving in peaceful and democratic communities and societies.

QUESTIONS FOR DISCUSSION

1. Garvin draws attention to the ways that persistent social injustices among young people often manifest themselves as interpersonal and intergroup conflicts. What knowledge do you have of inequalities and conflicts that arise among young people in your communities?

2. In what ways do social work practitioners engage (or fail to engage) with inequalities and conflicts among groups of young people? What examples of "social segregation" exist in social work settings? What tensions remain unaddressed?

3. How does the organization of this project challenge existing policies and practices with young people? How does it challenge our notions of youth?

4. What lessons does this effort offer us in our own practice with children and youth? What visions does it inspire?

NOTES

1. Some group development approaches incorporate a more cyclical and less linear conceptualization; however, our approach did not utilize these.

2. Examples of activities used in this section include an introduction to the concept and importance of dialogue, discussion of issues in the school and community that this

program might address, and a hope-fear exercise. The latter two activities are targeted toward helping to create group conditions that are supportive of challenging existing conditions in the broader community.

3. Examples of activities for this section included a "cross the line" exercise where students form a line and cross it if they identify with a category that is read aloud, and a conflict styles exercise where students identify with different conflict resolution strategies.

4. Examples of activities used in this section include a Star Power exercise and the use of negotiation to resolve conflicts.

REFERENCES

Garvin, C. (1997). *Contemporary group work.* 3rd edition. Boston: Allyn and Bacon.

Golombek, S. B. (2006). Children as citizens. In B. N. Checkoway and L. M. Gutiérrez, eds., *Youth participation and community change,* 11–30. New York: Haworth.

Gurin, P., G. Peng, G. Lopez, and B. Nagda. (1999). Context, identity, and intergroup relations. In D. A. Prentice and D. T. Miller, eds., *Cultural divides: Understanding and overcoming group conflict,* 133–72. New York: Russell Sage Foundation.

James, A., and A. Prout. (Eds.) (1990). *Constructing and reconstructing childhood: Contemporary issues in the sociological study of childhood.* New York: Falmer Press.

Lewin, K (1943–44/1951). Problems of research in social psychology. In D. Cartwright, ed., *Field theory in social science: Selected theoretical papers by Kurt Lewin,* 155–69. New York: Harper and Row.

———. (1946/1948). Action research and minority problems. In G..W.. Lewin, ed., *Resolving social conflicts,* 56–70, 201–16. New York: Harper and Row.

———. (1951) Frontiers in group dynamics. Part 2 in D. Cartwright, ed., *Field theory in social science: Selected theoretical papers by Kurt Lewin,* 188–237. New York: Harper and Row.

Nagda, B. A., C. Kim, and Y. Truelove. (2004). Learning about difference, learning from others, learning to transgress. *Journal of Social Issues* 60 (1): 195–214.

Reason, P., and H. Bradbury. (Eds.) (2001). *Handbook of action research.* Thousand Oaks, Calif.: Sage.

Spencer, M. S., and B. Nagda. (2002). Outcomes of intergroup dialogues for students in elective and required courses. Paper presented to the American Psychological Association Annual Conference, Chicago (August).

Stephan, W. G., and C. W. Stephan. (2001). *Improving intergroup relations.* Thousand Oaks, Calif.: Sage.

Strauss, A., and J. Corbin. (1990) *Basics of qualitative research: Grounded theory proce-dures and techniques.* Newbury Park, Calif.: Sage.

Toseland, R. W., and R. F. Rivas. (2005). *An introduction to group work practice.* 5th edi-tion. Boston: Pearson/Allyn and Bacon.

Tuckman, B. (1963). Developmental sequence in small groups. *Psychological Bulletin 63:* 384–99.

*Foster Youth as Teachers to
Transform Social Work*

Lori Fryzel and Jamie Lee Evans

Our hearts break as we write this chapter. Today is the memorial service for a young queer woman of color and former foster youth with whom we worked. Her name is Ali'ze, and she died tragically this week as a result of her homelessness. Ali'ze was a founding member of a foster youth–led evaluation project of group homes. She cared deeply about improving the group homes and foster care system that played such a huge part in her upbringing. Ali'ze survived poor schooling and poverty as well as scary and sometimes traumatizing foster care experiences to have a promising future as an advocate. Instead, this tragedy occurred only three years after she aged out of the foster care system. Ali'ze went to sleep in the back of an enclosed moving truck within which smoldered a barbecue pit. She died of smoke inhalation from the only thing keeping her warm that night. This tragedy is an example of what can happen to foster youth when we emancipate them, unprepared for "independence," without a safe space to live, families to belong to, and opportunities to succeed.

While child welfare programs can attempt to prepare transition-aged youth (TAY) for emancipation, the process is difficult even under the best circumstances. As authors of this chapter, we have discovered through our own experiences in care and through our interactions with countless foster youth that a foster care experience that truly prepares TAY for adulthood is, sadly, a rarity. Too often foster youth recount stories of physical and sexual abuse, discrimination, neglect, overmedication, misdiagnosis of mental illness, lack of opportunities for personal and professional growth, and "too many placements to even count." Most have spent years of their lives with limited opportunities for growth, and they are expected to emancipate into a world where they must be entirely self-sufficient. These unrealistic and unjust expectations set too many youth up for ongoing struggle in their young adult lives.

Most of us acknowledge that our nation's foster care system is producing poor outcomes for TAY. Studies of TAY have revealed bleak statistics. For example, youth transitioning to adulthood from the child welfare system are more likely to be involved in the juvenile justice system, less likely to be employed, less likely to have their high school diploma or GED, and less likely to go to college than those not involved in the system (Courtney et al. 2005). We must ask ourselves what can be done. While there are numerous public policy implications here, our project focuses on social work practice. We want social workers to be better equipped to work with youth, especially those who have experienced foster care. As stated on its website, www.youthtrainingproject.org, the fundamental mission of the Y.O.U.T.H. (Youth Offering Unique Tangible Help) Training Project is to teach and inspire social workers to take back the field and work in concert with young people to transform practice. If the system is ever going to change, it must start with changing the ways we view young people, the ways we talk to young people, and the ways we *include* young people—not only in the decision-making processes impacting their lives, but also in the system that is affecting their lives. Simply put, we call for a revolution from within.

THE BIRTH OF A YOUTH-LED SOCIAL WORKER TRAINING MOVEMENT

During the Clinton era, many of us making up the political Left were trying to distinguish the difference between the Democrats and the Republicans. After George W. Bush assumed the presidency in 2000, it became clear that social services had undoubtedly been more plentiful and diverse during the Democratic Clinton era, despite that administration's turn toward more regressive policies regarding the welfare of families and children. One positive opportunity occurred in 1999 when the Children's Bureau released a Request for Proposals (RFP) for groups to develop and deliver curriculum to child welfare workers that would support the improvement of outcomes for transition-aged foster youth. In short, policy makers and youth advocates recognized that life was tremendously difficult for the majority of youth emancipating from foster care and sought concrete action to address their plight.

We suggest that there may be two possible frameworks to explain why these funds were made available: (1) cynical pragmatism and (2) community responsibility. From a cynical and pragmatic perspective, when youth emancipate from care into homelessness and poverty, with ill health and lack of education, they are expensive. They may need medical assistance through programs such as Medicaid (MediCal in California) or government-subsidized housing; they may commit survival crimes in order to eat and thus end up incarcerated; they may have children early and without consistent incomes and need financial and child care support. Basically, from this perspective, it makes economic sense for the nation to assist these young people as they strive to reach adulthood. On the other hand, a community accountability-oriented perspective argues on behalf of societal responsibility for supporting children whose parents are unable to care for them. These are the state's children, and it is our community responsibility to support them with our tax dollars. This perspective also points to the ethical responsibility of social workers to ensure that youth enter adulthood with the skills and resources necessary to be self-sufficient.

There may be yet a third possible explanation for why the Children's Bureau offered this funding opportunity. The bureau is the arm of the federal government that has long been a champion of services to the most needy in the United States—mothers and their children. The Children's Bureau has historically provided leadership in research-based practice and training and has progressively become more committed to a philosophy of youth engagement and practice of positive youth development. Given the positive outcomes associated with youth engagement, the bureau required grant recipients to involve youth in meaningful ways in the development and delivery of the child welfare training curriculum. Without this initiative it is questionable whether such a dynamic and untraditional training program for social workers would have been created. When the funding for the initial projects ended, we asked the Children's Bureau to consider extending our program. Under the Bush administration, further funding for these programs, which had made substantial progress in curriculum development, was not available. Instead, we had to seek out other sources of funding from state and private sources. It is interesting to note, however, that at this same time there was an increase in federal funding of faith-based initiatives, including several million-dollar, five-year grants to create and deliver "marriage readiness" workshops for social workers who work with TAY.

The Y.O.U.T.H. Training Project is the result of a successful collaboration between the Bay Area Academy (BAA) and California Youth Connection

(CYC). The BAA, a social worker training academy sponsored by the School of Social Work at San Francisco State University, is one of five regional academies in California that designs and delivers training for county child welfare and probation staff to ensure that they have the knowledge, skills, and abilities necessary to improve outcomes in foster care. CYC is a statewide nonprofit foster youth advocacy organization guided and driven by current and former foster youth with the assistance of other committed community members. CYC promotes the participation of foster youth in child welfare policy development, legislative change, and the improvement of social work practice. Understanding the power of truly engaging in positive youth development to make changes in child welfare, these groups developed a thoughtful collaborative proposal that was awarded funding. Merging the grassroots activism of current and former foster youth that serves as the foundation of CYC with a well-respected and formal social work training institution resulted in a very successful partnership to spearhead this work.

Startup funding from the Children's Bureau allowed us to develop a unique training model unlike any other in the nation. The Y.O.U.T.H. Training Project, staffed almost entirely by former foster youth, educates and empowers current and former foster youth to share their experiences and expertise through self-written curriculum delivered in training to child welfare workers throughout California and beyond. Over the course of our first year of operation, we conducted statewide focus groups with both foster youth and child welfare social workers. Through this process, we were able to identify major areas in which practitioners lacked the knowledge and skills to support TAY. With this information, six current and former foster youth, ages 16–21, developed a two-day, 16-hour curriculum entitled *Youth Development, Empowerment, and Super Strategies for Supporting Transition-Aged Youth.* As part of our curricular journey, we invited curriculum development experts to train us, and we learned together about evaluation processes, adult learning styles, and transfer of learning methodology. We wrote, edited, wrote, and edited some more, ate meals together, shared hotel rooms and bus rides, engaged in debate, agreed and disagreed, and shared in this powerful, transformative collective process. Over the course of the year, we spent countless hours in hot tubs, in classrooms, across from each other at restaurants sharing stories, supporting one another, and growing together. During the last two years of our grant period, a pool of 12 youth trainers recruited from all over California learned the curriculum and trained more than 450 social workers statewide. Through our training we have developed a critical understanding of best practices for supporting TAY in educational arenas, for kinship care, for permanency planning, and for positive youth development.

We engage social workers in discussion of challenging and important subjects such as the experiences of lesbian, gay, bisexual, transgender, and queer youth; the challenges that pregnant and parenting foster youth face; mental health issues among foster youth; education and the school experience; the meaning of permanency in the lives of foster youth; foster youth culture; positive youth development; and the power of resiliency.

We invite readers to visit our website at www.youthtrainingproject.org to learn more.

GROWING A MOVEMENT

At the conclusion of our first grant period, we received two years of foundation funding to update and revise our curriculum and expand the project to include 40 additional youth trainers and train another 2,000 child welfare social workers. One additional staff member was hired, bringing the project to two full-time staff (the authors of this contribution), and 40 additional youth trainers were hired as contractors. We hired four teams of youth, 10 at a time, and organized "Leadership Institutes." The Leadership Institutes were designed to orient newly hired Y.O.U.T.H. trainers to the project, the curriculum, and facilitation skills. They came, all expenses paid, for two long weekends (eight total days) in order to become certified Y.O.U.T.H. trainers. Preparation for the Leadership Institutes was an enormous undertaking and included obtaining permission from group homes, social workers, and foster parents for youth still in care to travel for the long weekends, booking travel for youth coming from all parts of the state, and arranging the retreat / meeting space, among other logistical issues. Of major importance was, of course, developing the Leadership Institute's agenda and the training for trainers curriculum, which includes opportunities to reflect on personal experiences in care, facilitation skills training, teaching of the curriculum, team building, critical thinking, leadership activities, and, equally important, fun. Additionally, we contracted with outside facilitators and experts (people of color, women, and former foster youth were especially sought out) to expand the worldliness of the youth and also to enlarge our community. Learning from outside facilitators helped to break down the walls of adultism that are ever present when bringing adults and youth together. It makes the entire team—staff and youth—students together in a colearning process. Our Leadership Institutes conclude with a ceremony to bring closure to the intensive training time spent together. In a circle, the youth take turns offering "appreciations," where everyone has the opportunity to note something they appreciate about another person or the project, then awards and small graduation gifts are given to symbolize their new status as official Y.O.U.T.H. trainers.

Currently we have developed and are delivering three separate curricula. With a second cycle of funding from the Children's Bureau, we have developed a training curriculum for child welfare supervisors in California, Hawaii, Guam, and American Samoa. Another Y.O.U.T.H. curriculum was created with funding from the California Department of Social Services to provide training to child welfare workers and group home and probation staff in California on the topic of how best to serve youth who challenge social workers the most. Note that we deliberately changed the focus of the problem: the problem is not "difficult youth," as more typically framed from an adultist perspective. The problem we identify is that social workers are "most challenged" by some youth. In addition, we receive a small amount of private foundation funding and provide fee-for-service training on the topic of what one social work supervisor labeled the "alphabet kids," that is, LGBTQ, or lesbian, gay, bisexual, transgender, or queer and questioning youth. To date, we have trained over 4,000 workers in the child welfare system with these various curricula. While the project is unable to say what the future holds, we are working toward a sustainability plan to ensure the longevity of this work.

GUIDING PRINCIPLES OF THE Y.O.U.T.H. TRAINING PROJECT

The Y.O.U.T.H. Training Project has two primary goals: (1) to educate and build the capacity of a team of current and former foster youth, and (2) to change the practice of child welfare by providing the workers a chance to hear from the experts of care, those youth who have experienced foster care first hand and have absolutely relevant recommendations to make. However, the training of social workers comes with various obstacles to overcome, including adultism, racism, and homophobia. We have learned from experience that adults are not comfortable learning from youth. Too often, the primary training capacity social workers see foster youth able to occupy is tokenistic in nature, where youth are invited to come and tell a short personal (often tearful) narrative, which is then followed by in-depth, expert adult analysis and discussion. We challenge this view of youth, and we challenge social workers to let go of their assumptions and open themselves to listening to and learning from young people.

Perhaps the most significant part of our work lies in our model of working with youth. One core principle of the project is that we see ourselves in community. Our work started with a commitment to create an empowered foster youth community. Having adult staff members who are also former foster youth gives the Y.O.U.T.H. trainers an intimate opportunity to be in community with adults who can truly relate to many of their experiences, are down-to-earth, and are successful in their fields. Staff and youth engage in professional training and work with one another, we have roaring debates and touching discussions, and we live together for days at a time while training throughout California, Hawaii, and the greater United States. In addition, having grounded adults involved in the youths' life over time (the project is now over six years old) made for "permanency practice," and Y.O.U.T.H. trainers consistently identify their increased capacity to bond and connect with one another. This last realization, discovered and documented by an outside evaluator, was an unplanned but not surprising outcome of our project. It makes sense that community would come from a project that intentionally builds in opportunities for youth to make connections with one another. And while logic would tell us that these connections would and could become long term, the specific strengths of youth's overall connective abilities are an additional and happy unexpected outcome.

We have also learned to challenge dominant assumptions and practices regarding boundaries. In terms of our intentional community with youth and adults, there are boundaries in our work with youth, but we don't draw bold, thick lines to separate staff, youth, and social workers. Some might criticize our project for having loose boundaries. For example, we have been known to step out of professional roles with youth and develop a support team for youth in crisis (once for a homeless youth, once for a youth who attempted suicide), invite the team to our homes (for barbeques and meals as part of the Leadership Institute), donate our own money for youth in emergency situations (for example, homeless youth or a youth with no winter coat), engage our partners and friends in volunteer support of the project so the youth can meet them and build more supportive connections, and even house the older youth who at times sleep on our couches or in guest rooms to help save the project money. Although some might think these types of "boundary crossings" are dangerous, we have learned that the outcomes associated with these actions can be profoundly beneficial for youth with limited family support. We have learned that the positives outweigh the risks in these cases. We have found that once young people have received a boost of personal support from us, they are better able to seek and receive appropriate mental health services, get their first apartments, get better-paying jobs from interview practice, and take other steps toward the future.

The personal connectedness we have with youth also serves an important purpose directly related to our goals. The curriculum and training work we ask youth to do (on very fragile or painful aspects of their lives), can bring up many difficult feelings and traumatic memories for them. We depend on the strong bonds of the team to provide emotional support and demonstrate genuine caring. This connection and support have made a difference between life and death for some youth on our team. We demonstrate our love and concern in very concrete ways, such as picking up youth at airports (instead of forcing them to take a bus or subway after getting off an airplane that may have even been their first plane ride ever), providing the food that they prefer to eat (yes, that means eating at a lot of chain restaurants even in areas of fantastic cuisine like Napa, California), buying birthday cakes with candles and singing to them, playing fun games on our down time, sending e-mails to check in with them or just to say hi, sending postcards when we go on vacation, and sending birthday cards and cards for celebratory occasions such as holidays and graduations. Interestingly, the youth have already begun modeling the positive connectedness they have received back to the project staff. A recent example occurred in May 2007 when one of the authors received her master's degree in social work and several youth asked to attend the graduation ceremony. Stating that they wanted to experience a master's-level graduation, they also shared that they wanted to celebrate this former foster youth's achievements just as she had celebrated their accomplishments.

Another guiding principle of the project is our commitment to diversity. We deliberately recruit and hire foster youth from diverse backgrounds. And though racial, ethnic, and gender diversity is important to us, we don't stop there. We aim for regional diversity, diversity in perspective, personality, foster care experience, and achievement. Our training team consists of white, black, Asian, Native American, Pacific Islander, and youth born and raised abroad. We bring together youth from urban, suburban, and rural communities. Our team includes youth from kinship care, group homes, foster homes, adoption, guardianship, mental health placements, probation, and supervised care. We involve self-identified gay, lesbian, straight, bisexual, transgender, gender queer, and queer youth. Our team consists of college students from Stanford and Berkeley, community college students, high school students, high school dropouts, youth living in transitional housing, youth with self-identified mental health struggles, and youth who just want to get out of their foster homes and will join anything in order for that to be the case. And although bringing youth together from all of these different backgrounds could be a breeding ground for conflict and drama, we are proof that truly diverse projects can be successful at building something that foster youth are proud to be a part of and that many youth come to consider their family. One youth joined the team at age 16 and had never met an openly gay person before our first training weekend. On Friday night he confessed his disapproval of LGBTQ people identifying themselves to one another, preferring instead, he said when challenged on his opinion, to believe that only a few in the world identified as gay or lesbian. By Sunday night, our third night together, this young man bravely extolled insights into his own internalized homophobia—insights gained through conversations with another youth. Now, six years later at age 22, this young man who now lives in Miami keeps in touch with one of the authors, an out lesbian, and considers her one of his permanent connections!

Through our collective experience, we have learned important lessons about supporting youth in the process of establishing stable, enduring relationships in their lives, the hallmarks of "permanence." Our commitment to relationship, group process, and community building is key not only to healthy organizational development but also to positive youth development. Some of the lessons learned include:

• **Make a long-term commitment.** Our group has met for over seven years at this point, thus creating the time and space to sustain relationships over time. As addressed above, we put the concept of permanency to practice through caring, enduring relationships that create a sense of family among the youth participants in the organization. The intensive four-day workshops helped to build relationships and were the beginning of "practicing permanency." We continue our bonding through traveling together, presenting at conferences, and experiencing success after workshops.

• **Conflict is part of the process**. To truly embrace difference, we have learned to engage with and value conflict as a source of personal and organizational growth and transformation. Youth are encouraged to handle conflict and issues that come up with their cotrainers on their own, but they know that they can come to staff if they need help. Over time the youth have "called meetings" with each other to handle conflicts, express frustrations, and seek reconciliation. Group members get to experience relationships that are challenging at times and clearly rewarding and satisfying at other times.

• **Share knowledge and resources**. Members of our group have shared strategies, successes, resources, and ideas with one another on how to get along. By sharing our knowledge and resources, we have expanded our networks and helped one another secure housing, find jobs, continue in school, and build friendship. We connect through MySpace, open our homes to one another, and inform one another about college programs and scholarships for foster youth.

• **Engage in power analysis.** We recognize the importance of addressing the ways in which power works so that we can interrupt actions that exclude and silence youth and support possibilities for youth empowerment. This calls for examination of the workings of privilege and oppression on multiple fronts in the lives of young people. It means making sure young people have a right to participate in the decisions that affect their lives. We have learned to question adult-imposed decisions and to promote opportunities for youth empowerment to be practiced and achieved.

• **Build intergenerational alliances**. We have learned to identify and challenge adultism and to create ways in which adults can engage with youth as allies and colearners. We make a commitment to acknowledging adultist privilege and seeking out every possible opportunity to have equality in work with youth. We are all teachers and learners, and we recognize that youth have a lot to teach each other, the staff, and the social workers who serve them.

• **Operate from a strengths perspective**. Youth are not the equivalent of their problems. Youth are filled with talents, resilience, and strengths, making it essential that no one feels pathologized for having feelings come up throughout the process. Supporting positive youth development and a strength-based approach, then, is a vital aspect of this work.

• **Value use of self**. Foster youth are a disenfranchised group, marginalized and frequently not treated as anywhere near a peer by professionals. Coordinators participate in personal sharing as part of the process, and they created a structure in which mutual sharing is appropriate and allowed for each group to develop communication / understanding skills and expand their experience.

OUTCOMES AND THE MEANING OF OUR SUCCESS

What an awesome experience to have a team of foster youth translate an idea into groundbreaking success! It often baffles us that people think we are wizards who have accomplished a magical mystery tour by successfully creating a professional project that solely utilizes youth as curriculum developers and trainers. At the culmination of our first three-year grant funding, the project was highlighted as a triumph of ideas and hard work in the Children's Bureau publication *The Children's Express* (2004).

Being a part of the Y.O.U.T.H. Training Project, which was named by the youth, has undoubtedly reversed the internalization of the stigma associated with being a foster youth. Using their experiences in care coupled with professional training in facilitation and curriculum development, young people moved from the margins to the center and gave child welfare workers an opportunity to see foster youth as an empowered category of youth—not orphans, abandoned, or victims.

The youth have also had their own opportunity to explore what they think it means to "make it." Some of them have gone on to college, to graduate school, to "high-powered" professional positions. We didn't give youth a definition for success; it's not culturally or ethically possible to detail one definition of success, and we don't try. But we do let youth see examples of success throughout the project, and we encourage an environment of supportiveness around life issues, educational goals, and emotional connections / relationships. We seize every opportunity to go beyond talking about "positive youth development" to actually implement it.

QUESTIONS FOR DISCUSSION

1. How do changing political, economic, and social conditions alter the project of "coming of age" and "achieving independence" for young people? How might these conditions differentially impact young people who are aging out of the foster care system?

2. The authors give thoughtful attention to work with lesbian, gay, transgender, queer, and questioning youth. In your practice, are social workers engaged with questions of how to engage LGBTQ youth? What policy and practice changes in your arena of practice are needed to best serve these young people?

3. How do the "boundary crossings" described in this project redraw our notions of youth? What do we as social workers leave behind—and take with us—as we cross these boundaries?

4. The goal of achieving permanency is an often stated "certainty" of work in the foster care system. The authors talk about "practicing permanency" instead. What are the implications of this shift from "achieving permanency" to "practicing permanency"? How does this modification challenge our practice and expand the possibilities of work with foster youth?

5. Fryzel and Evans call for a "revolution from within" social work practice to change the way we view, talk with, and include young people. What vision do they offer of this revolution? How does this vision challenge the profession?

REFERENCE

Courtney, M. E., A. Dworsky, G. Ruth, T. Keller, J. Havlicek, and N. Bost. (2005). *Midwest evaluation of the adult functioning of former foster youth: Outcomes at age 19*. Chicago: Chapin Hall Center for Children at the University of Chicago.

Afterword

Janet L. Finn, Jeffrey J. Shook, and Lynn M. Nybell

In this book, we have invited you to wonder with us about the transformation of childhood, youth, and social work in the contemporary United States. The contributors offered us detailed portraits of social work practice with young people that provoked our curiosity about a wide assortment of issues. For example, they challenged us to think about the particular location and shape of our juvenile detention centers; the photographs of missing children on our milk cartons; the complex web of practices by which we determine that a particular young person will be held accountable as an adult in our criminal justice systems; the arrangement of suburban homes and shopping malls from the vantage point of the children who inhabit them; the meanings we assign to concepts such as "attachment," self-esteem," "permanency," or "morality"—and the meanings that we leave out.

These detailed accounts have been assembled here for their ability to "wake us up" to the ways in which contemporary social work policies and practices impact the minds, bodies, spirits, and experiences of young people. The authors also provoke our imaginations, opening up new conceptions with novel possibilities for practice. They draw new images of young people as rights-bearers, teachers, poets, advocates, and policy makers. Finally, the authors offer us models and methods of critically engaged scholarship, to be assessed not only by its trustworthiness and authenticity, but also by the extent to which it serves as a catalyst for action in the service of social justice (Guba and Lincoln 2005).

The basic premise of this volume is that childhood and adolescence are socially constructed categories that have been transformed over the last several decades by a variety of economic, political, and cultural forces. This transformation has altered both the experiences and representations of young people, resulting in significant changes in the way that we both view and treat young people. A collective goal of these contributions, then, has been to challenge social workers to appreciate the ways in which their practice with children and youth is inseparable from surrounding political and economic conditions. We are called upon to critically explore the complex interplay among policies, institutions, practices, and images regarding children and youth and our own involvement therein. Contributors to this volume provide us with tools for resisting the lure of simplistic solutions that avoid the nuances and complexities of the lived experiences of young people. Instead they call for "complexity thinking" (Adams, Dominelli, and Payne 2005: 6–7) and recognition of the richly textured lives and complicated life circumstances of children and youth today. When we are willing to "complexify" our thinking and practice, we are able to resist the tendency toward what Dennis Saleebey refers to as "context stripping." According to Saleebey, "When we transform persons into cases, we often see only them and how well they fit into a category. In this way, we miss important elements of a client's life—cultural, social, political, ethnic, spiritual, and economic—and how they contribute to, sustain, and shape a person's misery or struggles or mistakes" (2006:6).

Some contributors demonstrate ways to attend to how young people themselves conceive of their situations, striving to locate themselves alongside children and youth. They remind us that our practice with children and youth is an embodied experience, as we witness the struggles of young people in families, schools, and treatment centers or as we march beside young demonstrators toward city hall. Others maintain a disciplined conceptual attention to the place of children and youth in contemporary policy discourses, reminding us of the importance of critical reflection on our practice. Several authors speak to the ways they have found that allow young people to "talk back" to the powerful discourses in which they are framed, contrasting or aligning the diverse views of children and youth with the often more simplistic messages of social policy. They remind us that young people are not only social actors but also social critics, capable of insightful analysis and critique of the policies that affect their lives and of the material consequences that shape their everyday worlds.

An important theme raised by a number of contributors is the issue of children's rights. As discussed in a number of chapters in the volume, rights-based discourses have become increasingly prevalent in debates over the nature and needs of children and youth. Buoyed by the U.N. Convention on the Rights of the Child, child advocates have used rights-based arguments to attempt to address the protection and needs of children. In part, rights-based arguments can serve to reduce the ambiguity surrounding the cultural category of childhood by providing a specific set of rights, responsibilities, and entitlements. Several contributors, however, provide a note of caution regarding rights-based arguments by pointing to the ways that they can lead to more regimented and disciplined treatment of young people or by showing that rights-based claims can also lead to the exclusion of youth from the institutions of childhood. At the same time, other chapters reveal the vulnerability inherent in a lack of rights, such as the lack of a right to be a juvenile for justice system purposes or the lack of a right to an education. Critical, then, is the need to reflect upon the significance and consequences of rights-based arguments and actions in all aspects of social work practice with children and youth. This is especially important in the context of U.S. practice where an understanding of and commitment to human rights in general and the rights of the child in particular have been sorely neglected.

The contributors also encourage readers to imagine new possibilities for social work practice. The themes and ideas that emerge throughout these chapters suggest innovative courses of action for social work research, education, and practice with children and youth. These courses of action require social workers to critically examine the "certainties" and assumptions (Sarri and Finn 1992) that guide our practice with children and youth and to reflect on how our assumptions influence how we think about and treat young people. How do particular understandings of childhood and youth lead us toward particular sorts of intervention and limit our view of other possibilities? The contributors encourage us to seek new possibilities for practice that take into account different paradigms of thought and action, pushing us beyond traditional modes and strategies. In particular, they challenge us to look beyond immediate, personalized, depoliticized views of trouble and consider the history of structures and practices that have shaped the present situation. In so doing, we must also actively, intensively, and forcefully contest the production of ideas in different contexts and settings. Social work has a long history of advocacy and activism that is exemplified by the careers of researchers, teachers, and advocates such as Rosemary Sarri (foreword). What is needed now is a willingness to continue this tradition in everyday practice. Moreover, we also need a willingness to utilize multiple methods and sources of knowledge development regarding policy and practice with children and youth. "Evidence" cannot effectively inform policy and practice if it is partial or incomplete, reflecting the perspective of the dominant ideologies and methods. Thus, social workers must be willing to challenge traditional modes of "knowing" and to adopt methods that attend to context and provide a prominent place for the inclusion of "voice" and analysis of oppression.

The contributors take questions of power seriously and challenge readers to do the same. Several contributors provide concrete examples of the possibilities that emerge once we are able to recognize the agency and voices of young people and are willing to share power with them. But power sharing can be an unsettling proposition. It requires that we question our assumptions about expertise and open ourselves to learning from the wisdom of youth. It disrupts our received notions regarding professionalism, which are closely bound to beliefs about what constitutes the "best interests" of young people. And, perhaps most difficult of all, true power sharing demands humility and a willingness on the part of social workers to be transformed in the process. Meaningful participation of young people in the decisions that affect their lives is a key part of power sharing.

As contributors note, however, power sharing does not necessarily mean giving something up. In fact, these contributors show that through the embrace of power sharing and the recognition of young people as critical social actors, new and powerful organizational forms are emerging. Contributors offer concrete examples of the possibilities for innovative, justice-oriented action in which young people claim voice, rights, and moral authority. They take the reader beyond the rhetoric of participation to encounters with new forms of partnership, networks, and coalitions, which are not only inclusive of young people but also, at times, led by them. Young people are pushing the limits of adultist organizing models and inventing novel ways to frame issues and take action. In so doing, they are crafting new strategies for change that embrace diversity, media literacy, cultural expression, and the role of the arts in social and political change. Young people are looking locally and globally for inspiration. They are crafting alliances that cross and blur categorical boundaries of age, race, gender, class, and citizenship. They are cultivating untapped resources and creating "conspiracies of hope" (Deegan 1996). Social workers have a wealth of opportunities to join their efforts as allies, advocates, animators, and colearners. While these opportunities require social workers to resist the comfort of more traditional and familiar strategies and practices, they offer the potential of new possibilities of policy and practice that represent the complexity inherent in the lives of children and youth. Once social workers come to question the inevitability of current policies and practices regarding children and youth we face ethical challenges. Can we muster the moral courage and political will to engage in practice with children and youth guided by an ethics of participation that recognizes young people as bearers of rights? To do so poses a fundamental challenge to social work practice with children and youth.

We conclude by discussing ten lessons for practice that provide necessary tools for pursuing these opportunities. These "lessons" represent the ideas that have guided much of our own work. This list is not exhaustive and leaves substantial room for social work practitioners, educators, and researchers to add their own ideas in order to open up new possibilities for policy and practice. Are we up for the challenge?

TEN LESSONS FOR PRACTICE

1. **Question our certainties.** Effective practice with children and youth calls for ongoing critical reflection on our personal and professional assumptions about what is right and true, especially those beliefs that we hold most dear. Perhaps a rule of thumb for critical practice is that the more certain we are about the correctness of a diagnosis, policy, or intervention plan, the more important it is that we critically scrutinize our assumptions. With the power of 20/20 hindsight, we are able to see how our certainties have been challenged and changed over time. Too often, however, vulnerable young people have paid the price in the meantime.

2. **Appreciate complexity:** Throughout this book, contributors have illustrated the folly of narrow, simplistic thinking in the development of policies and practices with children and youth. They challenge us instead to acknowledge and confront the complexities of children's lives and our engagement with them. Doing so calls for humility and a willingness to acknowledge the partiality and limits of our own world views and knowledge bases. Appreciation of complexity requires that we grapple with the ambiguities of practice, listen to multiple points of view, and craft spaces of debate and dialogue wherein the richness of young peoples' lives and the tensions, contradictions, and challenges therein can be honored and addressed.

3. **Examine the discourses—who talks and how—in the production of childhood, youth, and trouble.** What "is" does not necessarily need to "be." Social workers must actively seek to examine why things are the way they are in order to fully understand existing policies and practices. By stepping back and critically analyzing the discourses surrounding these policies and practices,

social workers open up new opportunities for policy and practice that move beyond simplifications and acknowledge the complexity of the lives of young people. They also can begin to reflect upon their own practices and the effects of these practices on children and youth.

4. Link the personal to the political and structural. The contributors push us beyond the bounds of narrowly psychologized understandings of children and youth. Inspired by Robert Coles, they continually remind us that a nation's politics becomes a child's everyday psychology. The critical practice of social work must be continually cognizant of the myriad ways in which structural inequalities are insinuated into our bodies, psyches, and everyday worlds. As social workers we are not immune to or outside of these structural forces, but very much shaped by them. Thus, it is imperative that we critically examine the ways in which larger structural forces are realized in our institutions and systems of care, the values and language of public policies, the theoretical assumptions that guide understanding of problems and interventions, and the social relations among providers and recipients of services.

5. Take history seriously. In both implicit and explicit ways, the contributors challenge us to ground our practice in a critical historical perspective. They call on us to ask how the prior histories of our institutions, policies, discourses, and practices have contributed to particular sets of circumstances affecting the lives of children and their families today. How has the arbitrary become naturalized and external forces internalized in that process? They also remind us that children have histories. They are not blank slates to be molded by adult interventions but engaged actors drawing on their accumulated knowledge and resources to make sense of and act in the world.

6. Engage in power analyses and recognize rights. While couched in language regarding the "best interests" of the child, policies and practices are often as reflective of the needs and interests of adults as of young people. Acknowledging the power that adults have over the way young people are both defined and regulated is essential to the development of new policies and practices that move beyond the traditional control-oriented perspective of dealing with young people and opens up new avenues of power sharing.

7. Listen to the voices of children and youth. Throughout the book we hear the voices of children and youth, teaching us to wonder, claiming their rights to childhood, talking back to those who frame them through negative and constraining stereotypes, and rejecting adultist views of their worlds and interpretations of their experiences. Young people challenge tokenism and demand to have their voices heard in public forums, in their schools and home, and in the institutions dedicated to their "treatment" and "reform." As social workers we have an advocacy role to play here. We must push beyond tokenism to genuine attention to the words and worlds of young people.

8. Engage young people as partners in knowledge and policy development. As part of the process of listening to young people, social workers must actively use their voices in the development of knowledge and policy. Engaging young people as partners in this process represents a challenge to traditional and comfortable practices methods and strategies. Yet, it is an essential strategy if we are to develop policies and practices that will fully tap into the potential that young people offer.

9. Take courageous individual and collective action. Meanings of childhood are produced and reproduced across multiple locations and institutions at the macro and micro levels. By recognizing the continual production and reproduction of these meanings, social workers can become active participants in contesting existing discourses regarding the nature, needs, and interests of young people. For example, policies and practices that focus on the exclusion of young people from institutions of childhood based upon simplified ideas of the nature of children and youth can become accepted modes of action without challenge. Social workers are well situated to make these challenges and must bring their "voices" to the table.

10. Radicalize practice with conspiracies of hope. Through poetry, protest, and political action, young people themselves are leading the way to a bold and hopeful practice of social work and social change. Social workers would do well to join with young people in "conspiracies of hope" (Deegan 1996) through which we dare to imagine and create new possibilities of social work and social living in our communities, our nation, and our world.

REFERENCES

Adams, R., L. Dominelli, and M. Payne. (Eds.) (2005). *Social work futures: Crossing boundaries and transforming practice.* New York: Palgrave/Macmillan.

Deegan, P. (1996). Recovery and the conspiracy of hope. Presentation at the 6th Annual Mental Health Services Conference of Australia and New Zealand, Brisbane, Australia.

Guba, E. G., and Y. S. Lincoln. (2005). Paradigmatic controversies, contradictions, and emerging confluences. In N. K. Denzin and Y. S. Lincoln, eds., *The Sage handbook of qualitative research.* 3rd edition. Thousand Oaks, Calif.: Sage.

Link, R. (1999). Infusing global perspectives into social work values and ethics. In C. Ramanathan and R. Link, eds. *All our futures: Social work practice in a global era,* 69–93. Belmont, Calif.: Wadsworth.

Saleebey, D. (Ed.) (2006). *The strengths perspective in social work practice.* 4th edition. Boston: Pearson Education.

Sarri, R., and J. Finn. (1992). Child welfare policy and practice: Rethinking the history of our certainties. *Children and Youth Services Review* 14 (3/4): 219–36.

About the Contributors

Maryam Ahranjani is a regional director for Kaplan, Inc. and also serves as adjunct professor of law at the American University, Washington College of Law (WCL). Formerly the associate director of the program on Law and Government, Professor Ahranjani directs national and international expansion of the Marshall-Brennan Constitutional Literacy Project. She is coauthor of the textbook *Youth Justice in America* (2005), has authored numerous articles and lesson plans, is cofounder of the National Youth Justice Alliance, and received an American University Performance Award in 2006. A magna cum laude graduate of Northwestern University, Professor Ahranjani obtained her juris doctor degree from WCL and is fluent in Spanish and Farsi.

Luke Bergmann is currently a postdoctoral fellow in the School of Public Health at the University of California, Berkeley, where he is conducting research on substance abuse policy and prevention. He earned his Ph.D. degree in anthropology and social work and his MSW degree at the University of Michigan and is the author of *Owners, Occupants and Outcasts: Young Drug Hustlers in Detroit*, forthcoming from the New Press.

Linwood Cousins is a social worker and cultural anthropologist with a variety of teaching, research, and practice interests. He is associate professor of social work at Longwood University, where he teaches social work practice courses that focus on families and communities, human diversity, and human development. His research includes the sociocultural characteristics of race, ethnicity, and class as expressed by African American families and communities, with an emphasis on schooling and adolescents. His current practice activities include consultations and workshops that focus on developing social and cultural sensitivity for human service delivery to diverse populations and communities.

Jamie Lee Evans, MSW, is a longtime community builder and organizer for social justice. She is the project director for the Y.O.U.T.H. Training Project of the Bay Area Academy at San Francisco State University as well as the lead consultant for the emerging youth mental health consumer group Youth In Mind. She previously served as the director of recruitment and training and then director of teen education for San Francisco Women Against Rape. She holds a bachelor's degree from the University of California at Santa Cruz and a master's degree from San Francisco State University. She is also a survivor of the foster care system.

Janet L. Finn is professor of social work and director of the MSW Program at the University of Montana. She earned her MSW degree at Eastern Washington University and her Ph.D. degree in social work and anthropology at the University of Michigan. She is the author of numerous articles on gender, welfare, youth, and community and of the book *Tracing the Veins: Of Copper, Culture, and Community from Butte to Chuquicamata* (1998). Finn is coauthor of *Just Practice: A Social Justice Approach to Social Work* (2nd ed., 2008) and coeditor of *Motherlode: Legacies of Women's Lives and Labors in Butte, Montana* (2005). Her current projects include studies of women's grassroots organizations in Santiago, Chile, and of experiences of childhood in twentieth-century Butte, Montana.

Lori Fryzel is a 28-year-old survivor of both the foster care and international adoption system in South Korea and the United States. She began working in progressive social work efforts as a young organizer and then received her bachelor's degree in social work from Eastern Michigan University. She serves on the steering committee for Youth In Mind, a youth-guided leadership and advocacy group that promotes the involvement of youth voice in California's Mental Health System. Lori is attending San Francisco State University for her MSW degree and is also the field coordinator for the Y.O.U.T.H. Training Project of the Bay Area Academy at San Francisco State University.

Charles Garvin received his A.M. and Ph.D. degrees from the University of Chicago. He had been a social worker at Chapin Hall, Henry Booth House, and the Jewish Community Centers of Chicago. He taught at the School of Social Work of the University of Michigan from 1965 to 2002. He has written or cowritten such books as *Contemporary Group Work, Interpersonal Practice in Social Work, Social Work in Contemporary Society,* and *Generalist Practice: A Task-Centered Approach,* as well as over 50 articles. He is currently at work as coauthor of *Doing Justice: Working for Social Justice Goals in a Changing World.*

Kerrie Ghenie is a faculty member with the University of Montana School of Social Work and is a member of the Title IV-E Child Welfare Training Program. She earned her MSW degree at Walla Walla College and has experience as a child protective service social worker. Her areas of professional interest include children and families, child abuse/neglect, foster care and adoption, and social welfare policy and practice.

Sara Goodkind is assistant professor of social work at the University of Pittsburgh. She received her Ph.D. degree in social work and sociology and MSW degree from the University of Michigan. Her research focuses on programs and services for young people. She is interested in how beliefs and assumptions about gender, race/ethnicity, class, sexuality, and age shape service design and delivery and how that, in turn, affects the young people's and staff members' understandings of their lives, goals, and work. Much of her work has focused on girls in the juvenile justice system, and she is involved with efforts to improve the system and prevent and develop alternatives to girls' involvement with it.

Rachel Heiman is assistant professor of anthropology in the Bachelor's Program and Department of Social Sciences at the New School in New York City. She earned her Ph.D. degree in anthropology from the University of Michigan in 2004. She is the author of several articles on youth, middle-class anxieties, and suburban life. Her book, *Rugged Entitlement: Driving After Class in a Suburban New Jersey Town,* is forthcoming from the University of California Press. Her current projects include a collected volume on the global middle classes and an ethnographic study on the effect of diminishing fossil fuels on suburban middle-class life.

Derrick Jackson graduated from Eastern Michigan University with a bachelor's degree in social work. While working to pay his tuition, he found time to win ten Mid-American Conference championships in track and field, become an

All-American, and maintain his high academic standing. He would later go on to become one of the youngest recipients of the School of Social Work's Alumni of the Year award. While earning his MSW degree from the University of Michigan, Derrick worked with W. J. Maxey Training School. He then began his work at Ozone House, where Project SpeakOUT came to life. Currently, Derrick serves as the director of elections for the County of Washtenaw, teaches as an adjunct professor at Eastern Michigan University, continues his commitment to community by serving on numerous local boards and committees, and volunteers with several youth programs.

Patricia Jessup is an evaluation associate with InSites (www.insites.org), a non-profit organization promoting learning, growth, and change through inquiry-based evaluation, planning, and research. For InSites, her work includes evaluations of programs focused on Asian studies and professional development. She also is an independent evaluation consultant. This work has included studying the implementation of Middle Start—a comprehensive school improvement initiative developed through a partnership with the W. K. Kellogg Foundation, the Academy for Educational Development, and numerous Michigan-based organizations. Earlier in her career, she was a clinical social worker, counseling families, couples, and individuals. She holds a Ph.D. degree in education (2004) and an MSW degree (1975) from the University of Michigan, and a bachelor's degree in social work from the University of Wisconsin-Madison (1968).

Deborah Freedman Lustig is a research associate and graduate training coordinator at the Center on Culture, Immigration, and Youth Violence Prevention at the University of California, Berkeley. A cultural anthropologist, she earned her Ph.D. degree in anthropology from University of Michigan. She has conducted research on teenage mothers in the United States and on gender and education in Kenya and is beginning a new study of gentrification and youth violence in the United States.

Lynn Nybell is professor of social work at Eastern Michigan University. She holds an MSW degree and a Ph.D. degree in social work and anthropology from the University of Michigan. Her research interests include the social construction of childhood in social policy and practice, and the application of anthropological methods to the analysis of race, gender, and class in social work practice. She has published articles on shifting conceptions of childhood in social policy and (with Sylvia Sims Gray) on cultural competency in social work.

Jeffrey Shook is assistant professor of social work and law at the University of Pittsburgh. He received his juris doctorate from American University, Washington College of Law, and his Ph.D. degree in social work and sociology and MSW degree from the University of Michigan. His research involves the intersection of law, policy, and practice regarding children and youth. He has published on issues of juveniles in the criminal justice system, juvenile justice administration, and the intersection of juvenile justice and human rights. He is currently involved in research on juveniles in the criminal justice system and on youth transitioning to adulthood.

Ben Stride-Darnley is a Ph.D candidate (ABD) at McMaster University. His anthropological research focuses on young people's experience and participation in mental health programs that include education activities. His qualitative fieldwork was based in Ontario, Canada. His research interests include notions of agency and cultural (re)production, childhood and adolescence as life stages and social categories, the medicalization of behavior and mental health, incorporating young people's voices into research evidence and knowledge base, and power dynamics within institutional settings and policy (especially medical versus/ with educational discourses). He received a master's degree from McMaster University (2003) and a master's degree with honors from the University of St. Andrews, Scotland (2002). He has previously worked as an educational assistant supporting children and youth with special educational needs in Britain.

Jennifer Tilton is an urban anthropologist and an assistant professor of race and ethnic studies at the University of Redlands. She is completing revisions on a book entitled *Dangerous and Endangered Youth: Race and the Politics of Childhood in Urban America,* forthcoming from New York University Press. She is continuing her efforts to build links between her teaching, academic research, and the struggles of local communities for racial equality and social justice.

Charlie Wellenstein is on the faculty of the School of Social Work at the University of Montana as part of the Title IV-E Child Welfare Training Program. Wellenstein earned his MSW degree at Eastern Washington University. His areas of professional interest are child placement and substitute care, community treatment for at-risk youth, and juvenile justice.

Ruth Zweifler graduated in 1951 from Bryn Mawr College with an A.B. degree in biology. After a brief stint as a research assistant at Harvard Medical School, she devoted herself to raising her six children and to her lifelong commitment to work for world peace and justice. In 1975, acting on her long-held belief that citizens have a responsibility to participate in the public life of a community, she convened a group of like-minded citizens whose mission was to advocate on behalf of school children who were not receiving essential educational opportunities. This became the Student Advocacy Center of Michigan, where she served as executive director until her retirement in 2004.

Index